PARAMEDIC CARE: Principles & Practice

INTRODUCTION TO ADVANCED PREHOSPITAL CARE

Workbook

SECOND EDITION

BRADY

PARAMEDIC CARE: Principles & Practice

INTRODUCTION TO ADVANCED PREHOSPITAL CARE

Workbook

SECOND EDITION

Robert S. Porter

Bryan E. Bledsoe, D.O., F.A.C.E.P., EMT-P
Emergency Physician
Midlothian, Texas
and
Adjunct Associate Professor of Emergency Medicine
The George Washington University Medical Center
Washington, DC

Robert S. Porter, M.A., NREMT-P
Senior Advanced Life Support Educator
Madison County Emergency Medical Services
Canastota, New York
and
Flight Paramedic
AirOne, Onondaga County Sheriff's Department
Syracuse, New York

Richard A. Cherry, M.S., NREMT-P
Clinical Assistant Professor of Emergency Medicine
Director of Paramedic Training
SUNY Upstate Medical University
Syracuse, New York

PEARSON
Prentice Hall

Upper Saddle River, NJ 07458

Publisher: *Julie Levin Alexander*
Publisher's Assistant: *Regina Bruno*
Executive Editor: *Marlene McHugh Pratt*
Senior Managing Editor for Development: *Lois Berlowitz*
Project Manager: *Triple SSS Press Media Development*
Editorial Assistant: *Matthew Sirinides*
Director of Marketing: *Karen Allman*
Senior Marketing Manager: *Katrin Beacom*
Channel Marketing Manager: *Rachele Strober*
Marketing Coordinator: *Michael Sirinides*
Director of Production and Manufacturing: *Bruce Johnson*
Managing Editor for Production: *Patrick Walsh*
Production Liaison: *Faye Gemmellaro*
Production Editor: *Heather Willison/Carlisle Publishers Services*
Manufacturing Manager: *Ilene Sanford*
Manufacturing Buyer: *Pat Brown*
Creative Director: *Cheryl Asherman*
Senior Design Coordinator: *Christopher Weigand*
Cover Design: *Christopher Weigand*
Cover Photography: *Eddie Sperling*
Cover Image Manipulation: *Studio Montage*
Composition: *Carlisle Publishers Services*
Printing and Binding: *Banta-Harrisonburg*
Cover Printer: *Phoenix Color*

Studentaid.ed.gov, the U.S. Department of Education's Website on college planning assistance, is a valuable tool for anyone intending to pursue higher education. Designed to help students at all stages of schooling, including international students, returning students, and parents, it is a guide to the financial aid process. This Website presents information on applying to and attending college, as well as on funding your education and repaying loans. It also provides links to useful resources, such as state education agency contact information, assistance in filling out financial aid forms, and an introduction to various forms of student aid.

NOTICE ON CARE PROCEDURES

It is the intent of the authors and publisher that this Workbook be used as part of a formal EMT-Paramedic program taught by qualified instructors and supervised by a licensed physician. The procedures described in this Workbook are based upon consultation with EMT and medical authorities. The authors and publisher have taken care to make certain that these procedures reflect currently accepted clinical practice; however, they cannot be considered absolute recommendations.

The material in this Workbook contains the most current information available at the time of publication. However, federal, state, and local guidelines concerning clinical practices, including, without limitation, those governing infection control and universal precautions, change rapidly. The reader should note, therefore, that the new regulations may require changes in some procedures.

It is the responsibility of the reader to familiarize himself or herself with the policies and procedures set by federal, state, and local agencies as well as the institution or agency where the reader is employed. The authors and the publisher of this Workbook disclaim any liability, loss, or risk resulting directly or indirectly from the suggested procedures and theory, from any undetected errors, or from the reader's misunderstanding of the text. It is the reader's responsibility to stay informed of any new changes or recommendations made by any federal, state, and local agency as well as by his or her employing institution or agency.

NOTICE ON CPR AND ECC

The national standards for Cardiopulmonary Resuscitation (CPR) and Emergency Cardiovascular Care (ECC) are reviewed and revised on a regular basis and may change slightly after this manual is printed. It is important that you know the most current procedures for CPR and ECC, both for the classroom and your patients. The most current information may be obtained from the appropriate credentialing agency.

Pearson Education Ltd.
Pearson Education Singapore, Pte. Ltd.
Pearson Education Canada, Ltd.
Pearson Education—Japan
Pearson Education Australia PTY, Limited

Pearson Education North Asia Ltd.
Pearson Educación de Mexico, S.A. de C.V.
Pearson Education Malaysia, Pte. Ltd.
Pearson Education, Upper Saddle River, NJ

10 9 8 7 6 5 4 3 2 1
ISBN 0-13-117824-5

Dedication

To Kris and sailing: Pleasant distractions from writing about and practicing prehospital emergency medicine.

CONTENTS
Self-Instructional Workbook
Paramedic Care: Principles & Practice, 2nd Edition

INTRODUCTION TO ADVANCED PREHOSPITAL CARE

INTRODUCTION

To the Self-Instructional Workbook

Paramedic Care: Principles & Practice, 2nd Edition

Welcome to the self-instructional Workbook for *Paramedic Care: Principles & Practice*. This Workbook is designed to help guide you through an educational program for initial or refresher training that follows the guidelines of the 1998 U.S. Department of Transportation EMT-Paramedic National Standard Curriculum. The Workbook is designed to be used either in conjunction with your instructor or as a self-study guide you use on your own.

This Workbook features many different ways to help you learn the material necessary to become a paramedic, including those listed below.

Features

Review of Chapter Objectives

Each chapter of *Paramedic Care: Principles & Practice* begins with objectives that identify the important information and principles addressed in the chapter reading. To help you identify and learn this material, each Workbook chapter reviews the important content elements addressed by these objectives as presented in the text.

Case Study Review

Each chapter of *Paramedic Care: Principles & Practice* includes a case study, introducing and highlighting important principles presented in the chapter. The Workbook reviews these case studies and points out much of the essential information and many of the applied principles they describe.

Content Self-Evaluation

Each chapter of *Paramedic Care: Principles & Practice* presents an extensive narrative explanation of the principles of paramedic practice. The Workbook chapter (or chapter section) contains between 10 and 50 multiple-choice questions to test your reading comprehension of the textbook material and to give you experience taking typical emergency medical service examinations.

Special Projects

The Workbook contains several projects that are special learning experiences designed to help you remember the information and principles necessary to perform as a paramedic. Special projects include crossword puzzles, fill-in-the-blank, and a variety of other exercises.

Personal Benchmarking

This Workbook provides exercises that direct you to learn sites for drug administration on yourself. These exercises help you develop your medication administration skills and to use normal findings as benchmarks for reference when you begin your career as a paramedic.

Chapter Sections

Several chapters in *Paramedic Care: Principles & Practice* are extensive and contain a great deal of subject matter. To help you to grasp this material more efficiently, the Workbook breaks these chapters into sections with their own objectives, content review, and special projects.

Content Review

The Workbook provides a comprehensive review of the material presented in this volume of *Paramedic Care: Principles & Practice*. After the last text chapter has been covered, the Workbook presents an extensive content self-evaluation component that helps you recall and build upon the knowledge you have gained by reading the text, attending class, and completing the earlier Workbook chapters.

National Registry Practical Evaluation Forms

Supplemental materials found at the back of the Workbook include the National Registry Practical Evaluation Forms. These or similar forms will be used to test your practical skills throughout your training and, usually, for state certification exams. By reviewing them, you have a clearer picture of what is expected of you during your practical exam and a better understanding of the type of evaluation tool that is used to measure your performance.

Emergency Drug Cards

This Workbook contains alphabetized 3-inch × 5-inch cards that present the names/classes, descriptions, indications, contraindications, precautions, and routes and dosages of drugs the paramedic is most likely to encounter in prehospital care. Detach the cards and use them in flash card fashion. Practice until you can give the correct route, dosage, indications, and contraindications for each drug.

Acknowledgments

Reviewers
The following reviewers provided many excellent suggestions for improving this Workbook. Their assistance is greatly appreciated.

Edward B. Kuvlesky, NREMT-P
Battalion Chief
Indian River County, EMS
Indian River County, Florida

Steve Myers, RN, CEN, EMT-P
EMS Department Chair
Indian River Community College
Indian River County, Florida

Scott Vahradian, EMT-P
Santa Cruz, California

HOW TO USE

The Self-Instructional Workbook

Paramedic Care: Principles & Practice, 2nd Edition

The self-instructional Workbook accompanying *Paramedic Care: Principles & Practice* may be used as directed by your instructor or independently by you during your course of instruction. The recommendations listed below are intended to guide you in using the workbook independently.

- Examine your course schedule and identify the appropriate text chapter or other assigned reading.

- Read the assigned chapter in *Paramedic Care: Principles & Practice* carefully. Do this in a relaxed environment, free of distractions, and give yourself adequate time to read and digest the material. The information presented in *Paramedic Care: Principles & Practice* is often technically complex and demanding, but it is very important that you comprehend it. Be sure that you read the chapter carefully enough to understand and remember what you have read.

- Carefully read the Review of Chapter Objectives at the beginning of each Workbook chapter (or section). This material includes both the objectives listed in *Paramedic Care: Principles & Practice* and narrative descriptions of their content. If you do not understand or remember what is discussed from your reading, refer to the referenced pages and reread them carefully. If you still do not feel comfortable with your understanding of any objective, consider asking your instructor about it.

- Reread the case study in *Paramedic Care: Principles & Practice*, and then read the Case Study Review in the Workbook. Note the important points regarding assessment and care that the Case Study Review highlights and be sure that you understand and agree with the analysis of the call. If you have any questions or concerns, ask your instructor to clarify the information.

- Take the Content Self-Evaluation at the end of each Workbook chapter (or section), answering each question carefully. Do this in a quiet environment, free from distractions, and allow yourself adequate time to complete the exercise. Correct your self-evaluation by consulting the answers at the back of the workbook, and determine the percentage you have answered correctly (the number you got right divided by the total number of questions). If you have answered most of the questions correctly (85 to 90 percent), review those that you missed by rereading the material on the pages listed in the answer key and be sure you understand which answer is correct and why. If you have more than a few questions wrong (less than 85 percent correct), look for incorrect answers that are grouped together. This suggests that you did not understand a particular topic in the reading. Reread the text dealing with that topic carefully, and then retest yourself on the questions you got wrong. If incorrect answers are spread throughout the chapter content, reread the chapter and retake the Content Self-Evaluation to ensure that you understand the material. If you don't understand why your answer to a question is incorrect after reviewing the text, consult with your instructor.

- In a similar fashion, complete the exercises in the Special Projects section of the Workbook chapters (or sections). These exercises are specifically designed to help you learn and remember the essential principles and information presented in *Paramedic Care: Principles & Practice*.

- When you have completed this volume of *Paramedic Care: Principles & Practice* and its accompanying Workbook, prepare for a course test by reviewing both the text in its entirety and your class notes. Then take the Content Review examination in the Workbook. Again, review your score and any questions you have answered incorrectly by referring to the text and rereading the page or pages where the material is presented. If you note groupings of wrong answers, review the entire range of pages or the full chapter they represent.

If, during your completion of the Workbook exercises, you have any questions that either the text-book or Workbook doesn't answer, write them down and ask your instructor about them. Prehospital emergency medicine is a complex and complicated subject, and answers are not always black-and-white. It is also common for different EMS systems to use differing methods of care. The questions you bring up in class, and your instructor's answers to them, will help you expand and complete your knowledge of prehospital emergency medical care.

The authors and Brady Publishing continuously seek to ensure the creation of the best materials to support your educational experience. We are interested in your comments. If, during your reading and study of material in *Paramedic Care: Principles & Practice*, you notice any error or have any suggestions to improve either the textbook or workbook, please direct your comments via the Internet to the following address:

hiawatha@localnet.com

You can also visit the Brady Website at:
www.bradybooks.com/paramedic

GUIDELINES TO BETTER TEST-TAKING

The knowledge you will gain from reading the textbook, completing the exercises in the Workbook, listening in your paramedic class, and participating in your clinical and field experience will prepare you to care for patients who are seriously ill or injured. However, before you can practice these skills, you will have to pass several classroom written exams and your state's certification exam. Your performance on these exams will depend not only on your knowledge but also on your ability to answer test questions correctly. The following guidelines are designed to help your performance on tests and to better demonstrate your knowledge of prehospital emergency care.

1. Relax and be calm during the test.

A test is designed to measure what you have learned and to tell you and your instructor how well you are doing. An exam is not designed to intimidate or punish you. Consider it a challenge, and just try to do your best. Get plenty of sleep before the examination. Avoid coffee or other stimulants for a few hours before the exam, and be prepared.

Reread the text chapters, review the objectives in the Workbook, and review your class notes. It might be helpful to work with one or two other students and ask each other questions. This type of practice helps everyone better understand the knowledge presented in your course of study.

2. Read the questions carefully.

Read each word of the question and all the answers slowly. Words such as "except" or "not" may change the entire meaning of the question. If you miss such words, you may answer the question incorrectly even though you know the right answer.

EXAMPLE:
The art and science of Emergency Medical Services involves all of the following EXCEPT:

  A. sincerity and compassion.
  B. respect for human dignity.
  C. placing patient care before personal safety.
  D. delivery of sophisticated emergency medical care.
  E. none of the above.

The correct answer is C, unless you miss the "EXCEPT."

3. Read each answer carefully.

Read each and every answer carefully. While the first answer may be absolutely correct, so may the rest, and thus the best answer might be "all of the above."

EXAMPLE:
Indirect medical control is considered to be:

  A. treatment protocols.
  B. training and education.
  C. quality assurance.
  D. chart review.
  E. all of the above.

While answers A, B, C, and D are correct, the best and only acceptable answer is "all of the above," E.

4. Delay answering questions you don't understand and look for clues.

When a question seems confusing or you don't know the answer, note it on your answer sheet and come back to it later. This will ensure that you have time to complete the test. You will also find that other questions in the test may give you hints to answer the one you've skipped over. It will also prevent you from being frustrated with an early question and letting it affect your performance.

EXAMPLE:

Upon successful completion of a course of training as an EMT-P, most states will

    A. certify you. (correct)
    B. license you.
    C. register you.
    D. recognize you as a paramedic.
    E. issue you a permit.

Another question, later in the exam, may suggest the right answer:

The action of one state in recognizing the certification of another is called:

    A. reciprocity. (correct)
    B. national registration.
    C. licensure.
    D. registration.
    E. extended practice.

5. Answer all questions.

Even if you do not know the right answer, do not leave a question blank. A blank question is always wrong, while a guess might be correct. If you can eliminate some of the answers as wrong, do so. It will increase the chances of a correct guess.

A multiple-choice question with five answers gives a 20-percent chance of a correct guess. If you can eliminate one or more incorrect answers, you increase your odds of a correct guess to 25 percent, 33 percent, and so on. An unanswered question has a 0 percent chance of being correct.

Just before turning in your answer sheet, check to be sure that you have not left any items blank.

EXAMPLE:

When a paramedic is called by the patient (through the dispatcher) to the scene of a medical emergency, the medical control physician has established a physician/patient relationship.

    A. True
    B. False

A true/false question gives you a 50-percent chance of a correct guess.

The hospital health professional responsible for sorting patients as they arrive at the emergency department is usually the:

    A. emergency physician.
    B. ward clerk.
    C. emergency nurse.
    D. trauma surgeon.
    E. both A and C. (correct)

Introduction to Advanced Prehospital Care

Review of Chapter Objectives

With each chapter of the Workbook, we identify the objectives and the important elements of the textbook content. You should review these items and refer to the pages listed if any points are not clear.

After reading this chapter, you should be able to:

1. Describe the relationship between the paramedic and the other members of the allied health professions. pp. 5–6

The paramedic is the highest-level prehospital care provider and leader of the prehospital care team. He or she is a member of the allied health care professions and specifically a member of the ancillary health care professions, which include health care professionals other than physicians and nurses. Paramedics are credentialed or licensed by an appropriate state or provincial agency and approved by their system's medical directors.

2. Identify the attributes and characteristics of the paramedic. pp. 6–7

Paramedics must possess the knowledge, skills, and attitudes consistent with the expectations of the public and the profession. This includes recognizing that you are an essential component in the continuum of care and an advocate for the patient. As a paramedic, you must be flexible enough to work within the various types of EMS systems and adjust to the ever-changing emergency environment. You must be a confident leader, accept the challenges of your profession, have excellent judgement, communicate effectively, develop a rapport with a great diversity of patients, and function independently in a very unstructured environment.

3. Explain the elements of paramedic education and practice that support its stature as a profession. pp. 7–8

The 1998 U.S. Department of Transportation's *EMT-Paramedic: National Standard Curriculum* describes an intensive course of education with a great emphasis on anatomy, physiology, and pathophysiology. This material provides a broad foundation for your understanding of the human body and its injury and illness. Once you complete initial training, you are expected to continue your education, both to expand your knowledge of prehospital care and to ensure that you remain practiced and ready to employ those skills used less frequently. Further, you and other members of the profession must commit to supporting research both to define and improve skills and care procedures that benefit patients and identify those that do not. Only through research can the paramedic profession continue to grow and earn respect for the work of its members. Despite its relative youth, the field of emergency medical services enjoys growing public recognition as an important segment of the health care professions. However, this status must not be taken for granted.

4. Define and give examples of the expanded scope of practice for the paramedic.   pp. 7–8, 10

Currently there are four areas in which the scope of practice for EMT-Paramedics has been expanded. They include critical care transport, primary care, industrial medicine, and sports medicine. Critical care transport is a specialization directed at the needs of critically ill or injured patients as they are moved from one care facility to another. During this transport, paramedics often use equipment far more advanced and complex than that found on standard ambulances. With the changing nature of the health care market and increasing specialization of health care facilities, this realm of expanded scope is growing. Primary care is the movement of the paramedic into more traditional health care roles in such places as emergency departments, outpatient clinics, physicians' offices, urgent care centers, and patients' homes. Industrial medicine is the field in which specially trained paramedics provide on-site services, including emergency care, safety inspection, accident prevention, medical screening, and vaccinations in the work place. Sports medicine sets the paramedic as a partner with the athletic trainer while providing emergency care and advising whether an injured player should return to the game or continue competition.

Case Study Review

It is important to review each emergency response you participate in as a paramedic. Similarly, we will review the case study that precedes each chapter. We will address the important points of the response as addressed by the chapter. Often this will include the scene size-up, patient assessment, patient management, patient packaging, and transport.

Reread the case study on pages 3 through 5 in Paramedic Care: Introduction to Advanced Prehospital Care *and then read the following discussion.*

This case draws attention to some of the nontraditional aspects of the new and evolving emergency medical services system.

This extensive case study includes several elements that highlight the evolving nature and varying needs of prehospital emergency medical care. Stephen Fletcher finds himself far from home and distant from a population base large enough to support traditional emergency medical service. Yet, through a system in which emergency medical services personnel play somewhat unusual and nontraditional roles, he receives care substantially equal to that he would find at home.

Twenty years ago, Stephen would probably have denied his symptoms until later in the hike, which would have made his access to the system more difficult and his condition more serious. Public awareness programs highlighting the signs, symptoms, and dangers of myocardial infarction have made people recognize the condition more often and then seek help more quickly. As the EMS system continues to evolve, its members will become even more involved in increasing public awareness (through public education) of safe practices and risk-reducing behaviors.

The response to Stephen's call for help is typical of many EMS systems but is also specially designed for the needs of this wilderness area. In such a remote area, the system has been designed to get First Responders with some training quickly to the patient's side. Those First Responders begin the continuum of care, giving the paramedics a longer time to respond and while still being effective. In sparsely populated regions, the problem of getting timely paramedic care to patients may be obvious, but it may also emerge in heavily populated areas, where reaching the upper floors of a high rise or negotiating rush hour traffic may delay response times as well. A well-planned EMS system, like the one in the Case Study, recognizes these obstacles and makes the necessary adjustments.

The care that the paramedics first attending Stephen provide is very different from that commonly supplied by paramedics in urban centers. The Medic-2 personnel are over 200 miles from a major medical center and the intensive care that Stephen needs. Hence, they have been given special skills and the ability to perform them with limited supervision. At the same time, it is unlikely that Keith and Dudley will treat evolving myocardial infarctions very regularly. To maintain their skills for such care, they are required to participate in a regimen of practice for the important skills that they will use infrequently.

They may also rotate through more heavily populated and urban areas of their system to gain the experience needed to maintain their skills.

Keith and Dudley are supported in their work by both data transmission and radio or cell phone communication with medical direction. They work closely with their medical direction physician to obtain a second opinion and guidance regarding the care they are to offer. In a setting with a greater call volume, they would likely be less dependent on this communication because their exposure to more frequent medical and cardiac calls would probably keep their skills and judgment sharper. In addition, Stephen will be in Keith and Dudley's care for a prolonged period of time, and communication with medical direction will ensure optimal performance as the paramedics provide essential advanced procedures while the patient's blockage resolves and he exhibits some re-perfusion dysrhythmias.

As should be obvious from this case, technology greatly affects the environment in which EMS personnel operate. The paramedics transmit Stephen's ECG to the remote physician by radio fax. In many other systems, long-distance communication involves cell phones, which permit efficient, clear, and confidential communication with the medical direction physician. In the future, communication technologies such as video image transmission and global positioning systems will continue to reshape the way the EMS profession performs its service.

The system serving Stephen includes paramedics in the roles of critical care transport specialists. These specially trained paramedics are prepared both to assist the critical patient and to address the effects of the stresses placed on the patient during flight. Taking the patient high above ground level during flight reduces the atmospheric pressure. In the uninjured person, this has little effect, but in the seriously ill or injured patient, the consequences can be devastating. The two paramedics ensure that Stephen is well oxygenated during his trip and watch for signs of increasing dyspnea. They, too, will be at Stephen's side for longer than most "street" paramedics.

At the medical center, the continuum of care continues. The critical care transport paramedics smoothly hand off their patient to the staff of the coronary care unit without even passing through the emergency department. The care provided to Stephen continues to increase in sophistication, and it becomes clear that he has benefited from the type of EMS system that has been thoughtfully designed to meet the unique features of its population demographics.

This case study also points out that paramedics are now finding they have an expanding role in prehospital care. Once, paramedics were found only in urban centers. Today, their services are especially valuable in very remote and sparsely populated locations where access to any medical care is limited. Other areas into which the role of paramedics has extended include interfacility transports where intensive care is required and in nontraditional fields such as sports and industrial medicine.

Content Self-Evaluation

Each of the chapters in this Workbook includes a short content review. The questions are designed to test your ability to remember what you read. At the end of this Workbook, you can find the answers to the questions as well as the pages where the topic of each question was discussed in the text. If you answered a question incorrectly or are unsure of the answer, review the pages listed.

MULTIPLE CHOICE

1. The modern ambulance is best described as a:
   - A. rapid patient transport vehicle.
   - B. vehicle for horizontal transport.
   - C. mobile emergency room.
   - D. mobile intensive care unit.
   - E. automated care delivery center.

2. The licensing, registering, or credentialing of a paramedic is usually provided by a state or provincial agency.
   - A. True
   - B. False

_E_ 3. The expanding role of the paramedic may place him in the role of:
A. public educator.
B. health promoter.
C. injury and illness prevention advocate.
D. facilitator of access to care.
E. all of the above

_E_ 4. The paramedic is held accountable to which of the following?
A. the public
B. the system medical director
C. the employer
D. his or her peers
E. all of the above

_D_ 5. The best way to ensure you meet the expectations of the public, peers, and system medical director is to:
A. know your protocols.
B. attend all ongoing education sessions.
C. record everything well on the prehospital care report.
D. always act in the best interest of the patient.
E. act confident and in control while you provide care.

_C_ 6. Which of the following is NOT a characteristic of a professional paramedic?
A. confident leadership
B. excellent judgement
C. strong opinions about ethnic groups
D. ability to develop a rapport with a wide variety of patients
E. ability to function independently

_B_ 7. Which characteristic best describes the changes made in the profession by the 1998 DOT *National Standard Curriculum*?
A. It provided algorithms for most situations paramedics face.
B. It raised the standards of education for the paramedic.
C. It allowed the paramedic to prescribe more drugs.
D. It required stronger math, English, and communication skills.
E. all of the above

_B_ 8. You should consider the completion of your initial paramedic course as the end of your formal EMS education.
A. True
B. False

_B_ 9. A skill that is infrequently used in your career as a paramedic should be practiced less often during ongoing education.
A. True
B. False

_A_ 10. For years, paramedic practice was based on anecdotal data and tradition.
A. True
B. False

_C A_ 11. Ethics is best defined as:
A. a legal requirement of the profession.
B. good manners.
C. a standard of right or honorable behavior.
D. playing the role of a patient advocate.
E. a societal requirement.

_E_ 12. Which of the following is an example of the expanded scope of practice for paramedics?
A. critical care transport
B. primary care
C. industrial medicine
D. sports medicine
E. all of the above

_E_ 13. Which of the following types of facilities is likely to employ larger numbers of paramedics in the future?
A. physicians' offices
B. minor-care clinics
C. outpatient clinics
D. industrial medical clinics
E. all of the above

_A_ **14.** The expanding role of the paramedic may include releasing patients, after slight treatment at the scene, with minor injuries.

    A. True   **B.** False

_E_ **15.** An industrial paramedic is likely to provide which of the services listed below?

    A. safety inspections   **D.** accident prevention education

    B. assistance with sick calls   **E.** all of the above

    C. vaccinations

LISTING

16. List the major ways in which the 1998 DOT *National Standard Curriculum* has raised the education of paramedics to a higher level.

A&P are now a prerequisite to the paramedic course. The course requires more foundation of medical knowledge to underlie the required skills. Much more knowledge of pathophysiology illness & injury.

17. List the additional training associated with the following areas of the paramedic's expanded scope of practice.

A. Critical care transport

Advanced airway management, ventilator management, fluid & electrolyte therapy, advanced pharmacology, specialized monitoring, operation of n electrolyte therapy

B. Industrial medicine

Safty inspection, accident prevention, Medical screening of employees & vaccinations.

C. Sports medicine

Pregame preparation of players, provide any EMS care. Tell whether or not pleq can go back into game. May perform simple laceration repairs.

2

The Well-Being
of the Paramedic

Review of Chapter Objectives

After reading this chapter, you should be able to:

1. Discuss the concept of wellness and its benefits.   **pp. 16–17**

Wellness, or personal physical, mental, and emotional well-being, is the result of proper nutrition, basic physical fitness, safe practices to protect you from disease and injury, and the development of effective mechanisms to deal with the stress of the profession. The result of observing practices that promote wellness in your own life is a reduced incidence of work-related injury and illness, a good attitude toward the profession, and a long fruitful career in emergency medical services.

2. Define the components of wellness.   **pp. 17–23**

Basic physical fitness is the muscular strength, cardiovascular endurance (aerobic capacity), and flexibility that permit you to perform the tasks associated with prehospital emergency care without risk to the musculoskeletal system.

Good nutrition is the controlled and balanced consumption of carbohydrates, fats, proteins, vitamins, and minerals to meet the body's needs, yet not consumption in excess.

Personal protection from disease includes application of body substance isolation procedures and acquisition of proper immunizations for protection from contagious disease.

Stress and stress management involves the recognition that prehospital emergency care is a stressful profession and that stress management techniques are essential to a long career in EMS.

General safety considerations include such principles as safe lifting, ensuring a safe environment for EMS operations, safe driving practices, appropriate interpersonal relationships, and the proper dealing with habits and addictions.

3. Describe the role of the paramedic in promoting wellness.   **pp. 16–17**

The paramedic should, by example, promote basic physical fitness, proper nutrition, the following of safe practices, and the use of appropriate mechanisms to deal with job-related stress. He or she can be a model to peers, patients, and the community in general.

**4. Discuss how cardiovascular endurance, weight control, muscle
strength, and flexibility contribute to physical fitness.**   **pp. 17–20**

Cardiovascular endurance, weight control, muscular strength, and flexibility are all essential to the physical fitness required of the paramedic. Cardiovascular endurance is the measure of the heart's and blood vessels' ability to support physical exercise. Increased cardiovascular endurance improves the body's ability to accommodate the physical stress associated with patient lifting and movement and the carrying of equipment. Weight control is essential to limit cardiovascular and musculoskeletal stresses on the body. Muscular strength is achieved by regular exercise and helps keep the body ready for the stresses of lifting and moving the patient and EMS equipment. Flexibility is the strength and ease of motion through the normal range of motion of the body's major joints. Good flexibility will reduce back pain and the potential for joint and muscle injury during your EMS career.

5. **Describe the impact of shift work on circadian rhythms.** p. 35

Shift work disturbs the normal biorhythms of the body, called circadian rhythms. Dramatic changes in a person's daily time schedule disturb the normal sleep/awake, appetite, hormonal, and temperature fluctuation cycles of the body and may result in drowsiness and fatigue. To diminish the negative effects of shift work, it is best to maintain a regular 24-hour sleep/awake cycle (sleeping at about the same time), even on days when you do not work.

6. **Discuss the contributions that periodic risk assessments and warning sign recognition make to cancer and cardiovascular disease prevention.** p. 20

Periodic assessment of your risk for disease is important. Have frequent physical exams and examine your family history to determine the risk for cancer and cardiovascular disease. Know your cholesterol and triglyceride levels and keep them in check. Women past menopause might consider the use of hormonal therapy to reduce the risk of cardiovascular disease and have frequent mammograms and pap smears with advancing age. Males should have periodic prostate exams with advancing age. Also watch for blood in the stool, changes in moles, unexplained weight loss, unexplained chronic fatigue, and unusual lumps.

7. **Differentiate proper from improper body mechanics for lifting and moving patients in emergency and nonemergency situations.** pp. 21–23

Proper lifting and moving techniques, especially when coupled with good physical fitness and good nutrition, help protect the musculoskeletal system from the high risks for injury associated with prehospital emergency care. Good posture, lifting with the leg muscles, and keeping the back straight, the palms up, and the body close to the object being lifted will reduce the potential for injury. Exhale during a lift, keep your feet apart with one foot ahead of the other, take your time, and ask for help when you think you will need it. These principles will make lifting easier and help keep you from back injury during your years of service.

8. **Describe the problems that a paramedic might encounter in a hostile situation and the techniques used to manage the situation.** p. 40

Emergency responses occasionally put the caregiver into contact with hostile patients, family members, and bystanders. These individuals may affect your ability to provide care and, at the extreme, threaten you or your patient with physical harm. If there is a significant threat, remove yourself from the scene immediately. Often, however, the hostility of people at the scene can be overcome by appreciating the cultural diversity of those you treat and helping them understand that your reason for being there is to offer help. Treating everyone you attend with dignity and respect will go a long way toward establishing trust in you and in EMS providers in general.

9. **Describe the considerations that should be given to using escorts, dealing with adverse environmental conditions, using lights and siren, proceeding through intersections, and parking at an emergency scene.** pp. 39–40

Driving an emergency vehicle provides you with some privileges, but with them come some very important added responsibilities. In general you must remain especially aware of others on the roadway and remember that they may react unexpectedly to your approach and passage. Also consider the following steps when dealing with these specific situations:

- When following an escort, be aware that some drivers may not realize that you are following from behind and may pull out in front of you.
- Adverse driving conditions (rain, snow, ice, fog) reduce visibility and traction. Give other drivers more time to see you and stop, and respect the increased stopping time and reduced maneuverability of your ambulance in these conditions.
- Lights and sirens are used to alert others of your approach and ask them to yield the right of way. However, some drivers may neither see nor hear them or may react in an unexpected manner. Be alert while using lights and sirens and anticipate the actions of others.
- Intersections pose special problems for emergency vehicles. Driving through a red light or a stop sign is dangerous because other drivers may presume they have the right of way. The situation becomes more complicated and dangerous when multiple emergency vehicles are responding. When proceeding through an intersection, and especially when passing through a red light, slow to almost a stop and keep a good lookout for other vehicles not yielding right of way.
- Once at the scene, park so as to protect you and your crew, the patient, and other drivers. Place your emergency vehicle between traffic and the crash/care scene and be sure the lights can be seen by all oncoming traffic.

10. **Discuss the concept of "due regard for the safety of all others" while operating an emergency vehicle.** p. 40

The concept of exercising due regard for the safety of others recognizes that different drivers will react differently to the approach of emergency vehicles. This means that you must maintain an intense lookout for hazards while driving the emergency vehicle. You must anticipate the actions of other drivers on the highway, including those that are unexpected and not in keeping with the right of way given you under the law. Otherwise you may find yourself responsible for injury when your intent was to provide care or, worse, injure yourself.

11. **Describe the equipment available in a variety of adverse situations for self-protection.** pp. 24–25, 39–40

Equipment available to help protect you from the more common hazards of emergency medical service include helmets, footwear with toe and ankle support, body armor, reflective tape for night visibility, seatbelts, and personal protective equipment used for body substance isolation (gloves, masks, eyewear, respirators, gowns, resuscitation equipment).

12. **Describe the benefits and methods of smoking cessation.** p. 21

Smoking and the effects of nicotine are well known to be detrimental to respiratory and cardiovascular health and well linked to lung cancer. Smoking cessation programs using replacement therapy (nicotine patches), behavior modification, aversion therapy, hypnotism, and "cold turkey" approaches represent structured programs of controlled withdrawal from sociocultural, psychological, and physiological dependency on the drug. The result of a successful smoking cessation program is better respiratory and cardiovascular health and a reduced risk of respiratory infection and cancer.

13. **Describe the three phases of the stress response.** p. 34

There are three stages to the human response to stress: alarm, resistance, and exhaustion. Alarm is the initial response, more commonly known as the "fight-or-flight" response. The autonomic nervous system prepares the body to deal with a threat to its well-being by releasing hormones that increase cardiac output (increase heart rate, the strength of contraction, and preload) and blood pressure, induce pupil dilation, increase blood glucose, and relax the respiratory tree. Resistance begins as the body starts to adjust and cope with the stress. During this phase, the blood pressure and pulse rate may return to normal. The final stress response phase is exhaustion. If the exposure to stress is prolonged, the body may become exhausted and lose its ability to resist and adapt to the stressors. The individual becomes more susceptible to physical and psychological ailments.

14. List factors that trigger the stress response. p. 33

Stress is a stimulus from the environment that affects the body. Stress can have positive effects (eustress) or it can generate negative effects (distress). Factors that induce the stress response are anything that threatens (or is perceived to threaten) the well-being of the individual. These factors include physical ones, such as the threat of violence; emotional ones, such as the loss of a loved one; and physiological ones, such as physical fatigue or extreme hunger. Each person reacts differently to stressors, bringing his previous experiences into the equation.

15. Differentiate between normal/healthy and detrimental physiological and psychological reactions to anxiety and stress. pp. 35–37

The human stress response is the body's way of dealing with stress, and the outcome is either healthy or unhealthy. Healthy responses result in the individual's quickly adjusting to the stressor and physiologically and psychologically returning to normal. Unhealthy responses result in behavioral and physiological manifestations such as gastrointestinal disturbances, sleep disturbances, headaches, vision problems, fatigue, chest pains, confusion, a reduced attention span, poor concentration, disorientation, memory problems, inappropriate fear, panic, grief, depression, anxiety, and feelings of being overwhelmed, abandoned, or numb to emotion. A person with an unhealthy response may also experience withdrawal from normal social activities, increased use of drugs or alcohol, or inappropriate humor, silence, crying, suspiciousness, or activity levels.

16. Identify causes of stress in EMS. p. 37

EMS provides an abundant amount of stressors because of the nature of the profession. These stressors include: shift work; loud pagers and sounds; poor pay; long hours; periods of boredom followed by short periods of extreme excitement; scene violence; abusive patients; vomit; blood; gory scenes; chaotic scenes; personal fears; frustration; exhaustion; demands of family members, friends, or bystanders; inclement weather; conflicts with co-workers or supervisors; hunger and thirst; and physical demands on the body, such as heavy lifting. The personality traits commonly found in EMS members, a strong need to be liked and often unrealistically high self-expectations, also leave those individuals more likely to develop adverse responses to stress.

17. Describe behavior that is a manifestation of stress in patients and those close to them and describe how that behavior relates to paramedic stress. p. 33

Stress may become evident through almost any unusual behavior exhibited by the patient, family, or bystanders. It may manifest with hyperactivity or hypoactivity, withdrawal, suspiciousness, increased smoking, increased alcohol or drug intake, excessive humor or silence, crying spells, or any changes in behavior, communications, interactions with others, or eating habits. These behaviors can confound the assessment of the patient's mental status and place additional stress on the paramedic.

18. Identify and describe the defense mechanisms and management techniques commonly used to deal with stress. pp. 35–38

Constructive mechanisms and management techniques used to deal with stress can be divided into two categories; immediate and long term. Immediate coping mechanisms include controlling breathing to reduce adrenaline levels and reduce heart rate, reframing thoughts to encourage or support any needed behavior on your behalf (e.g., saying to yourself "I can do this!"), and focusing your concentration on the responsibilities at hand (i.e., the needs of the patient), not the stressful problem. For long-term well-being, ensure your physical, mental, and emotional health. Exercise, watch your diet, and ensure supportive and pleasant distractions from the stress such as a non-EMS circle of friends or a vacation away from the job.

19. **Describe the research about possible problems in the use of critical incident stress management (CISM) and the appropriate mental health services that should be available to EMS personnel.**   p. 38

In the past, Critical Incident Stress Management (CISM) was recommended for use in emergency medical services. However, current research suggests that CISM and critical incident stress debriefing (CISD) do not appear to mitigate the effects of stress and may actually interfere with the normal grieving/healing process. There remains an important role for competent mental health professionals at multi-casualty incidents. They should be on scene to provide psychological first aid, survey EMS providers and victims for stress-relates symptoms, and be available during the 2 months post-incident to screen and council anyone displaying stress-related symptoms.

20. **Describe the stages of the grieving process (Kübler-Ross).**   p. 30

The grieving patient is likely to progress through five stages of the grieving process as described by Elisabeth Kübler-Ross. Those stages include anger, denial, bargaining, depression, and acceptance. A grieving person usually progresses through these stages in order, though he may skip around or move back and forth between stages. In the anger stage, the person vents the frustration over the inability to control the situation or control the outcome. Denial represents the inability or refusal to accept the reality of the event or situation. Bargaining is an unrealistic attempt to change or put off the outcome. Depression represents despair over the inevitable and withdrawal into a private world. Acceptance is realization and acceptance of the event or patient's fate.

21. **Describe the unique challenges for paramedics in dealing with themselves, adults, children, and other special populations related to their understanding or experience of death and dying.**   pp. 29–33

Even though paramedics are exposed to death and dying, they don't necessarily handle these events better than other people. All people tend to move through the same stages of the grieving process, although age and the patient's special circumstances may alter the presentation of those stages. Children may not recognize the significance and finality of the event or may fear that death may soon happen to themselves or others. Adults react differently, usually experiencing a "paralyzing" feeling followed by intense grief for weeks. The intensity gradually subsides, with later peaks of feeling associated with anniversaries, birthdays, and the like. The elderly usually are concerned about the effects of the death on others and their loss of independence.

22. **Describe the body substance isolation steps to take for personal protection from airborne and bloodborne pathogens.**   pp. 24–26

Body substance isolation (BSI) practices include the use of personal protective equipment (PPE) to isolate the body from contaminants found in the air and body fluids while caring for a patient. These practices involve using protective latex or plastic gloves to protect yourself when touching a patient if there is reasonable expectation of contact with body fluids including tears, vomit, saliva, blood, urine, fecal material, cerebrospinal fluid, or any other body fluid or substance. Masks and protective eyewear should be used whenever there is a reasonable expectation that fluid or droplets will be splattered, as is the case with arterial hemorrhage, endotracheal intubation, intensive airway care, childbirths, and the cleaning of contaminated equipment. When a patient has or is suspected of having tuberculosis or another highly contagious airborne disease, use of a special type of mask, either the high-efficiency particulate air (HEPA) or N-95 respirator, offers protection by removing small infectious particles from the air. Gowns are worn to protect clothing and the body from contamination by splashing of body fluids in extreme circumstances (like childbirth). A gown impervious to fluid movement is recommended. When possible, use disposable equipment for patient ventilation and other invasive procedures.

23. **Given a scenario where equipment and supplies have been exposed to body substances, plan for the proper cleaning, disinfection, and disposal of the items.** pp. 27–28

When EMS equipment becomes contaminated (or possibly contaminated), it should be disposed of or properly cleaned and disinfected. Single-use devices, bandaging materials, and other disposable EMS equipment and materials should be placed in a sealed biohazard waste container and disposed of properly. Needles and other sharp contaminated items should be placed in a puncture-proof "sharps" container and disposed of properly. Equipment that has been in contact with a patient or otherwise becomes contaminated should be cleaned with soap and water, disinfected with an appropriate agent (commercial or a bleach solution), or sterilized (by heat, steam, or radiation) as per your service's policies and procedures. Any contaminated cleaning or disinfecting supplies should be disposed of properly.

24. **Given photos of various motor-vehicle collisions, assess scene safety and propose ways to make the scene safer.** pp. 39–40

The scene of an emergency is inherently dangerous, especially when it involves an auto crash. The roadway becomes a hazard because oncoming traffic may collide with your ambulance, personnel on the scene, and the wrecked auto(s). The crash produces broken glass, jagged metal, and spilled fluids that may be slippery, hot, caustic (battery acid), or flammable. The hostile patient involved in the crash may pose a threat to care providers, as may the patient's friends and family members or other bystanders. The incident may also affect utility poles, breaking their wires to create electrical hazards. The paramedic must use caution when approaching the scene and carefully rule out hazards. If any exist, you must eliminate them or not approach the scene. Do not attempt to correct a scene hazard unless you are specifically and properly trained and equipped to handle it. Place your vehicle to caution oncoming traffic and create a barrier between you and that traffic. At all scenes with jagged metal and broken glass, wear protective clothing including gloves, boots, helmet, and a protective coat (turnout gear). If need be, "blind" the occupants of a stopped vehicle with a spotlight until you are sure it is safe to enter the scene. If there is any possibility of blood or body fluid exposure, observe body substance isolation procedures.

25. **Given a scenario involving a stressful situation, formulate a strategy to help adapt to the stress.** pp. 33–38

When you are called to a situation that places you under stress, make a conscious decision to deal with it in an appropriate manner. Immediately control your breathing by taking deep breaths and letting the air out slowly through your mouth. Repeat this as needed, and then focus your energy on the essential tasks at hand. Tell yourself "I can do it" or "I can make it through this" and attend to the immediate needs of your patient. Once the immediate stressor is removed, ensure that you take care of yourself physically, emotionally, and mentally. Talk with members of your team about the event and identify what you have done well and areas in which you can improve. Exercise regularly, eat properly, and take a vacation or a few days off. Examine the situation and your options, decide how best to handle the situation in the long term, and go on with your life. If a situation is extremely stressful, take advantage of your system's mental health support services.

Case Study Review

Reread the case study on pages 15 and 16 in Paramedic Care: Introduction to Advanced Prehospital Care *and then read the following discussion.*

The case study presented identifies the evolution of Howard as a field paramedic. He came into the field with certain expectations and, through experience, has changed and developed a healthy attitude toward who he is, what he does, and the profession he has chosen. His short story, as presented here, can serve as a guide for what you can expect from a career in emergency medical services.

Howard has taken an active role in maintaining his own health so as to be able to help his patients and protect himself from injury. His choice to run and lift weights increases both his cardiovascular endurance and body strength. He can now function longer under stress and is less likely to sustain serious injury because his body is strong and flexible. But that's not all that Howard has learned and taken to heart.

Howard displays a mature view of his actions to reduce his risks for injury and disease. He consciously employs body substance isolation techniques and other safe practices to protect himself. He is aware that others are not as conscientious as he is, and he serves as a role model for others who are new to the profession. This attitude probably gains him the respect of his peers that he had tried to attain with his earlier "know-it-all" approach.

Howard has also gained an understanding of how stress affects both people in general and patients specifically. This gives him a demonstrable ability to interact with people and patients during emergencies. Howard learned about stress and its effects through an experience in his past. The incident changed him from a "cowboy" into the seasoned and caring paramedic he now is. It is this type of life-long learning that is essential to your growth and maturation as an EMT-Paramedic.

Content Self-Evaluation

MULTIPLE CHOICE

_A_ 1. Most EMS injuries occur during lifting or while in or around motor vehicles.
    A. True   B. False

_C_ 2. All of the following are benefits of physical fitness EXCEPT:
    A. decreased resting heart rate.
    B. decreased resting blood pressure.
    C. increased anxiety levels.
    D. enhanced quality of life.
    E. increased resistance to disease.

_A_ 3. The core elements of physical fitness include all of the following EXCEPT:
    A. disease resistance.   D. cardiovascular endurance.
    B. muscular strength.   E. aerobic capacity.
    C. flexibility.

 4. Exercise performed against stable resistance, in which muscles are exercised in a motionless manner, is called:
    A. isometric.   D. isotonic.
    B. polymeric.   E. polytonic.
    C. aerobic.

B _A_ 5. The target heart rate for a 50-year-old female with a resting heart rate of 65 is:
    A. 103.   D. 170.
    B. 139.   E. 220.
    C. 152.

_C_ 6. Flexibility is obtained by:
    A. isometric exercise.
    B. isotonic exercise.
    C. stretching.
    D. bouncing at the end of a range-of-motion exercise.
    E. weight lifting.

_E_ 7. Which of the following is NOT a major food group?
   A. grains and breads
   B. dairy products
   C. fruits
   D. meat and fish
   E. simple sugars

_C_ 8. A proper and healthy diet minimizes intake of which of the following?
   A. carbohydrates
   B. vitamins
   C. salt
   D. protein
   E. grains

_D_ 9. Water has what benefit over soft drinks?
   A. cheaper
   B. more thirst quenching
   C. better for you
   D. all of the above
   E. none of the above

_C_ 10. Which of the following does NOT increase your risk for cancer?
   A. prolonged, chronic, and unprotected sun exposure
   B. consumption of charcoal-grilled foods
   C. eating broccoli
   D. being a postmenopausal woman
   E. elevated cholesterol levels

_E_ 11. Which of the following can reduce the risk of back injury?
   A. doing abdominal crunches
   B. stopping smoking
   C. following good nutritional practices
   D. getting adequate rest
   E. all of the above

_C_ 12. Which of the following is NOT part of proper lifting?
   A. positioning the load as close to the body as possible
   B. locking your back in a slightly extended position
   C. reaching while twisting to distribute weight
   D. bending your knees
   E. keeping your palms up

_A_ 13. Because a person carrying a contagious disease may present without signs, you must consider the blood and body fluids of every patient you treat as infectious.
   A. True
   B. False

_A_ 14. Which of the following infectious diseases is NOT transmitted via airborne pathogens?
   A. hepatitis C
   B. pertussis
   C. tuberculosis
   D. varicella
   E. rubella

_D_ 15. Which of the following items of personal protective equipment is/are recommended when suctioning a patient?
   A. gloves
   B. eyewear and mask
   C. gown
   D. both A and B
   E. A, B, and C

_E_ 16. Which of the following items of personal protective equipment is/are recommended when assisting a mother with childbirth?
   A. gloves
   B. eyewear and mask
   C. gown
   D. both A and B
   E. A, B, and C

_B_ 17. HEPA and N-95 respirators are intended to protect against:
  A. HIV/AIDS.
  B. tuberculosis.
  C. hepatitis B.
  D. hepatitis C.
  E. bacterial meningitis.

_E_ 18. Proper handwashing requires:
  A. removing rings.
  B. lathering hands vigorously.
  C. scrubbing vigorously for at least 15 seconds.
  D. scrubbing under fingernails and in creases of the knuckles.
  E. all of the above

_E_ 19. Which of the following is a recommended immunization for the paramedic?
  A. tetanus/diphtheria
  B. polio
  C. hepatitis B
  D. rubella
  E. all of the above

_A_ 20. Used needles are to be disposed by:
  A. placing them in a properly labeled puncture-proof container.
  B. recapping them and placing them in a biohazard bag.
  C. returning them to the pharmacy for disposal.
  D. driving them deeply into the ground.
  E. breaking them and taping them together with the tips covered.

_E_ 21. Sterilization uses which of the following to kill pathogens?
  A. bleach
  B. radiation
  C. EPA-approved chemical agents
  D. pressurized steam
  E. all of the above except A

_C_ 22. Which of the following represent the standard progression through the stages of grieving?
  A. anger, denial, bargaining, acceptance, depression
  B. denial, bargaining, anger, depression, acceptance
  C. denial, anger, bargaining, depression, acceptance
  D. anger, denial, bargaining, depression, acceptance
  E. depression, anger, denial, bargaining, acceptance

_C B_ 23. A grieving patient who is withdrawing from friends and family and is unwilling to communicate with others is most likely in which stage of loss?
  A. denial
  B. anger
  C. depression
  D. bargaining
  E. acceptance

_B_ 24. Because paramedics experience death more often than the general population, they experience less stress and are better able to cope with it.
  A. True
  B. False

_B_ 25. At which age are children most likely to feel that death is a temporary absence from which the deceased person will return?
  A. newborn to age 3
  B. ages 3 to 6
  C. ages 6 to 9
  D. ages 9 to 12
  E. ages 12 to 18

_A_ 26. When informed of the death of a loved one, some family members may explode in anger, throwing things and screaming.
  A. True
  B. False

_A_ 27. When informing the family of the death of a member, use the words "dead" or "died" rather than less definitive ones such as "moved on" or "has gone to a better place."
  A. True
  B. False

28. The type of stress that has positive effects is:
   A. distress.
   B. halcion.
   C. stimulation.
   D. eustress.
   E. gravitas.

29. Which of the following is NOT a typical stressor for people working in emergency medical services?
   A. shift work
   B. violent people
   C. waiting for calls
   D. limited responsibilities
   E. thirst

30. The human response to stress progresses through three stages, in this order:
   A. resistance, alarm, exhaustion.
   B. alarm, resistance, exhaustion.
   C. alarm, exhaustion, resistance.
   D. resistance, exhaustion, alarm.
   E. exhaustion, alarm, resistance.

31. The U.S. Surgeon General estimated that stress-related diseases kill approximately what percentage of people who die of nontraumatic causes?
   A. 50%
   B. 60%
   C. 70%
   D. 80%
   E. 90%

32. The physiological phenomena that occur at approximately 24-hour intervals and regulate body temperature, sleepiness, and appetite are called:
   A. estrorhythms.
   B. circadian rhythms.
   C. lunar tidals.
   D. fatigue/rest cycles.
   E. solar epochs.

33. Drowsiness and fatigue account for approximately how many motor vehicle crashes per year?
   A. 56,000
   B. 34,000
   C. 14,000
   D. 5,000
   E. 2,000

34. When you work a regular night shift, a technique that may help you maintain the appropriate awake/sleep cycle is:
   A. sleeping during one "anchor time" for both on- and off-duty days.
   B. eating well before going to bed.
   C. sleeping during the day after you work a night shift and at night when off duty.
   D. sleeping in a warm place during the day.
   E. taking short naps rather than long sleep.

35. Which of the following is a warning sign of stress?
   A. withdrawal
   B. feeling of being abandoned
   C. difficulty making decisions
   D. aching muscles and joints
   E. all of the above

36. Which of the following is NOT a healthy behavior for dealing with or reducing stress?
   A. controlled breathing
   B. remaining distant from co-workers
   C. reframing
   D. creating a non-EMS circle of friends
   E. taking a vacation

37. Which of the following is a hazard commonly associated with auto crashes?
   A. downed power lines
   B. spilled hazardous chemicals
   C. moving traffic
   D. adverse weather conditions
   E. all of the above

_B_ 38. The paramedic attending the patient in the back of the ambulance is too busy and must move about too much to wear a seatbelt.
A. True   B. False

_D_ 39. The greatest risk when following an emergency escort is which of the following?
A. losing the escort in traffic
B. falling too far behind and losing the escort as it rounds a corner
C. running into the escort vehicle when it stops quickly
D. a vehicle pulling out after the first emergency vehicle passes
E. none of the above

_B_ 40. When driving an ambulance, a paramedic must:
A. ignore highway regulations as necessary to reach the patient.
B. practice due regard for the safety of others.
C. never exceed speed limits.
D. always use an escort vehicle.
E. none of the above

MATCHING

Body Substance Isolation Procedures

Write the letter or letters of the appropriate personal protective equipment necessary for each of the following procedures in the space provided.

A. gloves

B. mask and eyewear

C. HEPA or N-95 respirator

D. gown

_B A_ 41. Suctioning

BCD A 42. Childbirth

_B A_ 43. Endotracheal intubation

_C A_ 44. Patient with suspected TB

_D DA_ 45. Serious arterial blood loss

Special Project

Problem Solving

While transporting a patient to the hospital, you receive a needle stick from a used syringe that was left on the bench of your ambulance. List the steps you would take to reduce the chances of infection and complete the proper reporting process.

1. _Tell your officer_

_____

_____

2. Fill out exposer paper work

3. Call

4.

5.

Personal Benchmarking

Target Heart Rate

Your target heart rate is a heart rate at which you can maximize the benefits of exercise for your cardiovascular system. Exercise, by walking, riding a stationary or regular bike, or other activity, to raise your pulse rate to reach this target level. Exercising to your target level will significantly improve your cardiovascular fitness if done on a regular basis (three or more times per week).

Calculate your target heart rate using the following steps:

1. After resting (for a while), determine your heart rate.

2. Subtract your age from 220 (the resulting figure is your expected maximum heart rate).

3. Subtract your resting heart rate from your expected maximum heart rate.

4. Multiply the resulting number by 0.7.

5. Add the result to your resting heart rate to determine your target heart rate.

EMS Systems

Review of Chapter Objectives

After reading this chapter, you should be able to:

1. **Describe key historical events that influenced the national development of Emergency Medical Services (EMS) systems.** pp. 47–52

There is a long history of individuals providing care in the out-of-hospital setting, beginning in ancient times. The cardinal events in the history of EMS include the first organized use of patient transport (and the ambulance) by Jean Larrey, chief surgeon for Napoleon. While simply a horse-drawn cart called an *ambulance volante* (flying ambulance), it represented the first recognized attempt to bring the injured from the field to medical care. Wars continued to be the impetus to improve out-of-hospital care. The American Civil War, World Wars I and II, and the Korean and Vietnamese conflicts all brought substantial changes to field care and transport. The war in Vietnam saw a greater reduction in mortality associated with immediate care in the field and rapid access to surgery than was the case in any previous conflict. However, the single greatest event in the development of modern-day EMS was the National Highway Safety Act of 1966. This act, for the first time and on a national level, recognized emergency medical services and financially supported their development. Under that act, and its establishment of the Department of Transportation (DOT) as overseeing agency, the nation soon had the first national EMS training curriculum, new criteria for ambulance design (the KKK specifications), and the creation of state-led agencies to coordinate EMS development. Later federal legislation created EMS systems through the guidance of the Department of Health, Education, and Welfare, and since then several federal initiatives have continued to improve the nation's EMS system, mostly under the leadership of the DOT.

2. **Define the following terms:**

   a. **EMS systems** p. 46

   An emergency medical services system is a comprehensive network of personnel, equipment, and resources established to deliver aid and emergency medical care to the community.

   b. **Licensure** p. 59

   Licensure is a process by which a governmental agency grants permission to engage in an occupation based on an applicant's attaining a required competency sufficient to ensure the public's protection.

   c. **Certification** p. 59

   Certification is a process by which an agency or association grants recognition to an individual who meets its qualifications.

   d. **Registration** p. 59

   Registration is the listing of your name and essential information within a particular record of a certifying organization.

   e. **Profession** p. 59

   A profession is a vocation requiring advanced education or training in a specialized body of knowledge and/or skills.

f. Professionalism   p. 69

Professionalism is the conduct or qualities that characterize a practitioner in a particular field or profession.

g. Healthcare professional   p. 61

Healthcare professionals are properly trained and licensed or certified providers of health care.

h. Ethics   p. 69

Ethics are rules or standards for conduct of a particular group or profession.

i. Peer review   p. 69

Peer review is a process of evaluation of the quality of conduct or actions performed by members of a group or profession that is undertaken by other members of that group or profession.

j. Medical direction   p. 54

Medical direction is the guidance of the actions of prehospital care providers by a physician associated with the emergency medical services system. Medical direction may be on-line or off-line medical direction and includes the physician's involvement in and supervision of personnel education, personnel and equipment selection, protocol development, quality improvement, and advocacy for the EMS system and the patient.

k. Protocols   p. 55

Protocols are policies and procedures addressing primarily triage, treatment, transport, and transfer of patients as well as special circumstances and events within the EMS system.

3. Identify national groups important to the development, education, and implementation of EMS.   pp. 62–63

The National Association of EMTs, the National Registry of EMTs, the National Association of State EMS Directors, the National Association of Emergency Physicians, the National Council of State EMS Training Coordinators, and other similar associations provide leadership, advise national regulatory bodies, and establish standards for performance related to the provision of emergency medical care. These organizations serve to guide the continuing development, initial and ongoing EMS education, and implementation and coordination of EMS systems nationally.

4. Discuss the role of national associations, the National Registry of EMTs, and the roles of various EMS standard-setting agencies.   pp. 62–63

National associations identify standards for performance in EMS and advocate for patient care and the professional stature of their members. The National Registry of EMTs maintains a national standard, through testing, at the Basic, Intermediate, and Paramedic levels of EMT training. Other standard-setting agencies establish the criteria and standards for system performance. For example, the Joint Committee on Educational Programs for the EMT-Paramedic sets standards for institutions educating paramedics. The American Heart Association sets standards for basic and advanced cardiac life support. The American College of Emergency Physicians recommends a list of ALS equipment for ambulances. The American College of Surgeons establishes a listing of essential BLS ambulance equipment.

5. Identify the standards (components) of an EMS system as defined by the National Highway Traffic Safety Administration.   pp. 51–52

NHTSA has defined the following components for EMS systems:

- **Regulation and policy**—Each state must have laws, regulations, policies, and procedures that govern its EMS system.
- **Resources management**—Each state must have central control of health-care resources to ensure that all patients have equal access to emergency care.
- **Human resources and training**—Each state must require that all EMS providers are taught by qualified instructors using a standardized curriculum.
- **Transportation**—Each state must ensure that patients are safely and reliably transported by ground or air ambulance.
- **Facilities**—Each state must ensure that every seriously ill or injured patient is delivered to an appropriate medical facility in a timely manner.

- **Communications**—Each state must have a system for public access to EMS along with communications among dispatchers, ambulance crews, and hospital personnel.
- **Trauma systems**—Each state should develop a system of specialized care for trauma patients including the designation of trauma centers and systems to ensure patients arrive at the appropriate facility in a timely manner.
- **Public information and education**—EMS personnel should participate in programs designed to educate the public in injury prevention, emergency recognition, system access, and first aid.
- **Medical direction**—Each EMS system must have a physician medical director responsible for delegating medical practice to prehospital care providers and overseeing patient care.
- **Evaluation**—Each state must have a quality improvement system for continuing evaluation and upgrading of the EMS system.

6. Differentiate among the EMS provider levels: First Responder, Emergency Medical Technician-Basic, Emergency Medical Technician-Intermediate, and Emergency Medical Technician-Paramedic. pp. 59–60

- **First Responder**—The first responder is usually the first EMS-trained provider on the scene and is prepared to initially care for and stabilize the patient until personnel with higher levels of training arrive.
- **EMT-Basic**—The EMT-B is an EMS responder who meets the criteria of the U.S. DOT National Standard Curriculum for EMT-Basics and is prepared to assess, care for, and transport the patient at the basic life support level.
- **EMT-Intermediate**—The EMT-I is an EMS responder who meets the criteria of the U.S. DOT National Standard Curriculum for EMT-Intermediates and is prepared to assess, care for, and transport the patient using all EMT-Basic skills plus some advanced life support level skills such as advanced airway management, IV therapy, and administration of certain medications.
- **EMT-Paramedic**—The EMT-P is an EMS responder who meets the criteria of the U.S. DOT National Standard Curriculum for EMT-Paramedics and is prepared to assess, care for, and transport the patient using advanced patient assessment, trauma management, pharmacology, cardiology, and other medical skills. The paramedic should complete advanced cardiac life support and pediatric life support courses.

7. Describe what is meant by "citizen involvement in the EMS system." pp. 55–56

Citizen involvement in the EMS system means that average members of the public can recognize a medical or trauma emergency, know how to access the EMS system, and know how to provide basic life support assistance such as hemorrhage control, CPR, and, possibly, early defibrillation before the arrival of EMS personnel.

8. Describe the role of the EMS physician in providing medical direction. pp. 54–55

A paramedic functions only under the supervision and direction of a medical direction physician. That oversight is provided as either on-line medical direction or off-line medical direction. Off-line medical direction involves the physician's participation in personnel and equipment selection, training, protocol development, quality improvement, and acting as an EMS and patient advocate within the health profession. On-line medical direction consists of direct radio or phone consultation and oversight of paramedics and other prehospital care providers while they are caring for a patient. The ultimate responsibility for all care offered by the paramedic rests with the medical direction physician.

9. Discuss prehospital and out-of-hospital care as an extension of the physician. pp. 54–55

The medical director is a physician who is legally responsible for all clinical and patient care aspects of an EMS system. Prehospital care provided by the paramedic or other EMS personnel is provided under the license of the medical director, regardless of who their employer is.

10. Describe the benefits of both on-line and off-line medical direction. pp. 54–55

The benefits of both on-line and off-line medical direction include the medical supervision of the EMS system and prehospital and out-of-hospital patient care. Among these benefits are the opportunity to practice "prehospital medicine" under the license and supervision of the medical director including use of protocols, standing orders, and algorithms developed by the medical director. Additionally, on-line medical direction provides access to direct medical consultation for EMS personnel during the care of the emergency patient.

11. Describe the process for the development of local policies and protocols. pp. 54–55

Protocols are developed by the medical director (in cooperation with expert EMS personnel) to address the assessment and care offered during triage, treatment, transport, and transfer of the patient. The protocols and other system policies are developed to address not only commonly encountered circumstances but also special situations such as intervener physicians, child, spouse, or elderly abuse, DNR orders, patient refusals, and the like. The protocols and policies set the standards for accountability of EMS personnel and ensure uniform, medically approved care for each and every patient.

12. Describe the relationship between a physician on the scene, the paramedic on the scene, and the EMS physician providing on-line medical direction. p. 55

At the scene of a medical or trauma emergency, the health care professional with the highest training specific to emergency care should be responsible for patient care. When a non–system-affiliated physician is at the scene (an intervener physician), the on-line medical direction physician is ultimately responsible for the patient. When on-line medical direction is not available, the paramedic may relinquish patient care responsibility to the intervener physician as long as that individual identifies himself, demonstrates a willingness to assume patient care responsibilities, and agrees to provide the documentation required by the system. If treatment differs from system protocols, the intervener physician must agree to ride with the patient to the hospital.

13. Describe the components of continuous quality improvement and analyze its contribution to system improvement, continuing medical education, and research. pp. 67–70

Continuous quality improvement (CQI) is an ongoing effort to refine and improve the system to ensure the highest level of service possible. It involves six basic components: identifying system-wide problems, elaborating on the probable causes, listing solutions, outlining a plan of corrective action, providing resources and support to ensure success, and reevaluating the results and system performance continuously. CQI system review uses positive reinforcement and support to identify and improve patient care. It can identify areas for improvement and ways to allocate resources to make those improvements, frequently through continuing medical education. When questions arise about the benefits of care offered by a system, a CQI program can suggest research projects to investigate the real value of procedures, equipment, and protocols. The real key to effective CQI is the positive and reinforcing nature of its approach to system improvement.

14. Describe the importance, basic principles, process of evaluating and interpreting, and benefits of research. Appendix; pp. 70–71

Research is essential to ensuring that the equipment and procedures used in the out-of-hospital setting are safe, benefit the patient, and are worth any potential risks of employing them. Research attempts to objectively evaluate the performance of interventions in an unbiased way. Research begins by asking a question (stating a hypothesis), investigating any existing research, designing a study that is unbiased and fairly measures performance, collects and analyzes data, assesses and evaluates results against the hypothesis, and reports the findings. Evidence-based medicine (EBM) evaluates research to determine which procedures in emergency medicine have a positive impact on patient outcome and which do not. This process may cause us to re-evaluate the tools and procedures that were once considered standard in prehospital care.

Case Study Review

Reread the case study on pages 45 and 46 in Paramedic Care: Introduction to Advanced Prehospital Care *and then read the following discussion.*

This case study demonstrates the coming together of personnel from many agencies to meet the prehospital needs of a patient, an EMS system.

The case study highlights the different facets of EMS response. Observing the crash, you recognize the need for a response and access the system by using a cell phone to dial the universal entry number 911. The initial dispatcher quickly directs your call to the EMS area dispatcher, and the dispatcher starts numerous agencies en route to the scene—the fire department (BLS), the rescue service, and an ALS ambulance. The police are also notified and begin their response. The dispatcher gathers further information about the crash to update the responding personnel and possibly modify the response. Once on the scene, the BLS providers assume patient care responsibilities by ensuring that the scene is safe, analyzing the mechanism of injury, and taking information from you. From this information and the results of a quick physical assessment (the initial assessment) of the patients, they triage the patients and call the dispatcher for an additional ALS ambulance and air medical transport.

An additional arriving fire unit further ensures traffic control and scene safety and establishes a landing zone. The highest-trained EMS care provider assumes overall patient care coordination responsibilities. He calls for the patients to be distributed to the most appropriate facilities, ensuring that the patients receive the best of care and that no single facility is overloaded by the arrival of patients. This process, as established by the medical direction system and supervised by a resource hospital, also ensures that the most appropriate hospital resources are used for the most seriously injured patients. Patients are moved quickly to the appropriate facilities. The child is rushed by air to the pediatric trauma center, while the adults are rushed to other appropriate trauma centers. In this case study, various providers from various services work together efficiently to ensure that patients are removed from the crash scene quickly. This study is thus an excellent example of an EMS system operating as it should.

What is not mentioned here is that the care given by the providers is well coordinated because the various services practice working together in disaster drills and because continuous quality improvement programs have identified system weaknesses and have taken corrective action before these patients were placed in need. Ongoing education and skills maintenance exercises keep the providers current in skills and knowledge. Finally, the system's CQI committee will review this response, identify strengths and correct any weaknesses it reveals through education and revised protocols. Again, these are signs of a healthy EMS system.

Content Self-Evaluation

MULTIPLE CHOICE

___A___ 1. An Emergency Medical Services system is a network of personnel, equipment, and resources established to deliver aid and emergency care to the community.
   A. True   B. False

___A___ 2. The date of the earliest recorded medical care procedures is:
   A. about 5,000 years ago.   D. 1562.
   B. about 2,000 years ago.   E. 1666.
   C. 1497.

___E___ 3. In a well-developed EMS system, trained First Responders are likely to be:
   A. police officers.   D. teachers.
   B. firefighters.   E. all of the above
   C. lifeguards.

4. In a nontiered EMS system, in which order do care providers have contact with the patient?
   A. emergency physician, dispatcher, ALS provider, BLS provider
   B. dispatcher, ALS provider or BLS provider, emergency physician
   C. dispatcher, BLS provider, ALS provider, emergency physician
   D. dispatcher, BLS provider, emergency physician, ALS provider
   E. none of the above

5. The advent of the ambulance is generally credited to:
   A. Napoleon in 1812.
   B. Jean Larrey in 1797.
   C. Clara Barton in 1862.
   D. Cincinnati Ohio in 1865.
   E. Bellevue Hospital in 1869.

6. A report focusing on the problem of accidental death and legislation that began modern-day EMS dates to:
   A. 1950.
   B. 1966.
   C. 1972.
   D. 1981.
   E. 1988.

7. Which of the following was NOT a component of the Emergency Medical Services Systems Act of 1973?
   A. communications
   B. system financing
   C. training
   D. access to care
   E. system evaluation

8. The medical director is a physician who is legally responsible for all patient care offered by the system he oversees.
   A. True
   B. False

9. The intervener physician is a physician who is:
   A. not affiliated with the system of medical direction.
   B. at the scene of an emergency.
   C. a trained emergency physician.
   D. both A and B
   E. none of the above

10. When on-line medical control is established and an intervener physician is present, is willing to accept patient care responsibility, performs interventions consistent with the system protocols, and agrees to document the interventions as required by the system, the paramedic should:
   A. relinquish patient care responsibilities.
   B. retain patient care authority.
   C. relinquish patient care responsibilities only if the physician agrees to ride to the hospital.
   D. retain patient care responsibilities in cases of physician disagreement.
   E. none of the above

11. Off-line medical direction includes which of the following?
   A. protocols
   B. training guidelines
   C. personnel selection policies
   D. quality assurance
   E. all of the above

12. Which of the following is NOT one of the four "Ts" of emergency care?
   A. triage
   B. transfer
   C. termination of care
   D. transport
   E. treatment

_C_ 13. Which of the following statements is NOT true?
   A. The ability to recognize cardiac emergencies can save lives.
   B. Over 300,000 cardiac arrests per year occur before the patient reaches the hospital.
   C. Most cardiac arrests happen immediately upon onset of symptoms.
   D. If bystanders or the patient call in time, many cardiac arrests can be prevented.
   E. all of the above

_A_ 14. Current research suggests that automatic defibrillators in public places may reduce cardiac arrest mortality.
   A. True   B. False

_B_ 15. Multiple community phone numbers for citizen access to emergency medical services:
   A. ensure efficient system entry.
   B. add minutes to system entry.
   C. ensure callback capability.
   D. ensure instant routing to the proper agency.
   E. all of the above

_A_ 16. There are great disadvantages to dispatching EMS, fire, and police from a single control center.
   A. True   B. False

_C_ 17. The dispatch system that provides caller interrogation, predetermined response configurations, and prearrival instructions is:
   A. system status management.   D. caller interrogation.
   B. enhanced 911.   E. none of the above
   C. priority dispatch.

_A_ 18. There may be some increased liability for a system providing prearrival instructions.
   A. True   B. False

_D_ 19. The goal of dispatch and response in an effective EMS is to have:
   A. BLS units on the scene within 4 minutes.
   B. ALS units on the scene within 8 minutes.
   C. at least 90 percent of all responses within system time limits.
   D. all of the above
   E. none of the above

_B_ 20. The learning domain associated with skills is:
   A. cognitive.   D. didactic.
   B. psychomotor.   E. dexterous.
   C. affective.

_A_ 21. The process by which a state or other governmental agency grants permission to engage in a given occupation is:
   A. licensure.   D. reciprocity.
   B. certification.   E. tenure.
   C. registration.

_D_ 22. Granting someone recognition for meeting the qualifications of another agency is called:
   A. licensure.   D. reciprocity.
   B. certification.   E. tenure.
   C. registration.

_D_ 23. The U.S. DOT has developed curricula for how many levels of EMS providers?
   A. 1   D. 4
   B. 2   E. 5
   C. 3

_____E_____ 24. The EMS provider responsible for general patient assessment, CPR, hemorrhage control, and spinal immobilization is the:
- **A.** First Responder.
- **B.** EMT-Basic.
- **C.** EMT-Intermediate.
- **D.** EMT-Paramedic.
- **E.** all of the above

_____C_____ 25. An example of the expanded scope of practice in which paramedics work closely with law enforcement officers is:
- **A.** critical-care transport.
- **B.** industrial EMS.
- **C.** tactical EMS.
- **D.** primary care.
- **E.** all of the above

_____B_____ 26. The organization that administers practical and written exams and establishes qualifications for registration of EMT-Bs, EMT-Is, and EMT-Ps on a national level is the:
- **A.** National Association of EMTs.
- **B.** National Registry of EMTs.
- **C.** National Council of State EMS Training Coordinators.
- **D.** Joint Review Committee on Educational Programs for the EMT-Paramedic.
- **E.** American College of Emergency Physicians.

_____A_____ 27. The body that sets standards for paramedic education programs is the:
- **A.** Joint Review Committee on Educational Programs for the EMT-Paramedic.
- **B.** National Association of EMTs.
- **C.** National Registry of EMTs.
- **D.** National Council of State EMS Training Coordinators.
- **E.** American College of Emergency Physicians.

_____D_____ 28. Fixed-wing aircraft are usually used for patient transports exceeding:
- **A.** 25 miles.
- **B.** 50 miles.
- **C.** 150 miles.
- **D.** 200 miles.
- **E.** none of the above

_____C_____ 29. The agency responsible for establishing criteria for the design of ambulances is the:
- **A.** American College of Surgeons.
- **B.** American College of Emergency Physicians.
- **C.** U.S. General Services Administration.
- **D.** U.S. Military Assistance to Traffic and Safety Group.
- **E.** National Association of EMTs.

_____B_____ 30. A standard van with a raised roof that is configured as an ambulance is categorized as which type of ambulance?
- **A.** Type I
- **B.** Type II
- **C.** Type III
- **D.** Type A
- **E.** Type B

_____C_____ 31. A resource hospital is one that:
- **A.** accepts most patients for care.
- **B.** fulfills the role of the major trauma center.
- **C.** coordinates specialty services and ensures appropriate patient distribution.
- **D.** has the largest emergency department.
- **E.** provides restocking services for the system's ambulances.

_____E_____ 32. A hospital designated as a receiving facility for the EMS system should have which of the following?
- **A.** an emergency department
- **B.** 24-hour emergency physician coverage
- **C.** surgical facilities and coverage
- **D.** critical and intensive care units
- **E.** all of the above

_____ **33.** Which of the following is NOT a part of a well-designed disaster plan?
   A. mutual aid agreements among neighboring municipalities, services, and systems
   B. a rigid communications system
   C. frequent disaster plan tests and drills
   D. integration of all system components
   E. a coordinated central management agency

_____ **34.** A major complaint regarding quality assurance programs is that they tend to:
   A. be one-time efforts.
   B. address only procedural issues.
   C. be punitive in nature.
   D. not examine protocol issues.
   E. create divisions among care workers on staff.

_____ **35.** Continuous quality improvement differs from quality assurance in that it:
   A. emphasizes customer satisfaction.
   B. rewards or reinforces good behavior.
   C. examines billing practices.
   D. evaluates maintenance activities.
   E. all the above

_____ **36.** Which of the following is NOT one of the standard rules of evidence used to evaluate a proposed change in the EMS system?
   A. There must be a basis for change.
   B. The old procedure must be deemed no longer medically acceptable.
   C. The change must be clinically important.
   D. The change must be affordable, practical, and teachable.
   E. None of the above are standard rules of evidence.

_____ **37.** Ethics are best defined as:
   A. protocols and policies for conduct.
   B. rules or standards governing the performance of a profession.
   C. legal principles governing potential law suits.
   D. the four elements needed to determine negligence.
   E. justifications for actions.

_____ **38.** To the patient, it may be more important to receive care from a provider who seems to be interested in him and empathetic than to receive the most technically correct care.
   A. True   B. False

_____ **39.** The most common source of EMS funding is:
   A. voluntary donations.   D. tax subsidies.
   B. direct patient payments.   E. residual payments.
   C. third-party payers.

_____ **40.** The model for EMS operations that is becoming more and more popular for municipalities is the:
   A. public utility model.   D. volunteer model.
   B. third service model.   E. proprietary model.
   C. fire service model.

LISTING

Identify the agency or association most closely linked with the following guidelines for EMS:

41. National standard curricula for EMS providers

42. Criteria for ambulance design

U.S. General Services Administration.

43. Listing of standard equipment for Basic Life Support ambulances

_____

44. Listing of equipment and supplies for Advanced Life Support ambulances

_____

45. Criteria for paramedic education programs

_____

Special Project

The EMS Agenda for the Future

A. Describe the purpose of the EMS Agenda for the Future.

_____
_____
_____
_____
_____
_____
_____
_____
_____
_____
_____
_____
_____
_____
_____
_____

B. List at least 6 of the EMS attributes defined by the EMS Agenda for the Future.

_____
_____
_____
_____
_____
_____

4

Roles and Responsibilities of the Paramedic

Review of Chapter Objectives

After reading this chapter, you should be able to:

1. **Describe the attributes of a paramedic as a health care professional.** **pp. 86–92**

   The attributes of a paramedic are related to his stature as a health care professional and include leadership, integrity, empathy, self-motivation, appearance and personal hygiene, self-confidence, communication, time management, teamwork and diplomacy, respect, and patient advocacy.

   As a paramedic, you must demonstrate leadership in order to coordinate and direct other care providers in attending to the patient. You must know the abilities of your team and ask its members to do only what they are able to do. You must demonstrate integrity to earn the respect of your peers and the medical community. You must appreciate the plight of the patient and demonstrate an understanding of his situation. You must be both self-confident and self-motivated to employ life-saving procedures in the worst of conditions. You must strive for excellence in knowledge and skills and have and display confidence as you employ patient care skills. Your appearance must demonstrate a respect for both yourself and your patient. Remember that good grooming and personal hygiene are important in presenting a professional image. You must be able to communicate effectively both orally and in writing to patients, other care providers, and physicians. You must be able coordinate your efforts and those of others to quickly address the needs of the patient and to fulfill your responsibilities as a paramedic. You must respect others and, through demonstrating that respect, earn respect for yourself. One way of demonstrating that respect is showing a heightened sensitivity to your patient's rights as a person, including the right to confidentiality. You must become a patient advocate, promoting and ensuring that patients receive the care and attention their illness or injury requires. And, finally, you must ensure that you maintain the attributes of a professional through careful delivery of your service, including mastering and refreshing skills; following protocols, policies, and procedures; checking your equipment before its use; and operating the ambulance and equipment safely.

2. **Describe the benefits of paramedic continuing education and the importance of maintaining one's paramedic license/certification.** **pp. 86, 92**

   Continuing education helps you maintain the knowledge you acquired through your initial paramedic education and expands your own personal knowledge and skills. It helps you keep up with changes in prehospital care and is essential to maintaining your certification and ability to practice.

3. List the primary and additional responsibilities of paramedics.   pp. 78–86

The primary responsibilities of the paramedic include:

- **Preparation**—You must be mentally, physically, and emotionally ready to respond to the call; know your protocols, geography, and equipment; and ensure that your vehicle and equipment are all in proper working order.
- **Response**—You must drive responsibly, ensuring a timely yet safe response.
- **Scene size-up**—You must assess the scene to determine the safety of the scene, including identification of any hazards and the need for BSI; the number of ill or injured; the need for any additional resources; and the mechanism of injury or the nature of the illness.
- **Patient assessment**—Once at the patient's side, you must determine whether or not the patient needs cervical immobilization as well as his level of consciousness (or responsiveness) and the stability of the airway, breathing, and circulation. You will then assess for specific injury or illness signs through a focused or rapid trauma assessment. You will also evaluate the patient's medical history and perform ongoing assessments.
- **Recognition of injury or illness**—As a result of the scene size-up and patient assessment, you will identify the illness or injury and the patient's priority for care and transport.
- **Patient management**—You will employ appropriate care procedures, guided by protocols, with your patient and, at times, consult with medical direction to further guide your care.
- **Appropriate disposition**—Based on the results of your assessment, the effects of the care measures you have employed, and your system's protocols, you will determine the disposition of your patient. That disposition may be transport to a level I, II, or III trauma center or to another specialized hospital, the closest hospital, or an alternative care facility. An additional possible disposition is to treat and release the patient with instructions to seek the advice of a personal physician.
- **Patient transfer**—As the health care system becomes more complex and facilities become more specialized, you may be charged with the safe and efficient transfer of patients from one facility to another.
- **Documentation**—At the conclusion of your patient care, you will be required to document the results of your assessment and care to ensure the continuity of patient care.
- **Return to service**—At the end of your response, you must ensure that you, your crew, and your ambulance are ready to return to service. This includes cleaning and refueling the vehicle, maintaining equipment, and replacing supplies used during the call.

Additional responsibilities include:

- **Community involvement**—You should promote and participate in programs to help the community recognize when EMS is needed, how to access the system, and what to do until the ambulance arrives. Community involvement also includes participation in the development and presentation of programs to improve health—stressing a healthy diet, for example—and to reduce injury—such as promoting seat belt use.
- **Support for primary care**—Modern health care is evolving in ways aimed at ensuring that costly resources are best directed to serve the patient. In support of this aim, you may be responsible for transporting or directing patients with minor injury or illness to alternative facilities like urgent care centers or physicians' offices.
- **Citizen involvement in EMS**—Ordinary citizens can be highly important evaluators of the EMS system, because they are its consumers and can best say what elements of it are important to them. Pay attention to the comments, suggestions, and criticisms of patients/citizens you contact and pass what you learn along-to-the appropriate personnel in your system.
- **Personal and professional development**—To maintain and improve your ability to provide prehospital (and out-of-hospital) care, you must participate in professional development. This may include taking refresher and continuing education courses, engaging in skill maintenance exercises, and other activities.

4. **Define the role of the paramedic relative to the safety of the crew, the patient, and bystanders.** pp. 79–80

You must evaluate information obtained from the dispatcher and gathered during your scene size-up to identify any potential scene hazards. Then you must take action to ensure your safety and the safety of the patient, other crew members and rescue personnel, and bystanders. You must also monitor the scene during your care to ensure that no hazards develop to threaten you, your patient, fellow rescuers, or bystanders.

5. **Describe the role of the paramedic in health education activities related to illness and injury prevention.** p. 85

As EMS matures, its members will be expected to become more involved in both injury and illness prevention programs for the public. Such programs are the most effective ways of increasing overall public health and reducing both death and disability from accidents and injuries.

6. **Describe examples of professional behaviors in the following areas:** pp. 87–92

- **Integrity**—Be honest and trustworthy in your contacts with patients, crew members, and other health care professionals. Doing this is essential to maintaining personal integrity.
- **Empathy**—You can convey empathy by attempting to understand and appreciate a patient's situation.
- **Self-motivation**—Doing your job well without direct supervision represents self-motivation.
- **Appearance and personal hygiene**—A clean, pressed shirt and trousers and well-kept hair demonstrate a good appearance and appropriate personal hygiene.
- **Self-confidence**—Displaying comfort with the application of emergency skills demonstrates self-confidence.
- **Communications**—In emergency medical services, it is essential to communicate quickly, concisely, accurately, and effectively.
- **Time management**—An emergency scene is often a chaotic place. It is imperative that you be able to organize and direct your actions and those of others quickly and efficiently to ensure that your patient receives appropriate emergency care and transport to definitive care as rapidly as possible.
- **Teamwork and diplomacy**—The emergency response is a team event, and the paramedic, as team leader, must direct many individuals to work together in the patient's best interest.
- **Respect**—Respect is demonstrated by showing regard and consideration for patients, care providers, and others. Listening to these people and indicating that you really hear what they say shows your respect for them and earns you their respect.
- **Patient advocacy**—Ensuring that the needs of your patient remain the first priority of your pre-hospital emergency care will help you meet your responsibility as a patient advocate.
- **Careful delivery of service**—Demonstrate professional behavior by performing your job to the highest level of excellence, by mastering and maintaining your skills and knowledge, and by conscientiously carrying out equipment checks, driving safely, and following protocols, policies, and procedures.

7. **Identify the benefits of paramedics teaching in their community.** p. 85

Teaching in your community places you in front of your "consumers" before they call for help. This gives you an opportunity to develop a positive public image and explain the workings of the system. It will also help you integrate with the other members of the health care system.

8. **Analyze how the paramedic can benefit the health-care system by supporting primary care for patients in the out-of-hospital setting.** pp. 83, 85

With the increasing costs of health care, it has become necessary to ensure that the patient's needs are best matched to the available resources. This may mean that the paramedic, through assessment and consultation with the medical direction physician, may direct patients to facilities other than the emergency department.

9. Describe how professionalism applies to the paramedic while on and off duty. p. 87

It is essential that the paramedic display a professional attitude toward his patient and the profession as a whole. This applies while both on and off duty because the public often judges a profession by the actions of its members.

Case Study Review

Reread the case study on page 77 in Paramedic Care: Introduction to Advanced Prehospital Care *and then read the following discussion.*

The case study represents elements of an advanced EMS system and demonstrates how technology and improvements to health care can better serve the patient.

The efficient response demonstrated by this call began well before the dispatch of Medic 49. Bobby Moore has maintained his certification throughout his career as a paramedic and is a master of assessment and prehospital emergency care. He checked his ambulance thoroughly that morning to ensure it was stocked with the necessary supplies and that all equipment was working well. He checked the oil, tire pressure, and fluid levels and tested all lights, sirens, and radios. He was ready to respond when the call came in.

The computer linked the incoming phone call reporting the emergency to a database that identified the location (an exact address) of the caller and any elements of medical history (such as the number of responses to the address, serious past medical history of patients at the address, or potential for violence at the address) linked to that phone number and address. This information helped the paramedic better prepare for response and better ensure scene safety. A computer screen at the dispatch center displayed a map that highlighted the location of the caller and the closest police, ambulance, and fire units. Further enhanced CAD systems may highlight areas of likely traffic congestion, school zones, or road construction to help the dispatcher best direct the responding units to the scene.

Prearrival instructions helped the woman's husband regain his composure and take initial actions to ensure the airway and breathing. Without such steps, the stroke patient might have died before the arrival of EMS. The conversation between the caller and the dispatcher may also help guide paramedics to the patient's side.

Bobby Moore viewed the scene and ensured it was safe, then moved quickly to his patient's side. There he provided assessment, care, and transport according to protocol, policies, and procedures. As he did this, he demonstrated empathy and a sincere concern for his patient. He suspected that a stroke caused the patient's signs and symptoms and employed a quick stroke assessment that confirmed these suspicions. By doing this, he ensured that the patient would be quickly transported to the facility best suited to care for stroke care, bypassing a closer facility. As a result, the patient received quick therapy with agents best able to help her.

Paramedic Moore's communication with the emergency department and the medical direction physician was effective, alerting them to the patient's likely stroke condition. This sped the response as the "stroke team" was awaiting the patient's arrival. As Bobby transferred patient responsibility to the physicians, he provided a quick update of the patient's condition and any changes in her signs and symptoms.

Because of the quick care provided by this EMS system and its paramedic, this patient experienced the best outcome possible with today's technologies. She was integrated into a system of primary care and can move quickly back into the mainstream of society.

Content Self-Evaluation

MULTIPLE CHOICE

1. In the past ten years, the health care and EMS systems have seen dramatic changes in care delivery.
   A. True　　　　　　　　　　　　　B. False

_____ **E** 2. Before responding to a call, you must be:
   A. emotionally able to meet the demands of patient care.
   B. physically able to meet the demands of patient care.
   C. mentally able to meet the demands of patient care.
   D. sure the ambulance and equipment are ready for the response.
   E. all of the above

_____ **E** 3. Before responding to a call, you must be familiar with:
   A. local EMS protocols.
   B. the local communications system.
   C. local geography.
   D. neighboring EMS agencies.
   E. all of the above

_____ **A** 4. A call involving which of the following is least likely to require additional assistance?
   A. a single ill patient
   B. reported use of a weapon
   C. knowledge of previous violence
   D. hazardous materials
   E. a rescue situation

_____ **E** 5. Which of the following is an element of scene size-up?
   A. identifying potential scene hazards
   B. identifying the number of patients
   C. determining the nature of the illness
   D. requesting additional services
   E. all of the above

_____ **E D** 6. Which of the following is NOT an element of the initial assessment?
   A. determining an initial patient impression
   B. assessing patient responsiveness
   C. ensuring the patient's breathing
   D. investigating the patient's medical history
   E. treating any life threats

_____ **E D** 7. The recognition of the severity of injury occurs during:
   A. the scene size-up.   D. the ongoing assessment.
   B. the initial assessment.   E. both A and B
   C. the physical exam.

_____ **B** 8. The most common injuries to the paramedic involve:
   A. the neck.   D. the ankles.
   B. the back.   E. the hands.
   C. needle sticks.

_____ **A** 9. You are responsible for patient care and therefore also ultimately responsible for selecting the transport destination for your patient.
   A. True   B. False

_____ **B D** 10. When a patient receives a minor injury and is transported to an alternative care facility such as an outpatient clinic, this care is best described as:
   A. basic care.   D. diversion of care.
   B. primary care.   E. health maintenance.
   C. treat and release.

_C_ **11.** Which of the following items is NOT an essential part of the transfer of a patient between health care facilities?
   A. a verbal patient report from the transferring primary care provider
   B. a copy of the essential parts of the patient's chart
   C. the results of all diagnostic tests
   D. a summary of the patient's past medical history
   E. a summary of the patient's present medical history

_C_ **12.** The patient care report should normally be completed:
   A. before arrival at the emergency department.
   B. upon arrival at the emergency department.
   C. as soon as care is completed.
   D. upon arrival at your base station.
   E. either C or D

_E_ **13.** Why is it inappropriate for a paramedic to identify a patient as "being drunk"?
   A. It is an opinion.
   B. It is not an objective observation.
   C. It cannot be proven with the means available to the paramedic in the field.
   D. It subjects a paramedic to legal liability.
   E. all of the above

_E_ **14.** Which of the following is a component of returning to service after a call?
   A. refueling the ambulance   D. reviewing the call with the crew
   B. restocking supplies   E. all of the above
   C. stowing equipment

_B_ **15.** Which of the following is NOT a part of community involvement for the paramedic?
   A. teaching CPR
   B. transporting patients to alternative care facilities
   C. conducting EMS demonstrations
   D. providing prevention programs
   E. sponsoring programs that help the public recognize when to access EMS

_B_ **16.** What is the unique benefit of having citizen consumers involved in the development, evaluation, and regulation of the EMS system?
   A. They can help seek out alternative funding.
   B. They provide an outside objective view of the EMS system.
   C. They do not have the prejudices of most EMS providers.
   D. They can provide insight into new care procedures.
   E. all of the above

_B_ **17.** As the volume of EMS responses increases, so should the hours of training for EMS personnel.
   A. True   B. False

_E_ **18.** Participation in which of the following will help you maintain interest in EMS and maintain your skills and knowledge?
   A. in-hospital rotations   D. mass casualty drills
   B. case reviews   E. all of the above
   C. research projects

_B_ **19.** Ethics are laws that govern the conduct of members of a profession.
   A. True   B. False

_B_ **20.** Which of the following is NOT an attribute of a professional?
   A. leadership   D. self-motivation
   B. excited demeanor   E. diplomacy
   C. empathy

_____ A **21.** When presented with a complex situation, a self-confident paramedic will ask for
assistance.
    A. True   **B.** False

_____ D R **22.** Which of the following is NOT a method of displaying empathy?
    A. being supportive and reassuring
    B. demonstrating respect for others
    C. having a calm and helpful demeanor
    D. accepting constructive feedback
    E. understanding a patient's feelings

_____ B **23.** In general, the more patches you wear, the more respect you gain from patients.
    A. True   **B.** False

_____ E **24.** Personal biases that are appropriate while you practice as a paramedic include which of
the following?
    A. religious   **D.** ethical
    B. social   **E.** none of the above
    C. political

_____ C **25.** Placing the patient's needs above your own represents which professional attribute?
    A. empathy   **D.** initiative
    B. diplomacy   **E.** self-confidence
    C. patient advocacy

MATCHING

Write the letter of the paramedic responsibility in the space provided next to the action to which it applies.

Responsibility

A. Preparation

B. Response

C. Scene size-up

D. Patient assessment

E. Recognition of illness or injury

F. Patient management

G. Appropriate disposition

H. Patient transfer

I. Documentation

J. Return to service

Action

___ 26. Refuel the vehicle.

___ 27. Follow patient care protocols.

___ 28. Transport a patient to an outpatient center.

___ 29. Determine the mechanism of injury.

___ 30. Record the care you provided.

___ 31. Be familiar with local protocols.

___ 32. Determine the patient's medical history.

___ 33. Categorize the patient's priority for transport.

___ 34. Take a report from the sending facility.

___ 35. Drive responsibly and safely.

___ 36. Deliver a patient to a level II trauma center.

___ 37. Be mentally fit to respond to a call.

___ 38. Check crew members for signs of stress.

___ 39. Identify the nature of the illness.

___ 40. Determine the seriousness of the injury.

5 Illness and Injury Prevention

Review of Chapter Objectives

After reading this chapter, you should be able to:

1. **Describe the incidence, morbidity and mortality and the human, environmental, and socioeconomic impact of unintentional and allegedly unintentional injuries.** **p. 98**

   Injuries are the third leading cause of death in the United States overall and the leading cause of death for individuals between the ages of 1 and 44. Nearly 70,000 deaths are nonintentional, and the largest part of these are the result of vehicle collisions, fires, burns, falls, drownings, and poisonings. For every death there are approximately 19 hospitalizations and 254 emergency department visits. The lifetime cost of trauma exceeds $114 billion.

2. **Identify health hazards and potential crime areas within the community.** **pp. 99, 103–105**

   Health hazards are plentiful in a community. Homes are frequent sites of injuries to children from burns, falls, and firearm discharges. Geriatric patients also frequently fall in their homes. The home setting is also a place where paramedics are likely to encounter infants of low birth weight, patients discharged early from health care facilities, and patients having problems with medication noncompliance—all groups that are at greater likelihood for needing emergency care. Recreational and workplace injuries are also common in communities. Bars and areas with previous records of high crime rates should also be considered as potential crime areas.

3. **Identify local municipal and community resources available for physical, socioeconomic crises.** **pp. 99–101, 106–107**

   Establish a list of community resources in your locality that are available to assist patients in crisis. Such sites might include prenatal clinics, urgent care centers, and social services organizations that can offer food, shelter, clothing, and mental health counseling or services or referral to clinics or other forms of health care service.

4. **List the general and specific environmental parameters that should be inspected to assess a patient's need for preventive information and direction.** **pp. 103–105**

   Factors that should be considered when assessing the need for injury/illness prevention include the availability of prenatal care; level of public compliance with use of proper vehicular restraints for infants and children; awareness of proper firearm control measures; awareness of the dangers of drinking and driving; the home environments of geriatric patients (who are susceptible to falls);

awareness of the need for patients to comply with directions for using medications; and local hospital/health organization policies involving the early discharge of patients with illness or injury. By surveying your community in these areas, you may identify parameters where public education and direction may be beneficial in preventing illness and injury.

5. Identify the role of EMS in local municipal and community prevention programs.
pp. 97–98, 99–101, 103–107

The EMS provider can promote prevention by becoming an advocate of injury prevention. This may include teaching CPR and first aid courses for the public, teaching and supporting prevention programs, and being a role model and example by following safe practices (including BSI and ensuring scene safety) himself.

6. Identify the injury and illness prevention programs that promote safety for all age populations.
pp. 103–104

Childhood and flu immunization programs; prenatal, well baby, and elder-care clinics; defensive driving programs; workplace safety courses; and health clinics sponsored by hospitals or healthcare organizations are just some examples of injury and illness prevention programs available to people across a range of ages in the community.

7. Identify patient situations in which the paramedic can intervene in a preventive manner.
pp. 99, 101, 103–107

The paramedic can intervene at the scene of an illness or injury and take advantage of a teachable moment. In a nonjudgmental, nonthreatening way, the paramedic may identify behaviors that would prevent illness or injury—for example, wearing protective equipment such as seat belts in a car or helmets when biking—and instruct the patient in their use. The paramedic may also identify community risks such as improperly enclosed swimming pools, which are common sites of children drowning, or poorly protected railway crossings, which are likely sites of train-vs.-auto collisions.

8. Document primary and secondary injury prevention data.
pp. 99–109

Frequently, prehospital care reports contain or can be designed to collect information about the patient behavior regarding safe practices. Information on seat belt use, airbag deployment, medication compliance, and the like may be helpful in identifying areas in which programs promoting safe practices could reduce illness and injury. The patient care report may also identify mechanisms that frequently result in injury and suggest areas in which preventive practices or safety equipment may help reduce mortality and morbidity.

Case Study Review

Reread the case study on page 97 in Paramedic Care: Introduction to Advanced Prehospital Care *and then read the following discussion.*

This case study visits an incident that highlights the consequences of not having an injury and illness prevention program in the community and provides an opportunity to examine the impact such an incident might have on EMS providers.

A hot July day and the fun-loving antics of a couple of children have turned into disaster. And what appears to be an accident was truly a predictable and preventable incident. This incident also demonstrates the discouraging results of some EMS responses and the stress they may cause those who provide care.

How would this scenario have turned out if John's parents had insisted that the pool be fenced when it was installed to prevent the children from entering unsupervised? What if John and Timmy had had a water safety and swimming course when the pool was installed? Would the outcome have changed if the EMS system provided caller instructions and John's mom had performed mouth-to-mouth ventilations on Timmy for the 6 minutes before the ambulance arrived or, better yet, if she had completed a CPR course and provided rescue breathing and chest compressions? As you can see, there were many opportunities to improve the chances for a better outcome from this incident through illness and injury prevention.

This incident also presents what must have been a very discouraging call for the care providers. Initially the paramedics must have felt good about their actions. Timmy showed signs of responding to treatment and hopes were high. However, as time passes, they must be aware that their resuscitation was fruitless and has led to a costly and emotional burden on Timmy's parents as well as John and his parents. If the paramedics have children, they may be especially affected by the incident's result. If these providers, and the system they respond in, do not recognize this and deal with this stress, it may lead to job dissatisfaction and, eventually, to the paramedics leaving the profession.

As the EMS system matures, its members must become more responsible and active in identifying risks to the community and suggesting, supporting, and, possibly, sponsoring prevention education programs. We must also appreciate the impact critical incidents have on us as providers and be ready to request and accept assistance when they affect us.

Content Self-Evaluation

MULTIPLE CHOICE

C 1. Injury represents the _____ leading cause of death in the United States.
   A. first
   B. second
   C. third
   D. fourth
   E. fifth

A 2. While injuries are often considered to be caused by accident, they are most likely predictable and preventable.
   A. True
   B. False

E 3. The calculation made by subtracting a person's age at death from 65 produces a result called the:
   A. years of productive life.
   B. injury risk factor.
   C. secondary span.
   D. epidemiological age.
   E. vital factor.

E 4. Injury can result from:
   A. an unintentional act.
   B. an intentional act.
   C. acute exposure to thermal energy.
   D. acute exposure to electrical energy.
   E. all of the above

B 5. A systematic method to collect, analyze, and interpret information about injury data is a(n):
   A. injury risk program.
   B. injury surveillance program.
   C. epidemiological intervention.
   D. secondary prevention program.
   E. risk data analysis.

E 6. Under the guidelines of the Occupational Safety and Health Administration (OSHA), body substance isolation precautions are the responsibility of:
   A. the employee.
   B. the state health department.
   C. the state EMS authority.
   D. the employer.
   E. both the employer and employee.

A 7. EMS providers are well distributed throughout the population, are often considered to be champions of the health-care consumer, and are high-profile health care role models.
   A. True
   B. False

___A___ 8. A personal wellness program should include all of the following EXCEPT:
   A. professional counseling.
   B. a proper diet.
   C. strength training.
   D. cardiovascular fitness.
   E. a health-minded attitude.

___E___ 9. Which of the following is essential to safe emergency driving?
   A. being familiar with and obeying the traffic laws
   B. understanding the capabilities and limitations of your vehicle
   C. being able to handle weather and road conditions with precision
   D. using proper sound and visual warning devices
   E. all of the above

___B___ 10. A paramedic should enter a hazardous scene only when the proper rescue, utility, or hazardous materials teams are not available.
   A. True
   B. False

___B___ 11. Which of the following statements about premature and low-birth-weight infants is NOT true?
   A. There are close to 300,000 of these infants each year.
   B. These infants are far less likely to die in the first year of life.
   C. More than 4,000 of these infants die each year.
   D. Some of these infants have serious disabilities such as mental retardation.
   E. Inadequate prenatal care is often a major factor in these births.

___A___ 12. What percentage of child deaths are the result of injuries?
   A. one third
   B. one quarter
   C. one fifth
   D. one sixth
   E. one tenth

___B___ 13. The most serious injuries associated with pediatric bicycle collisions are to the:
   A. neck.
   B. head.
   C. abdomen.
   D. chest.
   E. extremities.

___C___ 14. The most common cause of injury to children younger than 6 years old is:
   A. bicycle collisions.
   B. auto crashes.
   C. falls.
   D. abuse.
   E. fire.

___A___ 15. The term *accident* does not accurately reflect the nature of auto collisions.
   A. True
   B. False

___C___ 16. The greatest cause of preventable injuries in the geriatric population is:
   A. skeletal failure.
   B. motor vehicle accidents.
   C. falls.
   D. intentional mechanisms.
   E. burns.

___A___ 17. The early release of patients from health care facilities to help control health care costs is likely to cause an increase in the number of EMS responses.
   A. True
   B. False

___E___ 18. Which of the following is an action you should take as an EMS responder to implement injury prevention strategies?
   A. Preserve response team safety.
   B. Recognize scene hazards.
   C. Engage in on-scene education.
   D. Know your community resources.
   E. all of the above

_____ 19. The opportunity presented by an emergency call to provide information to patients/bystanders about the future prevention of such an emergency is:

A. a prevention protocol.
B. a teachable moment.
C. EMS empowerment.
D. patient/provider prevention.
E. tertiary prevention.

_____ 20. Which of the following is a possible community resource for injury or illness prevention?

A. childhood and flu immunization program
B. elder-care clinic
C. workplace safety course
D. prenatal and well baby clinic
E. all of the above

Special Project

Understanding the Importance of Illness/Injury Prevention Programs

Reread the case study that opens this chapter and identify or explain the following based on it.

A. Is this a teachable moment, and why or why not?

_____

_____

_____

_____

_____

_____

_____

B. If Timmy was 7 years old, how many years of productive life were lost?

_____

C. Give an example of primary prevention for this scenario.

_____

_____

_____

_____

6 Medical/Legal Aspects of Advanced Prehospital Care

Review of Chapter Objectives

After reading this chapter, you should be able to:

1. **Differentiate between legal, ethical, and moral responsibilities of the paramedic.** pp. 113–114

   A paramedic's legal responsibility to the patient and others is defined by statute, regulation, and common law. Failure to meet this responsibility may result in criminal or civil liability. Ethical responsibilities are those actions expected of a paramedic by the health care profession and by the public. Moral responsibilities are personal values of right and wrong and are governed by conscience. Legal, ethical, and moral factors guide an individual in his actions as a paramedic.

2. **Describe the basic structure of the legal system and differentiate between civil and criminal law.** pp. 114–115

   There are four primary sources of law in the United States: constitutional, common, legislative, and administrative. Constitutional law defines governmental authority and gives the individual certain rights. Common law is based on past judge-decided cases (case law) and is a fundamental principle of our legal system. Legislative law consists of statutes enacted at the federal, state, or local level. Administrative law consists of the regulations and rules that a governmental agency uses to implement legislative law. These four sources of law affect the legal responsibilities of the practicing paramedic.

   Civil law is noncriminal legal action between individuals for such things as matrimonial, contract, and personal injury disputes. It may also include civil wrongs such as assault, battery, medical malpractice, and negligence. Criminal law addresses actions against society (crimes) such as rape, murder, and burglary and will fine or imprison those found guilty.

3. **Differentiate between licensure and certification as they apply to the paramedic.** p. 117

   Certification is the recognition of an individual who has met predetermined qualifications to participate in a certain activity. It may be given by a governmental or other agency or by a professional association. Licensure is a process whereby a governmental agency grants permission to an individual, after meeting certain qualifications, to engage in a particular profession. A particular state may choose to require certification, licensure, or both for a paramedic to practice.

4. List the specific reportable problems or conditions encountered while providing care and identify to whom the reports are to be made.   p. 117

Each state, through statutes and administrative regulation, may require prehospital care providers to report such matters as suspected spousal abuse, child neglect and abuse, abuse of the elderly, violent crimes, and public health threats such as animal bites and communicable diseases. Reports are made to the department of health, police, or other agencies as defined in statute or regulation.

5. Define the following terms:

a. Abandonment   p. 130

This is the termination of a patient-paramedic relationship while the patient still desires and needs care without the paramedic's providing for the appropriate continuation of care.

b. Advance directives   pp. 132–135

These are documents created to express the patient's treatment choices should he become incapacitated or otherwise unable to express a choice of treatment.

c. Assault   p. 130

This is placing a person in apprehension of immediate bodily harm without his consent.

d. Battery   p. 130

This is the unlawful touching of an individual without his consent.

e. Breach of duty   p. 119

This is the failure to act with the skill and judgment expected of a similarly trained paramedic under similar circumstances.

f. Confidentiality   pp. 123–124

This is the principle of law that prohibits the release of medical or other information about a patient without his permission.

g. Consent (expressed, implied, informed, involuntary)   pp. 125–127

Consent is the granting of permission to treat. Expressed consent occurs when a patient gives verbal or written permission to treat. Implied consent occurs when you presume the patient would give expressed consent if he or she were able. Informed consent is consent granted by the patient who knows the necessity, nature, and risks of treatment. Involuntary consent is consent to treat a patient given by the authority of a police agency or court.

h. Do not resuscitate (DNR) orders   pp. 132, 134–135

These are advance directives that define the life-sustaining equipment or procedures that may be used if the patient's heart or respirations cease.

i. Duty to act   p. 119

This is the formal or informal responsibility of the paramedic to provide care.

j. Emancipated minor   p. 126

This is generally someone under 18 years of age who is married, pregnant, a parent, a member of the armed forces, or financially independent and living away from home. Such a person is often considered legally able to give informed consent.

k. False imprisonment   p. 130

This is the restraint or transport of a patient without consent, proper justification, or authority.

l. Immunity   pp. 118, 121

This is the exemption from legal liability.

m. Liability   p. 113

This is the legal responsibility for one's actions. Any deviation from the duty to act or the standard of care exposes the care provider to liability.

n. Libel   p. 124

This is the act of injuring a person's character, name, or reputation by false and malicious written statements.

o. Minor   p. 126

A minor is a person under 18 years of age for whom a parent, legal guardian, or court-appointed custodian gives informed consent.

p. Negligence   pp. 118–121

This is the deviation from accepted standards of care recognized by the law for the protection of others against the unreasonable risk of harm.

q. Proximate cause   p. 120

This is the action or inaction of the paramedic that caused or worsened the damage suffered by the patient.

r. Scope of practice   pp. 116–117

This is the range of duties and skills paramedics are allowed and expected to perform.

s. Slander   p. 124

This is the act of injuring a person's character, name, or reputation by false and malicious spoken statements.

t. Standard of care   p. 119

This is the degree of skill and judgment expected of an individual when caring for a patient and is defined by training, protocols, and the expected actions of care providers with similar training and experience, working under similar conditions.

u. Tort   p. 115

This is a category of law dealing with civil wrongs against an individual such as negligence, medical malpractice, assault, battery, and slander.

6. Discuss the legal implications of medical direction, including off-line medical direction and on-line medical direction, and its relationship to the paramedic's standard of care.   pp. 116–117, 119

Medical direction, both on-line and off-line, helps define the paramedic's scope of practice. Protocols, policies, and procedures as well as medical direction from an on-line physician define what is the acceptable standard of care. The system medical director is responsible for supervising the protocols and continuing education of the paramedic. The on-line medical direction physician is responsible for supervising and directing the paramedic's actions at the scene and during transport. The paramedic is responsible for ensuring that the medical care given to the patient is appropriate and in keeping with the protocols. Any breach of duty or deviation from the standard of care that results in patient injury may result in charges of negligence.

7. Describe the four elements that must be present in order to prove negligence.   pp. 119–120

Four elements must exist before negligence can be proven. They include the duty to act, breach of duty, actual damages, and proximate cause. The duty to act is the direct or indirect responsibility to provide the patient with care. Breach of duty is the failure to meet the standard of care associated with the patient's needs. Damages are the actual physical, psychological, or financial harm suffered by the patient. Proximate cause means that the paramedic's action or inaction directly caused or worsened the harm suffered by the patient.

8. Explain liability as it applies to emergency medical service, including the physicians providing medical direction and the paramedic's supervision of other care providers.   pp. 113, 116–117, 119

Liability in EMS is the legal responsibility to provide appropriate assessment, care, and transport of the ill or injured patient. That liability extends to the system medical director and on-line medical direction physician as well as to the paramedic who supervises the actions of others while at the emergency scene. They must ensure that those they supervise follow the standard of care.

9. Discuss immunity, including Good Samaritan statutes and governmental immunity, as it applies to the paramedic.   pp. 118, 121

The Good Samaritan statute may offer some liability protection to someone who assists at the emergency scene if that person acts in good faith, is not grossly negligent, acts within his scope of practice, and does not receive payment for his services. In some states, Good Samaritan statutes have been expanded to include both paid and unpaid EMS providers.

Governmental immunity is a judicial doctrine that protects the government from liability unless it accepts that liability. However, most states have waived these rights, and courts are becoming increasingly likely to strike any remaining immunity down.

10. Explain the importance and necessity of patient confidentiality and the standards for maintaining patient confidentiality that apply to the paramedic. pp. 123–124

The paramedic, through his involvement in patient care, learns sensitive information about the patients he treats. To encourage patients to continue to divulge this information, paramedics must respect its confidential nature and divulge it only to those with a need to know. Information regarding a patient may be released to those continuing care, in accordance with the patient's consent to release information, as required by law, and as necessary for billing purposes.

11. Differentiate among the types of consent: expressed, informed, implied, and involuntary. pp. 125–126

Expressed consent is that given in writing or verbally, while implied consent is assumed consent from a patient who is unable to give expressed consent. Informed consent is the consent for treatment given by a patient when he understands the necessity, nature, risks, and alternatives to care. Involuntary consent is the consent given by the authority of a police agency or court to treat an individual.

12. Given various scenarios with a patient in need of care, describe the process used to obtain informed or implied consent. pp. 125–126

When a patient summons an ambulance, that action suggests that he is asking for help and consenting to treatment. However, a paramedic is obligated to explain what he is going to do to and for the patient and why he is going to do it. The paramedic must also determine if the patient is alert, oriented, and rational enough to make a competent decision to accept or refuse care. If the patient is not able to make a rational decision regarding care, the paramedic may need to invoke implied consent. If the patient is a minor and the legal parent or guardian cannot be reached, consent is assumed (implied consent).

13. Given several refusal-of-care scenarios, demonstrate appropriate patient interaction and documentation techniques. pp. 126–127

When a patient refuses care, the paramedic must ensure and document the following: the patient was legally able and competent to make the decision; the need for care and potential consequences of refusing care were explained; on-line medical direction was consulted; the patient was directed to see his own physician; and the patient was directed to call the ambulance if the symptoms return or get worse. The refusal form should be signed by the patient and either a family member or a police officer. If the patient refuses to sign a refusal of treatment form, then have his refusal witnessed by a family member or police officer.

14. Identify the legal issues involved in the decision not to transport a patient or to reduce the level of care being provided. pp. 126–128

A decision not to continue the care of a patient or to relinquish care to a lesser level of provider may expose the paramedic to charges of abandonment or negligence if the patient suffers harm. This is especially true if the paramedic has initiated advanced life support procedures such as starting an IV or administering a medication.

15. Describe how hospitals are selected to receive patients based on patient need and hospital capability and the role of the paramedic in such selection. p. 131

The patient's request to be transported to a particular hospital should be honored unless his particular care needs demonstrate otherwise. The decision to transport a patient to a facility other than the one requested must be based on the patient's care needs, the capabilities of the requested facility, protocols, and interaction with the on-line medical direction physician.

16. Differentiate between assault and battery and describe how to avoid committing each. pp. 130–131

Assault threatens bodily harm; battery is unauthorized touching. These civil and criminal actions can be avoided by the paramedic's making sure to obtain expressed consent for treatment and to explain what he is planning to do for the patient before doing it.

17. Describe the conditions under which the use of force, including restraint, is acceptable. pp. 130–131

The use of force to restrain a patient may be necessary when the patient is violent or poses a danger to himself or to others. Then only such force and restraint should be used as is required. In conditions in which force and restraint are necessary to care for a patient, the police should be involved.

18. Explain the purpose of advance directives and how they influence your patient care. pp. 132–135

Advance directives permit the patient to define what care he would desire should he become incapacitated. Advance directives include Do Not Resuscitate (DNR) orders, which limit care actions that can be taken should the patient go into cardiac or respiratory arrest. Living wills are legal documents that also prescribe the care a patient may receive, including his desire to donate organs and to die at home or elsewhere. State statutes usually define the authority of DNRs, living wills, and other advance directives.

19. Discuss the paramedic's responsibilities relative to resuscitation efforts for patients who are potential organ donors. p. 135

When presented with a patient who is a possible organ donor, it is essential for the paramedic to maintain adequate perfusion of that organ to ensure its viability. Employ resuscitation procedures including fluid therapy, cardiac compressions, and ventilation and notify the medical direction physician that you are transporting a possible organ donor.

20. Describe how a paramedic may preserve evidence at a crime or accident scene. pp. 135–136

Your responsibility at the crime scene is first to ensure your safety and that of your patient and then to ensure the health of the victim (your patient). If the patient is not obviously dead, initiate resuscitation and care directed at his injuries. Limit any movement of articles around the patient and at the scene and, if possible, document what you moved and from what location you moved it. Do not cut through clothing where objects entered the body; remove the clothing without cutting it, or cut around the openings.

21. Describe the importance of providing accurate documentation (oral and written) in substantiating an emergency medical service response. pp. 136–137

Documentation establishes what was found and what was done at the emergency scene. It must be completed promptly, thoroughly, objectively, and accurately. At the same time, the confidentiality of the information obtained must be maintained. The documentation will become a part of the patient's medical record and help guide continuing patient care. It will also become a record of what you did at the emergency scene and during transport should your actions ever come into question. It may also become a legal document in a court of law when someone feels he has been injured (damaged) by someone else.

22. **Describe the characteristics of a patient care report required to make it an effective legal document.**   pp. 136–137

A patient care report must be completed in a timely manner, must be thorough, must be objective, must be accurate, and must ensure patient confidentiality to be an effective legal document.

23. **Review several patient care reports and evaluate the content from a legal and liability perspective.**   pp. 136–137

Incomplete, inaccurate, subjective, or sloppy patient care reports suggest that patient care was incomplete, inaccurate, or sloppy or that your attention to the needs of the patient was not in keeping with your duty to act. Any modifications in the report, if not fully disclosed, suggest that you made an error and tried to cover it up.

24. **Given several scenarios in which a patient is injured while a paramedic is providing care, determine whether the four components of negligence are present.**   pp. 119–120

For a paramedic to be found negligent, the plaintiff must establish that the paramedic had a duty to act, that he breached that duty (did not provide the accepted standard of care), that the patient suffered damages, and that those damages were a result of the paramedic's actions.

25. **Given several scenarios, describe patient care behaviors that would protect the paramedic from claims of negligence.**   p. 121

Actions that may help prevent charges of negligence include participation in education, training, and continuing education programs, following on-line and off-line medical direction when appropriate, preparing accurate, thorough, and objective documentation, observing patient confidentiality, having a professional attitude and demeanor, acting in good faith, and using common sense. It is also advisable to obtain personal malpractice insurance.

Case Study Review

Reread the case study on pages 112 and 113 in Paramedic Care: Introduction to Advanced Prehospital Care *and then read the following discussion.*

This case study demonstrates the type of legal dilemma that many paramedics may encounter during their EMS responses.

The paramedics of EMS 117 are presented with a patient who is behaving bizarrely just before she becomes unconscious. They treat her, assuming that if she were conscious and alert she would recognize her need for treatment and consent to it (implied consent). Once she becomes conscious, she exercises her right to refuse treatment. The paramedics assess her and determine that she is able to make a rational decision and honor that decision. They recommend that she eat immediately to raise her glucose level and see her physician at the earliest opportunity. While all this seems reasonable, the paramedics are still exposed to legal responsibility for what happens to their patient after their care and release.

Some responsibility may fall upon the paramedics should their patient not obtain something to eat, suffer a later drop in blood-glucose level, and injure herself or others while driving. It is essential that the paramedics carefully explain to the patient that she was driving erratically and appeared intoxicated. They must identify that if she does not obtain something to eat, this behavior may occur again and cause her to do harm to herself or others. They should also explain that this incident indicates the need for a medical evaluation of her condition to ensure that episodes like it do not occur again. She truly needs to see a physician immediately, and her refusal of transport to the hospital is against their expert advice.

The paramedics will further protect themselves by thoroughly documenting the incident. They must carefully identify what their assessment revealed and their reasons for administering dextrose. They must identify the results of their care (the patient becoming alert and oriented) and her subsequent refusal of further care. They must document that they encouraged her to go to the hospital with them and receive evaluation by a physician and that, when she refused, they had her speak with an on-line medical direction physician. They must document their advising her to obtain food immediately and to see her physician at the earliest opportunity. They will also document her agreement to go to the mini-mart and obtain food as well as her assurance that she has an appointment with her physician. Finally, they must have her sign a "release-from-liability" form and document by what criteria they determined she was rational and able to make that decision.

In a situation of this type, a good working relationship with the police might be helpful. The woman was clearly driving while impaired and is likely to receive a moving violation from the officer. Indicating to him the risk of a later fall in glucose level (if she does not eat) and a return to her erratic behavior might cause him to encourage the patient to ride with the paramedics to the hospital.

Content Self-Evaluation

MULTIPLE CHOICE

_B_ 1. The term *liability* best refers to:
A. an illegal act.
B. legal responsibility.
C. an act of negligence.
D. civil responsibility.
E. responsibility for damages.

_C_ 2. Ethical responsibilities are best described as:
A. requirements of case law.
B. requirements of statute law.
C. standards of a profession.
D. personal feelings of right and wrong.
E. legal concepts of right and wrong.

_C_ 3. Which type of law is also called statutory law?
A. "case" law
B. common law
C. legislative law
D. administrative law
E. regulatory law

_A_ 4. Criminal law is best described as dealing with:
A. wrongs committed against society.
B. conflicts between two or more parties.
C. contract disputes.
D. negligence.
E. breaches of faith.

_E_ 5. Which of the following is a component of a paramedic's scope of practice?
A. protocols
B. system policies and procedures
C. on-line medical direction
D. training and continuing education
E. all of the above

_D_ 6. Which of the following is NOT a common mandatory reporting event?
A. rape
B. spousal abuse
C. child abuse
D. a seizure episode
E. animal bites

_B_ 7. Governmental immunity is a likely protection for the paramedic working for a municipality.
A. True
B. False

_A_ 8. The Ryan White CARE act provides what protection to the paramedic?
A. It requires a notification system for contagious disease exposure.
B. It compensates EMS providers who contract AIDS.
C. It permits EMS review of any patient records.
D. It grants immunity to civil litigation in cases of ordinary negligence.
E. It defines the restraints permissible while treating a violent patient.

_____D___ 9. Which of the following is NOT one of the elements required to prove a charge of negligence against a paramedic?
A. duty to act
B. proximate cause
C. actual damages suffered by the patient
D. payment to the paramedic
E. breach of duty

_____E___ 10. Which of the following is a duty expected of the paramedic?
A. to respond to the scene of an emergency
B. to conform to the expected standard of care
C. to provide care in accordance with the system's protocols
D. to drive, or ensure the emergency vehicle is driven, appropriately
E. all of the above

_____C___ 11. The degree of care, skill, and judgment that would be expected under like or similar circumstances by a similarly trained, reasonable paramedic is:
A. the duty to act.
B. the scope of practice.
C. the standard of care.
D. a proximate cause.
E. malfeasance.

_____C___ 12. *Res ipsa loquitur* is a legal term that refers to:
A. contributory negligence.
B. immunity from prosecution.
C. a matter that is self-evident.
D. the victim's liability.
E. the reliability of evidence.

_____E___ 13. Which of the following may protect a paramedic from charges of negligence?
A. Good Samaritan statute
B. governmental immunity
C. the statute of limitations
D. contributory negligence
E. all of the above

_____A___ 14. Although many employers and agencies carry insurance coverage, it is a good idea for a paramedic to obtain personal coverage because the agency's coverage may be inadequate.
A. True
B. False

_____A___ 15. In many states, a paramedic would be guilty of practicing without a license if, while off duty, he performed advanced life support skills outside his system of medical direction.
A. True
B. False

_____D___ 16. Which of the following is NOT an acceptable reason for the release of confidential patient information?
A. Medical providers need it to care for the patient.
B. A judge has signed a court order demanding its release.
C. It is necessary for third party billing.
D. Other paramedics, not on the call, have requested it.
E. The patient has made a written request for its release.

_____E___ 17. The act of injuring an individual's character, name, or reputation by false written statements and with malicious intent is:
A. slander.
B. breach of confidentiality.
C. malfeasance.
D. misfeasance.
E. libel.

_____B___ 18. Before beginning to treat a patient, a paramedic must obtain expressed consent.
A. True
B. False

_____C___ 19. The type of consent that is given by the authority of a court is:
A. expressed.
B. implied.
C. involuntary.
D. informed.
E. common.

_E_ **20.** For a patient's consent to be informed, the patient must be told and understand:
- **A.** the nature of the treatment.
- **B.** the necessity of the treatment.
- **C.** the risks of the treatment.
- **D.** the risks of refusing the treatment.
- **E.** all of the above

_B_ **21.** Once a patient has given consent for treatment, he may not withdraw that consent.
- **A.** True
- **B.** False

_B_ **22.** A minor is usually considered someone under the age of:
- **A.** 16.
- **B.** 18.
- **C.** 19.
- **D.** 21.
- **E.** 25.

_E_ **23.** Conditions that may define a person as an emancipated minor include being:
- **A.** married.
- **B.** pregnant.
- **C.** a parent.
- **D.** a member of the armed forces.
- **E.** all of the above

_B_ **24.** Once a patient has withdrawn his consent to care, it is may be considered assault to encourage the patient to go to the hospital.
- **A.** True
- **B.** False

_B_ **25.** Which of the following is NOT an essential element in accepting a patient's refusal of care?
- **A.** The patient is conscious, alert, and rational.
- **B.** The patient is a minor.
- **C.** The patient is aware of the possible consequences of his decision.
- **D.** The patient has been advised that he may call again for help if necessary.
- **E.** The patient and/or a disinterested witness has signed a release-from-liability form.

_A_ **26.** Ideally, a police officer should respond to the scene of all problem patients and sign the patient care report as a witness or, if the patient poses a threat to the paramedic, accompany the paramedic and patient to the hospital.
- **A.** True
- **B.** False

_D_ **27.** Ending a patient–caregiver relationship without providing the appropriate continuing care and without the patient's approval could be found to be:
- **A.** battery.
- **B.** defamation.
- **C.** nonfeasance.
- **D.** abandonment.
- **E.** assault.

_C_ **28.** The unlawful act of touching another person without permission is:
- **A.** assault.
- **B.** abandonment.
- **C.** battery.
- **D.** slander.
- **E.** libel.

_D_ **29.** An important question to ask yourself when considering the restraint of a patient is:
- **A.** Does the patient need immediate treatment?
- **B.** Does the patient pose a threat to himself?
- **C.** Does the patient pose a threat to others?
- **D.** All of the above
- **E.** None of the above

_A_ **30.** If you need to use force to restrain a patient, it is best to involve law enforcement whenever possible.
- **A.** True
- **B.** False

31. Under what situation should a paramedic NOT begin resuscitation of a pulseless, non-breathing patient?
   A. The patient is obviously dead.
   B. The patient has a valid DNR order.
   C. There is obvious tissue decomposition.
   D. There is extreme dependant lividity.
   E. all of the above

32. Do Not Resuscitate orders usually restrict care providers from:
   A. performing CPR in case of cardiac arrest.
   B. performing a "slow code."
   C. performing a "chemical code."
   D. leaving the scene until the coroner arrives.
   E. contacting medical direction.

33. If there is any doubt about the authenticity or applicability of a DNR order, a paramedic should initiate resuscitation immediately.
   A. True   B. False

34. Which of the following statements is NOT true regarding a paramedic's responsibility at the crime scene?
   A. He should contact law enforcement officers if they are not on the scene.
   B. He should not enter the scene unless it is safe.
   C. His primary responsibility is to preserve the evidence at the scene.
   D. He should not disturb the scene unless it is necessary for patient care.
   E. He should document the movement of any item at the scene.

35. Which of the following is NOT required when documenting a patient care response?
   A. Completing documentation promptly.
   B. Ensuring that documentation is accurate.
   C. Ensuring that documentation is subjective.
   D. Ensuring that patient confidentiality is maintained.
   E. Ensuring that documentation is thorough.

Special Project

Crossword Puzzle

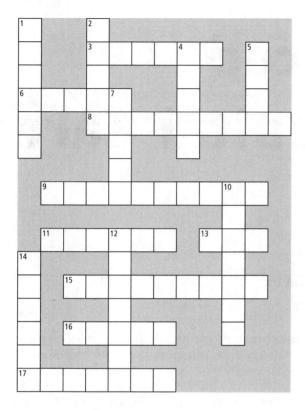

Across

3. Rules or standards of conduct that govern members of a profession

6. Right as determined by personal conscience

8. Legal responsibility

9. Deviation from the accepted standard of care

11. _____ will: document that allows a person to specify the kinds of treatment he would desire

13. _____ order: legal document indicating the life-sustaining measures to take during cardio-pulmonary arrest (abbr.)

15. _____ consent: communication from the patient indicating that he agrees to care

16. Component of a lawsuit in which both sides present testimony and evidence

17. Injuring a patient's character by false spoken statements

Down

1. _____ law: type of law derived from society's acceptance of customs and norms over time

2. Pertaining to the law

4. _____ law: division of the legal system that deals with noncriminal issues

5. A civil wrong committed by one individual against another

7. Injuring a patient's character by false written statements

10. A patient's permission to give care

12. _____ consent: type of permission to treat that is presumed from an otherwise incapacitated patient

14. Privileges that one is given by law and tradition

Ethics in Advanced Prehospital Care

Review of Chapter Objectives

After reading this chapter, you should be able to:

1. Define ethics and morals. p. 144

Morals are social, religious, or personal standards of right and wrong. Ethics are rules or standards that govern the conduct of a group or profession. Ethics and morals, along with common law, govern how we function in prehospital emergency care.

2. Distinguish between ethical and moral decisions in emergency medical service. pp. 144–151

Ethical decisions regarding patient care involve what the public and peers expect of the paramedic. Moral decisions involve the paramedic's own values of right and wrong.

3. Identify the premise that should underlie the paramedic's ethical decisions in out-of-hospital care. p. 146

Ultimately, the decisions made by the paramedic should be guided by the question: What is in the best interest of the patient?

4. Analyze the relationship between the law and ethics in EMS. p. 144

In general, the law takes a narrower and more specific look at behavior and identifies what is wrong in the eyes of society. Ethics takes a more general view of what is right or good behavior. Laws or the results of following them may be unethical, and the law often does not resolve ethical dilemmas.

5. Compare and contrast the criteria used in allocating scarce EMS resources. pp. 155–156

The most common situation regarding allocation of resources that a member of EMS is likely to face is a multiple-casualty incident (MCI). At an MCI, the triage process sorts casualties into priorities for care because patient needs outstrip the available resources. In the civilian environment, the person with the most need for care (except those with mortal injuries) receives care first. In the military domain, those with the least serious injuries receive care first to help maintain the fighting force (and win the battle).

6. **Identify issues surrounding advance directives in making a prehospital resuscitation decision.** pp. 151–153

Advance directives, such as living wills and Do Not Resuscitate orders, are ways that patients can indicate their desire for the type of medical care they wish to receive should they become incapacitated. Such directives often present ethical dilemmas for paramedics because they are trained and expected to do all that is necessary to preserve life. When a paramedic confronts a situation involving an advance directive, he must weigh the patient's right to autonomy against what he feels is in the patient's medical best interest. Whenever you are presented with an advance directive, ensure it is valid, current, and conforms to requirements in your state for such documents. When in doubt, resuscitate.

7. **Describe the criteria necessary to honor an advance directive in your state.** pp. 151–153

Each state has different laws that define the circumstances under which a paramedic can honor an advance directive. These laws also define the form and conditions that must be met before such a request is honored.

8. **Given several narrative circumstances, make decisions in keeping with the ethical principles associated with EMS.** pp. 140–156

Prehospital emergency care provides frequent circumstances that call for ethical decisions. The best guide is to provide what is in the best interest of the patient. Your first priority is to provide the best care you can. Then try to accommodate the patient's wishes to the best of your ability. Ultimately, do what you think is best for the patient.

Case Study Review

Reread the case study on page 143 in Paramedic Care: Introduction to Advanced Prehospital Care *and then read the following discussion.*

This case study shows the real potential for ethical dilemmas that can emerge during EMS responses. Here the care for the patient was not compromised because the paramedic caring for Mrs. Weinberg had equal or greater skill than the exchange student. The team worked together to accommodate the patient's medical needs and then the desires of Mrs. Weinberg.

What if Heinz was the paramedic of an EMT-B/Paramedic team? In the case described here, the patient needed only basic life support, but what if she needed IV fluids and pain medication? What if the case involved a female patient who has been physically abused or raped and was in need of advanced interventions? Can she request care from a female member of the team? Legally, the patient has the right to define his or her care (expressed consent). EMS members are obligated to accommodate the patient's requests, within legal limits, and if those requests diverge from good medical practice, they must carefully explain medical needs produced by the patient's condition and the risks of alternative therapy.

As ethics are defined as what society and professional peers expect, paramedics can be best guided by two principles: (1) provide the best medical care for the patient, and (2) then try to accommodate the patient's desires. Ethical decisions are not as black and white as most decisions in EMS, and system protocols do not address these situations. Often there is no one answer to an ethical question, and no two ethical situations are identical. However, paramedics who make decisions that do not meet the patient's medical needs or personal desires bring the profession into question and endanger its standing in the community.

Content Self-Evaluation

MULTIPLE CHOICE

_____ 1. Although ethical problems often have a legal aspect, most ethical problems are solved in the field and not in a courtroom.
A. True   B. False

_____ 2. Most codes of ethics provide specific guidance for performance of the professional.
A. True   B. False

_____ 3. When faced with an ethical challenge, the best guiding question is which of the following?
A. How would I like to be treated?
B. What would the patient want?
C. Which actions will account for the greatest good?
D. What is in the best interest of the patient?
E. What actions can I defend?

_____ 4. The term that means "desiring to do good" is:
A. benevolence.   D. autonomy.
B. justice.   E. euphylanthropnia.
C. beneficence.

_____ 5. The Latin phrase *primum non nocere* means:
A. "Do the best you can."
B. "Avoid mistakes."
C. "Maintain the patient's best interests."
D. "First, do no harm."
E. "Treat all patients fairly."

_____ 6. Which question best describes the impartiality test for analyzing an ethical situation?
A. Can you justify this action to others?
B. Would you want this procedure if you were in the patient's place?
C. Would you want this procedure performed on a family member if he were in similar circumstances?
D. Will you likely be questioned about the need for this procedure later?
E. none of the above

_____ 7. When in doubt about the validity of a DNR order or the patient's desire to be resuscitated, you should:
A. begin resuscitation immediately.
B. await arrival of the DNR to verify its validity.
C. contact medical direction for advice before beginning resuscitation.
D. do not resuscitate.
E. begin with CPR and delay advanced interventions.

_____ 8. There are no circumstances in which it is appropriate to breach patient confidentiality.
A. True   B. False

_____ 9. When presented with a patient who is enrolled in a health maintenance organization (HMO) whose policy states that the patient must be cared for at a member institution, you are responsible to act in the patient's best interest.
A. True   B. False

_____ **10.** When presented with orders from a physician that do not comply with your protocols and that you believe are not in the patient's best interest, you should:

    A. follow the physician's order and report your concerns to the medical director.

    B. ask the physician to repeat or confirm the order.

    C. ask the physician for an explanation of the order.

    D. do not follow the physician's order.

    E. do all except A.

Special Project

Ethics and the Mass-Casualty Incident

Answer the following questions about the ethical dilemmas presented by mass-casualty incidents.

A. Define the normal approach to caring for a patient and explain why it differs at the disaster scene.

_____

_____

_____

_____

_____

_____

_____

_____

_____

_____

_____

_____

B. At a mass-casualty incident, a patient in cardiac arrest would not receive immediate care. Explain the reasoning behind this and the ethical dilemma it presents.

_____

_____

_____

_____

_____

_____

_____

_____

_____

_____

_____

_____

8 General Principles of Pathophysiology

Because Chapter 8 is lengthy, it has been divided into parts to aid your study. Read the assigned textbook pages, then progress through the objectives and self-evaluation materials as you would with other chapters. When you feel secure in your grasp of the content, proceed to the next section.

Part 1: The Cell and the Cellular Environment, begins on p. 166

Review of Chapter Objectives

After reading this part of the chapter, you should be able to:

1. List the types of tissue. pp. 174–180

Epithelial tissue lines internal and external body surfaces. It provides protection and specialized functions such as secretion, absorption, diffusion, and filtration. Major examples are the skin and the lining of the digestive tract.

Muscle tissue has the capability to contract when stimulated. It is of three types: cardiac muscle, found only in the heart; skeletal muscle, which is under voluntary control; and smooth muscle, found in the intestines and blood vessels, which is not under voluntary control.

Connective tissue is the most abundant tissue in the body and provides support, connection, and insulation. Connective tissue includes bone, cartilage, and fat. Blood may also be classified as connective tissue.

Nerve tissue is specialized tissue capable of transmitting electrical impulses throughout the body and makes up the brain, spinal cord, and peripheral nerves.

2. Discuss cellular adaptation, injury, and death. pp. 174–180

Cellular adaptation involves the ability of the body cell to change and adapt based on normal and abnormal stresses. Cellular adaptation includes atrophy, hypertrophy, hyperplasia, metaplasia, and dysplasia.

- Atrophy is the process of decreasing cell size due to a decrease in cell workload.
- Hypertrophy is an increase in cell size resulting from an increase in workload.

- Hyperplasia is an increase in the number of cells in response to an increase in workload.
- Metaplasia is a replacement of one type of cell with another type of cell not normal for that tissue.
- Dysplasia is an abnormal change in cell size, shape, and appearance due to an external stressor.

Cellular injury is most commonly due to hypoxia, chemicals, infectious agents, inflammatory reactions, physical agents, nutritional factors, or genetic factors.

- Hypoxic injury results when a cell is deprived of oxygen due to a respiratory or cardiovascular problem. Ultimately, the cell cannot efficiently produce its energy source, ATP, and acids and fluids accumulate.
- Chemical injury results when agents such as ethanol, lead, carbon monoxide, drugs, or insecticides enter the body and injure the cell.
- Infectious injury causes cell damage when disease-causing agents (pathogens) enter the body. These agents damage and destroy cells, create toxins, or instigate an allergic reaction.
- Immunological/inflammatory injury results as the body attempts to ward off invading foreign substances. Although the response is intended to attack the foreign substance, it also damages body cells.
- Physical injury results from exposure to temperature extremes, electrical current, pressure, radiation, noise, and mechanical stresses.
- Injuries due to nutritional imbalance include atherosclerosis; exacerbation of diabetes; insufficient intake of proteins, carbohydrates, lipids, vitamins, and minerals; or malnutrition and starvation.
- Genetic injury results from defective DNA that creates a predisposition toward (like diabetes) or directly causes (like sickle cell disease) a disease.

Cellular death occurs through one of two processes. They are apoptosis and necrosis.

- Apoptosis is a natural elimination of damaged, destroyed, or nonfunctioning cells. This response involves scattered individual cells and allows tissue to repair itself.
- Necrosis is the result of a pathological process and generally involves a grouping or region of cells. In necrosis, cells swell and rupture and take on a different appearance. The process disrupts the normal physiological activity of the tissue.

3. **Describe the cellular environment and factors that precipitate disease in the human body.** pp. 180–200

The body goes to great lengths to maintain a constant internal and cellular environment (homeostasis). Major factors of this environment include hydration, the movement of substances into and out of the cell, and acid/base balance.

- **Hydration**—Water composes about 60 percent of the total body weight and plays a very important role in the body's internal environment. Some 75 percent of the body's water is contained within the cells (intracellular fluid), while 7.5 percent is contained within the vascular system (intravascular fluid). The remaining water is found between cells (interstitial fluid) and in other spaces within the body. An abnormal decrease in body hydration (dehydration) may be caused by increased gastrointestinal losses, sweating, internal (third space) losses, plasma losses, or other types of losses. An abnormal increase in body water is called overhydration.
- **Electrolytes**—Electrolytes are molecules that dissociate into negatively and positively charged particles (called ions) when dissolved in water. The normal distribution of body water is dependent on the distribution of electrolytes among the body spaces (intravascular, interstitial, and intracellular).
- **Osmosis and diffusion**— Diffusion is the movement of molecules from an area of higher concentration to one of lower concentration. Osmosis is the movement of a solvent (like water) through a membrane to equalize the concentration of electrolytes on each side of the membrane. The body also moves electrolytes through cell membranes (against the osmotic gradient) by active transport and facilitated diffusion. These processes are responsible for maintaining a fluid electrolyte balance among the intravascular, interstitial, and intracellular spaces.

- **Acid/base balance**—The concentration of free hydrogen ions in a fluid reflects its acidity and is noted as a logarithmic value called pH. A pH of 1 is extremely acidic, while a pH of 14 is without hydrogen ions and extremely basic (or alkalotic). The body maintains a slightly alkalotic environment by regulating the quantity of free hydrogen ions. Normal body pH ranges from 7.35 to 7.45. The body maintains its pH through a bicarbonate buffer system, the respiratory system, and the kidneys.

Case Study Review

Reread the case study on pages 164 and 165 in Paramedic Care: Introduction to Advanced Prehospital Care *and then read the following discussion.*

This case study demonstrates the important link between understanding the disease process (pathophysiology) and the assessment and care of the patient.

Paramedics Terry Martinez and Mark Westbrook are called to attend to a patient who displays the signs and symptoms of a serious emergency. These signs and symptoms are from several body systems and seem unrelated. They include a reduced mental status (CNS), difficulty swallowing (gastrointestinal), cold, pale, diaphoretic skin and a rash (integumentary), and difficulty breathing, with wheezes and chest tightness (respiratory). These paramedics might begin treating each symptom as a separate problem if they did not recognize how the symptoms are related. The crew can recognize this relationship, however, because of their understanding of the pathophysiology of disease.

The patient presents with some signs and symptoms of inadequate tissue perfusion, also known as shock. These include the anxiousness and confusion, difficulty breathing (dyspnea), the rapid and weak pulse, the diaphoresis, and cold and clammy skin. These assessment findings are a result of the body's attempts to compensate for the migration of fluid out of the vascular system and into the lungs, skin, and other tissue and the reduced respiratory efficiency caused by the airway restrictions and fluid build-up (pulmonary edema). The lowered level of consciousness and agitation occur because the brain is not well perfused or oxygenated. The air hunger occurs as the body tries to increase the oxygen available to the blood and body cells. The rapid, weak pulse is a result of the body increasing the heart rate to compensate for a reduced blood volume and cardiac output. Finally, the cool, clammy (diaphoretic), and pale skin represents the body directing blood away from noncritical organs to the brain, heart, and kidneys. Mark and Terry recognize these assessment findings as indications of the serious medical condition we call shock. They know something is seriously wrong with the 34-year-old female.

Their assessment reveals signs and symptoms specific to the patient's problem. They discover complaints of tightness in the chest, difficulty swallowing, and a hoarse voice and notice wheezes in the lung fields and hives on her chest and abdomen. These symptoms and signs are consistent with the body's overly aggressive response to an invading agent. The term for a mild reaction to an invading agent is "allergy," while the drastic response this patient displays is called "anaphylaxis." To prevent further absorption of the toxin, the body constricts the airways and begins the inflammatory response by allowing fluid to leak into the interstitial spaces. These responses are initiated by the body's release of a powerful hormone called histamine.

Understanding the significance of this problem and knowing that it can rapidly lead to death, Mark and Terry immediately intervene. They administer another body hormone, epinephrine, to counteract the effects of histamine and then administer fluids to replace the fluid shifting into the interstitial spaces. Providing the patient with oxygen helps increase respiratory efficiency. Once the immediate effects are addressed, the paramedics administer diphenhydramine (Benadryl) to negate the more long-term effects of the histamine. Knowing that this patient could go into respiratory arrest at any moment, they prepare to protect the upper airway using rapid sequence intubation. They will ventilate the patient via bag-valve mask to ensure adequate oxygenation, if needed.

Mark and Terry are able to recognize and treat this serious emergency only because they understand the pathophysiology of anaphylaxis. To be a good paramedic, you must understand the pathological processes at work behind the signs and symptoms of the most frequent diseases threatening life. Understanding the material in this chapter is a good beginning.

Content Self-Evaluation

MULTIPLE CHOICE

_A_ 1. The fundamental unit of life is:
A. the cell.
B. tissue.
C. the organ.
D. the organism.
E. DNA.

_A_ 2. One of the three main elements of a typical cell is the:
A. cell membrane.
B. cilia.
C. leukocyte.
D. eosinophil.
E. basophil.

_C_ 3. The characteristic ability of a cell membrane to selectively permit material to pass through it is called:
A. diffusiveness.
B. imperviousness.
C. semipermeability.
D. cytoplasmicism.
E. isotonicism.

_E_ 4. The thick viscous fluid that fills the cell and gives it shape is called:
A. ribosome.
B. lysosome.
C. cytoplasm.
D. protoplasm.
E. either C or D

_C_ 5. The structure that contains the genetic material including the cell's DNA is the:
A. endoplasmic reticulum.
B. Golgi apparatus.
C. nucleus.
D. mitochondria.
E. cytokine.

_E_ 6. Which of the following is NOT one of the major cell functions?
A. movement
B. respiration
C. excretion
D. conductivity
E. dialysis

_D_ 7. The compound that provides the cell with most of its energy is:
A. DNA.
B. phosgene.
C. carbon dioxide.
D. ATP.
E. carbohydrate.

_A_ 8. The tissue type that covers the internal and external body surfaces is:
A. epithelial.
B. smooth muscle.
C. nerve.
D. connective.
E. skeletal muscle.

_E_ 9. The tissue type that is mostly under voluntary control is:
A. epithelial.
B. cardiac muscle.
C. nerve.
D. connective.
E. skeletal muscle.

_D_ 10. The tissue type that provides support and insulation is:
- A. epithelial.
- B. cardiac muscle.
- C. nerve.
- D. connective.
- E. skeletal muscle.

_A_ 11. The body organ system that produces most body heat is:
- A. muscular.
- B. gastrointestinal.
- C. genitourinary.
- D. endocrine.
- E. lymphatic.

_E_ 12. The body organ system that is important in fighting disease and filtration is the:
- A. muscular.
- B. gastrointestinal.
- C. genitourinary.
- D. endocrine.
- E. lymphatic.

_E_ 13. The term that is applied to the building up and tearing down of biochemical substances to produce energy is:
- A. anatomy.
- B. physiology.
- C. catabolism.
- D. anabolism.
- E. metabolism.

_A_ 14. Ductless or endocrine glands secrete directly into the circulatory system.
- A. True
- B. False

_B_ 15. The natural tendency of the body to maintain a constant internal environment is:
- A. cellular equilibrium.
- B. homeostasis.
- C. metabolism.
- D. physiology.
- E. paracrine signaling.

_A_ 16. The body's major baroreceptors are located in the:
- A. arch of the aorta.
- B. brain stem.
- C. lung tissue.
- D. inner ears.
- E. medulla oblongata.

_B_ 17. Most of the input affecting body organs and homeostasis occurs via the positive feedback loop.
- A. True
- B. False

_B_ 18. The feedback system that decreases stimulation as the target organ responds is the:
- A. positive feedback loop.
- B. negative feedback loop.
- C. decompensation system.
- D. beta adrenergic system.
- E. cholinergic loop.

_C_ 19. The "dance with death" is a phrase associated with which of the following signs of shock?
- A. rapid, weak pulse and warm, dry skin
- B. dyspnea and hypotension
- C. tachycardia and hypotension
- D. bradycardia and cool, moist skin
- E. lowered level of consciousness and hypotension

_B_ 20. A cell size that increases due to an increase in workload is an example of the process known as:
- A. atrophy.
- B. hypertrophy.
- C. hyperplasia.
- D. metaplasia.
- E. dysplasia.

_E__ 21. An abnormal change in cell size or shape due to some external stressor is an example of the process known as:
   A. atrophy.
   B. hypertrophy.
   C. hyperplasia.
   D. metaplasia.
   E. dysplasia.

_D__ 22. A blockage or reduction in the delivery of oxygenated blood to body cells is:
   A. hypoxia.
   B. anoxia.
   C. hypoperfusion.
   D. ischemia.
   E. infarction.

_E__ 23. Which of the following types of cellular injuries is caused by pathogens?
   A. hypoxic
   B. chemical
   C. inflammatory
   D. immunological
   E. infectious

_E__ 24. A pathogen's virulence is described as its ability to:
   A. invade cells.
   B. destroy cells.
   C. produce toxins.
   D. produce hypersensitivity reactions.
   E. all of the above

_D__ 25. A change in cellular structure due to an alteration in the permeability of the cell's membrane is:
   A. fatty alteration.
   B. anabolism.
   C. catabolism.
   D. cellular swelling.
   E. apoptosis.

_A__ 26. Cellular destruction caused by an internal release of enzymes is:
   A. apoptosis.
   B. fatty change.
   C. necrosis.
   D. gangrene.
   E. hemoptysis.

_C__ 27. Which of the following is NOT a type of necrosis?
   A. fatty
   B. liquefactive
   C. bilateral
   D. coagulative
   E. caseous

_C__ 28. The amount of water in the adult male is approximately what percentage of body weight?
   A. 25 percent
   B. 35 percent
   C. 60 percent
   D. 75 percent
   E. 80 percent

_C__ 29. Extracellular fluid accounts for what percentage of total body water?
   A. 75 percent
   B. 60 percent
   C. 25 percent
   D. 17.5 percent
   E. 7.5 percent

_B__ 30. The fluid space found between the vascular and cellular compartments is the extracellular compartment.
   A. True
   B. False

_D__ 31. A fluid that dissolves other substances is a:
   A. solute.
   B. electrolyte.
   C. hydrate.
   D. solvent.
   E. anhydrous.

_E__ 32. Which of the following is a source of body fluid loss and dehydration?
   A. diarrhea
   B. hyperventilation
   C. pancreatitis
   D. poor nutritional states
   E. all of the above

_B_ 33. The term *turgor* refers to:
  A. intense thirst.
  B. skin tension.
  C. highly concentrated urine.
  D. sunken fontanelles.
  E. extreme obesity.

_A_ 34. Which element is most common in the human body?
  A. hydrogen
  B. oxygen
  C. carbon
  D. nitrogen
  E. sodium

_B_ 35. A positively charged ion is a(n):
  A. anion.
  B. cation.
  C. electrolyte.
  D. dissociated element.
  E. reagent.

_E_ 36. The most prevalent cation in the human body is:
  A. magnesium.
  B. chloride.
  C. potassium.
  D. bicarbonate.
  E. sodium.

_D_ 37. Which of the following ions is responsible for buffering the acid concentrations in the body?
  A. magnesium
  B. chloride
  C. potassium
  D. bicarbonate
  E. sodium

_D_ 38. Which of the following is an electrolyte?
  A. glucose
  B. urea
  C. protein
  D. sodium bicarbonate
  E. serum

_A_ 39. A solution that contains more solute concentration on one side of a semipermeable membrane than on the other is said to be:
  A. hypertonic.
  B. isotonic.
  C. hypotonic.
  D. osmotic.
  E. diffused.

_B_ 40. When an isotonic solution is placed in the human bloodstream, water moves in which direction?
  A. into the vascular space
  B. does not move
  C. out of the vascular space
  D. in both directions
  E. none of the above

_A_ 41. When a hypertonic solution is placed in the human bloodstream, water moves in which direction?
  A. into the vascular space
  B. does not move
  C. out of the vascular space
  D. in both directions
  E. none of the above

_B_ 42. The movement of a solvent from an area of higher concentration through a semipermeable membrane to an area of lower concentration is termed:
  A. diffusion.
  B. osmosis.
  C. active transport.
  D. facilitated transport.
  E. oncosis.

_A_ 43. The movement of water out of and then back into the capillary as it travels through the capillary is regulated by the protein concentration within the blood and the pressure as the blood is pushed through the capillary.
  A. True
  B. False

©2006 Pearson Education, Inc.
Paramedic Care: Principles & Practice, Vol. 1

_D_ 44. The pressure that draws water into the blood because of the proteins there is called:
A. osmolarity.
B. osmotic pressure.
C. hydrostatic pressure.
D. oncotic force.
E. filtration.

_E_ 45. The movement of water out of the plasma across the capillary membrane into the interstitial space is:
A. osmolarity.
B. osmotic pressure.
C. hydrostatic pressure.
D. oncotic force.
E. filtration.

_D_ 46. Which of the following is a common cause of edema?
A. an increased plasma oncotic force
B. decreased hydrostatic pressure
C. decreased capillary permeability
D. lymphatic channel obstruction
E. all of the above

_A_ 47. The blood component that contains proteins, electrolytes, and clotting factors is:
A. plasma.
B. platelets.
C. erythrocytes.
D. leukocytes.
E. none of the above

_E_ 48. Which of the blood components below is/are responsible for a portion of the clotting process?
A. plasma
B. platelets
C. erythrocytes
D. leukocytes
E. A and B

_B_ 49. The most desirable fluid for blood loss replacement is normal saline.
A. True
B. False

_B_ 50. The percentage of blood accounted for by red blood cells is termed the:
A. component count.
B. hematocrit.
C. hemoglobin level.
D. oncotic pressure.
E. leukocyte level.

_E_ 51. Common signs of a transfusion reaction include:
A. fever.
B. chills.
C. hives.
D. nausea.
E. all of the above.

_A_ 52. A small volume of colloid solution can be administered to a patient with a greater than expected increase in the intravascular volume.
A. True
B. False

_D_ 53. Which of the following is NOT a colloid solution?
A. plasmanate
B. hetastarch
C. dextran
D. Ringer's solution
E. salt-poor albumin

_C_ 54. Which of the following solutions will cause a net movement of water into erythrocytes?
A. a colloid solution
B. a hypertonic solution
C. a hypotonic solution
D. an isotonic solution
E. both A and B

_A_ 55. Which of the following solutions contains a concentration of electrolytes that is very similar to plasma?
A. lactated Ringer's solution
B. normal saline
C. 1/2 normal saline
D. D_5W
E. dextran

_A_ 56. The higher the pH value, the lower the concentration of hydrogen ions.
A. True
B. False

_B___ 57. The normal pH range in the human body is:
   A. 6.9 to 7.35.
   B. 7.35 to 7.45.
   C. 7.45 to 7.8.
   D. 6.9 to 7.8.
   E. none of the above

_C___ 58. Which of the following would be considered alkalosis in the human?
   A. 6.9 to 7.35
   B. 7.35 to 7.45
   C. 7.45 to 7.8
   D. 6.4 to 6.9
   E. none of the above

_C___ 59. A decrease in pH of 1 would reflect which change in the concentration of hydrogen ions?
   A. 100 times as great
   B. 10 times as great
   C. 1/10th as great
   D. 1/100th as great
   E. a doubling

_B___ 60. The cellular environment of the human body is slightly acidic.
   A. True
   B. False

_D___ 61. The body system that responds most rapidly to a change in the pH is the:
   A. respiratory system.
   B. cardiovascular system.
   C. digestive system.
   D. buffer system.
   E. genitourinary system.

_A___ 62. The addition of hydrogen ions to the bloodstream will result in an increase in carbon dioxide.
   A. True
   B. False

_B___ 63. Respiratory alkalosis is caused by an increased retention of carbon dioxide in the lungs.
   A. True
   B. False

_A___ 64. In addition to treating the underlying cause, the care of metabolic acidosis includes ensuring adequate ventilation.
   A. True
   B. False

_D___ 65. A common cause of metabolic alkalosis is the administration of:
   A. sedatives.
   B. analgesics.
   C. bronchodilators.
   D. diuretics.
   E. antibiotics.

Special Project

Crossword Puzzle

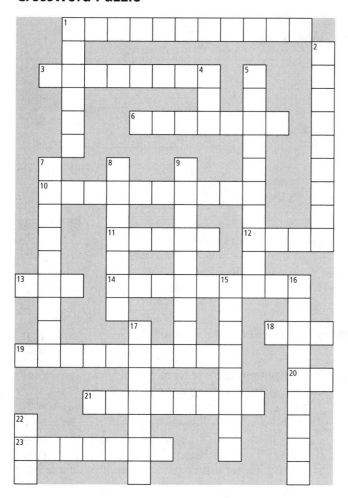

Across

1. Platelet important in blood clotting
3. Describing solutions that have the same solute concentration on both sides of a semipermeable membrane
6. The structure of an organism
10. Type of tissue lining the internal and external body surfaces
11. A group of tissues functioning together
12. An agent that can neutralize hydrogen ions
13. The fluid inside body cells (abbr.)
14. Describing a solution that has a lower solute concentration than a solution on the other side of a semipermeable membrane
18. High-energy compound present in all cells, especially the muscles (abbr.)
19. Replacement of cells of one type by cells of another type not normal for that tissue
20. The potential for hydrogen (abbr.)
21. An agent that increases urine output
23. The passage of a solvent through a membrane

Down

1. A grouping of cells that perform a similar function
2. Structure that performs a specific function within a cell
4. The root word meaning "cell"
5. Iron-based compound that binds with oxygen
7. White blood cell that plays a key role in the immune system
8. Decrease in cell size due to a decrease in cell workload
9. An excess of alkaline substances or a deficit in acids
15. The sum of all the cells, tissues, and organ systems of a living being
16. Thick, viscous fluid that fills and gives shape to the cell
17. Protein commonly present in plant and animal tissues
22. An electrically charged atom or group of atoms

Part 2: Disease—Causes and Pathophysiology, begins on p. 200

Review of Chapter Objectives

After reading this part of the chapter, you should be able to:

1. Analyze disease risk.   pp. 200–205

Disease risk arises from several sources including genetic, environmental, lifestyle, age, and gender factors. Genetic factors are transferred from parents to offspring through genes and may cause frank disease or predispose an individual to disease. Environmental factors include violence, toxins, climate, socioeconomic conditions, exposure to bacteria, and other factors. Lifestyle factors include diet, exercise, smoking, and drug use. Age results in a progressive diminution of body functions and the increasing presence of progressive diseases. Gender risk is associated with hormonal protection or predisposition to disease. Often disease risk is associated with a combination of genetic, environmental, lifestyle, age, and gender factors.

2. Describe environmental risk factors and combined effects and interactions among risk factors.   pp. 200–201

Environmental risk factors include violence that may induce trauma, toxins that may cause chemical trauma, poisoning, or cancers, and adverse climates that may cause UV skin and eye damage as well as hyperthermia and hypothermia, frostbite, and freezing injuries. Poor water supplies, poor nutrition, inadequate housing, and poor medical care may also increase the risk for disease. Frequently, environmental and other disease risk factors combine to induce disease. Type II diabetes, for example, is associated with a familial history but is also associated with a high-fat and high-carbohydrate diet, lack of exercise, and obesity. Heart disease is associated with a familial history, diet, gender, and age factors.

3. Discuss familial diseases and associated risk factors.   pp. 201–205

Diseases such as allergies, asthma, rheumatic fever, some cancers, diabetes, cardiovascular disease, cystic fibrosis, sickle cell disease, and some neuromuscular diseases are caused directly by defective genes or related to a genetic predisposition to the disease. Often these predispositions are then triggered by environmental or lifestyle factors that lead to the frank disease. For example, a familial history of heart disease is exacerbated with smoking, obesity, poor diet, and a sedentary lifestyle.

4. Discuss hypoperfusion.   pp. 205–219

Hypoperfusion is inadequate blood flow to and past the body cells. This means that blood flow is insufficient to provide oxygen and necessary nutrients and to remove carbon dioxide and other metabolic wastes. If permitted to continue, hypoperfusion progresses and leads to failure of compensatory mechanisms, decompensation, irreversible shock, and death. Hypoperfusion (or shock) may be caused by trauma, fluid loss, myocardial infarction, infection, allergic reaction, spinal cord or brain injury, and other causes.

5. Define cardiogenic, hypovolemic, neurogenic, anaphylactic, and septic shock.   pp. 214–219

Cardiogenic shock is due to the inability of the heart to pump enough blood to meet the body's needs. It is commonly caused by severe left ventricular failure secondary to a myocardial infarction or congestive heart failure. Cardiac output decreases and workload increases, while coronary artery flow decreases and myocardial oxygen demand increases. These factors begin a vicious cycle that often ends in complete heart failure.

Hypovolemic shock is due to the loss of blood volume through internal or external hemorrhage, dehydration, plasma losses from burns, excessive sweating, or third space losses. As the vascular volume decreases, the body compensates by releasing catecholamines, increasing heart rate and inducing vasoconstriction. This produces the classical signs and symptoms of shock—a rapid weak pulse, cool, clammy, ashen skin, dyspnea, anxiety, combativeness—and, ultimately, hypotension.

Neurogenic shock results from injury to the brain or spinal cord that interrupts the body's control over the vascular system. The vessels lose tone and dilate, increasing the size of the vascular container and producing a relative hypovolemia. The body's normal response is muted because the adrenal glands do not secrete catecholamines and the central nervous system cannot induce vasoconstriction. The injury may also affect the heart and respiratory system.

Anaphylactic shock is an exaggerated and severe allergic reaction to a foreign substance that enters the body. It usually occurs rapidly and may be triggered by many substances. The most severe of anaphylactic reactions are triggered when substances are injected directly into the bloodstream, as with bee and wasp stings and injected medications.

Septic shock is caused by an infection that progresses and enters the bloodstream. The toxins produced by the overwhelming infection increase capillary permeability and overcome the compensatory mechanisms, and shock results.

6. Describe multiple organ dysfunction syndrome.   pp. 219–221

Multiple organ dysfunction syndrome (MODS) is a progressive impairment of two or more body organs, usually after an initial insult and apparently successful resuscitation. It is caused by an uncontrolled inflammatory response and occurs most commonly after septic shock. The syndrome is caused by an exaggerated immune response in which hormones are released, causing vasodilation, increased capillary permeability, and increased metabolic demands. The syndrome usually begins within 24 hours of the initial insult and progresses over several weeks.

Content Self-Evaluation

MULTIPLE CHOICE

_____ 1. Which of the following is a factor that can influence disease risk?
  A. family history
  B. environment
  C. gender
  D. lifestyle
  E. all of the above

_____ 2. Which of the following is a disease with a genetic predisposition?
  A. septic shock
  B. rubella
  C. cystic fibrosis
  D. Hansen's disease
  E. all of the above

_____ 3. Most disease processes are simply caused by either an environmental or genetic factor, rarely both.
  A. True
  B. False

_____ 4. The death rate from disease is reported as its:
  A. prevalence.
  B. morbidity.
  C. mortality.
  D. incidence.
  E. none of the above

_____ 5. People with genetic predispositions to certain diseases can frequently take actions that modify the risk factors associated with acquiring the disease.
   A. True   B. False

_____ 6. Which of the following is a disease with both a genetic predisposition and modifiable risk factors?
   A. allergies   D. breast cancer
   B. asthma   E. all of the above
   C. heart disease

_____ 7. The risk of acquiring heart disease for a person with a familial history of coronary artery disease is how many times greater than for someone without such a family history?
   A. two   D. five
   B. three   E. eight
   C. four

_____ 8. Hypertension is a risk factor for which of the following?
   A. stroke   D. cardiovascular disease
   B. kidney disease   E. all except C
   C. cancer

_____ 9. What percentage of lung cancers in women are associated with smoking?
   A. 40 percent   D. 80 percent
   B. 60 percent   E. 90 percent
   C. 70 percent

_____ 10. Obesity is defined as having a body weight that is over ideal body weight by:
   A. 20 percent.   D. 35 percent.
   B. 25 percent.   E. 40 percent.
   C. 30 percent.

_____ 11. For which of the following diseases is obesity NOT a risk factor?
   A. hypertension   D. vascular disease
   B. heart disease   E. diabetes
   C. breast cancer

_____ 12. Perfusion involves the exchange of which of the following between the bloodstream and body cells?
   A. carbon dioxide   D. waste products
   B. oxygen   E. all of the above
   C. nutrients

_____ 13. The term _shock_ is synonymous with:
   A. hypotension.   D. hyperperfusion.
   B. hypoperfusion.   E. hypervolemia.
   C. hypovolemia.

_____ 14. Stroke volume of the heart is directly related to all of the following EXCEPT:
   A. preload.   D. cardiac contractile force.
   B. afterload.   E. circulating catecholamines.
   C. oxygen saturation.

_____ 15. Of the factors listed below, the one with the greatest influence on cardiac preload is:
   A. total blood volume.   D. systolic blood pressure.
   B. venous return.   E. circulating volume.
   C. heart rate.

_____ 16. The stretching of the myocardial wall increases the strength of cardiac contraction in the mechanism known as:
  A. peripheral vascular resistance.
  B. the Hering-Breuer response.
  C. the Frank-Starling mechanism.
  D. cardiac preload.
  E. the catecholamine response.

_____ 17. When baroreceptors detect a fall in blood pressure, they cause a(n):
  A. decrease in heart rate.
  B. increase in the strength of myocardial contraction.
  C. venous dilation.
  D. arteriolar dilation.
  E. all of the above

_____ 18. The cardiovascular container includes:
  A. arteries.
  B. veins.
  C. capillaries.
  D. arterioles.
  E. all of the above

_____ 19. The arteriole has the ability to change its diameter up to fivefold.
  A. True
  B. False

_____ 20. Contraction of the venous blood vessels will:
  A. increase preload.
  B. decrease arterial pressure.
  C. increase blood pressure.
  D. increase vascular volume.
  E. none of the above

_____ 21. The oxygen concentration in air within the alveoli is approximately:
  A. 10 percent.
  B. 14 percent.
  C. 17 percent.
  D. 19 percent.
  E. 21 percent.

_____ 22. Which of the following is NOT one of the conditions for movement and utilization of oxygen described by the Fick principle?
  A. adequate inspired oxygen
  B. adequate cardiac stretching
  C. proper tissue perfusion
  D. efficient oxygen off-loading
  E. adequate red blood cells

_____ 23. Hypoperfusion may occur with all of the following EXCEPT:
  A. low heart rate.
  B. dilated vascular container.
  C. excessive vascular constriction.
  D. reduced blood volume.
  E. excessive afterload.

_____ 24. The second stage of cellular metabolism that breaks glucose down into energy that can be used by the body requires the presence of:
  A. sodium bicarbonate.
  B. glucagon.
  C. oxygen.
  D. pyruvic acid.
  E. sodium chloride.

_____ 25. The Krebs cycle produces a chemical energy form used by the body that is called:
  A. adenosine triphosphate.
  B. lactic acid.
  C. pyruvic acid.
  D. citric acid.
  E. sodium bicarbonate.

_____ 26. Inadequate perfusion may lead to increased sodium and water in the body's cells and eventually the bursting of cell membranes.
  A. True
  B. False

_____ 27. The process by which glycogen is converted into glucose in the cells is:
  A. glycolysis.
  B. glycogenesis.
  C. glycogenolysis.
  D. gluconeogenesis
  E. lipolysis.

_____ 28. The body's process of compensation for hypoperfusion is initiated by:
  A. glucose.   D. pyruvic acid.
  B. oxygen.   E. cortisol.
  C. norepinephrine.

_____ 29. The catecholamines epinephrine and norepinephrine are responsible during the body's
       response to hypoperfusion for:
  A. decreasing heart rate.
  B. decreasing cardiac contractile strength.
  C. arteriolar dilation.
  D. increasing blood pressure.
  E. decreasing blood volume.

_____ 30. During shock, the spleen may expel blood back into the circulatory system up to a
       volume of:
  A. 200 mL.   D. 500 mL.
  B. 300 mL.   E. 600 mL.
  C. 400 mL.

_____ 31. During hypoperfusion, the renin-angiotensin compensatory system:
  A. increases red blood cell production.
  B. causes the spleen to release blood.
  C. produces a potent vasoconstrictor.
  D. induces beneficial fluid shifts.
  E. reduces the production of lactic acid.

_____ 32. The stage of shock in which medical intervention is no longer effective is:
  A. compensated shock.   D. irreversible shock.
  B. decompensated shock.   E. septic shock.
  C. progressive shock.

_____ 33. During decompensated shock, which of the following is likely to occur?
  A. fluid shift from the interstitial spaces
  B. systemic alkalosis
  C. cardiac excitation
  D. dropping blood pressure
  E. all of the above

_____ 34. What type of shock is due to plasma loss from burns?
  A. cardiogenic   D. septic
  B. hypovolemic   E. anaphylactic
  C. neurogenic

_____ 35. What type of shock is due to a severe allergic reaction?
  A. cardiogenic   D. septic
  B. hypovolemic   E. anaphylactic
  C. neurogenic

_____ 36. Which type of shock results from infection that enters the bloodstream and is carried
       throughout the body?
  A. cardiogenic   D. septic
  B. hypovolemic   E. anaphylactic
  C. neurogenic

_____ 37. A relaxing of the blood vessel walls is the cause of which type of shock?
  A. cardiogenic   D. septic
  B. hypovolemic   E. anaphylactic
  C. neurogenic

©2006 Pearson Education, Inc.
Paramedic Care: Principles & Practice, Vol. 1

_____ 38. The reason we are aware of multiple organ dysfunction syndrome (MODS) is that modern medicine is able to help patients survive the initial serious illness or injury.
      A. True   B. False

_____ 39. The first evidence of MODS usually presents within:
      A. 12 hours.   D. 7 to 10 days.
      B. 24 hours.   E. 14 to 21 days.
      C. 72 hours.

_____ 40. Death from MODS usually occurs after:
      A. 24 hours.   D. 14 days.
      B. 48 hours.   E. 21 days.
      C. 72 hours.

MATCHING

Match the type of shock with the characteristic of its presentation.

Type of shock

A. cardiogenic

B. hypovolemic

C. neurogenic

D. septic

E. anaphylactic

Pathology or presentation

_____ 41. pulmonary edema

_____ 42. warm, red skin

_____ 43. itching and skin flushing

_____ 44. history of recent illness

_____ 45. hives

_____ 46. possible high fever

_____ 47. classic signs of shock

_____ 48. laryngeal edema

_____ 49. dry skin

_____ 50. history of diarrhea

Part 3: The Body's Defenses Against Disease and Injury, begins on p. 221

Review of Chapter Objectives

After reading this part of the chapter, you should be able to:

1. Define the characteristics of the immune response.   pp. 225–239

Foreign and invading cells or substances often have unique proteins on their surfaces called antigens. The immune system detects these antigens as being unlike those of the body's cells and initiates a response. This response uses antibodies to selectively control or destroy the foreign substance. As a result of the first contact with the foreign agent, the body develops a "memory" that produces a more rapid and effective response should the same antigen be recognized again. This response is called immunity.

Immunity can be acquired or natural. Natural immunity is not generated by the immune response but is a genetically inhospitable environment for a particular organism—for example, human resistance to canine distemper. Active acquired immunity is that immunity gained from a response to an invading antigen and is long-lasting. Passive immunity is acquired from an outside source such as an immunization or from maternal blood during gestation and is temporary.

The primary immune response occurs with the first exposure to an antigen and lags from five to seven days after exposure. The secondary response occurs as the immune system is sensitized to the antigen by the first response. If it is again exposed to the antigen, it presents a more aggressive and faster response.

Humoral immunity is immunity resident in the blood and lymphatic fluid, primarily from B lymphocytes that produce antibodies. Cell-mediated immunity is immunity provided by T lymphocytes that recognize and directly attack the foreign antigen.

2. Discuss induction of the immune system.   pp. 226–230

The immune system must be triggered or induced. This may occur as a result of the actions of antigens and immunogens, histocompatibility, and blood groupings.

Antigens that induce an immune response are called immunogens. Generally an antigen must be sufficiently foreign and sufficient in size, complexity, and number to generate an immune response.

Histocompatibility locus antigens are antigens that the body recognizes as either foreign or self. Those that are recognized as self (or non-foreign) do not generate an immune response, whereas those that are recognized as foreign (non-self) stimulate an immune response. It is extremely important to find compatible tissue for organ donation, or tissue rejection may result.

Blood group antigens are associated with a different grouping of antigens than those associated with the histocompatibility response. The major blood group antigens consist of the Rh factor (present in about 85% of the population) and the A and B antigens associated with the ABO blood typing system.

3. Discuss fetal, neonatal, and geriatric immune function.   pp. 238–239

The developing fetus does generate some immune response capabilities during gestation, but the immune system is not fully mature at birth. The fetus receives some protection from maternal antibodies that cross the placenta, but those diminish with time. At five to six months the infant is most susceptible to disease, especially respiratory infections.

The immune functions begin to deteriorate after sexual maturity as the thymus decreases in size and may reduce the effectiveness of T cells. Decreased hypersensitivity and diminished T cell response to infection generally occur in individuals over the age of 60.

4. Describe the inflammation response and its systemic manifestations.   pp. 223–225, 240–253

The inflammatory response is a swift, short-acting, nonspecific internal response to cellular injury from trauma or disease. It involves several plasma protein systems and provides four major functions. They are destroying and removing the unwanted substances, walling off the infected or inflamed area, stimulating the immune response, and promoting the healing process.

There are three major manifestations of the acute inflammatory response. They are fever, an increase in circulating white blood cells, and an increase in circulating plasma proteins. Fever is a result of fever-causing chemicals (endogenous pyrogens) released during phagocytosis and is caused by toxins released by bacteria or as a response to an antigen-antibody complex. The elevation in body temperature may make the environment less hospitable to the invading pathogen. Both the number of circulating white blood cells and plasma proteins increase as the body tries to defeat the infection.

The chronic inflammatory response is a response that lasts longer than two weeks. During chronic inflammation, the body tries to isolate the agent by forming a barrier around it. Sometimes this cavity is filled with a fluid mixture of cellular debris, dead white blood cells, and tissue fluid called pus.

5. **Discuss the role of mast cells, the plasma protein system, and cellular components as part of the inflammation response.** pp. 241–251

Mast Cells. Specialized cells called mast cells that resemble bags of granules are the chief activators of the inflammatory response. When injured, they initiate the inflammatory response by releasing their granules (degranulation) or by constructing substances that play important roles in the inflammatory response (synthesis).

Degranulation occurs as the mast cell is injured and releases vasoactive amines and chemotactic factors. The principle vasoactive amine is histamine, a potent agent that increases blood flow through the affected area and increases capillary permeability to permit fluid and white blood cells to migrate into the interstitial space. Chemotactic factors are agents that attract white blood cells to the site of inflammation.

Synthesis is the construction of leukotrienes and prostaglandins to enhance the inflammatory response. Leukotrienes have actions similar to histamine and chemotactic factors; however, they promote a slower and longer lasting response. Prostaglandins cause increased perfusion and capillary permeability but limit the effects of histamine and reduce the release of enzymes from some white blood cells.

Plasma Protein Systems. In addition to the antigen-antibody system, there are three plasma protein systems that complement the inflammatory response system. They are the complement system, the coagulation system, and the kinin system.

The complement system is a complicated cascade system that is activated by antigen-antibody complexes, by products released by the invading bacteria, or by components of other plasma protein systems. The later portions of the cascade produce proteins that may coat the invading agent (opsonization), ingest the agent (phagocytosis), rupture the bacteria's cell membrane (lysis), cause the invading agents to clump together (agglutination), or neutralize the virus through actions similar to the degranulation of the mast cell. Complement proteins may also clog the tissues surrounding the infection and isolate it.

The coagulation or clotting system produces fibrin at the end of a clotting cascade. Fibrin is a sticky protein fiber that traps red blood cells to form a clot, prevents microorganism movement, increases vascular permeability, and produces some chemotactic substances.

The kinin system produces bradykinin, a protein that causes vasodilation, extravascular smooth muscle contraction, increased vascular permeability, and some chemotaxis.

Cellular components of the inflammatory response include the vascular response, increased capillary permeability, and exudation of white blood cells. The vascular response causes blood to flow more strongly into the injured area and helps push both plasma and white blood cells into the inflamed area. The increased capillary permeability is due to a constriction in the capillary wall cells that opens the spaces in between the cells and permits the large white blood cells to squeeze through (diapedesis). The white blood cells are phagocytes that engulf and digest invading cells and debris.

6. **Describe the resolution and repair from inflammation.** pp. 251–252

The tissue repair process begins with a generalized cleaning up of the injured and inflamed tissue called debridement. Here phagocytes remove dead cells and debris and dissolve any formed scab. Then resolution or repair occurs. Resolution is the complete restoration of the structure and function of injured tissue. If the injury was more than minor and complete restoration is not possible, then repair will take place. Repair replaces original tissue with scar tissue.

7. **Discuss the effects of aging on the mechanisms of self defense.** pp. 252–253

The very young and very old are most susceptible to insufficient immune and inflammation responses. The infant, at around 5 or 6 months, has immature immunity, and maternal immune agents are on the decline. The elderly have reduced T and B cell effectiveness after age 60 as the thymus shrinks in size. They also have impaired wound healing as a result of the normal aging process, an increased likelihood of chronic disease, and their frequent use of antiinflammatory drugs that reduce the body's immune and inflammatory responses. Decreased perfusion also contributes to tissue hypoxia and poor inflammatory and immune response.

8. **Discuss hypersensitivity.** pp. 253–258

Usually, hypersensitivity triggers an inflammation response that injures healthy tissue. There are four types of hypersensitivity that cause this destructive reaction. They are IgE-mediated reactions (type I), tissue-specific reactions (type II), immune complex-mediated reactions (type III), and cell-mediated reactions (type IV).

Type I reactions involve the immunoglobulin (antibody) IgE. These antibodies are created in great numbers with the first exposure to an antigen and are released with subsequent exposures, leading to a release of histamine and triggering of the inflammatory response. This results in skin flushing, itching, urticaria and edema, dyspnea, laryngeal edema, laryngospasm, bronchospasm, vasodilation and increased permeability, tachycardia, hypertension, nausea, vomiting, cramping and diarrhea, dizziness, headache, convulsions, and tearing. This type of reaction (anaphylactic) may be life threatening.

Type II reactions are directed to specific types of tissue. The tissue is destroyed by the complement cascade, which causes destruction of the target cell's membrane; by clearance of the target cell by macrophage action; by the antigen binding cytotoxic cells to the target cell; and finally by the antigen disabling receptor sites on the target cell.

Type III reactions are either localized or systemic reactions as the complement cascade system attracts neutrophils. They are unable to destroy the invading pathogen and release agents that destroy neighboring healthy cells.

Type IV reactions are activated directly by T cells and do not involve antibodies. The T cells activate other immune cells and attack antigen-bearing cells directly with toxins they produce.

9. **Describe deficiencies in immunity and inflammation.** pp. 258–260

Congenital or primary immunity deficiencies occur when the development of lymphocytes is impaired during fetal development. Differing immune deficiencies may develop depending on whether T cells, B cells, or both are affected. In some cases just a small portion of the immune system is deficient and the body is unable to respond to one or a few antigens.

Acquired deficiencies occur after birth and do not result from genetic factors. Nutritional, iatrogenic (caused by medical care), trauma, and stress factors may also result in a decrease in the body's resistance to illness. A specific type of immune deficiency is acquired immune deficiency syndrome (AIDS). AIDS develops from an infection caused by human immunodeficiency virus (HIV). It carries its genetic information on RNA that converts into DNA when it invades a cell and then becomes part of the infected cell's genetic material. The virus may remain dormant for years until it becomes active and kills the host cell and infects other cells. It results in a pervasive invasion of the body's immune defenses.

10. **Describe homeostasis as a dynamic steady state.** p. 262

Homeostasis is often defined as a constant environment within the body and one that the body tries to maintain. In reality, this state is always changing due to turnover of body cells, to the aging process, to continuing body processes such as synthesis and breakdown of all body substances, and to the effects of stressors. The body tries, however, to maintain a relatively constant environment.

11. **Describe neuroendocrine regulation.** pp. 263–266

When a psychological stressor affects an individual, the sympathetic nervous system is stimulated and there is a release of catecholamines, cortisol, and other hormones.

Catecholamines (norepinephrine and epinephrine) are released when sympathetic nerve impulses (from the thoracic and lumbar portions of the spinal cord) stimulate the adrenal medulla. These catecholamines act on four different receptors: Alpha 1, alpha 2, beta 1, and beta 2. Alpha 1 receptors cause peripheral vasoconstriction and mild bronchoconstriction and increase metabolism. Alpha 2 receptors mediate the actions of alpha 1 agents. Beta 1 receptors increase the heart rate, contractile strength, automaticity, and conductivity. Stimulation of beta 2 receptors causes vasodilation and bronchodilation.

©2006 Pearson Education, Inc.
Paramedic Care: Principles & Practice, Vol. 1

Sympathetic stimulation also causes the adrenal cortex to produce a steroid hormone, cortisol. Cortisol stimulates the creation of glucose (gluconeogenesis) and limits glucose uptake by cells, increasing blood glucose levels. It also promotes the breakdown of proteins and lipids and acts as an immunosuppressant. While its effects do not support the inflammation and immune responses, cortisol ensures there are adequate energy sources and may help direct blood flow to critical organs during stress.

12. Discuss the interrelationships between stress, coping, and illness.   pp. 266–269

The ability to cope with stress appears to have an impact on how effectively the body deals with disease. Positive coping mechanisms support the resolution of disease, whereas ineffective coping mechanisms exacerbate symptoms and the illness.

Content Self-Evaluation

MULTIPLE CHOICE

_____ 1. Which of the following are single-cell organisms consisting of cytoplasm surrounded by a rigid cell membrane?
A. viruses
B. bacteria
C. fungi
D. parasites
E. prions

_____ 2. Which of the following are more like plants than animals and rarely cause serious human disease?
A. viruses
B. bacteria
C. fungi
D. parasites
E. prions

_____ 3. Which of the following are released by bacterial cells during their growth?
A. antibiotics
B. gram-negative material
C. exotoxins
D. endotoxins
E. none of the above

_____ 4. The body's anatomical barrier against infection (the skin and linings of the respiratory and digestive systems) is considered:
A. an external, specific barrier.
B. an external, nonspecific barrier.
C. an internal, specific barrier.
D. an internal, nonspecific barrier.
E. none of the above

_____ 5. The body's immune response against infection is considered:
A. an external, specific response.
B. an external, nonspecific response.
C. an internal, specific response.
D. an internal, nonspecific response.
E. none of the above

_____ 6. The immune response to infection is more rapid than the inflammatory response and is not specific to the invading organism.
A. True
B. False

_____ 7. The proteins located on the surface of many substances that enter the body and are used during the immune response to identify foreign organisms are:
A. antigens.
B. antibodies.
C. B cells.
D. T cells.
E. lymphocytes.

_____ 8. Which of the types of immunity listed below is genetic?
- **A.** primary
- **B.** acquired
- **C.** natural
- **D.** secondary
- **E.** extrinsic

_____ 9. Which type of immunity refers to the body's initial response to exposure to an antigen?
- **A.** primary
- **B.** acquired
- **C.** natural
- **D.** secondary
- **E.** humoral

_____ 10. The type of immunity, resident in the blood, that produces antibodies and remembers a specific antigen is:
- **A.** cell-mediated.
- **B.** humoral.
- **C.** natural.
- **D.** primary.
- **E.** extrinsic.

_____ 11. Which of the following is NOT an essential characteristic of an antigen required to trigger an immune response?
- **A.** sufficient foreignness
- **B.** sufficient size
- **C.** sufficient complexity
- **D.** sufficient quantity
- **E.** sufficient lability

_____ 12. The antigens that help the body recognize a substance as "self" or "nonself" are called HLA (human leukocyte antigens) antigens.
- **A.** True
- **B.** False

_____ 13. What percentage of the North American population has the Rh factor present in their blood?
- **A.** 15 percent
- **B.** 25 percent
- **C.** 45 percent
- **D.** 75 percent
- **E.** 85 percent

_____ 14. Under the ABO classification system, the universal blood donor is identified as having blood type:
- **A.** A.
- **B.** B.
- **C.** O.
- **D.** AB.
- **E.** B and O.

_____ 15. Individuals with which of the following blood types would have the anti-A antibody?
- **A.** A
- **B.** B
- **C.** O
- **D.** AB
- **E.** answers B and C

_____ 16. The time delay between the initial introduction of an antigen and the first detectable appearance of antibodies in the blood is about:
- **A.** 24 hours.
- **B.** 2 to 4 days.
- **C.** 5 to 7 days.
- **D.** 1 to 2 weeks.
- **E.** 2 to 4 weeks.

_____ 17. Antibodies are immunoglobulin molecules consisting of Y-shaped chains that respond to a specific antigen.
- **A.** True
- **B.** False

_____ 18. An antibody attaching to an antigen may result in all of the following EXCEPT:
- **A.** agglutination.
- **B.** debridement.
- **C.** neutralization.
- **D.** enhancement of phagocytosis.
- **E.** precipitation.

_____ 19. Which of the following is NOT a function of antibodies?
  A. opsonization of bacteria
  B. activation of inflammatory processes
  C. generation of stem cells
  D. neutralization of bacterial toxins
  E. neutralization of viruses

_____ 20. Some antibodies are present in tears, saliva, and breast milk.
  A. True   **B.** False

_____ 21. Which cells are associated with the cell-mediated response of the immune system?
  A. B cells   **D.** Y cells
  B. T cells   **E.** both A and B
  C. phagocytes

_____ 22. The infant's antibody levels are lowest at what age?
  A. birth   **D.** 6 to 8 months
  B. 1 to 2 months   **E.** 10 to 12 months
  C. 5 to 6 months

_____ 23. Which of the following is NOT true of inflammatory response?
  A. It is of relatively short duration.
  B. It begins after five to seven days.
  C. It involves many types of cells.
  D. It involves several protein systems.
  E. It is considered part of the body's immune system.

_____ 24. Which of the following is NOT a function of the inflammatory response?
  A. to destroy and remove unwanted substances
  B. to wall off the infected and inflamed area
  C. to stimulate the immune response
  D. to promote healing
  E. to agglutinate viruses

_____ 25. Degranulation by the mast cells occurs when the cell is stimulated by all of the following EXCEPT:
  A. physical injury.   **D.** histamines.
  B. toxins.   **E.** venoms.
  C. allergic reactions.

_____ 26. The attraction of white blood cells to the site of infection is called:
  A. synthesis.   **D.** the complement system.
  B. chemotaxis.   **E.** agglutination.
  C. allergy.

_____ 27. The action of histamine during the inflammatory response is to:
  A. increase capillary permeability.
  B. increase blood flow to the injured area.
  C. attack the invading cells.
  D. attract white blood cells.
  E. both A and B

_____ 28. The plasma protein systems produce results through a series of interactions called a(n):
  A. chain reaction.   **D.** interrelational exchange.
  B. sequential series.   **E.** neutralization.
  C. cascade.

_____ 29. Which of the following is an expected action against an invading organism resulting from the complement system?
A. opsonization
B. phagocytosis
C. lysis
D. agglutination
E. all of the above

_____ 30. The kinin system produces bradykinin that causes which of the following actions?
A. increased capillary permeability
B. vasoconstriction
C. smooth muscle relaxation
D. degranulation
E. increased cardiac output

_____ 31. The first action of the inflammatory response is:
A. an increase in vascular permeability.
B. increased circulation to the affected area.
C. white blood cells adhering to blood vessel walls.
D. white blood cells traversing the capillary wall.
E. all of the above occur simultaneously

_____ 32. The movement of white blood cells through gaps in the capillary wall is called:
A. margination.
B. diapedesis.
C. granulocytosis.
D. active transport.
E. exudation.

_____ 33. Which of the following cells release histamine and other chemicals during the inflammation response?
A. monocytes
B. neutrophils
C. basophils
D. eosinophils
E. all of the above

_____ 34. Occasionally, when macrophages are unable to destroy foreign invaders, a granuloma will form to isolate the infection.
A. True
B. False

_____ 35. The best outcome from the wound healing process is:
A. debridement.
B. repair.
C. resolution.
D. scarring.
E. granulation.

_____ 36. Healthy tissue grows inward from the edges of a wound to fill it in during which stage of the wound healing process?
A. initial response
B. granulation
C. epithelialization
D. contraction
E. debridement

_____ 37. The process in which scar tissue is modified and strengthened after the initial wound repair is:
A. epithelialization.
B. granulation.
C. maturation.
D. reconstruction.
E. debridement.

_____ 38. The impaired wound healing experienced by the elderly is thought to be a natural consequence of aging.
A. True
B. False

_____ 39. Which of the following describes a disturbance in the body's normal tolerance for self antigens?
A. allergy
B. anaphylaxis
C. autoimmunity
D. isoimmunity
E. granulation

©2006 Pearson Education, Inc.
Paramedic Care: Principles & Practice, Vol. 1

_____ 40. Which of the following is a hypersensitivity response associated with antigens from another person?
A. allergy
B. anaphylaxis
C. autoimmunity
D. isoimmunity
E. monoimmunity

_____ 41. The common allergic and anaphylactic responses are caused by which immunoglobulin (antibody)?
A. IgM
B. IgG
C. IgA
D. IgE
E. IgD

_____ 42. The common clinical signs of a severe allergic reaction include all of the following EXCEPT:
A. skin flushing.
B. dyspnea.
C. nausea.
D. dizziness.
E. bradycardia.

_____ 43. An allergy is an immune response to an environmental antigen.
A. True
B. False

_____ 44. The type of immunity that causes rejection of donated organs is:
A. allergy.
B. anaphylaxis.
C. autoimmunity.
D. isoimmunity.
E. monoimmunity.

_____ 45. Most cases of infection by the human immunodeficiency virus (HIV) in the United States result from:
A. injection.
B. droplet inhalation.
C. skin contamination.
D. body fluids during sexual intercourse.
E. both A and D

_____ 46. A state of physical or psychological arousal to stimuli is:
A. disease.
B. homeostasis.
C. stress.
D. general adaptation syndrome.
E. turnover.

_____ 47. The initial stage of the general adaptation syndrome in response to stress is:
A. exhaustion.
B. resistance.
C. withdrawal.
D. alarm.
E. turnover.

_____ 48. The second stage of the general adaptation syndrome in response to stress is:
A. exhaustion.
B. resistance.
C. withdrawal.
D. alarm.
E. turnover.

_____ 49. The final stage of the general adaptation syndrome in response to stress is:
A. exhaustion.
B. resistance.
C. withdrawal.
D. alarm.
E. turnover.

_____ 50. During the initial stage of stress, which of the following is NOT likely to occur?
   A. tachycardia
   B. levels of circulating hormones returning to normal
   C. hypertension
   D. digestion slowing
   E. blood flow to skeletal muscles increasing

_____ 51. Homeostasis can be described as a constantly changing yet steady environment.
   A. True   B. False

_____ 52. The interactions that contribute to the alteration of the immune system as an outcome of a stress response are called:
   A. GAS alliance.
   B. homeostatic return.
   C. turnover response.
   D. stress-stressor combination.
   E. pyschoneuroimmunological regulation.

_____ 53. The continual synthesis and breakdown of body substances that results in homeostasis is:
   A. autocombustion.   D. oxidation.
   B. turnover.   E. plasmodynamics.
   C. recycling.

_____ 54. Catecholamines include which of the following hormones?
   A. endorphins   D. norepinephrine
   B. epinephrine   E. both B and D
   C. cortisol

_____ 55. The hormone released in the greatest quantity by the adrenal medulla is norepinephrine.
   A. True   B. False

_____ 56. Stimulation of the alpha 1 receptors will cause:
   A. increased heart rate.
   B. inhibition of the effects of norepinephrine.
   C. vasoconstriction.
   D. bronchodilation.
   E. all of the above

_____ 57. Stimulation of the beta 2 receptors will cause:
   A. increased heart rate.
   B. inhibition of the effects of norepinephrine.
   C. vasoconstriction.
   D. bronchodilation.
   E. increase contractility.

_____ 58. Cortisol has harmful immunosuppressive actions that, unless mediated, worsen the effects of stress.
   A. True   B. False

_____ 59. The hormone associated with decreased pain sensitivity and increased feelings of well-being is:
   A. growth hormone.   D. beta-endorphin.
   B. prolactin.   E. estrogen.
   C. testosterone.

_____ 60. Effective stress coping mechanisms have an apparent impact on how people deal with disease but do not effect the seriousness of the associated illness.
   A. True   B. False

Special Project

Complete the diagram below summarizing the immune response process. Write the letter of the label in the appropriate place on the diagram.

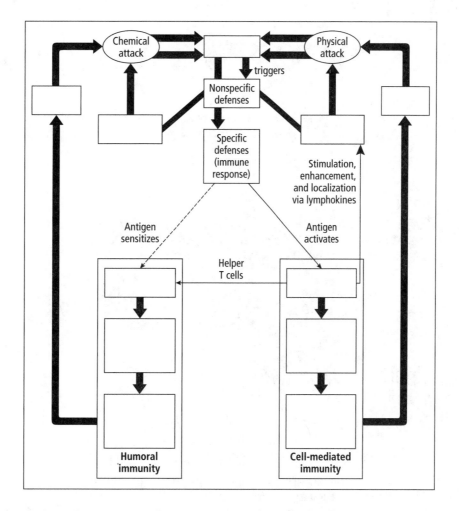

A. Activation of B cells

B. Cytotoxic T cells

C. Maturation of plasma cells and production of antibodies

D. Production of memory T cells and cytotoxic T cells

E. Antigen

F. Complement system

G. NK cells/macrophages

H. Production of memory B cells and plasma cells

I. Activation of T cells

J. Maturation and migration of cytotoxic T cells

K. Circulating antibodies

General Principles of Pharmacology

Because Chapter 9 is lengthy, it has been divided into parts to aid your study. Read the assigned textbook pages, then progress through the objectives and self-evaluation materials as you would with other chapters. When you feel secure in your grasp of the content, proceed to the next section.

Part 1: Basic Pharmacology, p. 278

Review of Chapter Objectives

After reading this part of the chapter, you should be able to:

1. Describe important historical trends in pharmacology. p. 278

The use of herbs and minerals has been documented in the treatment of illness and injury as early as 2000 B.C. Before that, the ancient Egyptians, Arabs, and Greeks probably passed formulations down through the generations by word of mouth. During the 17th and 18th centuries, tinctures of opium, coca, and digitalis were available, and the concept of inoculation with biological extracts was developed by the late 19th century. By the end of that century, atropine, chloroform, codeine, ether, and morphine were in use. This past century has seen an explosion in the number and types of pharmaceuticals in use. As we begin the 21st century, recombinant DNA technology has produced human insulin and tissue plasma activator (tPA).

2. Differentiate among the chemical, generic (nonproprietary), official (USP), and trade (proprietary) names of a drug. pp. 278–279

The chemical name of a drug represents its chemical composition and molecular structure. An example is 7-chloro-1,3-dihydro-1-methyl-5-phenyl-2H-1,4-benzodiazepine-2-one.

The generic name of a drug is suggested by the original manufacturer and confirmed by the United States Adopted Name Council. An example, for which the chemical name is given above, is diazepam.

The official name of a drug is established by the Federal Drug Administration when it is listed in the *United States Pharmacopeia* (USP). An example is diazepam, USP.

The brand, trade, or proprietary name of a drug is the name given the drug by a specific manufacturer. This name is a proper name and should be capitalized and may be followed by a trademark insignia. An example is Valium®, a brand name for diazepam.

3. **List the four main sources of drug products.** p. 279

There are four main sources of drugs. They are plants, animals, minerals, and synthetic substances (laboratory).

4. **Describe how drugs are classified.** pp. 284–285

The Food and Drug Administration classifies a new drug using one-digit and one-letter designations. The numerical classification describes its origin: a new molecular drug, a new salt of a marketed drug, a new formulation or dosage, a new combination not previously marketed, a generic duplication of an existing drug, a new indication for an already marketed drug, and a drug on the market before the existence of the FDA. The letter classification identifies the treatment or therapeutic potential of a drug: an important therapeutic gain, a similarity to an existing drug or drugs, whether the drug is indicated in the treatment of AIDS and HIV disease, whether the drug has been developed to treat a severely debilitating or life-threatening disease, or whether the drug is an orphan drug (a drug developed for a relatively uncommon disease).

5. **List the authoritative sources for drug information.** p. 279

Drug inserts usually accompany prescription drugs and list information as required by the United States Food and Drug Administration.

The *Physician's Desk Reference* (PDR) is a compilation of materials supplied by drug manufacturers (usually the drug insert material). It also contains indexing and some drug photos.

Drug Information is a publication of the Society of Health System Pharmacists. It is an authoritative listing of virtually every drug used in the United States.

The *Monthly Prescribing Reference* is a periodic publication designed to keep physicians informed regarding the prescription of medications and which prescription drugs are used for which diseases.

The *AMA Drug Evaluation* is published by the American Medical Association and is a comprehensive listing of commonly used medications.

6. **List legislative acts controlling drug use and abuse in the United States.** pp. 280–282

The Pure Food and Drug Act of 1906 was enacted to improve the quality and labeling of drugs and named the *United States Pharmacopeia* as the country's official source for drug information.

The Harrison Narcotic Act of 1914 restricted the use of addictive drugs by controlling importation, manufacture, sale, and use of opium, cocaine, and their derivatives.

The Federal Food, Drug and Cosmetic Act of 1938 empowered the Food and Drug Administration (FDA) to establish and enforce standards for drugs.

In 1951, the Durham-Humphrey Amendments to the Federal Food, Drug and Cosmetic Act required pharmacists to have written or oral orders (prescriptions) for certain drugs and created a category of over-the-counter drugs.

The Comprehensive Drug Abuse Prevention and Control Act of 1970 repealed the Harrison Narcotics Act, established five schedules of controlled substances, and identified levels of control and required record keeping for each.

7. **Differentiate among Schedule I, II, III, IV, and V substances and list examples of substances in each schedule.** p. 281

Schedule I drugs include heroin, LSD, and mescaline drugs with a high potential for abuse and no medical indications. These drugs are used for research, analysis, and instruction only.

Schedule II drugs include opium, cocaine, morphine, codeine, oxycodone, methadone, and secobarbital. These drugs have a high potential for abuse and may lead to severe dependence, though they have some medical indications.

Schedule III drugs include opioids in limited amounts or combined with noncontrolled substances like Vicodin or Tylenol with codeine. These drugs have accepted medical indications.

Schedule IV drugs include diazepam, lorazepam, and phenobarbital. These are drugs of lower abuse potential compared to those in Schedule III and also have accepted medical indications.

Schedule V drugs include limited amounts of opioids. These drugs are often used for cough or diarrhea. They have less potential for abuse than Schedule IV drugs and have accepted medical indications.

8. Discuss standardization of drugs.   p. 282

Drugs may contain the same active ingredient yet be far different in the way they are delivered to the body. To recognize this, an assay of the drug determines the amount and purity of the drug in the preparation. A bioassay determines the amount of drug that is available in a biological model and thereby establishes its bioequivalence, or relative therapeutic effectiveness compared with drugs with chemically equivalent compositions.

9. Discuss investigational drugs, including the Food and Drug Administration (FDA) approval process and the FDA classifications for newly approved drugs.   pp. 282–285

All new drugs must go through extensive testing to ensure they both provide their intended therapeutic action and present no significant risk to patients. The FDA requires and regulates this testing. Animal testing precedes human testing, and once the drug's pharmacokinetics and therapeutic index have been evaluated in animals, human testing begins. Human testing involves four phases. Phase 1 testing is carried out on relatively healthy volunteers to determine human pharmacokinetics and establish the drug's safety. Phase 2 testing occurs on limited numbers of patients with a disease to determine the therapeutic drug levels and toxic and side effects. Phase 3 testing refines the dosage and further investigates side effects. Phase 4 is postmarketing testing to monitor the drug's performance.

The FDA classifies drugs according to their relationship to other drugs. Classifications include the following: a new molecular drug; a new salt of a marketed drug; a new formulation or dosage of a drug; a new combination not previously marketed; a generic duplication of a drug already on the market; a new indication for a drug already on the market; a drug marketed before 1938. Other classifications indicate the following: whether a drug offers an important therapeutic gain; whether a drug is similar to others already on the market, whether a drug is indicated for AIDS and HIV; whether a drug has been developed for life-threatening or severely debilitating disease; and whether a drug is intended for a relatively limited population (orphan drugs).

10. Discuss special consideration in drug treatment with regard to pregnant, pediatric, and geriatric patients.   pp. 286–289

Pregnancy alters the mother's physiology and also adds a second party, the developing fetus, to the concerns regarding medication administration. The increased maternal heart rate, cardiac output, and blood volume can affect the onset and actions of many medications. Drugs may also alter fetal development and result in fetal injury, deformity, or death. During the third trimester, some drugs may pass through the placenta and affect the fetus directly.

Several anatomical and physiological differences between pediatric patients and adults result in differences in the ways drugs are absorbed and metabolized. Differences in gastric pH and emptying time and lower digestive enzyme levels in children change the way enteral medications are absorbed. A child's thinner skin causes topical agents to be absorbed more quickly. Lower plasma protein levels in children affect the availability of agents that usually bind to them. Higher water content in the neonate also affects drug absorption and distribution, as does the slower, then faster metabolism of the neonate and child, respectively. Organ maturity also affects drug metabolism and elimination. For children, drug administration is often guided by weight and in some cases guided by height (the Broselow tape).

With advancing age, the body's metabolism, gastric motility, decreased plasma proteins, reduced body fat and muscle mass, and depressed liver function all affect the absorption, metabolism, and elimination of drugs. Older patients are also likely to be on multiple medications for multiple diseases, thereby increasing the likelihood of adverse medication interactions.

11. Discuss the paramedic's responsibilities and scope of management pertinent to the administration of medications. pp. 285–286

There are six basic "rights" of drug administration that indicate the paramedic's essential responsibilities and practices. They are the right medication, the right dose, the right time, the right route, the right patient, and the right documentation.

The right medication. Ensure the medication is what is intended for the patient. Review your standing orders or, if an order is received from medical direction, repeat the order back to the physician so you are both clear on the medication, dose, route, and timing of the administration. Also examine the drug packaging to ensure it is the medication you wish to administer.

The right dose. Carefully calculate the dose (usually weight dependent) for the patient before you draw up the medication and again just before you administer it. Prehospital medications are usually packaged to accommodate a single administration. If the drug package you select has much more or less than you intend to use, recheck the packaging to ensure it is the right drug and right concentration and recheck your calculations to ensure the right dosage.

The right time. Usually prehospital medications are given rather rapidly and not on a schedule. Check the packaging and your protocols for administration rate and ensure you follow the sequencing, time intervals, and drip rates for emergency drugs.

The right route. While most emergency drugs are administered by the IV route, be aware of the alternative routes of drug administration, the drugs administered via those routes, and the circumstances requiring the use of those routes. With each medication administration, ensure you are using the right route.

The right patient. It is imperative to ensure that the patient is properly matched to medication. A patient/drug mismatch is an infrequent problem in prehospital care, but as EMS moves to the out-of-hospital environment, paramedics may be treating some patients on a routine basis. Always ensure that the medication order is for the patient you are attending.

The right documentation. Thoroughly document all aspects of patient care, including what drugs (medication, dose, time and route) were administered in what dosage.

12. Review the specific anatomy and physiology pertinent to pharmacology. pp. 289–300

Drugs modify or exploit the existing functions of cells; they do not confer any new properties. They also often have several sites of action throughout the body and must be thought of for their systemic actions. Drugs may cause their effects by binding to cell receptor sites, changing the physical properties of a cell, chemically combining with other chemicals, or altering a normal metabolic pathway.

The most common mechanism of action for drugs administered in the prehospital setting involves drugs that bind to receptor sites. These receptor sites are most commonly associated with the nervous system because this system is responsible for overall body control. Drugs frequently affect the receptors for pain and those of the autonomic nervous system, including the sympathetic and parasympathetic nervous systems. Autonomic effects include changes in the rate and strength of cardiac contraction, in the degree of peripheral vascular contraction (resistance), and in bronchoconstriction or dilation to name just a few.

Other drugs act by changing the physical properties of the body, for example, by altering the osmolarity of the blood or by chemically combining with other substances to change the internal environment (as sodium bicarbonate combines with acids to make the blood more alkaline). Finally, some drugs alter a metabolic pathway to obtain their intended effect. Some anticancer drugs act in this way.

13. List and describe general properties of drugs. pp. 295–297

- **Affinity** is the force of attraction between the drug and the receptor site.
- **Efficacy** is the drug's ability to cause its expected effect.
- An **agonist** is a drug that causes the expected effect when bound to the receptor site.
- An **antagonist** is a drug that does not cause the expected effect when bound to the receptor site.
- An **agonist-antagonist** is a drug that binds to a receptor site, causing some expected effects and blocking others.

- A **competitive antagonist** is a drug that causes some effects as it binds to a receptor site but blocks the binding of another drug.
- A **noncompetitive antagonist** is a drug that binds to and deforms a receptor site so other drugs cannot bind there.

14. List and describe liquid and solid drug forms. pp. 294–295

Drugs come in many different forms. Solid drug forms include the following:

- **Pills** are drugs that are shaped spherically for easily swallowing.
- **Powders** are drugs simply in a powder form.
- **Tablets** are powders compressed into a disk-like form.
- **Suppositories** are drugs mixed with a wax-like base that melts at body temperature. They are usually inserted into the rectum or vagina.
- **Capsules** are gelatin containers filled with the drug powder or tiny pills. When the container dissolves, the drug is released into the gastrointestinal tract.

Liquid forms include the following:

- **Solutions** are drugs dissolved in a solvent, usually water or oil based.
- **Tinctures** are medications extracted using alcohol with some alcohol usually remaining.
- **Suspensions** are mixtures of a solvent and drug in which the solid portion will precipitate out.
- **Emulsions** are suspensions with an oily substance in the solvent that remains as globules even when mixed.
- **Spirits** are solutions of volatile drugs in alcohol.
- **Elixirs** are drugs mixed with alcohol and water, often with flavorings to improve taste.
- **Syrups** are solutions of sugar, water, and drugs.

15. List and differentiate routes of drug administration. pp. 293–294

Enteral routes deliver medications by absorption through the gastrointestinal tract. There are several routes of enteral administration. Oral routes are the most common for drug administration and are well suited for self-administration of medication. Nasogastric or orogastric tube administration uses either type of tube to direct medications into the stomach. Sublingual administration permits the drug to be absorbed by the capillaries under the tongue. Buccal (between the cheek and gum) absorption is similar to sublingual drug administration. Rectal administration is a route used for unconscious, vomiting, seizing, or uncooperative patients.

Routes outside the gastrointestinal tract are referred to as parenteral and typically use needles to inject medications into the circulatory system or tissues. With intravenous drug administration, a drug is injected directly into the veins, leading to rapid distribution of the medication. Endotracheal medication administration uses the endotracheal tube to place the medication into the lung field, where it is quickly absorbed by the bloodstream. Intraosseous administration directs medication into the medullary space of a long bone in the pediatric patient. Umbilical drug administration uses the umbilical artery or vein as an alternative IV site in the neonate. With intramuscular administration, the medication is injected into the muscle tissue, where it is rapidly absorbed by the bloodstream. Subcutaneous administration is just slightly slower than intramuscular administration. Transdermal administration is slightly slower than subcutaneous, and topical administration has the slowest absorption rate of all routes. With administration by inhalation/nebulization, a drug is introduced into the lung field, where it is absorbed. Nasal medications are introduced into the mucous membranes of the nose and are rapidly absorbed. With instillation, a drug is placed (topically) into a wound or the eye. Intradermal medications are delivered between dermal layers.

16. Differentiate between enteral and parenteral routes of drug administration. pp. 293–294

Enteral routes of administration are those that direct drugs into the gastrointestinal system and include oral (PO), orogastric or nasogastric tube (OG/NG), sublingual (SL), buccal, and rectal. Parenteral routes are routes of administration outside the gastrointestinal tract and include intravenous (IV), endotracheal (ET), intraosseous (IO), umbilical, intramuscular (IM), subcutaneous (SC), inhalation/nebulization, topical, transdermal, nasal, instillation, and intradermal.

17. Describe mechanisms of drug action. pp. 295–297

How a drug interacts with the body to cause its effects is referred to as pharmacodynamics. Drugs induce their effects by binding to a receptor site, changing the physical properties of the cell, chemically combining with other substances, or altering a normal metabolic pathway.

18. List and differentiate the phases of drug activity, including the pharmaceutical, pharmacokinetic, and pharmacodynamic phases. pp. 289–300

The pharmaceutical phase of drug activity addresses the drug's intrinsic characteristics such as how the drug dissolves or disintegrates once injected or ingested. Pharmacokinetics refers to the processes by which a drug is absorbed, distributed, biotransformed, and eliminated by the body. Pharmacodynamics is the mechanism (or mechanisms) by which a drug interacts with the body to accomplish its action.

19. Describe the processes called pharmacokinetics and pharmocodynamics, including theories of drug action, drug-response relationship, factors altering drug responses, predictable drug responses, iatrogenic drug responses, and unpredictable adverse drug responses. pp. 289–300

There are two important elements of pharmacology: how drugs are transported into or out of the body (pharmacokinetics) and how drugs interact with the body to cause their effects (pharmacodynamics).

Pharmacokinetics examines the absorption, distribution, biotransformation, and elimination of drugs.

For a drug to perform its action, it must first reach its site of action, a process referred to as **absorption**. While some drugs affect target tissue directly (such as antacids in the stomach), most must first find their way to the bloodstream. Drugs administered directly into a venous or arterial vessel are quickly transported to the heart, mixed with the blood, and distributed throughout the body. A drug injected into the muscle tissue and, to a somewhat lesser degree, into the subcutaneous tissue, is transported quickly to the bloodstream because of the more than adequate circulation in these tissues. However, shock and hypothermia may slow the process, whereas fever and hyperthermia may speed it. Oral medications must survive the gastric acidity and be somewhat lipid soluble to be transported across the intestinal membrane. The differing acid content of the digestive tract also affects the dissociation of the drug into ions that are more difficult to move into the circulation. And, finally, the drug's concentration affects its uptake by the bloodstream and, ultimately, its distribution. The end result of the absorption process is the concentration of the drug in the bloodstream and its availability for activation of the target tissue, called its bioavailability.

Once a drug enters the bloodstream, it must be carried throughout the body and to its site of action. This term for this process is **distribution**. Many factors affect the release and uptake of a drug by the body's cells. Some drugs bind to the plasma proteins of the blood and are released over a prolonged period of time. An increase in the blood's pH may increase the rate of release of the drug, or competition from other drugs for binding sites may cause more of a drug to become available. Distribution of some drugs is dependent on their ability to cross the blood-brain or placental barriers. Other drugs are easily deposited in fatty tissue, bones, and teeth.

Once in the body, drugs are broken down into metabolites in a process called **biotransformation**. This process makes the drug more or less active and can make the drug more water soluble and easier to eliminate. Some drugs are totally metabolized, some are partially metabolized, and still others are not metabolized at all. The liver is responsible for most biotransformation, while the lungs, kidneys, and GI tract do some limited biotransformation.

Elimination is the excretion of the drug in urine, expired air, or in feces. Renal excretion is the major mechanism for eliminating drugs from the body. Drugs are eliminated as the blood pressure pushes and filters blood through kidney structures. This effect is enhanced by special cells that "pump" (active transport) some metabolites into the tubules. Kidney reabsorption also plays a part in drug excretion. Protein-soluble molecules and electrolytes are easily absorbed, but the uptake may be affected by the blood's pH.

A drug's effects on the body are referred to as **pharmacodynamics.** Drugs may cause their effects by binding on a receptor site, by changing physical properties, by chemically combining with other substances, or by altering a normal metabolic pathway.

Most drugs effect their actions by binding to receptor sites, especially those of the autonomic nervous system. The drug either inhibits or stimulates the cells or tissue. The force of attraction of a drug is referred to as its **affinity.** Affinity becomes important when different drugs compete for a site. The drug's **efficacy** is its ability to cause the expected response. Binding to a receptor site causes a change within the cell and induces the drug's effect. However, some drugs may establish a chain-reaction effect whereby other drugs are released and cause the desired effect. The number of receptor sites may change as the drug becomes available and uses them, thereby reducing the drug's continuing effect. Chemicals that bind to the receptor and cause the expected response are termed **agonists. Antagonists** bind to the site and do not cause the expected response. Some drugs have both properties. Often drugs compete for a receptor site in a process called **competitive antagonism,** while a situation in which a drug attaches to a receptor, effectively locking out other drugs, is termed **noncompetitive antagonism.** Permanent binding to a receptor site is **irreversible antagonism.**

Drugs also may act by modifying the physical properties of a part of the body. For example, the drug mannitol changes the blood's osmolarity and increases urine output.

Some drugs chemically combine with other substances to cause their desired effect. For example, antacids interact with the hydrochloric acid in the stomach to reduce the pH.

Other drugs act by altering normal biological processes and the metabolic pathways. Such drugs are used to treat cancers and viral infections.

The **drug-response relationship** is the relationship between a drug's pharmaceutical, pharmacokinetic, and pharmacodynamic properties. It most commonly relates to the blood plasma level of the drug. Other important factors include the speed of onset, duration of action, minimum effective concentration, and biological half-life. Another very important factor in the drug-response relationship is the **therapeutic index,** or the ratio between the drug's lethal and effective doses.

Factors altering drug response include the patient's age, body mass, gender, pathological state, genetic factors, and psychological factors, as well as environmental considerations and the time of administration. These factors may increase or decrease the drug's ability to generate its desired affect.

Responses to drug administration may include unintended responses, or **side effects.** These are care-provider induced (iatrogenic) and include allergic reactions, idiosyncratic (unique to an individual) reactions, tolerance, cross tolerance, tachyphylaxis, cumulative effects, dependency, drug interactions, drug antagonisms, summation, synergistic reactions (a result greater than the expected additive result of two drugs administered together), potentiation, and interference. Some of these effects may be predictable and desired and some may be unexpected.

20. Differentiate among drug interactions. p. 300

Drugs have the potential to interact, cause, and alter the effects of other drugs taken by a patient. One drug may alter the effects of another by altering the rate of intestinal absorption, by competing for the same plasma protein binding site, by altering the other's metabolism and hence bioavailability, by causing an antagonistic or synergistic action at a receptor site, by altering the excretion rate of another drug through the kidneys, or by altering the electrolyte balance necessary for the other drug's actions.

21. Discuss considerations for storing and securing medications. p. 295

Temperature, humidity, ultraviolet radiation (sunlight), and time affect the potency of many drugs. It is important that they be stored under proper conditions and that they are rotated so they are utilized (or discarded) before their shelf life expires.

22. List the components of a drug profile by classification. p. 280

Names: The generic, trade, and sometimes the chemical names.
Classification: The broad group to which the drug belongs.

Mechanism of action: The way the drug causes its desired effects (its pharmacodynamics).

Indications: The conditions appropriate for the drug's administration.

Pharmacokinetics: How the drug is absorbed, distributed, and eliminated, including its onset and duration of action.

Side effects/adverse reactions: The drug's untoward or undesired effects.

Routes of administration: How the drug is given.

Contraindications: Conditions that make it inappropriate to administer a drug (including conditions in which administration is likely to cause a harmful outcome).

Dosage: The amount of drug that should be given.

How supplied: The typical concentrations and preparations of the drug.

Special considerations: How the drug may affect pregnant, pediatric, and geriatric patients.

Case Study Review

Reread the case study on pages 276 to 278 in Paramedic Care: Introduction to Advanced Prehospital Care *and then read the following discussion.*

Paramedics Jo Henderson and Scott Parker are presented with a classical myocardial infarction patient in Reverend Allen. They treat Reverend Allen with a great spectrum of drugs in an attempt to relieve discomfort and help the heart continue its coordinated and effective pumping action. These drugs include oxygen, nitroglycerin (NitroStat), promethezine (Phenergan), morphine sulfate, and reteplase (Retavase). To administer these drugs safely, Jo and Scott must understand the pharmacological principles behind their safe and appropriate administration.

They administer supplemental oxygen by the inhalation route to increase the percentage of inspired oxygen, thereby increasing the oxygen available to the hemoglobin of the blood and increasing its saturation. The increased oxygen concentration at the capillary level helps it diffuse into the interstitial compartment and then into the body cells. Oxygen is a very safe drug to use; however, both Jo and Scott know that it may cause the chronic obstructive lung disease (emphysema or chronic bronchitis) patient to slow or stop respirations.

They give Reverend Allen oral chewable aspirin, which they know reduces the tendency of platelets to aggregate and blood to clot. It prevents the creation of new thrombi and helps maintain circulation through the restricted coronary arteries. It, like oxygen, is a very safe drug, though it can contribute to or exacerbate ulcer disease (a problem in chronic, not emergency, administration) and may prolong clotting times in the trauma patient.

They begin an intravenous infusion of normal saline to provide a rapid and direct route for drug administration. The IV line provides a direct route to the venous circulation, then to the heart and lungs, and then to the entire body through the arterial system. They can then use this route to rapidly make their drugs available to the Reverend Allen's bloodstream and body tissue systems.

Nitroglycerin is given sublingually because it is easily absorbed through the capillary beds found there. It dilates the venous system, reducing cardiac preload and oxygen consumption. Nitroglycerin also may reduce coronary vessel spasm in Prinzmetal's angina. Jo and Scott must be very careful to ensure that Reverend Allen's blood pressure is above 100, because a common side effect of nitroglycerin is orthostatic hypotension. Jo and Scott know that nitroglycerin loses its effectiveness quickly once the container is opened or when it is exposed to light. They ensure the pill has a bitter taste and remember that patients often complain of headaches when the drug is potent.

Phenergan is a dopamine antagonist that is given to reduce the nausea associated with the heart attack and to potentiate (increase the effects of) morphine sulfate. Once given, Jo and Scott must be especially careful to titrate the morphine dosage they administer.

As Reverend Allen's chest pain continues, the paramedics administer morphine sulfate to further reduce pain and cardiac workload. Morphine is an opium derivative that reduces the ability of neurons to propagate pain impulses to the spinal cord and brain. Morphine also decreases both cardiac preload and afterload, thereby reducing myocardial oxygen demand in the patient suffering a heart attack. However, morphine's major side effects are respiratory depression and hypotension. Jo and Scott must carefully monitor Reverend Allen's respirations and blood pressure. They must also carefully document the administration of this drug, since it is a controlled substance.

Finally, Jo and Scott administer reteplase (Retavase), one of the clot-busting, or thrombolytic drugs, to dissolve the clot in Reverend Allen's coronary arteries and restore myocardial circulation. While this drug can reduce the impact of a coronary occlusion due to a clot, its administration poses the risk of serious internal bleeding and possible stroke. Jo and Scott evaluate a 12-lead ECG to determine the location of the probable infarct and ask Reverend Allen numerous carefully worded questions to rule out the various internal hemorrhage risks before the drug is administered. They also carefully document the administration of this medication, because its use will continue during Reverend Allen's hospital stay.

While the steps in the care for Reverend Allen are linear and straightforward, they must be applied with a full understanding of pharmacology. Jo and Scott must ensure that they are giving the right drug to the right patient at the right time through the right route and in the right dose and concentration. They must watch for the expected therapeutic actions as well as expected side effects and untoward (unwanted and nonbeneficial) effects. However, by judiciously using medications, Jo and Scott can relieve Reverend Allen's symptoms, stabilize his vital signs, and begin to treat his disease well before he arrives at the emergency department.

Content Self-Evaluation

MULTIPLE CHOICE

____ 1. The study of drugs and their interactions with the body is:
    A. pharmaceutics.   D. pharmacology.
    B. pharmacokinetics.   E. pharmacopedia.
    C. pharmacodynamics.

____ 2. Which of the following types of drug names is 7 chloro-1,3-dihydro-1-methyl-5-phenyl-2H-1,4 benzodiazepine-2-one?
    A. chemical name   D. brand name
    B. generic name   E. common name
    C. official name

____ 3. Which of the following types of drug names is diazepam?
    A. chemical name   D. brand name
    B. generic name   E. common name
    C. official name

____ 4. Digitalis is an example of a drug derived from:
    A. a plant.   D. synthetic production.
    B. an animal.   E. a lipid base.
    C. a mineral.

____ 5. Bovine insulin is an example of a drug derived from:
    A. a plant.   D. synthetic production.
    B. an animal.   E. a lipid base.
    C. a mineral.

____ 6. The drug reference that presents manufacturer-provided drug information and some photos of drugs is the:
    A. *EMS Guide to Drugs.*   D. *Monthly Prescribing Reference.*
    B. *Physician's Desk Reference.*   E. all of the above
    C. *AMA Drug Evaluations.*

_C_ 7. The broad group to which a drug belongs is its:
   A. indication.
   B. pharmacokinetics.
   C. classification.
   D. mechanism of action.
   E. none of the above

_C_ 8. Conditions in which it is inappropriate to give a drug are referred to as its:
   A. mechanisms of action.
   B. indications.
   C. contraindications.
   D. side effects.
   E. special considerations.

_E_ 9. Which of the following drugs is classified as a Schedule II controlled substance?
   A. heroin
   B. morphine
   C. codeine
   D. diazepam
   E. B and C

_B_ 10. The assay of a drug in a preparation determines its:
   A. potency.
   B. amount and purity.
   C. effectiveness.
   D. availability in a biological model.
   E. effectiveness compared to other like drugs.

_E_ 11. The bioequivalence of a drug in a preparation refers to its:
   A. potency.
   B. amount and purity.
   C. effectiveness.
   D. availability in a biological model.
   E. effectiveness compared to other like drugs.

_E_ 12. Which of the following is NOT one of the six rights of medication administration?
   A. right dose
   B. right patient
   C. right documentation
   D. right time
   E. right mechanism

_A_ 13. Dosages of many emergency drugs are based on patient weight, so unit dose packaging may not contain the right amount for every patient.
   A. True
   B. False

_B_ 14. Children are, for the most part, just small adults, so drug dosages just need to be reduced proportionally by weight.
   A. True
   B. False

_D_ 15. Which of the following is NOT true regarding the newborn patient?
   A. The neonate has less gastric acid than an adult.
   B. The neonate has diminished blood plasma levels.
   C. The neonate has immature renal and hepatic systems.
   D. The neonate has less body water than an adult.
   E. The neonate has lower enzyme levels than an adult.

_E_ 16. Drugs in which of the following FDA categories have demonstrated definite risks to the fetus?
   A. R
   B. A
   C. B
   D. C
   E. D

_D_ 17. Which of the following is NOT true regarding the geriatric patient?
   A. The geriatric patient has decreased gastrointestinal motility.
   B. The geriatric patient has decreased body fat.
   C. The geriatric patient has decreased muscle mass.
   D. The geriatric patient is more likely to be disease free.
   E. The geriatric patient has decreased liver function.

_A_ 18. Drugs do not confer any new properties on cells or tissues; they only modify or exploit existing functions.
A. True
B. False

_C_ 19. Which of the following is NOT one of the four basic processes of pharmacokinetics?
A. absorption
B. distribution
C. receptor binding
D. biotransformation
E. elimination

_B_ 20. Which of the following represents an energy-consuming movement of ions against the concentration gradient?
A. diffusion
B. active transport
C. osmosis
D. filtration
E. facilitated transport

_D_ 21. Which of the following represents movement of molecules across a membrane from an area of higher pressure to an area of lower pressure?
A. diffusion
B. active transport
C. osmosis
D. filtration
E. facilitated transport

_A_ 22. The measure of the amount of a drug that is still active after it reaches the target organ is its:
A. bioavailability.
B. biotransformativity.
C. metabolism.
D. pro-drug effect.
E. active distribution.

_D_ 23. Which of the following is NOT a significant medium for elimination of drugs from the body?
A. urine
B. respiratory air
C. feces
D. sweat
E. all are significant

_B_ 24. Which of the following is not an enteral route of drug administration?
A. oral
B. umbilical
C. buccal
D. sublingual
E. rectal

_D_ 25. Which of the following is the preferred route for medication administration in most emergencies?
A. intramuscular
B. inhalation
C. endotracheal
D. intravenous
E. subcutaneous

_A_ 26. Drugs that are spherically shaped to be easy to swallow are:
A. pills.
B. suppositories.
C. tablets.
D. capsules.
E. suspensions.

_C_ 27. Drugs that are powders compressed into disks are:
A. pills.
B. suppositories.
C. tablets.
D. capsules.
E. suspensions.

_C_ 28. Preparations in which the solid does not dissolve in the solvent are:
A. solutions.
B. tinctures.
C. suspensions.
D. spirits.
E. elixirs.

_E_ **29.** Preparations made with alcohol and water solvent, often with flavorings, are:
  A. solutions.
  B. tinctures.
  C. suspensions.
  D. spirits.
  E. elixirs.

_C_ **30.** Pharmacodynamics are best described as:
  A. interactions between drugs.
  B. the processes by which drugs are eliminated from the body.
  C. the effects of a drug on the body.
  D. the processes by which drugs bind to receptor sites.
  E. the process by which a drug is administered.

_C_ **31.** The location where a drug combines with a protein, resulting in a biochemical effect, is a:
  A. second messenger.
  B. antagonist.
  C. receptor.
  D. agonist.
  E. protein block.

_B_ **32.** A drug's ability to cause its expected response is referred to as its:
  A. affinity.
  B. efficacy.
  C. agonism.
  D. antagonism.
  E. equilibrium.

_D_ **33.** A chemical that binds to a receptor site but does not cause the expected effect is a(n):
  A. partial-antagonist.
  B. competitive antagonist.
  C. agonist.
  D. antagonist.
  E. noncompetitive antagonist.

_B_ **34.** A chemical that binds to a receptor site, causes the expected effect, and prevents other drugs from activating the receptor site is a(n):
  A. partial antagonist.
  B. competitive antagonist.
  C. agonist.
  D. antagonist.
  E. noncompetitive antagonist.

_C_ **35.** The drug morphine sulfate is an example of a(n):
  A. agonist-antagonist.
  B. competitive antagonist.
  C. agonist.
  D. antagonist.
  E. noncompetitive antagonist.

_A_ **36.** The drug nalbuphine (Nubain) is an example of a(n):
  A. agonist-antagonist.
  B. competitive antagonist.
  C. agonist.
  D. antagonist.
  E. noncompetitive antagonist.

_A_ **37.** A drug reaction that is unique to an individual is referred to as:
  A. idiosyncrasy.
  B. tachyphylaxis.
  C. antagonism.
  D. synergism.
  E. potentiation.

_D_ **38.** A drug reaction that is greater than expected from the administration of two drugs that have the same effect at the same time is referred to as:
  A. idiosyncrasy.
  B. tachyphylaxis.
  C. antagonism.
  D. synergism.
  E. potentiation.

_E_ **39.** The time span between when a drug drops below its minimum effective concentration and its complete elimination from the body is its:
  A. onset of action.
  B. duration of action.
  C. therapeutic index.
  D. biological half-life.
  E. termination of action.

40. The ratio between a drug's lethal dose and its effective dose is its:
   A. onset of action.
   B. duration of action.
   C. therapeutic index.
   D. biological half-life.
   E. termination of action.

Special Project

Crossword Puzzle

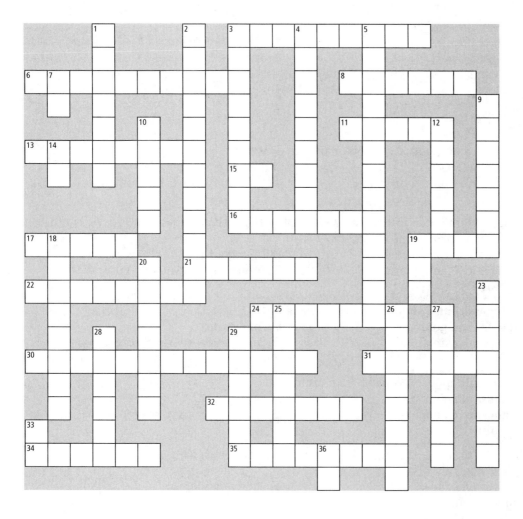

Across

3. Type of drug created in the laboratory

6. Movement of molecules across a membrane down a pressure gradient

8. _____ transport: mechanism to move a substance that requires energy

11. A sugar, water, and drug solution

13. Test that determines a drug's bioequivalency

15. Drug administration to the medullary spaces of bones (abbr.)

16. Generic term for the inorganic source of a drug

17. Route of drug administration via the nose

19. Route of drug administration via the mouth

21. Solution of a volatile drug in alcohol

22. A drug's ability to cause the expected response

24. An agent that binds to a receptor site to cause its intended response

30. Chemically equal to and having the same therapeutic effect as another drug

31. Generic term for the source of drugs extracted from living creatures

32. Drug drawn from a compound by withdrawing a carrier

34. A powder compressed into a disk-like form

35. A protein molecule on the cell wall to which a drug attaches, resulting in a biochemical effect

Down

1. Route of medication delivery via the gastrointestinal tract

2. Drug effect that is unique to an individual

3. Two drugs together producing a response greater than the expected sum of responses

4. Decreased response to the same amount of drug after repeated doses

5. Rapidly occurring tolerance to a drug

7. Route of drug administration that is slower than intravenous injection because the drug passes into the capillaries (abbr.)

9. Route of drug administration via the surface of the skin

10. Test to determine the amount and purity of a chemical in a preparation

12. Fine granular form of a drug

14. Preferred route of drug administration in most emergencies (abbr.)

18. Force of attraction between a drug and a receptor

19. Type of drugs available to the public without a prescription (abbr.)

20. Gelatin container filled with powder or small spheres of drug

23. Suspension of an oily substance in a solvent

25. Name for a drug, suggested by the manufacturer and confirmed by the United States Adopted Name Council

26. Form of a drug prepared by an alcohol extraction process

27. Movement of a solvent, through a semipermeable membrane from an area of lower to one of higher solute concentration

28. Route of drug administration via the terminal end of the enteral route

29. Drug that is a combination of alcohol and water solvent, commonly mixed with flavorings

33. Endotracheal route of drug administration (abbr.)

36. Oral route of drug administration (abbr.)

Review of Chapter Objectives

After reading this part of the chapter, you should be able to:

1. **Review the specific anatomy and physiology pertinent to pharmacology with additional attention to autonomic pharmacology.**   **pp. 301–364**

Drugs affect many systems of the body, including the central nervous system, the autonomic nervous system, the cardiovascular system, the respiratory system, the gastrointestinal system, and the endocrine system. Drugs are also used to treat infectious disease and inflammation.

Central Nervous System Pharmacology

The central nervous system consists of the brain and spinal column and all neurons that both originate and terminate within these structures. Since this system is responsible for conscious thought and affects many bodily functions, it is the target for many drugs used in medical care. These agents include analgesics, anesthetics, antianxiety and sedative-hypnotic drugs, antiseizure and antiepileptic drugs, CNS stimulants, and psychotherapeutic drugs.

Analgesics are used to reduce the sensation of pain. These drugs include the opioid and nonopioid analgesics, adjunctive medications (to enhance the effects of the analgesics), and opioid agonists-antagonists. Agents that block the actions of analgesics, opioid antagonists and in some cases analgesic antagonists, are used in cases of overdose or to reverse or negate the undesired effects of analgesics.

Anesthetics are used to decrease the sensation of both touch and pain. Anesthetics may be given locally or systemically and in lower doses may produce a decreased sensation of pain while the patient may remain conscious. At higher doses, anesthetics generally induce unconsciousness.

Antianxiety and sedative-hypnotic drugs are used to reduce anxiety, induce amnesia, assist sleeping, and may be used as a part of a balanced approach to anesthesia. These drugs include the benzodiazepines, barbiturates, and alcohol. They decrease (depress) the central nervous system's response to stimuli.

Antiseizure and antiepileptic agents are used to prevent seizure activity and are often associated with undesirable side effects. Antiseizure agents generally act on the sodium and calcium channels in the neural membrane and include phenytoin, carbamazepine, valproic acid, and ethosuximide.

CNS stimulants are used to treat fatigue, drowsiness, narcolepsy, obesity, and attention deficit disorders. They cause their actions by either increasing the release and effectiveness of excitatory neurotransmitters or decreasing the release or effectiveness of inhibitory neurotransmitters. These agents include amphetamines, methylamphetamines, and methylxanthines.

Psychotherapeutic medications treat mental dysfunction, including schizophrenia, depression, and bipolar disorder. Schizophrenia is treated with neuroleptic (affecting the nerves) and antipsychotic drugs (phenothiazines and butyrophenones), which block numerous peripheral neuroreceptor sites. Antidepressants increase the availability, release, or effectiveness of norepinephrine and serotonin and are used to treat depression. These medications include the tricyclic antidepressants (TCAs), the selective serotonin reuptake inhibitors (SSRIs), and monoamine oxidase inhibitors (MAOIs). Bipolar disorder (manic depression) is manifested by dramatic mood swings and is treated with lithium.

Parkinson's disease is another central nervous system disorder caused by the destruction of dopamine-releasing neurons in the portion of the brain controlling fine motor movements. This disease is treated by stimulating the dopamine release (Sinemet) or with anticholinergic agents (benztropine).

Autonomic Nervous System Pharmacology

See objective 2.

Cardiovascular System Pharmacology

The cardiovascular system consists of the heart, blood vessels, and the blood. The heart is a four-chambered muscular organ that pumps most of the blood around the body. It is controlled by an intrinsic electrical system that coordinates cardiac muscular response and pumping action. The myocardium is unique in that it has the ability to generate an electrical impulse (automaticity) and conduct an impulse to surrounding tissue (conductivity). The heart muscle contracts and relaxes (depolarizes and repolarizes) as sodium, calcium, and potassium ions flow into and out of the cell.

Antidysrhythmic drugs are used to prevent or treat abnormal variations in the cardiac electrical cycle. Sodium channel blockers slow the influx of sodium back into the cell and, in effect, slow conduction through the atria and ventricles. Class IA sodium channel blockers (quinidine, procainamide, and disopyramide) slow repolarization, while class IB drugs (lidocaine, phenytoin, tocainide, mexiletine) speed repolarization and reduce automaticity in the ventricles. Class IC drugs (flecainide, propafenone) decrease conduction velocity through the atria, ventricles, bundle of His, and the Purkinje network and delay ventricular repolarization. Beta blockers (propranolol, acebutolol, esmolol) are antagonistic to the beta$_1$ actions of the sympathetic nervous system. Since the beta receptors are attached to the calcium channels of the heart, these agents act in a manner very similar to the calcium channel blockers. Potassium channel blockers (bretylium, amiodarone) block the efflux of calcium; these agents prolong repolarization and the effective refractory period (the period before the myocardium can contract again). Calcium channel blockers (verapamil, diltiazem) decrease conductivity through the AV node and slow conduction of atrial flutter or fibrillation to the ventricles. Other antidysrhythmics include adenosine (a fast and short-acting potassium and calcium blocker), digoxin (decreases SA node firing rate and conduction velocity through the AV node), and magnesium (effective in treating a polymorphic ventricular tachycardia—torsade de pointes).

Antihypertensive drugs manipulate peripheral vascular resistance, heart rate, or stroke volume to reduce blood pressure. Diuretics reduce the amount of circulating blood (and hence the cardiac preload and stroke volume) by increasing the urine output of the kidneys. They include loop diuretics (furosemide), thiazides (HydroDIURIL), potassium-sparing diuretics (spironolactone), and the osmotic diuretics (mannitol). Beta-adrenergic antagonists (metoprolol) act by reducing the heart's rate and contractility as well as by reducing the release of hormones (renin) from the kidneys that ultimately cause vasoconstriction (through the renin-angiotensin-aldosterone system). Centrally acting adrenergic inhibitors (clonidine) stimulate alpha$_2$ receptors and inhibit the release of norepinephrine. Alpha$_1$ antagonists (prazosin, terazosin) competitively block the alpha$_1$ receptors, mediating sympathetic increases in peripheral vascular resistance. Finally, some drugs (labetalol, carvedilol) have combined alpha and beta antagonistic effects. Angiotensin converting enzyme (ACE) inhibitors (captopril, enalapril, lisinopril, enalaprilat) block the production of angiotensin II, a very potent vasoconstictor, through the renin-angiotensin-aldosterone system. Angiotensin II receptor antagonists act on the renin-angiotensin-aldosterone system by blocking the actions of angiotensin II at its receptor site. Calcium channel blockers (nifedipine) are also effective at controlling hypertension by selectively acting on the smooth muscles of the arterioles and reducing peripheral vascular resistance without reducing cardiac preload. Direct vasodilators (hydralazine, minoxidil, sodium nitroprusside) selectively dilate arterioles and decrease peripheral vascular resistance. Hypertension may also be controlled by agents that block the autonomic nervous system (trimethaphan) or with cardiac glycosides (digoxin, digitoxin) that affect the ion pumps of the myocardium and increase cardiac contraction strength but reduce heart rate.

Angina is treated with calcium channel blockers (verapamil, diltiazem, nifedipine) because they reduce cardiac workload and slow the heart rate. Organic nitrates (nitroglycerin, isosorbide, amyl nitrite) relax vascular smooth muscle, decreasing cardiac preload and workload, and, in Prinzmetal's angina, may increase coronary blood flow.

Three agents are used to prevent and break up blood clots that obstruct either the heart chambers or the blood vessels. Antiplatelet drugs (aspirin, dipyridamole, abciximab, ticlopidine) decrease the formation of platelet plugs during the clotting process. Anticoagulants (heparin, warfarin) interrupt the clotting cascade. Fibrinolytics (streptokinase, alteplase, reteplase, anistreplase) dissolve the fibrin mesh of clots and thereby help break apart clots after they form.

Antihyperlipidemic agents (lovastatin, simvastatin, cholestyramine) are used to reduce the level of low-density lipoproteins, a causative factor for coronary artery disease.

Respiratory System Pharmacology

The respiratory system is basically a pathway through which air travels in from the exterior to the air-exchange sacs, the alveoli, and then out again. Indications for pharmacological intervention include asthma, rhinitis, and cough.

Asthma is a pathological condition caused by an allergy to pet dander, dust, or mold that causes respiratory restriction or obstruction. The allergic response releases histamine, leukotrienes, and prostaglandins, producing immediate bronchoconstriction and then inflammation. Treatment includes beta$_2$ agonists (albuterol) to reduce bronchoconstriction and epinephrine for severe reactions not responding to beta$_2$ agonists. Anticholinergic agents (ipratropium) act along different pathways to the beta$_2$ agonists and may provide an additive effect in limiting bronchoconstriction. Glucocorticoids (beclomethasone, methylprednisolone, cromolyn) have antiinflammatory properties that reduce the amount of mucus and the edema in the airway and alveolar walls. Lastly, leukotriene antagonists (zileuton) block the formation of, or the receptors for (zafirlukast), leukotriene. Leukotrienes are mediators released from mast cells that contribute powerfully to both bronchoconstriction and inflammation.

Rhinitis is the inflammation of the mucosa of the nasal cavity and may cause nasal congestion, itching, sneezing, and rhinorrhea (runny nose). Nasal decongestants (phenylephrine, pseudoephedrine, phenylpropanolamine) are alpha$_1$ agonists that reduce vasodilation and are given in mist or oral form. Antihistamines (alkylamines, ethanolamines, clemastine, phenothiazines, loratadine, cetirizine, fexofenadine) are used for more serious allergic reactions and block the action of histamine and thereby relieve bronchoconstriction, capillary permeability, and vasodilation. Cough suppressants (antitussive agents, both opioid and nonopioid) dull the cough reflex and are designed to treat unproductive coughing due to an irritated oropharynx. Expectorants are intended to increase the productivity of the cough while mucolytics make the mucus more watery and possibly more effective.

Gastrointestinal System Pharmacology

Drugs used to treat the gastrointestinal system are primarily for gastric ulcers, constipation, diarrhea, emesis, and to aid digestion. Peptic ulcer disease occurs as the balance between the protective coating of the stomach and its acidity is no longer maintained. The acid may then eat away at the intestinal lining and tissues underneath. The injury may result in internal hemorrhage. Peptic ulcer disease is treated with antibiotics (bismuth, metronidazole, amoxicillin, tetracycline) to treat the underlying cause and drugs (cimetidine, ranitidine, famotidine, nizatidine, omeprazole, lansoprazole, antacids, pirenzepine) that block or decrease the secretion of acid. Constipation is treated with bulk-forming (methlycellulose, psyllium), surfactant (docusate sodium), stimulant (phenolphthalein, bisacodyl) or osmotic (magnesium hydroxide) laxatives. Diarrhea is often caused by an underlying disease and is usually self-correcting. In severe cases, it is treated with antibiotics. Input from the inner ear, nose, and eyes or a response to anxiety or fear triggers the vomiting reflex (emesis), which can be useful for certain poisonings and overdoses. Antiemetics that reduce the vomiting reflex include serotonin antagonists (Ondansetron), dopamine antagonists (phenothiazines, butyrophenones, metoclopramide), anticholenergics, and cannabinoids (dronabinol, nabilone). Finally, drugs used to aid ingestion are enzymes (pancreatin, pancrelipase) similar to endogenous enzymes found in the intestinal tract.

Endocrine System Pharmacology

The endocrine system provides the body with hormones essential to maintaining homeostasis and controlling overall body activity. It consists of the following glands: pituitary, pineal, thyroid, thymus, parathyroid, adrenal, pancreas, ovaries, and testes. These organs produce hormones that then circulate throughout the body and affect target organs. Drugs can affect the anterior and posterior pituitary, parathyroid and thyroid, adrenal, pancreas, and reproductive glands or simulate the hormones they produce.

The pituitary gland is made up of the anterior and posterior lobes and resides deep within the skull. The anterior pituitary gland releases hormones related to growth. Dwarfism results from a deficiency in growth hormone and is treated with somatrem and somatropin. Gigantism and acromegaly usually result from a tumor and are treated by surgical removal of the tumor or with the drug octreotide, which inhibits the release of the growth hormone. The posterior pituitary produces oxytocin and antidiuretic hormone (ADH). Oxytocin induces uterine contractions and precipitates delivery, while antidiuretic hormone increases water reabsorption in the kidneys and thereby regulates electrolyte balance, blood volume, and blood pressure. Diabetes insipidus is caused by inadequate circulating ADH and is treated with vasopressin, desmopressin, and lypressin.

The parathyroid gland regulates the levels of calcium and vitamin D. Chronic low calcium and vitamin D levels are treated with supplements, while high levels (usually due to tumors) are treated with surgical removal of all or part of the parathyroid gland.

The thyroid gland hormones play vital roles in growth, maturation, and metabolism. Childhood-onset hyperthyroidism results in dwarfism and mental retardation, while adult-onset hyperthyroidism manifests with a decreased metabolism, weight gain, fatigue, and bradycardia. Hypothyroidism is treated with levothyroxine, a synthetic analogue of thyroxine, the major thyroid hormone. Goiters occur as a result of inadequate iodine in the diet and are treated with iodine supplements. Thyroid tumors often cause hyperthyroidism and are treated with surgery, radiation therapy, or the drug propylthiouracil or a combination of therapies.

The adrenal cortex secretes glucocorticoids that increase the glucose in the bloodstream, mineralocorticoids that regulate the salt/water balance, and androgens that regulate sexual development and maturity. Cushing's disease results in increased glucocorticoid secretion and hyperglycemia, obesity, hypertension, and electrolyte imbalances. It is usually treated surgically, with pharmacological intervention aimed at the symptoms; drugs used for this include antihypertensive agents (spironolactone), ACE inhibitors (captopril), and drugs that inhibit corticoid synthesis. Addison's disease is characterized by hyposecretion of corticoids and presents with hypoglycemia, emaciation, hypotension, hyperkalemia, and hyponatremia. It is treated with cortisone, hydrocortisone, and fludrocortisone.

The pancreas produces two hormones important to glucose metabolism. They are insulin and glucagon. Insulin is essential for the transport of glucose, potassium, and amino acids into the cells. It stimulates cell growth and division and converts glucose into glycogen in the liver and skeletal muscles. Glucagon increases blood glucose levels by promoting the synthesis of glucose from glycerol and amino acids and from breaking down glycogen into glucose. Diabetes is an inappropriate carbohydrate metabolism due to an inadequate release of insulin (type I, juvenile onset) or a decreased responsiveness to insulin (type II, adult onset). Oral hypoglycemic agents stimulate insulin release from the pancreas and are administered to the type II diabetic. They are from four classes: sulfonylureas (tolbutamide, chlorpropamide, glipizide, glyburide), biguanides (metformin), alpha-glucosidase inhibitors (acarbose, miglitol), and thiazolidinediones (troglitazone). Pork, beef, or human insulin is injected subcutaneously daily for the type I diabetic. Hyperglycemic agents (glucagon and diazoxide) act to increase blood glucose levels while 50 percent dextrose in water ($D_{50}W$) is an intravenous sugar solution intended to supply carbohydrates to the hypoglycemic patient.

The genitalia release hormones that regulate human sexuality and reproduction. In the female, the ovaries, ovarian follicles, and, during pregnancy, the placenta release these hormones. Drug therapy can supplement these hormones, provide contraception, stimulate or relax the pregnant uterus, or assist in fertility. Estrogen is administered post menopause to reduce the risk of osteoporosis and coronary artery disease. It is also administered in delayed puberty. Progestins counteract the untoward effects of estrogen and are used to treat amenorrhea, endometriosis, and dysfunctional uterine hemorrhage. Estrogen and progestin (or progestin alone) are commonly used as contraceptives. Their side effects include a predisposition to thromboembolisms, hypertension, and uterine bleeding. Oxytocic agents (oxytocin) induce uterine contractions to induce or speed up labor, while tocolytics (terbutaline, ritodrine) relax the smooth muscle of the uterus and delay labor. Female infertility is treated with agents (clomiphene, urofollitropin, menotropin) that promote maturation of ovarian follicles. In the male, testosterone replacement therapy (testosterone enanthate, methyltestosterone, fluoxymesterone) is provided for deficiency or delayed puberty. An enlarged prostate is cared for with surgery or drug (finasteride) therapy. Recent drugs, such as sildenafil (Viagra), vardenafil (Levitra) and tadalafil (Cialis), are used for erectile dysfunction and act by relaxing vascular smooth muscle. However, in combination with nitrates, these drugs may lead to decreased cardiac preload and profound hypotension.

Pharmacology of Infectious Disease

Infectious diseases are typically caused by bacteria, viruses, or fungi and are treated by antimicrobial drugs including antibiotics and antifungal, antiviral, and antiparasitic agents. Symptoms of microbial infection are treated with nonsteroidal antiinflammatory drugs (NSAIDs), and some diseases are treated prophylactically with serums and vaccines.

Antibiotics either kill the offending bacteria or decrease their ability to grow and reproduce. Penicillin, cephalosporin, and vancomycin act by inhibiting cell wall synthesis and causing the walls to rupture. Macrolide, aminoglycoside, and tetracycline antibiotics prevent cells from replicating.

Antifungal agents inhibit fungal growth (ketoconazole), while antiviral drugs act through various mechanisms (indinavir, acyclovir, zidovudine). Antiparasitic agents are used to treat malaria (chloroquine, mefloquine, quinine), amebiasis (paromomycin, metronidazole), and helminthiasis (mebendazole, niclosamide).

Other antimicrobials are used to treat diseases such as tuberculosis (isoniazid, refampin) and leprosy (dapsone, clofazimine).

Nonsteroidal antiinflammatory drugs (ketorolac, piroxicam, naproxen) limit the fever (antipyretics) and pain (analgesics) associated with headache, arthritis, dysmenorrhea, and orthopedic injuries.

2. Review autonomic pharmacology.   pp. 310–325

The autonomic nervous system is located within the peripheral nervous system and consists of the sympathetic (fight-or-flight) and parasympathetic (feed-and-breed) systems. These systems are antagonistic and provide control over body functions. The autonomic nervous system controls virtually every organ and body structure not under conscious control and is responsible for maintaining the internal human environment. The nerves of the two systems do not actually touch other nerves or target organs. Messages are carried through the small space between them (synapse) via chemical messengers (neurotransmitters). Acetylcholine is the neurotransmitter at the target organs of the parasympathetic nervous system, while norepinephrine is the neurotransmitter at the target organs for the sympathetic nervous system.

Stimulation of the parasympathetic nervous system causes pupillary constriction, digestive gland secretion, decreased cardiac rate and strength of contraction, bronchoconstriction, and increased digestive activity. Cholinergic (effecting the acetylcholine receptors) drugs stimulate the parasympathetic nervous system and produce salivation, lacrimation, urination, defecation, gastric motility, and emesis (signs suggested by the acronym SLUDGE). They cause their actions directly by acting on the receptor sites (bethanechol and pilocarpine) or indirectly by inhibiting the degradation of acetylcholine (neostigmine and physostigmine). Anticholenergic (parasympatholytic) drugs oppose the actions of acetylcholine and the parasympathetic nervous system. Atropine is the prototype anticholinergic drug, while scopolamine is used to treat motion sickness and ipratropium bromide (Atrovent) is inhaled to treat bronchoconstriction caused by asthma. Ganglionic blocking agents compete for the acetylcholine receptors at the ganglia and can effectively turn off the parasympathetic nervous system. Neuromuscular blocking agents produce a state of paralysis without inducing unconsciousness. Ganglionic stimulating agents (nicotine) stimulate the ganglia of both the parasympathetic and sympathetic nervous systems yet have no therapeutic purpose.

Stimulation of the sympathetic nervous system causes an increased heart rate and strength of contraction, bronchodilation, increased blood flow to the muscles, decreased blood flow to the skin and abdominal organs, release of glucose stores from the liver, increased energy production, decreased digestive activity, and the release of epinephrine and norepinephrine. Sympathetic receptors include four adrenergic receptors ($alpha_1$, $alpha_2$, $beta_1$, and $beta_2$) and dopaminergic receptors. $Alpha_1$ stimulation causes peripheral vasoconstriction, mild bronchoconstriction, and increased metabolism. $Alpha_2$ stimulation prevents the over-release of norepinephrine at the synapse. $Beta_1$ stimulation exclusively affects the heart and causes increased heart rate, cardiac

©2006 Pearson Education, Inc.
Paramedic Care: Principles & Practice, Vol. 1

contractile force, automaticity, and conduction. Beta$_2$ stimulation causes bronchodilation and selective vasodilation. Dopaminergic stimulation causes increased circulation to the kidneys, heart, and brain. Sympathomimetic (adrenergic) drugs stimulate the effects of the sympathetic nervous system, while sympatholytic drugs block the actions of the sympathetic nervous system. Alpha$_1$ drugs increase peripheral vascular resistance, preload, and blood pressure. Alpha$_1$ agonists are used to control blood pressure or to control injury due to the infiltration of an alpha$_1$ drug. Beta$_1$ drugs stimulate the heart and are primarily used in cardiac arrest or cardiogenic shock. Beta$_1$ antagonists are used to control blood pressure, suppress tachycardia, and reduce cardiac workload in angina. Beta$_2$ agonists are used to treat asthma.

3. List and describe common prehospital medications, including indications, contraindications, side effects, routes of administration, and dosages.   **pp. 301–364**

At the back of this workbook you will find a series of pages with drug cards. Each card contains the name/class, description, indications, contraindications, precautions, routes of administration, and dosages for a drug commonly used in prehospital emergency care. Detach the cards and begin to use them as flash cards. This will help you learn essential information about the drugs you will use during your career as a paramedic.

4. Given several patient scenarios, identify medications likely to be prescribed and those that are likely to be a part of the prehospital treatment regimen.   **pp. 301–364**

Prescribed Medications
As you arrive at the side of and begin to assess and treat a patient, an important aspect of assessment will be to determine what medications the patient is taking (both prescribed and over-the-counter). Since many drugs are given for specific pathologies, the drugs prescribed may give you clues as to the patient's underlying problem. The general pathology classification and the drugs used to care for that pathology are listed below. As you progress through your training, and especially as you enter the medical emergencies portion of your training, the classification of pathologies and the drugs prescribed for such will become more specific and extensive.

Central Nervous System

Analgesics	Opioid agonists	opium, morphine
	Nonopioids	aspirin, NSAIDs, ibuprofen, acetaminophen
	Benzodiazepines	diazepam, lorazepam, midazolam
	Antihistamines	promethazine, caffeine
	Opioid agonist-antagonists	pentazocine, nalbuphine, butorphanol
Antianxiety agents	Benzodiazepines	diazepam, lorazepam, midazolam
	Barbiturates	phenobarbital
Antiseizure agents	Benzodiazepines	diazepam, lorazepam, midazolam
	Barbiturates	phenobarbital
	Hydantoins	phenytoin, fosphenytoin
	Succinimides	ethosuximide
	Miscellaneous	valproic acid
CNS stimulants	Amphetamines	amphetamine sulfate, methamphetamine, dextroamphetamine
	Methyphenidates	methyphenidate
	Methylxanthines	caffeine, aminophylline, theophylline
Antipsychotics	Phenothiazines	chlorpromazine
	Butyrophenones	haloperidol
	Miscellaneous	clozapine, risperidone
Antidepressants	TCAs	imipramine, amitriptyline, desipramine, nortriptyline
	SSRIs	fluoxetine, sertraline, paroxetine

	MAOIs	phenelzine
Agents used in bipolar disorder		lithium (bipolar disorder)
Agents used in Parkinson's disease		levodopa, Sinemet, amantadine, bromocriptine
	MAOIs	selegiline
	Anticholenergics	benztropine, diphenhydramine

Autonomic Nervous System

Parasympathetic nervous system	Cholinergics	bethanechol, pilocarpine, neostigmine, physostigmine, echothiophate
	Anticholinergics	atropine, scopolamine, ipratropium bromide, dicyclomine, benztropine
Sympathetic nervous system	Adrenergics	norepinephrine, epinephrine, dopamine, dolbutamine, isoproterenol, ephedrine, phenylephedrine, terbutaline
	Antiadrenergics	phenoxybenzamine, prazosin, phentolamine
	Beta blockers	propranolol, metoprolol, atenolol
	Skeletal muscle relaxants	baclofen, cyclobenzaprine, carisoprodol, dantrolene

Sense Organs

Eyes	Glaucoma	timolol, betaxolol, pilocarpine
	Diagnostic procedures	atropisol, scopolamine, phenylephrine
	Anesthetic	tetracaine
Ears	Antibiotics	chloramphenicol, gentamicin sulfate
	Wax removal	carbamide peroxide and glycerin

Cardiovascular System

Antidysrhythmics	Sodium channel blockers	quinidine, procainamide, disopyramide, lidocaine, phenytoin, mexiletine, flecainide, propafenone, moricine
	Beta blockers	propranolol, esmolol
	Potassium channel blockers	bretylium, amiodarone
	Calcium channel blockers	verapamil, diltiazem
	Miscellaneous	adenosine, digoxin, magnesium
Diuretics	Loop	furosemide
	Thiazides	hydrochlorothiazide
	Potassium sparing	spironolactone
Antihypertensives	Adrenergic inhibitors	clonidine, methyldopa, reserpine, guanethidine, guanadrel, prazosin, terazosin, labetalol, carvedilol, nifedipine
	ACE inhibitors	captoril, enalapril, lisinopril
	Angiotension II antagonist	losartan
	Calcium channel blockers	nifedipine
	Vasodilators	hydralazine, minoxidil, sodium nitroprusside, trimethaphan, digoxin, digitoxin
	Antianginals	verapamil, diltiazem, nifedipine, nitroglycerin
Hemostatic agents	Antiplatelets	aspirin, dipyridamole, abciximab, ticlopidine
	Anticoagulants	heparin, warfarin

| | Thrombolitics | streptokinase, alteplase, reteplase, anistreplase |
| | Antihyperlipidemics | lovastatin, simvastatin, cholestyramine |

Respiratory System

Antiasthmatics	Beta$_2$ agents	albuterol, terbutaline
	Sympathomimetics	epinephrine, ephedrine, isoproterenol
	Methylxanthines	methylxanthine, theophylline, aminophylline
	Anticholinergics	ipratropium
	Glucocorticoids	methylprednisolone, cromolyn
	Leukotriene antagonists	zileuton, zafirlukast
Rhinitis and cough	Nasal decongestants	phenylephedrine, pseudoephedrine, phenylpropanolamine
	Antihistamines	
	Alkylamines	chlorpheniramine
	Ethanolamines	diphenhydramine, clemastine
	Phenothiazines	promethiazine, dimenhydrinate, loratadine, cetirizine, fexofenadine
	Cough suppressants antitussive	codeine, hydrocodone, dextromethorphan, diphenhydramine, benzonatate

Gastrointestinal System

Peptic ulcer disease	H$_2$ receptor agonists	cimetidine, ranitidine, famotidine, nizatidine
	Proton pump inhibitors	omeprazole, lansoprazole
	Antacids	aluminum, magnesium, calcium, or sodium compounds
	Anticholinergics	pirenzepine
Laxatives	Bulk-forming	methylcellulose, psyllium
	Surfactant	docusate sodium
	Stimulant	phenolphthalein, bisacodyl
	Osmotic	magnesium hydroxide
Antidiarrheal	Antibiotics	
Antiemetics	Serotonin antagonists	ondansetron
	Dopamine antagonists	
	Phenothiazines	prochlorperazine, promethazine
	Butyrophenones	haloperidol, droperidol
	Miscellaneous	metoclopramide
	Cannabinoids	dronabinol, nabilone
To aid digestion		pancreatin, pancrelipase

Endocrine System

Pituitary gland	Anterior pituitary	somatrem, somatropin, octreotide
	Posterior pituitary	vasopressin, desmopressin, lypressin
Parathyroid glands		calcium and vitamin D supplements
Thyroid gland		levothyroxine
Adrenal cortex	Cushing's disease	spironolactone, captopril
	Addison's disease	cortisone, hydrocortisone, fludrocortisone
Pancreas	Insulin	
	Oral hypoglycemics sulfonylureas	tolbutamide, chlorpropamide, glipizide, glyburide

	Biguanides	metformin
	Alpha-glucosidase inhibitors	acarbose, miglitol
	Thiazolidinediones	troglitazone
	Hyperglycemic agents	glucagon, diazoxide

Reproductive System

Female	Estrogen/Progestins	
	Oral contraceptives	
	Oxytocics	oxytocin, ergonovine
	Tocolytics	terbutaline, ritodrine
	Infertility agents	clomiphene, urofollitropin, menotropin
Male	Testosterone	enanthate, methyltestosterone, fluoxymesterone
	Enlarged prostate	finasteride
Sexual performance		levodopa, sildenafil

Cancer Drugs

	Antimetabolites	fluorouracil
	Alkylating agents	cyclophosphamide, mechlorethamine
	Mitotic inhibitors	vinblastine, vincristine

Infectious Disease

	Antibiotics	penicillin, cephalosporin, vancomycin
	Antifungals	ketoconazole
	Antivirals	acyclovir, zidovudine, indinavir
	Antiparasitics	
	Malaria	chloroquine, mefloquine, quinine
	Amebiasis	paromomycin, metronidazole
	Helminthiasis	mebendazole, niclosamide
	Antimicrobial	
	Tuberculosis	isoniazid, rifampin
	Leprosy	dapsone, clofazimine
	Nonsteroidal antiinflammatories	acetaminophen, ibuprofen, ketorolac, piroxicam, naproxen

Immune System

	Immunosuppressants	azathioprine
	Immunomodulators	zidovudine, rotonavir, saquinavir

Note that this is not a complete list of common prescription drugs. As you continue your studies and career as a paramedic, many prescription drugs will become familiar to you. It is also recommended that you obtain a small pocket book that lists common prescription drugs and the conditions for which they are normally prescribed.

Prehospital Medications

Indications for the drugs commonly used in prehospital emergency medical care are contained on the drug cards at the end of this workbook. Review them with special attention to the conditions in which each drug is used.

5. **Given various patient medications, assess the pathophysiology of a patient's condition by identifying classifications of drugs.**   pp. 300–364

Within the discussion of the previous objective and throughout the text of this part of Chapter 9, drugs prescribed frequently for each common medical condition are noted. Finding one or more of these drugs with a patient might suggest preexisting medical conditions and, possibly, the underlying reason the patient called for your assistance. Whenever you find prescription drugs with a patient, you should determine what they were prescribed for and if the patient has been compliant with his or her drug administration. There are numerous pocket EMS drug guides that identify the most common prescription drugs by their various names and give the common reasons they are prescribed. If you are ever unsure of the nature and use of a patient's medication, contact your medical direction physician.

Content Self-Evaluation

MULTIPLE CHOICE

E 1. Drugs can be classified by:
   A. the body system they affect.
   B. the mechanism of their action.
   C. their indications.
   D. their source.
   E. all of the above

B 2. The drug that demonstrates the common properties of a class of drugs is called a:
   A. root drug.
   B. prototype drug.
   C. characteristic drug.
   D. primary drug.
   E. none of the above

E 3. Which of the following is NOT a division of the nervous system?
   A. central nervous system
   B. peripheral nervous system
   C. autonomic nervous system
   D. sympathetic nervous system
   E. antagonistic nervous system

A 4. Which nervous system controls motor functions?
   A. somatic
   B. autonomic
   C. sympathetic
   D. parasympathetic
   E. antagonistic

D 5. Which nervous system is responsible for the "feed-or-breed" response?
   A. somatic
   B. autonomic
   C. sympathetic
   D. parasympathetic
   E. antagonistic

C 6. A drug that relieves pain only is termed a(n):
   A. anesthetic.
   B. endorphin.
   C. analgesic.
   D. opioid.
   E. antimanic.

B 7. The prototype opioid drug is:
   A. heroin.
   B. morphine.
   C. aspirin.
   D. ibuprofen.
   E. acetaminophen.

C 8. Naloxone (Narcan) is the principle:
   A. nonopioid analgesic.
   B. opioid agonist.
   C. opioid antagonist.
   D. prehospital anesthetic.
   E. opioid agonist-antagonist.

C 9. Anesthetics, as a group, tend to cause which of the following?
   A. reconfigured sensation
   B. respiratory stimulation
   C. central nervous system depression
   D. cardiovascular stimulation
   E. endorphin stimulation.

_A___ 10. When using neuromuscular blocking agents, it is common to use antianxiety, amnesic, and analgesic agents as well.
   A. True   B. False

_D___ 11. Which of the following is the only anesthetic gas given in the prehospital setting?
   A. ether   D. nitrous oxide
   B. halothane   E. sodium pentothal
   C. enflurane

_B___ 12. Hypnotic is a term that describes a drug that:
   A. decreases anxiety.   D. decreases pain sensation.
   B. instigates sleep.   E. is an opioid antagonist.
   C. reduces sensation.

_B___ 13. The antagonist for the benzodiazepines is:
   A. naloxone.   D. diazepam.
   B. flumazenil.   E. midazolam.
   C. thiopental.

_B___ 14. Amphetamines cause which of the following?
   A. release of epinephrine   D. increased appetite
   B. release of dopamine   E. weight gain
   C. decreased wakefulness

_A___ 15. Caffeine is classified as a(n):
   A. methylxanthine.   D. opioid.
   B. methylphenidate.   E. endorphin.
   C. amphetamine.

_B___ 16. The drug class used to care for patients with mental dysfunctions is:
   A. neuroleptic.   D. schizophrenic.
   B. psychotherapeutic.   E. antimanic.
   C. extrapyramidal.

_A___ 17. It appears that dopamine, norepinephrine, and serotonin play a role in psychotic pathologies.
   A. True   B. False

_C___ 18. As a result of the extrapyramidal effects of antipsychotic drugs, these drugs are termed:
   A. Parkinsonian agents.   D. dopamine agonists.
   B. extrapyramidogenics.   E. neurotransmitters.
   C. neuroleptics.

_D___ 19. The drug of choice for treating the extrapyramidal symptoms associated with antipsychotic drugs is:
   A. diazepam.   D. diphenhydramine.
   B. furosemide.   E. epinephrine.
   C. chlorpromazine.

_D___ 20. Which of the following is NOT a sign or symptom of depression?
   A. weight loss   D. excessive energy
   B. weight gain   E. inability to concentrate
   C. sleep disturbances

_D___ 21. Expected side effects of tricyclic antidepressants include all of the following EXCEPT:
   A. blurred vision.   D. bradycardia.
   B. dry mouth.   E. orthostatic hypotension.
   C. urinary retention.

_____B_____ 22. Tricyclic antidepressants (TCAs) raise the seizure threshold and are effective antiseizure medications.
   A. True   B. False

_____B_____ 23. The drug of choice for the management of bipolar disorder is:
   A. valium.   D. phenelzine.
   B. lithium.   E. morphine sulfate.
   C. imipramine.

_____B_____ 24. Parkinson's disease may present with which characteristic signs and symptoms?
   A. elation   D. tachykinesia
   B. unsteady gait   E. aggressiveness
   C. postural rigidity

_____A_____ 25. Parkinson's disease is caused by a reduced number of presynaptic terminals that release dopamine.
   A. True   B. False

_____B_____ 26. Dopamine is given directly to the Parkinson's disease patient to help balance the dopamine/acetylcholine balance.
   A. True   B. False

_____B_____ 27. Which nervous system works in opposition to the parasympathetic nervous system?
   A. central   D. somatic
   B. sympathetic   E. antagonistic
   C. autonomic

_____B_____ 28. The agents that transport impulses through the synapse between neurons and between nerve cells and the target organs are called:
   A. neuroeffectors.   D. neuroleptic ions.
   B. neurotransmitters.   E. transport cells.
   C. intrasynaptic agents.

_____A_____ 29. The cholinergic neurotransmitter is:
   A. acetylcholine.   D. muscarinic antagonist.
   B. epinephrine.   E. muscarinic agonist.
   C. norepinephrine.

_____A_____ 30. Which neurotransmitter serves both the sympathetic and parasympathetic nervous systems?
   A. acetylcholine   D. dopamine
   B. epinephrine   E. none of the above
   C. norepinephrine

_____D_____ 31. A drug that stimulates the parasympathetic nervous system is called a(n):
   A. sympatholytic.   D. parasympathomimetic.
   B. sympathomimetic.   E. antiemetic.
   C. parasympatholytic.

_____D_____ 32. A cholinergic drug is also which of the following:
   A. a sympatholytic.   D. a parasympathomimetic.
   B. a sympathomimetic.   E. an antiemetic.
   C. a parasympatholytic.

_____C_____ 33. The acronym that describes the effects of cholinergic stimulation is:
   A. SARIN.   D. ALPHA.
   B. 2-PAM.   E. BETA.
   C. SLUDGE.

_B_ 34. The effects of cholinergic stimulation include all of the following EXCEPT:
   A. salivation.
   B. tachycardia.
   C. defecation.
   D. urination.
   E. emesis.

_D_ 35. The prototype anticholenergic drug is:
   A. epinephrine.
   B. norepinephrine.
   C. acetylcholine.
   D. atropine.
   E. dopamine.

_B_ 36. Neuromuscular blockade produces paralysis and amnesia to the event.
   A. True
   B. False

_D_ 37. Which of the following is NOT an action caused by nicotine?
   A. tachycardia
   B. increased salivation
   C. vasoconstriction
   D. hypotension
   E. increased gastric secretion

_D_ 38. The sympathetic nervous system originates from which regions of the spinal cord?
   A. cranial and sacral
   B. cranial and lumbar
   C. cranial and thoracic
   D. thoracic and lumbar
   E. thoracic and sacral

_A_ 39. Approximately what percentage of the hormones released by the stimulated adrenal medulla constitute norepinephrine?
   A. 20 percent
   B. 40 percent
   C. 60 percent
   D. 80 percent
   E. 90 percent

_B_ 40. Which of the following receptors is inhibitory?
   A. alpha$_1$
   B. alpha$_2$
   C. beta$_1$
   D. cholinergic
   E. dopaminergic

_D_ 41. Stimulation of which of the following receptors causes both vasodilation and bronchodilation?
   A. alpha$_1$
   B. alpha$_2$
   C. beta$_1$
   D. beta$_2$
   E. dopaminergic

_E_ 42. Stimulation of which of the following receptors causes dilation of the renal, coronary, and cerebral arteries?
   A. alpha$_1$
   B. alpha$_2$
   C. beta$_1$
   D. beta$_2$
   E. dopaminergic

_B_ 43. Alpha$_1$ antagonist drugs are used almost exclusively to control hypertension.
   A. True
   B. False

_E_ 44. What effect does alpha stimulation have on the heart?
   A. increases heart rate
   B. increases automaticity
   C. increases contractile strength
   D. increases oxygen consumption
   E. none of the above

_B_ 45. Which type of drug decreases cardiac contractility and heart rate?
   A. beta$_2$ agonists
   B. beta$_1$ antagonists
   C. beta$_1$ agonists
   D. alpha$_1$ antagonists
   E. alpha$_1$ agonists

_D_ **46.** The prototype beta blocker is:
- **A.** isoproterenol.
- **B.** dopamine.
- **C.** atropine.
- **D.** propranolol.
- **E.** none of the above.

_D_ **47.** Which of the following is NOT a naturally occurring catecholamine?
- **A.** dopamine
- **B.** epinephrine
- **C.** norepinephrine
- **D.** isoproterenol
- **E.** A and C

_A_ **48.** Which type of drug causes bronchodilation?
- **A.** beta$_2$ agonists
- **B.** beta$_1$ antagonists
- **C.** beta$_1$ agonists
- **D.** alpha$_1$ antagonists
- **E.** alpha$_1$ agonists

_D_ **49.** Which response contains the proper order of an electrical impulse as it travels through the cardiac conduction system?
- **A.** bundle of His, SA node, AV node, Purkinje fibers, internodal pathways
- **B.** AV node, internodal pathways, SA node, bundle of His, Purkinje fibers
- **C.** internodal pathways, AV node, SA node, Purkinje fibers, bundle of His
- **D.** SA node, internodal pathways, AV node, bundle of His, Purkinje fibers
- **E.** bundle of His, SA node, internodal pathways, AV node, Purkinje fibers

_B_ **50.** The unique property of myocardial muscle tissue that permits it to generate an electrical impulse is:
- **A.** inotropy.
- **B.** automaticity.
- **C.** contractility.
- **D.** autonomic firing.
- **E.** depolarization.

_B_ **51.** The heart's dominant pacemaker is the:
- **A.** AV node.
- **B.** SA node.
- **C.** Purkinje fibers.
- **D.** bundle of His.
- **E.** internodal pathways.

_A_ **52.** Beta blockers and calcium channel blockers have similar effects on the heart.
- **A.** True
- **B.** False

_B_ **53.** Adenosine produces which of the following?
- **A.** facial pallor
- **B.** chest pain
- **C.** bronchodilation
- **D.** marked tachycardias
- **E.** all of the above

_C_ **54.** Hypertension affects about how many people in the United States?
- **A.** 10 million
- **B.** 25 million
- **C.** 50 million
- **D.** 100 million
- **E.** 250 million

_D_ **55.** Which of the following is an osmotic diuretic?
- **A.** hydrochlorothiazide
- **B.** furosemide
- **C.** potassium chloride
- **D.** mannitol
- **E.** spironolactone

_C_ **56.** The renin-angiotensin-aldosterone system performs what function?
- **A.** increasing hepatic function
- **B.** decreasing blood volume
- **C.** increasing vasoconstriction
- **D.** causing severe bronchoconstriction
- **E.** all of the above

_C_ **57.** Which of the following drug types is used in the treatment of hypertension?
- **A.** antihyperlipidemics
- **B.** glucocorticoids
- **C.** calcium channel blockers
- **D.** cardiac glycosides
- **E.** all of the above

_C_ 58. Which of the following are actions caused by the administration of digoxin?
   A. decreases intracellular sodium levels
   B. decreases intracellular calcium
   C. increases the strength of cardiac muscle contraction
   D. increases ventricular engorgement during left heart failure
   E. all of the above

_A_ 59. The primary action of nitroglycerin in angina is to:
   A. reduce preload.
   B. reduce peripheral vascular resistance.
   C. dilate the coronary arteries.
   D. reduce the anginal pain.
   E. increase blood pressure.

_D_ 60. The enzyme responsible for breaking down the fibrin of a clot once an injury has been repaired is:
   A. adenosine diphosphate.   D. plasmin.
   B. thromboxane.   E. none of the above
   C. vitamin K.

_E_ 61. Thrombi are the primary pathologies for which of the following?
   A. stroke   D. hypertension
   B. myocardial infarction   E. all of the above except D
   C. pulmonary embolism

_E_ 62. Which of the following prevents thrombi by interrupting the clotting cascade?
   A. antiplatelets   D. hemostatic agents
   B. anticoagulants   E. all of the above
   C. fibrinolytics

_B_ 63. All of the following are used to treat or prevent thrombi EXCEPT:
   A. antiplatelets.   D. oral anticoagulants.
   B. antihyperlipidemic agents.   E. parenteral anticoagulants.
   C. thrombolitics.

_B_ 64. Warfarin is contraindicated in pregnant mothers because it is likely to cause:
   A. uterine bleeding.   D. vitamin K toxicity.
   B. birth defects.   E. placenta previa.
   C. maternal hypertension.

_D_ 65. Of the hemostatic agents, which can dissolve clots once they have formed?
   A. aspirin   D. streptokinase
   B. heparin   E. thrombarin
   C. warfarin

_C_ 66. Which of the following is of greatest help in reducing cholesterol levels in the blood?
   A. low density lipoproteins (LDL)
   B. very low density lipoproteins (VLDL)
   C. high density lipoproteins (HDL)
   D. intermediate density lipoproteins (IDL)
   E. neutral density lipoproteins (NDL)

_E_ 67. Which of the events below occurs first in an asthma attack?
   A. inflammatory response
   B. mast cell rupture
   C. release of histamine and leukotrienes
   D. immediate bronchospasm
   E. allergen binding to antibody on the mast cell

_C__ 68. Which of the following groups is NOT used to treat asthma?
   A. leukotriene antagonists   D. methylxanthines
   B. glucocorticoids   E. anticholinergics
   C. ganglionic blocking agents

_A__ 69. Which of the following is the first line therapy for asthma?
   A. selective beta₂ agonists   D. glucocorticoids
   B. nonselective sympathomimetics   E. leukotriene antagonists
   C. anticholinergics

_C__ 70. Nasal decongestants act by which of the following actions?
   A. restricting histamine release   D. thinning nasal mucus
   B. blocking histamine action   E. all of the above
   C. constricting nasal capillaries

_B__ 71. Histamine is a major agent in the severe anaphylactic reaction.
   A. True   B. False

_A__ 72. Antihistamine drugs are not indicated for asthma patients because they thicken
         bronchial secretions.
   A. True   B. False

_C__ 73. A drug that suppresses the urge to cough is a(n):
   A. expectorant.   D. surfactant.
   B. mucolytic.   E. cannabinoid.
   C. antitussive.

_E__ 74. Most peptic ulcer disease is caused by:
   A. over-secretion of gastric acid. D. decreased gastric circulation.
   B. stress.   E. a bacterium.
   C. alcohol consumption.

_E__ 75. Which of the following is a type of laxative?
   A. bulk-forming   D. stimulant
   B. osmotic   E. all of the above
   C. surfactant

_A__ 76. The drug chloramphenicol is used to treat what condition involving the ears?
   A. bacterial infections   D. inflammation/irritation
   B. viral infections   E. all of the above
   C. impacted wax

_E__ 77. Which of the following drugs have ototoxic properties?
   A. aspirin
   B. other nonsteroidal antiinflammatory drugs
   C. some antibiotics
   D. furosemide
   E. all of the above

_A__ 78. The gland of the endocrine system that is regarded as the master gland is the:
   A. pituitary.   D. pancreas.
   B. thyroid.   E. adrenal.
   C. parathyroid.

_C__ 79. The hormones produced by the thyroid play vital roles in growth, maturation, and:
   A. acromegaly.   D. gastric secretion regulation.
   B. electrolyte balance.   E. all of the above
   C. metabolism.

_C_ 80. Goiters are typically caused by an insufficiency in:
  A. potassium.
  B. calcium.
  C. iodine.
  D. vitamin K.
  E. hemoglobin.

_B_ 81. The adrenal cortex is responsible for the production of hormones for all the following purposes EXCEPT:
  A. to regulate salt balance.
  B. to regulate immunity.
  C. to regulate glucose production.
  D. to regulate water balance.
  E. to regulate sexual maturity.

_B_ 82. The type of diabetes that typically manifests during childhood is:
  A. gestational.
  B. type I.
  C. type II.
  D. type III.
  E. type IV.

_A_ 83. The pancreas secrets two hormones important to the regulation of glucose. They are insulin and:
  A. glucagon.
  B. glycogen.
  C. dextrose.
  D. cortisol.
  E. orinase.

_D_ 84. Which of the following forms of insulin is not likely to cause an allergic reaction?
  A. lente
  B. pork
  C. beef
  D. recombinant
  E. bovine

_A_ 85. The principle indication for estrogen replacement therapy in women is:
  A. postmenopause replacement.
  B. contraception.
  C. to delay childbirth.
  D. in delayed puberty.
  E. all of the above

_B_ 86. Serious hypotension may occur in a patient who takes sildenafil when also taking:
  A. glucagon.
  B. nitrates.
  C. $D_{50}W$.
  D. antibiotics.
  E. thyroxine.

_E_ 87. Antibiotics act by:
  A. killing the bacteria outright.
  B. creating antigens to deactivate the bacteria.
  C. engulfing the bacteria.
  D. decreasing the bacteria's growth rate.
  E. both A and D

_B_ 88. A solution containing whole antibodies for a specific pathogen is called a(n):
  A. vaccine.
  B. serum.
  C. immunogen.
  D. rotovirus.
  E. none of the above

_B_ 89. The best age for vaccination against disease is:
  A. under 6 months.
  B. under 2 years.
  C. from 2 to 5 years.
  D. over 5 years of age.
  E. over 8 years of age.

_A_ 90. The number associated with each B vitamin relates to:
  A. its order of discovery.
  B. its molecular size.
  C. its importance to the body.
  D. its point of absorption.
  E. none of the above

Special Project

Practicing as a paramedic involves the administration of numerous medications for patients with serious medical conditions. To be able to administer these medications safely, you must know each medication's indications, contraindications, precautions, routes of administration, and dosages. This information is not easy to commit to memory.

At the end of this workbook is a series of Emergency Drug Cards with indications, contraindications, precautions, routes of administration, and dosages for the drugs. Detach them and select those cards that represent drugs used by your EMS system or educational program. If there are drugs that your system or educational program uses that are not included in the drug cards, use index cards to create additional drug cards. Enter the important information for each drug under the listed categories and enter the drug name on the reverse side of the card. Review the material on each card from this workbook and on the cards that you create with your instructor and medical protocols. Ensure that they document the indications, dosages, and routes consistent with your protocols and with prehospital practice in your system. It is not unusual for systems to use slightly different indications, contraindications, and dosages. Also note that continuing research may change the types of medications and the way they are administered.

Once you have assembled the drug cards and they are consistent with your system protocols, review them to begin learning the important drug information. Once you feel comfortable with each drug's information, shuffle the cards and then check your ability to recognize the indications, contraindications, side effects, routes of administration, and dosages for each medication. Review these drugs from time to time during your education and with specific classroom sessions regarding the medical emergencies and trauma emergencies. Ultimately, you should know all the information listed for each drug in your stack of cards.

10

Intravenous Access and Medication Administration

Because Chapter 10 is lengthy, it has been divided into parts to aid your study. Read the assigned textbook pages, then progress through the objectives and self-evaluation materials as you would with other chapters. When you feel secure in your grasp of the content, proceed to the next section.

Part 1: Principles and Rates of Medication Administration, begins on p. 372

Review of Chapter Objectives

After reading this part of the chapter, you should be able to:

1. **Review the specific anatomy and physiology pertinent to medication administration.** **pp. 376–406**

   Chapter 9 reviewed human anatomy as it pertains to the absorption, distribution, metabolization, and elimination of the drugs we use to treat disease and trauma. This chapter identifies the anatomy and physiology related to medication administration.

   The percutaneous routes of drug administration include transdermal and mucous membrane administration. Transdermal administration permits drug absorption through the skin via topical application in which the medication is slowly and steadily absorbed. Mucous membrane administration methods include sublingual, buccal, ocular, nasal, and aural administration, in which a drug is given under the tongue, between the cheek and gum, in the eye, into the nose, or into the ear respectively. Sublingual and buccal routes result in systemic absorption, while the remaining routes result in more local effects.

   Pulmonary administration introduces a drug by nebulizer or metered dose inhaler or through an endotracheal tube. All three methods direct the drug to the lung tissue for action; however, endotracheal administration is an emergency route for systemic administration.

   Enteral administration delivers a drug to the gastrointestinal tract, where it is absorbed. This is a relatively safe and simple route for drug administration and is the most common route for over-the-counter and prescription drug administration. The disadvantage of this route is that many factors can affect absorption including stress, diet, and metabolic rate. Liver function metabolizes some drugs, and a dysfunctional liver may alter the medication's metabolization or distribution. The enteral methods of administration include oral, gastric tube, and rectal administration. (Rectal administration is not subject to hepatic [liver] alteration.)

With parenteral administration, a drug is injected into the dermis (intradermal), the subcutaneous layer (subcutaneous), muscle (intramuscular), or veins (intravenous). The intradermal route provides little or no systemic absorption and is used for diagnostic testing and for the administration of local anesthetic. Subcutaneous injection promotes slow, sustained systemic absorption of a drug, while intramuscular injection permits systemic drug absorption at a moderate rate. Because intravenous drug administration injects the drug directly into the bloodstream, where it is directed to the heart, mixed with the returning venous blood, and then distributed systemically, it is the fastest parenteral administration route.

Anatomically, subcutaneous injections may be made into the skin regions over the deltoid muscle, the thighs, and, in some cases, the upper abdomen. Intramuscular injections may be given into the deltoid muscle, 2 inches below the acromial process; into the gluteal muscle, in the upper outer quadrant of the buttocks; into the anterolateral aspect of the thigh muscle (vastus lateralis); and into the central and lateral segment of the mid-thigh (rectus femoris).

2. **Describe the indications, equipment needed, technique used, precautions, and general principles for the following.**

All administration of medication requires the use of body substance isolation measures and medically clean techniques. The six rights of medication administration must be observed (see objective 5). With drug administration, you must watch carefully for the desired and adverse effects of the drug administration.

a. **Inhalation routes of medication administration.** pp. 380–384

Pulmonary medications are administered via nebulizer, metered dose inhaler, and endotracheal tube. Drugs indicated for inhalation include those that cause bronchodilation, mucolytics, antibiotics, and topical steroids for respiratory emergencies, congestion, infection, and inflammation respectively.

A nebulizer aerosolizes a small volume of liquid (or dissolved) medication using oxygen, which is then inhaled into the lungs and absorbed quickly. The device is assembled (mouth piece, medication reservoir, oxygen port, relief valve, and oxygen tubing and source), and 3 to 5 mL of solution (or a medication dissolved in 3 to 5 mL of sterile water) is placed in the medication reservoir. Oxygen is set to run at 5 to 8 lpm (without a humidifier), and the mouthpiece is placed in the patient's mouth. The patient should hold the nebulizer and inhale slowly and deeply with each breath, then hold the breath for one to two seconds before exhaling. The patient should continue doing this until the medication is gone (about three to five minutes). For nebulized medications to be effective, the patient must have an adequate tidal volume and respiratory rate, although nebulizers can be connected to an endotracheal tube during positive pressure ventilation.

Metered dose inhalers are frequently used in patients with COPD and asthma to deliver agents to induce bronchodilation. The device consists of a pressurized medication canister, plastic shell and mouthpiece, and possibly a spacer. The patient self-administers the drug by assembling the inhaler, shaking it for two to five seconds, inverting it, placing the mouthpiece in the mouth, and sealing the lips against the mouthpiece. Then, during the beginning of a deep inhalation, the patient presses the canister downward to release a dose of medication. A second dose may be necessary. Nebulizers are preferable to metered dose inhalers in acute respiratory emergencies because they administer the drug over more time and are less dependent on a single deep inspiration.

Endotracheal administration of a drug involves expressing the drug down the endotracheal tube (in a volume of 10 mL and from 2 to 2.5 times the normal intravenous dose). Narcan, atropine, lidocaine, and epinephrine can be administered this way in an emergency when IV access is not otherwise available. Once the drug is injected down the endotracheal tube, the ventilator provides several deep ventilations to deliver the drug to the pulmonary tissue.

b. **Parenteral routes of medication administration.** pp. 390–406

Parenteral administration includes the routes utilizing needles to administer drugs into the tissues or vascular system—intradermal, subcutaneous, intramuscular, intravenous, and intraosseous routes. Begin the parenteral administration process by cleansing the patient's skin at the injection site with an antiseptic such as alcohol or a povidone-iodine solution. The medication for injection is in solution and drawn up in a syringe, then injected with a needle (bevel up). For subcutaneous and intramuscular injection, consider injecting a 0.1-mL air bubble after the medication to limit leakage, and then massage the region to enhance absorption. Most emergency medications are injected via the intravenous route because of its rapid distribution throughout the body. Intradermal drug administration calls for insertion of a 25- to 27-gauge needle at a 10- to 15-degree angle just into a segment of skin that is pulled taut. Slow injection of up to 1 mL of solution will create a small wheal of medication. Then remove the needle. Intradermal injection results in a very slow absorption rate greatly affected by local perfusion rates and is used for diagnostic testing and the administration of local anesthetics.

For subcutaneous administration, place a 24- to 26-gauge needle into a 1-inch "pinch" of the patient's skin at a 45° angle and inject no more than 1 mL of medication. The skin must be free of scarring, superficial nerves, blood vessels and tendons, tattoos, and bruising. Pulling the plunger back ensures the needle is not in a blood vessel (aspiration of blood indicates a blood vessel entry). Subcutaneous injection may be given at many locations around the body, including the tissue under the tongue.

For intramuscular injections, use a 21- to 23-gauge needle inserted at a 90° angle into the deltoid (up to 2 mL), dorsal gluteal (up to 5 mL), vastus lateralis (up to 5 mL), or rectus femoris (up to 5 mL) muscle. Again, pulling back on the plunger ensures the needle is not in a blood vessel. Intramuscular injection provides a predictable systemic absorption and is used for several prehospital drugs including glucagon and morphine. Careful placement of parenteral needles is important because of potential damage to nerves and arteries. Needles for intradermal, subcutaneous, and intramuscular injection are ⅜ to 1 inch in length.

c. Percutaneous routes of medication administration. pp. 376–380

Transdermal drug administration is indicated for drugs that are readily absorbed through the skin, when slow, steady absorption is required, or for topical administration for local effects (antiinflammatories, bacteriostatics, and softening agents). Transdermal medications include lotions, creams, foams, wet dressings, adhesive-backed applications, and suppositories. The medication is applied to a clean, dry portion of skin according to the manufacturer's instructions. The medication is left for the required time and watched for the desired and adverse effects, and a dressing is placed over the application if necessary. Care must be taken not to get the drug on your skin and to watch for overdosing due to thin skin, increasing absorption rates, or for underdosing due to thick skin, scar tissue, or peripheral vascular disease, slowing absorption.

The mucous membrane route for drug administration permits drug absorption through the capillaries of the sublingual, buccal, ocular, nasal, or aural mucous membranes. With the sublingual route, a spray is applied or a tablet placed beneath the tongue, where the patient must let it dissolve and be absorbed. Nitroglycerin is a drug commonly administered via the sublingual route. With buccal administration a pill or other preparation is placed between the cheek and gum to permit absorption. Hormonal and enzyme preparations are commonly administered via the buccal route. Ocular administration involves one or both eyes. The patient lies supine or tips his head back and looks at the ceiling. The eyelid is pulled down, and the droplet of a liquid medication (using an medicine dropper) or an ointment is placed into the conjunctival sac. Do not touch the eye or administer drugs directly on the eye unless specifically instructed to do so. Medications administered via this route include agents to treat eye pain, infection, or increased intraocular pressure or to lubricate the eyelid. Nasal administration involves the topical absorption of drops or sprays through the nasal mucosa for nasal congestion, hemorrhage, or infection. The patient is directed to blow his nose and tilt his head back. A medicine dropper or squeezable nebulizer expresses the drug into the nare(s), then the nare(s) is (are) held shut and/or the head is tilted forward to enhance the distribution of the medication. Aural administration is used to treat local infection or ear pain. Droplets or medicated gauze are placed into the affected ear while the patient lies supine with his head turned. The adult's pinna is pulled up and back, while the child's is pulled down and back to expose the auditory canal. Do not pack the canal tightly.

d. Enteral routes of medication administration, including gastric tube administration and rectal administration. pp. 384–390

Enteral drug administration includes oral, gastric tube, and rectal administration routes and results in drug absorption through the gastrointestinal tract. Medications administered this way (excepting the rectal route) are processed through the liver, affecting their metabolism and elimination.

Oral medications are introduced as capsules, tablets, pills, time release capsules, elixirs, emulsions, lozenges, suspensions, or syrups introduced into the oral cavity and swallowed with four to eight ounces of water. This is the most common method of over-the-counter and prescription drug administration because of its ease of administration.

Gastric tube administration introduces a drug down the nasogastric or orogastric tube and into the stomach. It is used when the patient has difficulty swallowing and in instances of overdose, trauma, upper gastrointestinal bleeding, or the need for nutritional support. Drugs in solid forms may be crushed (so as to move easily down the tube), mixed with water, and administered through the gastric tube, although such action will destroy the time release action of coated drugs. When administering a drug via the gastric tube route, ensure proper placement by injecting air and auscultating over the epigastric area and by aspirating gastric contents through the tube. Flush the tube with 50 to 100 mL of saline, then prepare a volume of about 30 mL of medication (diluted to volume with normal saline) and administer the solution through the gastric tube. Follow administration with 50 to 100 mL of normal saline and clamp off the tube for about 30 minutes.

Rectal administration involves topical administration of a medication to the rectal mucosa and provides rapid, predictable absorption. Use a syringe and 14-gauge needleless catheter (or small endotracheal tube) to introduce the medication into the rectum, then hold the buttocks closed to promote retention and absorption. A suppository is a soft, pliable form of drug that melts at body temperature and is inserted into the rectum for absorption. An enema is a liquid bolus of medication introduced through the rectum.

3. Describe the indications, contraindications, side effects, dosages, and routes of administration for medications commonly administered by paramedics. pp. 376–406

There are many drugs used in the prehospital setting to care for the common medical and trauma emergencies. The Emergency Drug Cards at the back of this workbook list many of these drugs, including the drug name/class, indications, contraindications, precautions, dosages, and routes of administration. Detach these cards and review them frequently to become familiar with the medications you will use during your prehospital patient care.

4. Discuss legal aspects affecting medication administration. pp. 372–373, 375–376

The administration of the wrong medication or withholding the right medication or providing it in the wrong dose or by the wrong route can have catastrophic consequences. Hence, medication administration is an area of paramedic practice in which the paramedic is exposed to legal liability. You must ensure that you receive informed and expressed consent from the patient (when possible), provide medications in strict compliance with system protocols and the direction of on-line medical control, and follow proper administration techniques. Once a medication is administered, it is essential that you document the indication for the drug, any on-line authorization for the administration, the name of the person who delivered the drug, the drug name, dose, route, time and rate of delivery, and the resulting patient response, whether positive or negative. These actions will go a long way to limiting your liability in drug administration.

5. Discuss the "six rights" of drug administration and correlate them with the principles of medication administration. pp. 372–373

There are basically six rights of drug administration. They are the right patient, the right drug, the right dose, the right time, the right route, and the right documentation.

The right patient. Ensure that the patient is the right person and properly matched to the medication. This is an infrequent problem in prehospital care, but as EMS moves to the out-of-hospital environment, we may be treating some patients on a routine basis. Ensure the medication order is for the patient you are attending.

The right drug. Ensure the drug is what is intended for the patient. Review your standing orders or, if the order is received from medical direction, repeat ("echo") the order back to the physician so you are both clear on the drug, dose, route, and timing of the order. Also examine the drug packaging to ensure that it contains the medication you wish to administer and that the medication is still sterile, has not expired, and is not contaminated or discolored.

The right dose. Carefully calculate the exact dose (usually weight dependent) for the patient before you draw up the medication and again just before you administer it. If the drug package you select has significantly more or less of the drug than you intend to use, recheck the packaging to ensure it is the right drug and right concentration, and recheck your calculations to ensure the right dosage. Never overdose or underdose your patient.

The right time. Usually prehospital medications are given rather rapidly and not on a schedule. Check the packaging and your protocols for administration rates and ensure that you follow the sequencing, time intervals between, and drip rates for emergency drugs.

The right route. Specific drugs require specific routes of administration. While most emergency drugs are administered by the IV route, be aware of alternative drug administration routes, the drugs that can be administered by those routes, and the circumstances requiring the use of those routes. With each medication administration, ensure you are using the right route.

The right documentation. Documentation of drug administration is of paramount importance. You must carefully record the patient's condition (the circumstances that require the drug's administration), the drug name, dose, and route of administration, and who administered the drug and at what time. It is also essential that you record the patient's response to the drug, whether good or bad.

6. Differentiate among the percutaneous routes of medication administration.   pp. 376–380

The **transdermal** route of medication administration promotes slow, steady absorption of the drug across the dermis. Nitroglycerin is frequently administered for its systemic effects via this route, while lidocaine, antiinflammatories, and bacteriostatic solutions are administered for their local effects.

Sublingual drugs are absorbed through the mucous membranes beneath the tongue, where the medication is rapidly absorbed by the extensive vasculature there. Tablets or sprays are often used, and nitroglycerin is frequently administered this way in the emergency setting.

Buccal medications (usually tablets) are placed between the cheek and gums for absorption. Enzymes and hormonal preparations are also administered this way.

Ocular drug administration involves topical administration of a medication (usually drops or ointment) into one or both eyes. This route is typically used for treating eye pain or local infections, decreasing intraocular pressure, or lubrication of the eyelid.

Nasal medications are usually drops or sprays given through the nares to treat nasal congestion, hemorrhage, or infection.

Aural medications are delivered into the auditory canal using a medicine dropper (solution) or medicated gauze. These drugs are used to treat localized infection and ear pain.

7. Discuss medical asepsis and the differences between clean and sterile techniques.   p. 374

Medical asepsis describes a medical environment free of pathogens. The most aseptic environment is a sterile one, one free of all living organisms. However, in prehospital care we frequently cannot attain such a state. We utilize equipment and supplies that are sterile when packaged and then use medically clean techniques to reduce the risk of spreading infection. These techniques include the use of disinfectants to kill microorganisms on equipment and in the ambulance and of antiseptics to reduce the bacterial load on the patient's skin when we utilize procedures like venipuncture.

8. Describe uses of antiseptics and disinfectants.   p. 374

Antiseptics are agents are designed for topical use to destroy or inhibit pathogenic microorganisms already on living tissue. They are used to cleanse the skin before parenteral drug administration to prevent infection secondary to the needle stick.

Disinfectants are powerful agents that are toxic to living tissue. They are not designed for topical administration but for the direct cleaning of durable patient care equipment.

9. **Describe the use of body substance isolation (BSI) procedures when administering a medication.** pp. 373–374

Any time there is the possibility of contact with body substances or patient wounds, you must use body substance isolation measures. Gloves, at a minimum, provide barrier protection to the caregiver from possibly infectious material at the scene and to the patient from the caregiver. Goggles and a mask also provide protection, as does hand washing after contact with a patient or possibly infected material.

10. **Describe disposal of contaminated items and sharps.** p. 375

Sharps and contaminated materials pose a risk for the spread of infection. Do not recap needles unless absolutely necessary and, in such instance, do so using only one hand. Used needles represent a real risk for introducing pathogens from the patient's blood into someone stuck with the needle. Dispose of all needles in a puncture-proof biohazard container. Ensure all medical waste is placed in a biohazardous waste bag and is not left at the scene. Follow your service's biohazard exposure plan should you receive a needle stick.

11. **Synthesize a pharmacological management plan including medication administration.** p. 375

As you care for patients with serious medical and trauma emergencies, you will often need to administer medications to them via the sublingual, oral, pulmonary, subcutaneous, intramuscular, intravenous, and interosseous routes. The procedures described in this chapter must become an integral part of your patient management skills.

The following objective, while not listed in the chapter, will help in your understanding of the chapter content.

12. **Describe the equipment and procedures for preparing and drawing up a medication in anticipation of parenteral administration.**

A syringe is a plastic, hollow, calibrated barrel into which fits a plunger that is used to draw up and administer very accurate volumes of a solution or liquid. Syringes range in size from 1 to 100 mL. A hypodermic needle is a hollow metal tube, one end of which is beveled and very sharp while the other end is equipped with an adapter to fit a syringe. Needles are measured in diameter or gauge from 14 (largest) to 27 (smallest) and vary in length from $\frac{3}{8}$ to $1\frac{1}{2}$ inch.

Medications come packaged for administration in glass ampules, single and multidose vials, nonconstituted vials, prefilled syringes, and premixed IV solutions. Ampules are sealed glass containers that must be broken to obtain the drug. A sterile gauze pad is wrapped around the ampule neck and the top is broken off. The needle from a syringe is placed within the ampule to draw out the necessary volume of solution. Single and multidose vials are glass containers with self-sealing rubber tops, usually protected with a metal cap. The cap is removed and the stopper cleansed with alcohol. A syringe is filled with a volume of air, equivalent to the desired volume of drug. The needle is inserted into the vial, the air is expressed inside, and the drug is withdrawn. The needle is then withdrawn from the vial, and the drug is ready for administration. Nonconstituted drug vials come either in the form of pairs of vials (the drug and solvent) that require you to introduce the solvent into the powdered drug vial or in specially designed vials (Mix-o-Vials) that permit mixing after you pop the seal between the drug and solvent. Once the drug is constituted, you withdraw it as from a standard vial. Preloaded syringes are vials containing the drug that screw into a syringe barrel and permit direct administration of the drug by pushing the vial barrel into the syringe. Intravenous premixed solutions for IV infusion come in bottles or plastic bags (plastic bags are use for prehospital administration). They contain a solution of drug and solvent for direct administration via an intravenous line with administration volume (and hence dose) controlled by setting the rate of administration.

Case Study Review

Reread the case study on pages 370 to 371 in Paramedic Care: Introduction to Advanced Prehospital Care *and then read the following discussion.*

Susan and Todd are presented with a typical emergency patient in this scenario. While Susan anticipated asthma from the patient's wheezing, her positioning, and her general appearance (all determined during the first impression of the patient), she is meticulous in her complete patient evaluation and determination of baseline vital signs, ECG, pulse oximetry, and patient (SAMPLE) history. This information is essential to identify the pathology affecting the patient and to identify and document the indications, and rule out possible contraindications, for medication administration.

Susan and Todd identify that the patient attempted to use a metered dose inhaler for relief from the asthma attack. Because of their knowledge of various medication administration techniques and their respective advantages and disadvantages, they know that in severe attacks of respiratory distress, the ventilatory exchange is poor and limits the effectiveness of the inhaler. They employ albuterol nebulization because the prolonged and humidified inhalation may be more effective in delivering the drug to the deeper respiratory tissue. They also recognize the seriousness of the attack and administer epinephrine subcutaneously to ensure rapid delivery of a bronchodilator. Finally, Susan administers methylprednisolone via an intravenous line as an antiinflammatory agent to combat that component of the severe asthma condition. This drug comes in a special two-part vial that permits an increased shelf life but requires that Susan be familiar with special aspects of the drug's preparation and administration.

For each of these drug routes, Susan must be familiar with the specific equipment used, the location for injections, and the technique of drug injection and must recognize what common complications may be associated with a particular route of administration. Susan must also be able to calculate the proper dose of the drug and the volume of drug on hand that contains that dose.

During each medication administration, Susan must follow the proper protocol, identify the six rights of drug administration, and employ the appropriate technique to draw up and deliver the medication. She must also observe body substance isolation measures and aseptic and medically clean techniques; dispose of sharps, drug containers, and other biohazards properly; and document the indications, administration, and effects of each drug she used. While this is a complicated process, it will become second nature to you once you begin your career as a paramedic.

Content Self-Evaluation

MULTIPLE CHOICE

1. Medication administration is an important part of the medical care provided by paramedics.
   - A. True
   - B. False

2. Which of the following is NOT one of the six rights of drug administration?
   - A. the right dosage
   - B. the right indication
   - C. the right time
   - D. the right documentation
   - E. the right patient

3. The process you use to ensure you hear and correctly understand the medical direction physician's order to administer a medication is:
   - A. protocol compliance.
   - B. order confirmation with your partner.
   - C. redundant physician orders.
   - D. echoing the order back to the physician.
   - E. asking the physician to repeat the order.

4. Which of the following must you know about the drugs you are authorized to administer?
   A. their usual dosages
   B. their contraindications
   C. their common side effects
   D. their routes of administration
   E. all of the above

5. When you administer drugs, which of the following body substance isolation measures should you always employ?
   A. gloves
   B. a mask
   C. goggles
   D. a gown
   E. A and D

6. The condition in which a medical environment is free of all pathogens is described as:
   A. asepsis.
   B. uncontaminated.
   C. medically clean.
   D. disinfection.
   E. none of the above

7. The environment that paramedics should strive to maintain while delivering prehospital emergency care is:
   A. aseptic.
   B. sterile.
   C. medically clean.
   D. disinfected.
   E. none of the above

8. To cleanse the site of a parenteral injection, you would use a(n):
   A. aseptic.
   B. disinfectant.
   C. detergent.
   D. antiseptic.
   E. dilutant.

9. When possible, you should recap needles:
   A. as a last resort.
   B. in a moving ambulance only.
   C. except in a moving ambulance.
   D. only when they have not been used on a patient.
   E. when directed by a physician.

10. Documentation regarding the administration of a drug should include all of the following EXCEPT the:
    A. time of administration.
    B. route of administration.
    C. class of drug administered.
    D. positive patient responses.
    E. negative patient responses.

11. Transdermal medications are provided in which of the following forms?
    A. ointments
    B. wet dressings
    C. foams
    D. lotions
    E. all of the above

12. Which of the following factors can decrease the absorption rate with transdermal medication administration?
    A. thin skin
    B. overdose
    C. penetrating solvents
    D. peripheral vascular disease
    E. all of the above

13. Which of the following is a common emergency drug administered sublingually?
    A. sodium bicarbonate
    B. epinephrine
    C. nitroglycerin
    D. aspirin
    E. magnesium

14. The route in which a drug is administered between the cheek and gum is:
    A. transdermal.
    B. sublingual.
    C. buccal.
    D. aural.
    E. inhalation

15. Ocular medications are given for which conditions?
    A. eye pain
    B. eye infection
    C. increased intraocular pressure
    D. lubricating the eyelid
    E. all of the above

16. Ocular medications are most commonly administered:
    A. over the pupil.
    B. over the iris.
    C. over the sclera.
    D. into the conjunctival sac.
    E. all of the above

17. Nasal administration of medication is used frequently because of its rapid absorption rate and systemic effects.
    A. True
    B. False

18. The small volume nebulizer often used in prehospital emergency medical service administers what volume of medication?
    A. 1 to 2 mL
    B. 3 to 5 mL
    C. 5 to 10 mL
    D. 10 to 15 mL
    E. 15 to 20 mL

19. The small volume nebulizer's major advantage over the metered dose inhaler is that the patient does not need an adequate tidal volume for effective medication delivery.
    A. True
    B. False

20. The metered dose inhaler is activated to release its medication:
    A. just before the patient seals his lips to the mouthpiece.
    B. as the patient exhales.
    C. as the patient inhales.
    D. during both inhalation and exhalation.
    E. between inhalation and exhalation.

21. Nebulizers and metered dose inhalers are advantageous in respiratory emergencies because they deliver their medication to the exact site of action.
    A. True
    B. False

22. Endotracheal medication administration calls for drugs to be diluted to what volume?
    A. 1 mL
    B. 2 mL
    C. 3 mL
    D. 5 mL
    E. 10 mL

23. Which of the following drugs is NOT administered via the endotracheal route?
    A. meperidine
    B. naloxone
    C. atropine
    D. lidocaine
    E. epinephrine

24. Enteral medications are absorbed through the:
    A. liver.
    B. gastrointestinal tract.
    C. mucous membranes.
    D. portal system.
    E. accessory organs.

25. Liver function is an important factor in the effectiveness of enteral drug administration.
    A. True
    B. False

26. When using a medicine cup to measure an oral dose of medication, you should use what aspect of fluid level to determine the fluid volume?
    A. the highest point of the meniscus
    B. the lowest point of the meniscus
    C. between the high and low point of the meniscus
    D. one calibration below the lowest level of the meniscus
    E. none of the above

©2006 Pearson Education, Inc.
Paramedic Care: Principles & Practice, Vol. 1

_____ 27. The normal teaspoon holds about what volume of fluid?
A. 2 mL   D. 10 mL
B. 3 mL   E. 12 mL
C. 5 mL

_____ 28. The advantage of rectal administration over the other enteral drug routes is that:
A. the rectal route is easier to administer drugs through.
B. there is no hepatic alteration of the drug.
C. the rectal route can absorb more medication.
D. rectal irritation is rare.
E. all of the above

_____ 29. To inject a drug rectally you may use:
A. a large catheter with needle removed.
B. a special enema container with a rectal tip.
C. a small endotracheal tube attached to a syringe.
D. all of the above
E. none of the above

_____ 30. A syringe should be chosen for drug administration that is slightly smaller than the volume of drug to be administered.
A. True   B. False

_____ 31. The smaller the gauge of a hypodermic needle, the smaller the diameter of its lumen.
A. True   B. False

_____ 32. What is the total dose of a drug contained in an ampule with 5 mL of a drug in a 0.3 mg/mL concentration?
A. 0.3 mg   D. 15 mg
B. 1.5 mg   E. none of the above
C. 5 mg

_____ 33. Which of the following drug containers may contain multiple doses of a drug?
A. vial   D. preloaded syringe
B. ampule   E. medicated solutions
C. Mix-o-Vial

_____ 34. Prior to drawing medication from a vial, you must first inject an equal volume of air into the vial.
A. True   B. False

_____ 35. Which of the following must be cleansed with an alcohol swab before the drug is withdrawn?
A. vial   D. preloaded syringe
B. ampule   E. A and C
C. Mix-o-Vial

_____ 36. The drug route that calls for insertion of the needle at 10 to 15 degrees is:
A. intradermal.   D. intraosseous.
B. subcutaneous.   E. none of the above
C. intramuscular.

_____ 37. Which of the following is most likely to be an acceptable site for subcutaneous injection?
A. forearms   D. buttocks
B. calves   E. all of the above are acceptable
C. abdomen

_____ 38. Through which of the following routes should you inject no more than 1 mL of a drug?
A. intradermal   D. A and B
B. subcutaneous   E. all of the above
C. intramuscular

_____ 39. For intradermal and subcutaneous injections, the needle is inserted with the bevel down.
  A. True   B. False

_____ 40. At which of the following intramuscular injection sites should you administer a maximum of 2 mL of a drug?
  A. deltoid   D. rectus femoris
  B. gluteal   E. both B and C
  C. vastus lateralis

_____ 41. When you pull back on the syringe plunger during subcutaneous or intramuscular injection and blood appears, you should:
  A. inject the drug.
  B. inject the drug followed by a small bubble of air.
  C. insert the needle 1 cm further.
  D. attempt the injection at another site.
  E. consider the appearance of blood insignificant.

_____ 42. The drug route that calls for use of a 21- to 23-gauge needle is:
  A. intradermal.   D. intraosseous.
  B. subcutaneous.   E. none of the above
  C. intramuscular.

_____ 43. The drug route that calls for use of a needle ⅜ to 1 inch long is:
  A. intradermal.   D. all of the above
  B. subcutaneous.   E. none of the above
  C. intramuscular.

_____ 44. The recommended angle of insertion for the needle when administering an intramuscular injection is:
  A. 10 degrees.   D. 90 degrees.
  B. 15 degrees.   E. between 10 and 15 degrees.
  C. 45 degrees.

_____ 45. After injecting an intramuscular drug, massaging the site is contraindicated because it will slow absorption.
  A. True   B. False

Part 2: Intravenous Access, Blood Sampling, and Intrasseous Infusion, begins on p. 407

Review of Chapter Objectives

After reading this part of the chapter, you should be able to:

1. **Review the specific anatomy and physiology pertinent to medication administration.**   pp. 407–449

   Various veins are found close to the surface of the skin and are relatively easy to locate because of their prominence, color, and/or feel. Common vessels used for peripheral venipuncture include those of the back of the hand, those of the arms, the vein of the antecubital fossa, and those of the feet and legs. An additional large vein available for catheter insertion is the external jugular vein on the lateral neck. The more distal veins should be used, when possible, as using a vein generally limits the use of veins distal to the site. Large veins must be used for blood administration, in the administration of some drugs, and in cases in which large volumes of drugs must be administered.

Central veins are not usually used in the prehospital setting because of the time needed to initiate the access, the difficulty in determining proper placement, and the incidence of complications.

Intraosseous infusion directs the flow of fluid or a drug into the medullary space of a long bone, where it is available to the venous circulation. The tibia is the most frequent location of cannulation, with the proximal anterior and medial tibia just below the tibial tuberosity used for pediatric patients and the distal tibia just above the medial malleolus and just medial to the tibial crest for adults. A special needle is inserted through the compact bone and into the medullary space.

2. Describe the indications, equipment needed, technique used, precautions, and general principles for the following:

a. Peripheral venous or external jugular cannulation. pp. 407–437

Peripheral venous access is the preferable route for medication administration in the emergency prehospital setting. Most emergency drugs are administered this way because it provides a direct route into the venous system, then to the heart, where the drug and blood are further mixed, and then to the body as distributed by the arterial system. Vascular access can be obtained using a steel needle with a beveled sharp edge. Most commonly, an over-the-needle catheter is advanced into the vein, with the needle then withdrawn, leaving the catheter to permit introduction of drugs or fluid or withdrawal of blood for diagnostic testing. The veins of the hands, arms, antecubital fossa, feet, and legs and the external jugular veins are common sites for intravenous cannulation.

The equipment used for intravenous therapy includes a venous constricting band to help engorge the veins; the needle for venipuncture; an antiseptic to cleanse the site; administration tubing to direct and control fluid administration from an IV bag or a syringe to draw up, then administer medication; tape or commercial devices to secure the intravenous catheter; and bacteriostatic ointment to protect the site from infection. An ideal location for venipuncture is free of injury and with relatively prominent veins. The caregiver should take appropriate body substance isolation measures before beginning the procedure. Then the venous constricting band is secured just proximal to the selected site and a vein is chosen. The area is cleansed with an alcohol or povidone-iodine swab, using concentric circles moving outward from the selected site. An over-the-needle catheter is selected, with 14- to 18-gauge for blood, thick medications such as glucose, or fluid volume administration or a 20- to 22-gauge catheter for pediatric or geriatric patients or patients who do not need a larger catheter. The catheter is directed, bevel up, through the skin at an angle of 10° to 30° until a "pop" is felt or blood appears in the flash chamber. Once in the vein, the catheter is advanced an additional 0.5 cm and then the catheter is threaded into the vein. The needle is withdrawn, the constricting band is released, and the administration set or saline or heparin lock is attached. A small amount of fluid is run to ensure that the catheter is patent. Watch for edema around the site, which is suggestive of infiltration. Intravenous cannulation and infusion may result in local pain, infiltration, pyrogenic reactions, allergic reactions, catheter shear and embolism, inadvertent arterial puncture, circulatory overload, thrombophlebitis, thrombus formation, air embolism, and necrosis.

Fluid is infused through a venipuncture site to hydrate the patient or to keep the drug route open and quickly available. Most prehospital infusions use isotonic (same osmotic pressure as the plasma) solutions such as normal saline, 5 percent dextrose in water, or lactated Ringer's solution. These solutions flow through the administration set, where their rate of administration is regulated by adjusting the drip rate in a chamber. Most commonly 10 (macro) or 60 (micro) drops traveling through a drip chamber equal 1 mL. The administration set contains one or more injection ports to accommodate the administration of drugs or additional fluid administration. A special type of administration set is the measured volume administration set, which contains a calibrated chamber that will permit the discrete administration of a volume of fluid.

The external jugular vein is an alternative venous access site located on the lateral anterior neck. It is a large, easily found vein that permits venous access when other veins are collapsed due to hypovolemia or other vascular problems. It is close to the central circulation, so it provides almost immediate absorption of any drugs administered through it. The jugular vein can be engorged by placing digital pressure along the vein just above the clavical. External jugular cannulation is painful and risks damage to the airway or arterial structures in the neck.

b. Intraosseous needle placement and infusion. pp. 441–449

Intraosseous needle placement is indicated for the critical pediatric patient under five years of age when you cannot establish other IV access sites or for the adult patient when you also cannot perform peripheral venous access because of disease or extreme hypovolemia. A special needle is introduced through the compact bone of the tibia and into the medullary space. There fluids or drugs are readily available for absorption and distribution by the venous system.

In the child, the needle is placed at 90° to the tibial plateau, just medial and about two finger widths below the tibial tuberosity (the anterior bump just below the patella). Don gloves and cleanse the site with an antiseptic swab. With a firm twisting motion, introduce the needle into the bone for a few centimeters until you feel a "pop" or reduced resistance. Remove the trocar, attach a syringe, and draw back on the syringe to aspirate bone marrow and blood. Rotate the plastic disk to engage the skin and secure the needle. Connect the IV fluid administration set and secure the needle with bulky dressings and tape. Adult or geriatric IO administration uses the flat tibial plate just two finger widths above the medial malleolus. IO infusion may result in bone fracture, infiltration, growth-plate damage, pulmonary embolism, and the problems associated with venous cannulation. This site is not very effective for extensive fluid resuscitation in the adult.

c. Obtaining a blood sample. pp. 437–441

Blood composition, the presence of toxins, and blood gas levels are important values to determine for learning what is wrong with a patient. Since emergency care may alter these figures, it is sometimes important to draw blood in the prehospital setting. Blood is withdrawn from a vein through either a needle or catheter and is either directly placed in special containers (blood tubes) or into a syringe for distribution into the blood tubes. A large vein must be used, because the withdrawal of blood may collapse smaller veins. A needled vacutainer is introduced into an engorged vein and blood tubes are introduced, one at a time. The vacuum withdraws blood from the vein and into the tubes, which are then manually agitated to mix the blood with an anticoagulant (all but the red-top tube). If a vacutainer is not available, 20 mL of blood may be drawn up in a syringe and distributed among the containers. It is important to fill the containers in order of red, blue, green, purple, and gray (as available), because they contain various anticoagulants and another order may cross-contaminate the blood.

Content Self-Evaluation

MULTIPLE CHOICE

_____ 1. Which of the following is an indication for intravenous administration?
  A. fluid replacement
  B. blood replacement
  C. drug administration
  D. need of blood for analysis
  E. all of the above

_____ 2. Both central venous and peripheral venous cannulation are common in prehospital care.
  A. True
  B. False

_____ 3. Which of the following is a likely site for intravenous cannulation?
  A. the hands
  B. the arms
  C. the legs
  D. the neck
  E. all of the above

_____ 4. Which of the following is NOT a central venous vessel?
  A. the internal jugular
  B. the subclavian
  C. the femoral
  D. the antecubital
  E. all of the above are central venous vessels

_____ 5. The solution that contains large proteins is a(n):
   A. colliod.
   B. crystalloid.
   C. isotonic.
   D. hypotonic.
   E. hypertonic.

_____ 6. The solution that contains an electrolyte concentration close to that of plasma is a(n):
   A. colliod.
   B. crystalloid.
   C. isotonic.
   D. hypotonic.
   E. hypertonic.

_____ 7. The solution that contains an electrolyte concentration greater than that of plasma is a(n):
   A. colliod.
   B. crystalloid.
   C. isotonic.
   D. hypotonic.
   E. hypertonic.

_____ 8. One example of a hypotonic solution is:
   A. normal saline.
   B. lactated Ringer's solution.
   C. plasmanate.
   D. 5 percent dextrose in water.
   E. dextran.

_____ 9. The most desirable replacement for blood lost during trauma is:
   A. normal saline.
   B. lactated Ringer's solution.
   C. plasmanate.
   D. 5 percent dextrose in water.
   E. none of the above

_____ 10. Which intravenous fluid bag would you discard?
   A. one that is cloudy
   B. one that is discolored
   C. one that is leaking
   D. one that is expired
   E. all of the above

_____ 11. For optimal fluid delivery, the drip chamber should be how full?
   A. $\frac{1}{4}$
   B. $\frac{3}{8}$
   C. $\frac{1}{2}$
   D. $\frac{2}{3}$
   E. none of the above

_____ 12. The administration set most appropriate for administration of intravenous solutions for fluid replacement is the:
   A. macrodrip administration set.
   B. microdrip administration set.
   C. measured volume administration set.
   D. blood tubing set.
   E. none of the above

_____ 13. The most common microdrip setting equaling 1 mL is:
   A. 10 gtt.
   B. 20 gtt.
   C. 45 gtt.
   D. 60 gtt.
   E. none of the above

_____ 14. The administration set most appropriate for administration of a very specific volume of intravenous solution or drug is the:
   A. macrodrip administration set.
   B. microdrip administration set.
   C. measured volume administration set.
   D. blood tubing set.
   E. none of the above

_____ 15. The major difference between blood tubing and a standard intravenous administration set is that blood tubing has a filter to remove clots and particulate matter.
   A. True
   B. False

_____ 16. Blood is not administered with fluids like lactated Ringer's solution because such solutions increase blood's potential for coagulation.
   A. True
   B. False

_____ 17. Many patients are prone to develop hypothermia during fluid administration.
   A. True   B. False

_____ 18. The most common intravenous cannula used in the prehospital setting is the:
   A. over-the-needle.   D. angiocatheter.
   B. through-the-needle.   E. A and D
   C. hollow needle.

_____ 19. A needle gauge of 18 is smaller than a needle gauge of 22.
   A. True   B. False

_____ 20. A venous constricting band should be left in place no longer than:
   A. 1 minute.   D. 5 minutes.
   B. 2 minutes.   E. 10 minutes.
   C. 3 minutes.

_____ 21. Leaving the constricting band on for too long is likely to cause:
   A. collapse of the vein.
   B. damage to the distal blood vessels.
   C. damage to the vessels under the band.
   D. changes in the distal venous blood.
   E. all of the above

_____ 22. When cleansing the site for intravenous cannulation, you should make one swipe over
   the intended site with a povidone-iodine or alcohol swab.
   A. True   B. False

_____ 23. The angle of insertion for intravenous cannulation is:
   A. 10 degrees.   D. 60 degrees.
   B. 10 to 30 degrees.   E. 60 to 90 degrees.
   C. 45 degrees.

_____ 24. After you feel the "pop" associated with intravenous cannulation, you should:
   A. advance the catheter.
   B. advance the needle 0.5 cm, then advance the catheter.
   C. advance the needle 1 cm, then advance the catheter.
   D. advance the needle 2 cm, then advance the catheter.
   E. withdraw the needle, then advance the catheter.

_____ 25. You should consider using the external jugular vein as an IV access site only after you
   have exhausted other means of peripheral access or when the patient needs immediate
   fluid administration.
   A. True   B. False

_____ 26. During external jugular vein cannulation, the patient's head should be:
   A. moved to the sniffing position.
   B. turned toward the side of access.
   C. turned away from the side of access.
   D. hyperextended.
   E. hyperflexed.

_____ 27. To fill the jugular access site and make the vessel easier to both locate and cannulate,
   you should:
   A. apply a venous constricting band, tightly.
   B. apply a venous constricting band, loosely.
   C. occlude the vein gently with a finger.
   D. perform the procedure without occluding the vein.
   E. have the patient take a deep breath and hold it.

_____ 28. When establishing an IV with blood tubing, you must be careful to:
   A. fill the drip chamber ⅓ full.
   B. completely cover the blood filter with blood.
   C. fill the set with normal saline first.
   D. fill the drip chamber ¾ full.
   E. both A and B above

_____ 29. Which of the following is a factor that may affect intravenous flow rates?
   A. failure to remove a venous constricting band
   B. edema at the access site
   C. the cannula tip up against a vein valve
   D. a clogged catheter
   E. all of the above

_____ 30. The complication of peripheral venous access in which a plastic embolus can form is:
   A. pyrogenic reaction.   D. catheter shear.
   B. pain.   E. all of the above
   C. thrombophlebitis.

_____ 31. The most common cause of catheter shear is:
   A. cannulating thick veins.
   B. cannulating underneath the constricting band.
   C. withdrawing the needle from within the catheter.
   D. withdrawing the catheter from the needle.
   E. faulty catheter construction.

_____ 32. If a blood clot appears to stop or slow intravenous fluid flow, forcefully inject a small amount of heparin into the catheter and continue the infusion.
   A. True   B. False

_____ 33. You should change a large (500- to 1,000-mL) infusion bag when the volume remaining in the bag is:
   A. 10 mL.   D. 50 mL.
   B. 20 mL.   E. 100 mL.
   C. 30 mL.

_____ 34. If air becomes entrained in the administration set when you are changing an IV bag or bottle, you should:
   A. continue the infusion, because the volume of air is negligible.
   B. discard the set and use a new one.
   C. use a syringe placed between the bubbles and patient to withdraw the air.
   D. reverse the fluid flow until the bubbles enter the fluid bag or drip chamber.
   E. squeeze the tubing to push them into the drip chamber or bag.

_____ 35. Never administer an intravenous drug infusion as the primary IV line.
   A. True   B. False

_____ 36. Which of the following is NOT true regarding infusion pumps?
   A. They deliver fluids under pressure.
   B. They are large and difficult to carry.
   C. Most pumps contain alarms for occlusion.
   D. Most pumps contain alarms for fluid source depletion.
   E. They deliver fluids at precise rates.

_____ 37. The reason venous blood sampling is important in the prehospital setting is that our interventions may alter the blood's composition or erase important information about it.
   A. True   B. False

_____ 38. The color of the blood tube container that must be drawn first is:
   A. blue.   D. purple.
   B. red.   E. gray.
   C. green.

_____ 39. Drawing blood and injecting it into the blood tubes in the wrong order may result in:
   A. leaving the wrong volume of blood in a tube.
   B. cross-contamination of the blood with anticoagulants.
   C. depletion of the vacuum in the tubes at too early a stage.
   D. coagulation in the last tubes to be filled.
   E. all but C

_____ 40. Do not use a blood tube after its expiration date because the anticoagulant and vacuum may have become ineffective.
   A. True   B. False

_____ 41. The device that accepts the blood tube to permit its filling is:
   A. the Luer Lot.   D. the Luer-sampling needle.
   B. the Huber needle.   E. either A or C
   C. the vacutainer.

_____ 42. You should fill the blood tube to between a third and a half of its volume because the anticoagulant is measured for this amount of blood.
   A. True   B. False

_____ 43. When using a syringe to fill your blood tubes, you should draw a volume of blood of about:
   A. 5 mL.   D. 35 mL.
   B. 10 mL.   E. 50 mL.
   C. 20 mL.

_____ 44. The complication from drawing blood in which red blood cells are destroyed is:
   A. hematocrit.   D. hemotypsis.
   B. hemoconcentration.   E. hematuria.
   C. hemolysis.

_____ 45. Hemoconcentration occurs during drawing blood:
   A. when the constricting band is left in place too long.
   B. when blood is drawn back through a needle that is too small.
   C. with premature mixing of the anticoagulant.
   D. with too vigorous a mixing of the blood and anticoagulant.
   E. with too forceful an aspiration of blood into the syringe.

_____ 46. When an IV catheter is withdrawn, place pressure on the venipuncture site with a sterile gauze pad for about five minutes.
   A. True   B. False

_____ 47. The intraosseous site of infusion is most commonly used for which category of patient?
   A. geriatric patients   D. patients with nonskeletal injuries
   B. cardiac patients   E. all of the above
   C. children under five years of age

_____ 48. The proper site for intraosseous needle placement in the child is one to two finger widths:
   A. below and medial to the tibial tuberosity.
   B. below and lateral to the tibial tuberosity.
   C. above the medial malleolus.
   D. above the lateral malleolus.
   E. above and lateral to the tibial crest.

©2006 Pearson Education, Inc.
Paramedic Care: Principles & Practice, Vol. 1

_____ 49. Confirmation that you are in the medullary space is achieved by:
   A. feeling the bone "pop."
   B. pushing the needle 2 to 4 mm.
   C. aspirating bone marrow and blood.
   D. feeling resistance to the twisting of insertion.
   E. none of the above

_____ 50. Complications of intraosseous cannulation include all of the following EXCEPT:
   A. pulmonary embolism.
   B. fracture.
   C. growth plate damage.
   D. aspiration of bone marrow.
   E. complete insertion.

Special Project

Medication Administration: Personal Benchmarking

To administer medications to the patient experiencing a trauma or medical emergency, you must be familiar with the subcutaneous, intramuscular, and intravenous administration sites located around the body. By locating these various sites on your own body, you can become accustomed to the texture and feel of the various sites used for administration of medications and fluids. This personal benchmarking can help you identify these locations as you begin to treat patients.

Subcutaneous Injection Sites: Medications such as epinephrine are injected subcutaneously because of the slow, steady, and dependable absorption associated with that method. The hypodermic needle is inserted into a "pinch" of skin located on the proximal arm, lateral thigh, and, in some cases, the abdomen (as shown in the illustration on page 401 of the textbook). Examine each of these areas on yourself or a friend and locate possible administration sites where you can easily pinch the skin and feel it separate from the muscular tissue below. Inspect the tissue to ensure it is free of superficial blood vessels, nerves, and tendons, and avoid areas of bruising, scar tissue, or tattoos.

Intramuscular Injection Sites: Medications such as glucagon and morphine are administered into the muscular tissue because it has both the ability to accept a relatively large (2 to more than 5 mL) amount of the drug and a moderate and predictable absorption rate. A hypodermic needle is inserted directly (at an angle of 90° to the skin surface) through the skin and subcutaneous tissue and into the muscle mass directly beneath. Muscle masses for IM medication administration are chosen carefully to reduce the risk of injecting the drug into a blood vessel or nerve. Common IM sites include the deltoid muscle, the dorsal gluteal muscle, the vastus lateralis muscle and the rectus femoris muscle. These muscle locations are diagrammed on page 404 of your textbook. Palpate each muscle on yourself and a friend to identify the proper locations for IM needle insertions and medication administration. You should be able to feel the firm muscle mass as pictured on page 404 and locate the safe regions to inject medications. Avoid areas of scar tissue and bruises and try to select ones that are free of superficial blood vessels.

Intravenous Injection Sites: Most medications during prehospital care are administered through the intravenous route. This route allows rapid introduction of a drug into the bloodstream, where it is mixed with blood and then distributed throughout the body. The most common venipuncture sites include the veins of the back of the hand, the arm, the antecubital fossa, and the legs and the external jugular vein (see page 408 of the textbook). It is preferable to initiate an IV cannulation with the smallest vein needed at the most distal site, because infiltration or blood vessel injury limits the usefulness of the vein distal to the injury. Obtain a venous constricting band and place it just proximal to the area you will examine for veins. Wait a few seconds until the veins engorge with blood and become more prominent. Then look at the skin below the band for a prominent bump along the course of the vein and a possible bluish discoloration due to the accumulation of blood. Palpate the vessel and appreciate the spongy feel of the blood-filled tube. As you collapse the vessel with your finger pressure, you should feel it compress easily and form a hollow depression beneath your finger. Close your eyes and palpate a region, trying to locate veins by touch. In many patients you will not see the prominence of veins and may only have the characteristic feel of the skin's surface to go by. Palpate the antecubital fossa to locate the antecubital vein. Note that it is rather central in the fold of the elbow and has the spongy feel. This vessel may be the only one you can locate on the patient with severe hypovolemia.

Stand in front of a mirror and look for the external jugular vein. Turn your head to the side and place digital pressure on the jugular vein just above the clavicle. The vein should initially be collapsed and difficult to see in a standing patient, but occluding the vein should cause it to rapidly engorge and become prominent. Notice the course the vein takes as it travels down from the angle of the jaw to the clavicle.

Intraosseous Injection Sites: When other injection sites are unavailable in pediatric, geriatric, and adult patients, an alternative site is the tibia (intraosseous). This site has the advantages of permitting the injection of any intravenous drug or fluid and of being easily located when the patient is otherwise in vascular collapse and the veins are very difficult to find. It is only used when another intravenous site cannot be established. Two sites are used, the proximal site for the pediatric patient and the distal site for the adult or geriatric patient (see pages 441–443 of the textbook). Locate the proximal site by identifying the prominent bump at the top of the tibia (the tibial tuberosity) and then locating the flat surface one to two finger widths below and medial to it. Locate the distal site by locating the medial malleolus (the medial prominence of the ankle) and then the flat surface one to two finger widths above and anterior to it (medial to the anterior tibial crest).

Part 3: Medical Mathematics, begins on p. 449

Review of Chapter Objectives

After reading this part of the chapter, you should be able to:

1. **Review mathematical equivalents.**   **pp. 449–452**

The basic units used for most of medicine are metric: the gram for weight, the liter for volume, and the meter for distance. The metric system is a decimal system that uses suffixes and prefixes to delineate larger and smaller quantities, most commonly kilo (1,000), milli (1/1,000), and micro (1/1,000,000). Pharmacology math involves working with addition, subtraction, multiplication, and division, as well as working extensively with ratios, fractions, and formulas.

2. **Differentiate temperature readings between the centigrade and Fahrenheit scales.**   **pp. 451–452**

The centigrade (officially known as Celsius) scale graduates the temperature between the point at which ice melts and the point at which water boils into 100°. The Fahrenheit scale graduates the range between the lowest temperature at which a salt-water mixture would remain a liquid (0°) and the boiling point of water into 212°. The Celsius scale is used in medicine, and the conversion between the two is demonstrated by the formulas below.

$$°F = 9/5 \ °C + 32 \qquad °C = 5/9 \ (°F - 32)$$

3. **Discuss formulas as a basis for performing drug calculations.** pp. 452–458

The major formula for determining the amount of a drug to be administered is as follows:

$$Dh = \frac{Vh \times Dd}{Va}$$

The formula is mathematically manipulated so that the unknown element can be computed using the known values.

Other elements of drug calculation call for determining the volume flowing through an intravenous administration set by monitoring the number of drops falling in a drip chamber per minute. Conversion is based upon the number of drops that equal one milliliter of fluid.

$$\text{Dose on hand} = \frac{\text{Volume on hand} \times \text{Desired dose}}{\text{Volume to be administered}}$$

You may also be required to convert pounds to kilograms (if the patient dosing is in weight of drug per kilogram of body weight). To do this you should know that:

$$1 \text{ pound} = 2.2 \text{ kilograms}$$

In some cases, it is important to administer a volume of medication over time, and the associated formula for such administration is:

$$\text{Drops/Minute} = \frac{\text{Volume to be administered} \times \text{Drip factor}}{\text{Time in minutes}}$$

4. **Describe how to perform mathematical conversions from the household system to the metric system.** pp. 451–452

Weight. Weight conversion between household and metric measures is accomplished by dividing a weight in pounds by 2.2 to find the equivalent metric weight in kilograms. Conversely, if you know a weight in kilograms, multiply it by 2.2 to get the weight in pounds

$$kg = lb/2.2 \qquad lb = kg \times 2.2$$

Volume. Volume conversion between household and metric measures is based on the recognition that 1 quart is about equal to 1 liter, 1 cup to 250 milliliters, and so on.

Special Project

Pharmacology (Drip and Drug) Math

Guide to Easier Drug Calculations

Although there might be more rapid systems to calculate drip rates and concentrations, the following stepwise approach is designed to help you understand the math so you are able to solve almost any problem. While math is an essential skill for the paramedic, most drip calculations are simple, standard, and easy to perform once you become familiar with the drugs and drip rates used in your system.

Step I.: Identify all known elements.

Elements for most drug dose calculations:

C = Concentration (g, mg, or mcg per mL)
Dd = Desired dose
Va = Volume to be administered
Dh = Weight (Dose on hand) (g, mg, or mcg)
Vh = Volume on hand (convert to mL)

Elements for most drip calculations:

> R = Rate (either in gtt/min, gtt/mcg, or mL/min)
> V = Volume (convert to mL)
> T = Time (convert to minutes)
> D = Drip conversion (gtt per mL)

Step II.: Select the proper formula.

The element that you don't know (and need to find) should be equal to the remainder of the formula.

Concentration = Dose on hand/Volume on hand $\qquad$ C = Dh/Vh
Dose on hand = Volume on hand × Concentration $\qquad$ Dh = Vh × C
Volume on hand = Dose on hand/Concentration $\qquad$ Vh = Dh/C

$$\text{Volume to be administered} = \frac{\text{Volume on hand} \times \text{Desired dose}}{\text{Dosage on hand}} \qquad Va = \frac{Vh \times Dd}{Dh}$$

$$\text{Dose on hand} = \frac{\text{Volume on hand} \times \text{Desired dose}}{\text{Volume to be administered}} \qquad Dh = \frac{Vh \times Dd}{Va}$$

$$\text{Desired dose} = \frac{\text{Volume to be administered} \times \text{Dosage on hand}}{\text{Volume on hand}} \qquad Dd = \frac{Va \times Dh}{Vh}$$

$$\text{Volume on hand} = \frac{\text{Volume to be administered} \times \text{Dosage on hand}}{\text{Desired dose}} \qquad Vh = \frac{Va \times Dh}{Dd}$$

Rate = Volume/Time (R = V/T)
Volume = Rate × Time (V = R × T)
Time = Volume/Rate (T = V/R)

Step III.: Convert all variables into common terms.

Use the drip conversion figure or other conversion formula to convert all values to metric and standard values.

> Rate—into milliliters or milligrams/minute
> Volume—into milliliters
> Concentration—into milligrams/milliliter
> Time—into minutes
> Weight—into milligrams

Step IV.: Plug in the known values.

Complete the formula, inserting the values identified in Step I.

Step V.: Cancel out labels.

Cross multiply labels to cancel them out. The result should leave you with the label in terms of the unknown value.

$$??? \text{ Volume} = \frac{\text{Rate} \times \text{Time}}{\text{min}} = \frac{X \text{ mL} \times Y \text{ min}}{\text{min}} = X \text{ mL} \times Y = X \times Y \text{ mL}$$

Step VI.: Do the mathematical operations.

Multiply, divide, add, or subtract as necessary.

$$3 \times 7 = 21 \qquad 3/7 = 0.43 \qquad 7 + 3 = 10 \qquad 7 - 3 = 4$$

Step VII.: Apply any needed conversions.

Use the mathematical conversions needed, such as the drip conversion, to give you the final answer. Ensure that your answer is provided in the form and label the question asks for.

$$\frac{X \text{ mL/min}}{\min} \text{ using a } \frac{Y \text{ gtt/mL}}{\text{mL}} = X \text{ mL} \times \text{gtt} = \frac{X \times Y \text{ gtt}}{\min} = X \times Y \text{ gtt/min}$$

There are two particular types of math used in prehospital care. One deals with continuous intravenous infusions (drip math) and the other deals with parenteral bolus or enteral administration (drug math). Included within this and the following workbooks are exercises for drip and drug math.

Drip Math Worksheet I

Formulas

Rate = Volume/Time	mL/min = gtt per min/gtt per mL
Volume = Rate × Time	gtt/min = mL per min × gtt per mL
Time = Volume/Rate	mL = gtt/gtt per mL

Please complete the following drip math problems.

1. You are running a D_5W drip (60 gtt/mL) into a patient at 15 gtt/min. During a 25-minute trip to the hospital, how much fluid would you infuse?

2. Medical Control requests that you infuse 250 mL of a solution during a 1-hour transport. What rate do you need to set:

    A. for a 60 gtt/mL infusion set?

    B. for a 10 gtt/mL infusion set?

3. If a 50 mL bag of normal saline is hung and running through a 45 gtt/mL administration set at 32 drops per minute, how long will the fluid last?

4. If you are running a macro drip (10 gtt/mL) at 4 drops per second, how much fluid could you infuse in 45 minutes?

5. Medical control orders you to infuse 1.5 mL of a solution every minute. What drip rate would you set:

    A. with a 60 gtt/mL set?

    B. with a 45 gtt/mL set?

    C. with a 10 gtt/mL set?

Drug Math Worksheet I

Formulas

Concentration = Dose on hand/Volume on hand	C = Dh/Vh
Dose on hand = Volume on hand × Concentration	Dh = Vh × C
Volume on hand = Dose on hand/Concentration	Vh = Dh/C
Volume to be administered = $\dfrac{\text{Volume on hand} \times \text{Desired dose}}{\text{Dose on hand}}$	$Va = \dfrac{Vh \times Dd}{Dh}$

$$\text{Dose on hand} = \frac{\text{Volume on hand} \times \text{Desired dose}}{\text{Volume to be administered}} \qquad Dh = \frac{Vh \times Dd}{Va}$$

$$\text{Desired dose} = \frac{\text{Volume to be administered} \times \text{Dose on hand}}{\text{Volume on hand}} \qquad Dd = \frac{Va \times Dh}{Vh}$$

$$\text{Volume on hand} = \frac{\text{Volume to be administered} \times \text{Dose on hand}}{\text{Desired dose}} \qquad Vh = \frac{Va \times Dh}{Dd}$$

$$1 \text{ kg} = 2.2 \text{ lb} \quad 1 \text{ g} = 1{,}000 \text{ mg} \quad 1 \text{ mg} = 1{,}000 \text{ mcg}$$

Please complete the following drug math problems.

1. What volume of atropine, provided as 1 mg in 5 mL, would you administer to provide 0.5 mg of drug to the patient?

2. The medical direction physician asks you to administer 40 mg of furosemide to a patient. It comes in an ampule with 80 mg in 4 mL. What volume will you administer?

3. What volume of epinephrine would you administer to provide a patient with 1 mg of the drug:

   A. if provided as a 1:1,000 solution? (1 g/1,000 mL)

   B. if provided as a 1:10,000 solution? (1 g/10,000 mL)

4. Protocol calls for the administration of 0.2 mg/kg of adenosine for a pediatric patient. Your patient weighs 6 kilograms, and the drug is supplied in a vial with 6 mg in 2 mL. What volume would you administer to your patient?

11

Therapeutic Communications

Review of Chapter Objectives

After reading this chapter, you should be able to:

1. Define communication. p. 446

Communication is the exchange of information through the use of common symbols—written, spoken, or of other kinds. The basic elements of communication include a sender, an encoded message, a receiver, and feedback. The sender encodes a written, spoken, signed, or other message to the receiver. The receiver decodes the message to derive his interpretation of the content. He then provides feedback to the sender. If, because of the feedback, the sender believes the communication was accurately received, the communication was successful.

2. Identify internal and external factors that affect a patient/bystander interview. pp. 466–467

There are several reasons why communications can be ineffective or fail. They include prejudice, lack of empathy or understanding, lack of (or a perceived invasion of) privacy, or internal or external distractions. If the sender, receiver, or both are subject to these influences, the communication is likely to be ineffective. On the other hand, trust and rapport between sender and receiver can facilitate communication.

3. Identify the strategies for developing rapport with the patient. pp. 467–468, 473–474

Developing rapport with a patient is dependent upon truly feeling empathy for the patient and observing several principles of good interpersonal communication. Use your patient's name frequently with the proper form of address (Mr., Ms., or Mrs.). Use a professional but compassionate tone of voice and explain what you are doing and why, and be honest about what is happening. Keep a kind, calming, and caring facial expression, use the appropriate style of communication, and listen carefully to what your patient says.

Using the following techniques can provide feedback to your interviewee and thus help develop rapport:

- **Silence** gives your patient time to gather his thoughts and complete his answer.
- **Reflection**, your echoing of the patient's response, assures you understand the interviewee's answer.
- **Facilitation** encourages the patient to make further responses.
- **Empathy** is using your body language and your speech to assure the patient you are interested and concerned.
- **Clarification** involves asking the interviewee to explain answers you don't understand.

- **Confrontation** is a technique in which you ask direct questions about confusing or contradictory statements by the patient.
- **Interpretation** is a statement of your understanding of the events and circumstances of which the interviewee has offered an explanation.
- **Explanation** is a technique in which you share objective information you gather with the interviewee.
- **Summarization** is your brief review of all the pertinent information you have gathered from the interviewee.

4. **Provide examples of open-ended and closed, or direct, questions.** pp. 471–472

Open-ended questions provide the patient with the opportunity to respond to your question with an unguided, spontaneous answer. An example is "What happened to cause you to call for an ambulance?" or "Describe what you had for lunch." Closed, or direct, questions guide the patient to an answer of yes or no or some other short response. The question does not allow for an explanation of the circumstances. Examples of closed or direct questions are "Do you have any chest pain?" and "Does it hurt to breathe?"

5. **Discuss common errors made when interviewing patients.** p. 474

Common errors associated with interviewing include providing false assurance, giving inappropriate advice, using authority inappropriately, using avoidance language, improperly distancing yourself from the interviewee, using professional jargon, talking instead of listening, interrupting the interviewee, and using questioning language that implies guilt (using "why" questions).

6. **Identify the nonverbal skills used in patient interviewing.** pp. 469–471

Distance. The distance at which you place yourself from the patient during the interview process is an important tool in making the patient comfortable and in defining your role as a caregiver. The closer you come to the patient, the more personal and intimate your conversation. However, unwanted entry into someone's personal space can be perceived as threatening.
Relative level. The relative difference between a caregiver's eye level and the patient's is important. When the caregiver's eye level is above the patient's, it reflects a state of authority; an eye level equal with the patient's indicates equality; while an eye level below the patient's indicates a willingness to let the patient have some control over the interview. Each position has advantages and disadvantages when interviewing the emergency patient.
Stance. A closed stance (arms crossed, fists clenched, and the body square to the patient) suggests disinterest, discomfort, fear, or anger. An open stance (open hands, relaxed muscles, and a nodding head) suggests comfort, interest, and confidence.
Eye contact. Eye contact with a patient suggests interest and an entry into the patient's personal space. It is a powerful communication tool and a way to convey the care giver's empathy with the patient.
Touching. Touching is also a way to communicate empathy and concern. Like eye contact, however, it can be threatening when not used in the right circumstances.

7. **Summarize methods used to assess mental status based on interview techniques.** pp. 472–473

By carefully watching the patient's body language and attending to his verbal and nonverbal responses to questioning, you can assess his level of responsiveness and his ability to concentrate. Be especially watchful of speech and how the patient phrases sentences and articulates. Also note how well he answers questions and the appropriateness of questions he asks.

8. **Discuss strategies for interviewing a patient who is not motivated to talk.** pp. 473, 474–475

Be sure the patient understands your questions and why you are asking them. Use the feedback techniques explained in objective 3. Take the time to develop rapport and trust with the patient and to communicate your empathy toward his situation. Ensure there is no language barrier and that you and the patient are isolated so that information given is confidential. Provide supportive feedback to encourage freer communication. If information is unavailable from the patient, ask family or bystanders to help provide it.

9. Differentiate strategies used when interviewing a patient who is hostile compared to one who is cooperative. pp. 473, 479

The uncooperative patient is one who simply does not want to help with, participate in, or permit your assessment or care for him. A hostile patient displays anger and may be a risk to you. Work carefully to establish rapport with each type, but recognize that the hostile patient may endanger you and your crew. Always maintain distance from the hostile patient and have an escape route ready should a threat of violence become an attempt.

10. Summarize the developmental considerations of various age-groups that influence patient interviewing. pp. 469, 472, 475–477

Your interviewing techniques must be flexible to accommodate the developmental considerations that influence patient assessment and care. Be patient, understanding, and empathetic and listen carefully to what the patient says. Adjust your interviewing technique, intensity, eye contact, eye level, touch, and stance to meet the needs of your patient. Be simple and straightforward with young children, and build a good rapport with their caregivers, because they are the ones the children look to for guidance. With age, children become more objective, realistic, trusting, and cooperative. With the elderly, show respect and appreciate the difficulties preexisting diseases and reduced hearing and eyesight can have on their ability to understand what is happening to them.

11. Define the unique interviewing techniques for patients with special needs. pp. 474–479

Patients with special needs include children, the elderly, patients with sensory impairments, and those with language or cultural considerations. Generally an empathetic and calm approach to any of these patients will be helpful, combined with special strategies for each group.

Children. Effective interviewing techniques depend on a child's age, as children grow quickly from infancy to childhood, to adolescence, and to adulthood. Begin by talking with and establishing a rapport with the child's caregivers (parents and family) and gradually approach the patient. Keep your eye level close to the child's and speak choosing your words carefully so the patient can understand and is not threatened. Explain what you are doing and why, being honest and truthful. Build trust and use a toy to distract younger children from their symptoms and your intrusion into their personal space.

Elderly patients. The elderly require respect, the proper form of address, slower explanations, and patience. Take along their living assists—eyeglasses, hearing aids, and so on—if you must transport them, and always respect their dignity.

Sensory impaired. Sensory impairments can make communication more difficult and requires careful explanations of what is going to happen to the patient and why. Guide the sightless patient with an arm, and provide written or signed communication for the hearing impaired. If the patient can lip read, ensure your face is illuminated and facing directly toward him when you speak.

Language and cultural barriers. Language and cultural barriers are obstacles to effective communication that can be overcome only with patience and compassion. Do not judge a patient's values or try to impose yours on him. Use an interpreter (family member or sibling) and phrase questions and statements carefully, addressing both the patient and interpreter. Recognize that eye contact and personal distances may mean different things in different cultures. Respect cultural folk medicines and beliefs.

12. Discuss interviewing considerations used in cross-cultural communications. pp. 477–479

When interviewing across cultures, be patient, understanding, and empathetic. Understand the differences in how the culture perceives eye contact and personal distances and resist making judgements due to stereotyping. Respect folk medicine practices and beliefs.

13. Given several preprogrammed simulated patients, provide a patient interview using therapeutic communications. pp. 466–479

During every day of your career as a paramedic, you will attend patients and their families to determine what is wrong with the patient and then to provide care. These encounters will, from time to time, be with patients who do not trust you, do not understand you, are threatened by you, are frightened by you, or do not understand what is happening to them. They present a challenge to good communication that you must overcome to extract information from them and begin your care. The impression you leave with these patients is the impression they will carry of the emergency medical service system until they again call on the system for assistance. During your classroom, practical, and clinical experience, work to develop your interviewing skills, especially with troublesome patients, so you present a good image to the people who use our services.

Case Study Review

Reread the case study on pages 465 and 466 in Paramedic Care: Introduction to Advanced Prehospital Care *and then read the following discussion.*

The case study in this chapter describes the impact that caregivers can have, both good and bad, on other caregivers, patients, and families. Though this case is described by a paramedic student, it clearly demonstrates the different ways emergency caregivers can influence patients and families.

What will the result of the actions of the first paramedic team be? Will this patient be less likely to complain about "indigestion" to her family? Will this patient's family discourage calls for EMS when she again reports a burning sensation in his chest? The answer to both questions is likely to be "yes." An incident like this may undo years of community education efforts to encourage the public to call the ambulance early when people in the community experience chest pain. If this family does call for help again, what will they expect? Will they expect empathetic caregivers or arrogant intruders? Will the patient freely communicate his signs and symptoms or be resistant because of previous ridicule? The answers to these questions tell the real impact of an inappropriate attitude toward the people who call for emergency medical service. How would you like to be the next paramedic to treat this patient or a family member?

On the other hand, the two paramedics (and First Responders) from the second call treated the patient and family much differently and left them with a very different impression of the team who cared for them and the EMS system in general. If there is a need to call for assistance again, the patient and family who were a part of the second call will not be likely to hesitate. They will expect to be treated well, and they will have confidence in those who arrive. They will probably relate their signs and symptoms freely and be cooperative with patient care. How would you like to be the next paramedic to treat this patient and his family?

What makes the difference between the paramedic teams on these two calls? Is it that the first team does not know how to approach the patient and conduct appropriate patient and family communications? The answer is probably "no." It is more likely a failure to appreciate the importance of good patient interviewing and communications. It is an under-appreciation of the judgements made about us, and our systems, by the people we touch (both directly and indirectly). Do the members of the first team recognize that they are held in poor esteem by the student that rode with them? Probably not. This case study firmly demonstrates that the first step toward accomplishing good patient communication skills is having a sincere empathy and appreciation for the needs of the patient.

140 PARAMEDIC CARE *Introduction*

©2006 Pearson Education, Inc.
Paramedic Care: Principles & Practice, Vol. 1

Content Self-Evaluation

MULTIPLE CHOICE

_____ 1. Creating a message is also known as:
   A. alliterating.
   B. encoding.
   C. receiving.
   D. interpreting.
   E. drafting.

_____ 2. Empathy is the identification with and understanding of another's situation, feelings, and motives.
   A. True
   B. False

_____ 3. Which of the following represents an example of why EMS communications fail? communication?
   A. lack of empathy
   B. prejudice
   C. loud music
   D. thinking about family or the job
   E. all of the above

_____ 4. Which of the following is NOT one of the elements necessary for a paramedic to make a good first impression?
   A. clean, neat uniform
   B. arrogant demeanor
   C. interested and caring facial expression
   D. consideration for the patient
   E. good personal hygiene

_____ 5. Which of the following techniques is NOT considered to be a way to build patient trust and rapport?
   A. using your patient's name
   B. explaining what you are doing and why
   C. addressing your patient as "Honey" or "Sweetie"
   D. modulating your voice
   E. using an appropriate style of communication

_____ 6. The interpersonal zone that extends 4 to 12 feet from the patient is:
   A. the intimate zone.
   B. personal distance.
   C. social distance.
   D. public distance.
   E. none of the above

_____ 7. Which of a caregiver's eye levels imparts authority and may intimidate the patient?
   A. one higher than the patient's eye level
   B. one lower than the patient's eye level
   C. one on the same level with the patient's
   D. both A and B
   E. Both B and C

_____ 8. Closed questions direct the patient and elicit very specific responses; since this is not desired during an interview, these questions should be avoided at all costs.
   A. True
   B. False

_____ 9. The listening and feedback technique in which the interviewer encourages the speaker to provide more information is:
   A. summarization.
   B. explanation.
   C. reflection.
   D. clarification.
   E. facilitation.

_____ 10. Common errors made when interviewing patients include all of the following EXCEPT:
   A. using professional jargon.
   B. echoing back the patient's statements as part of the reflection technique.
   C. inappropriate distancing.
   D. inappropriate advice.
   E. providing false assurances.

_____ 11. Interrupting a patient to guide him to the information you need is both a useful tool in the interview process and a good listening skill.
   A. True   B. False

_____ 12. A difficult patient interview may stem from which of the following?
   A. a disease process   D. cultural differences
   B. fear   E. all of the above
   C. language differences

_____ 13. At which childhood development level is the patient most likely to be fearful, distrustful, and uncooperative?
   A. infant   D. school age
   B. toddler   E. adolescent
   C. preschooler

_____ 14. At which childhood development level does the patient consider modesty to be very important?
   A. infant   D. school age
   B. toddler   E. adolescent
   C. preschooler

_____ 15. The viewing of one's own life as more desirable or acceptable or best is:
   A. ethnicity.   D. cultural imposition.
   B. cultural diversity.   E. cultural arrogance.
   C. ethnocentrism.

©2006 Pearson Education, Inc.
Paramedic Care: Principles & Practice, Vol. 1

Life-Span Development

Review of Chapter Objectives

After reading this chapter, you should be able to:

1. **Compare and contrast the physiological and psychosocial characteristics of the following life-span development stages.**

Infant   pp. 484–489

Infancy is the period from birth to one year of age in which the vital signs are pulse rate 100 to 160, respiratory rate 30 to 60, systolic blood pressure 87 to 105, and body temperature of 98 to 100°F. The weight of the infant decreases immediately after birth and then increases, doubling birth weight after 4 to 6 months and tripling it after 9 to 12 months. Immediately after birth, the cardiovascular system changes dramatically from the maternal circulation, with the left ventricle increasing in strength throughout the first year. The infant airway is less stable than the adult's, and the infant is an obligate nasal breather and has delicate lung tissue that is prone to barotrauma. Acquired immunity from the mother somewhat protects the infant from six months up to about one year. The infant has well-developed reflexes including the startle (Moro), palmar grasp, rooting, and sucking reflexes, which usually disappear after the first few months. The infant's skull is not completely closed, and the openings (the fontanelles) may demonstrate dehydration when sunken. They close by 9 to 18 months.

Psychosocially, the infant develops based on instincts, drives, capacities, and interactions with the environment. Bonding occurs as the infant senses that his needs will be met by caregivers and develops attachments to family. The infant learns as caregivers gradually increase their expectations of the infant and child. In crisis, the infant will often follow a predictable sequence of responses: protest, despair, and withdrawal.

Toddler and preschooler   pp. 489–492

The toddler is a child from one to three years of age with vital signs normally of a pulse rate of 80 to 110, respirations at 24 to 40, systolic blood pressure at 95 to 105, and temperature of 96.8 to 99.6°F. The preschooler is between three and six years of age and has vital signs of a pulse rate of 70 to 110, respirations of 22 to 34, a systolic blood pressure between 95 and 110, and a body temperature of 96.8 to 99.6°F. The toddler and preschooler gain about 2 kg in body weight per year. Their cardiovascular systems are better developed, and thermoregulation is more efficient than in infants. The lungs are increasing in surface area, yet rapid respirations will tire the child quickly. Passive immunity is lost, and the toddler and preschooler become more susceptible to minor respiratory and gastrointestinal infections, though they now begin to develop their own immunities.

Psychosocially, the toddler and preschooler begin to use words and understand their meaning. By the age of three or four years they have mastered the basics of language. They begin to understand cause and effect, develop separation anxiety, and engage in play-acting and magical thinking. They become progressively more influenced by peers and television. Divorce may have an important impact on their psychosocial development, because they may feel abandoned or responsible.

School-age   p. 493

The school-aged child is between 6 and 13 years old and has vital signs of a pulse rate of 65 to 110, respirations of 18 to 30, systolic blood pressure of 97 to 112, and a body temperature of 98.6°F. As the vital signs continue to move toward normal adult values, the school-aged child grows at a rate of 6 cm and 3 kg per year. Brain function continues to increase, and primary teeth are replaced by permanent ones.

The school-aged child develops advanced decision-making skills and develops his own self-concept. Factors in this development include self-esteem, moral reasoning and judgment, and self-control.

Adolescent   pp. 494–495

The adolescent is between 13 and 19 years of age and has normal vital signs of a pulse rate of 60 to 90, respirations of 12 to 26, a systolic blood pressure of 112 to 128, and a body temperature of 98.6°F. The adolescent may experience a rapid growth spurt, with maximum growth occurring for the female by age 16 and by age 18 for the male. During this stage, children reach reproductive maturity. In females, the breasts enlarge and menstruation begins.

Adolescence is a time of great psychosocial change. The adolescent strives for autonomy, becomes interested in the opposite sex, and develops an individual identity. The development of logical, analytical, and abstract thinking continues, and the adolescent becomes disappointed when others, especially adults, do not live up to their personal code of ethics.

Early adult   p. 495

The early adult years are between ages 19 and 40. During this stage of life, normal vital signs are a pulse rate of 60 to 100, respirations of 12 to 20, blood pressure of 120/80, and body temperature of 98.6°F. The body reaches peak performance between 19 and 26 years of age, then begins to slow. Spinal disks settle, leading to a loss in body height, and fatty tissues increase, leading to weight gain.

During this time period, most lifelong habits and routines develop and job stress is at its greatest. The family is also stressed by childbirth and the challenges it brings.

Middle-age adult   pp. 495–496

The middle-aged adult years are between 40 and 60. During this stage, normal vital signs include a pulse rate of 60 to 100, respirations of 12 to 20, a blood pressure of 120/90, and a body temperature of 98.6°F. During middle age, some degradation of vision and hearing occur, and cardiovascular disease and cancer become health risks.

Middle-aged adults become concerned about the social clock and become more task oriented, aiming to accomplish their lifelong goals. They may experience the "empty-nest syndrome," in which the children leave home and parental responsibilities become much reduced. Financial commitments associated with elderly parents and young children may add stress.

Late-age adult   pp. 496–501

The late-aged adult is older than 60 years and has vital signs that are dependent on individual health status. The walls of the blood vessels thicken, increasing peripheral vascular resistance and reducing blood flow to the organs. The heart begins to show signs of disease of the valves, coronary arteries, electrical system, and the heart muscle itself. Blood volume decreases, as does the number of platelets and red blood cells. The respiratory surface area decreases, as does lung elasticity. The chest expands, and the chest wall stiffens. Respiratory workload increases, while efficiency decreases and coughing becomes less effective. The endocrine system works less efficiently,

©2006 Pearson Education, Inc.
Paramedic Care: Principles & Practice, Vol. 1

and glucose metabolism and insulin production decrease. The senses continue to deteriorate, including smell, eyesight, and hearing. Reaction time also diminishes.

Late-aged individuals are affected by concerns regarding housing, self-reliance, and financial burdens. They may be "forced" into retirement while they are still able to perform.

Case Study Review

Reread the case study on page 483 in Paramedic Care: Introduction to Advanced Prehospital Care *and then read the following discussion.*

This case study helps us appreciate the life-span differences that paramedics must be prepared to address with any emergency response.

This call requires you and your partner to care for a newborn infant and her mother. These are two very different patients with very different normal vital signs, different abilities to respond to environmental stimuli, and different levels of physiological and psychosocial development. Your assessment and care must be different for each, but so must your understanding of the physiological differences between the two. A pulse rate of 140 and a respiratory rate of 46 would signal extreme distress in the mother but are considered in the normal range in the newborn. It is also important to understand that a good active cry is a good sign of adequate respiration in the newborn, while slow, quiet respiration in the toddler may be a sign of respiratory exhaustion and failure.

While the human body maintains a relatively uniform anatomy and physiology throughout life, we must appreciate the subtle differences associated with the infant, toddler, preschooler, school-aged child, adolescent, and the early, middle-aged, and late-aged adult. Not only do vital signs change with age, but the effectiveness of the cardiovascular, respiratory, gastrointestinal, and endocrine systems do also. Further, psychosocial development affects the way the various age-grouped individuals respond to the environment and to the stresses of life and disease. Understanding life-span development will make your understanding of patients and their responses to disease easier.

Content Self-Evaluation

MULTIPLE CHOICE

_____ 1. In which age-group does normal body temperature become that found in adults?
    A. infant   D. school-aged
    B. toddler   E. adolescent
    C. preschooler

_____ 2. The toddler represents a child between the ages of:
    A. birth and 1 year.   D. 6 and 12 years.
    B. 1 and 3 years.   E. 13 and 18 years.
    C. 3 and 5 years.

_____ 3. The adolescent represents a child between the ages of:
    A. birth and 1 year.   D. 6 and 12 years.
    B. 1 and 3 years.   E. 13 and 18 years.
    C. 3 and 5 years.

_____ 4. Blood pressure generally rises with age.
    A. True   B. False

_____ 5. The respiratory rate generally rises with age.
    A. True   B. False

B   6. During the first week of life, the infant's weight is expected to:
- A. increase by 2 kg per week.
- B. decrease by 5 to 10 percent.
- C. double.
- D. triple.
- E. none of the above

E   7. When compared to the airway at any other stage of life, the infant's airway is:
- A. shorter.
- B. narrower.
- C. less stable.
- D. more easily obstructed.
- E. all of the above

A   8. The reflex sometimes referred to as the "startle reflex" is the:
- A. Moro reflex.
- B. palmar reflex.
- C. rooting reflex.
- D. sucking reflex.
- E. reflux reflex.

C   9. The anterior fontanelle closes between:
- A. 1 and 2 months.
- B. 2 and 4 months.
- C. 9 and 18 months.
- D. 1 and 2 years.
- E. none of the above

C   10. The process of learning used by children in which they build upon what they already know is called:
- A. bonding.
- B. secure attachment.
- C. scaffolding.
- D. benchmarking.
- E. modeling.

A   11. The toddler is very susceptible to minor respiratory and gastrointestinal infections.
- A. True
- B. False

D   12. The weight of the toddler's brain is approximately what percentage of the weight of the adult brain?
- A. 60 percent
- B. 70 percent
- C. 80 percent
- D. 90 percent
- E. 96 percent

B   13. Children begin to develop magical thinking at about:
- A. 1 to 2 years.
- B. 2 to 3 years.
- C. 3 to 4 years.
- D. 4 to 5 years.
- E. 5 to 6 years.

C   14. The school-aged child gains about how much weight per year?
- A. 1 kg
- B. 2 kg
- C. 3 kg
- D. 4 kg
- E. 5 kg

C   15. At what age does the female generally finish growing?
- A. 12
- B. 14
- C. 16
- D. 18
- E. 20

A   16. In late adolescence, the average male is taller and stronger than the average female.
- A. True
- B. False

D   17. Peak physical condition occurs among:
- A. the preschool-aged.
- B. the school-aged.
- C. adolescents.
- D. early adults.
- E. middle-aged adults.

A   18. The leading cause of death among early adults is:
- A. accidents.
- B. cardiovascular disease.
- C. cancer.
- D. respiratory disease.
- E. drug overdose.

19. The maximum life span for a human being is about:
  A. 76 years.   D. 100 years.
  B. 84 years.   E. 120 years.
  C. 96 years.

20. By the age of 80, the vessels of the cardiovascular system decrease their elasticity by about 50 percent.
  A. True   B. False

21. During late adulthood, which of the following is expected?
  A. decreased blood volume   D. poor iron levels
  B. decreased platelet count   E. all of the above
  C. decreased number of red blood cells

22. Which of the following is NOT expected of the respiratory system during late adulthood?
  A. enlarged alveoli
  B. decreased airway diameter
  C. reduced lung surface area
  D. stiffening of the chest wall
  E. increased likelihood of respiratory disease

23. Which of the following is a likely result of tooth loss in the elderly?
  A. an increased swallowing time
  B. decreased peristalsis
  C. less effective esophageal sphincter
  D. the swallowing of larger pieces of food
  E. all of the above

24. The individual in late adulthood is likely to be sensitive to loud noises and yet less able to hear indistinct speech or normal conversation in the presence of loud noise.
  A. True   B. False

25. Arteriosclerotic heart disease is the major killer after age 40 in all age, gender, and racial groups.
  A. True   B. False

MATCHING

Write the letter of the development stage in the space provided next to the characteristic most commonly associated with that age-group.

A. Infant   E. Adolescent

B. Toddler   F. Early adult

C. Preschooler   G. Middle-aged adult

D. School-aged   H. Late-aged adult

_____ 26. Highest level of job stress

_____ 27. Concerned with "social clock"

_____ 28. Baby teeth begin to appear

_____ 29. Sexual maturity

_____ 30. Permanent teeth

_____ 31. Hearing loss for pure tones

_____ 32. Development of self-concept

_____ 33. Understanding of cause and effect

_____ 34. Hearing maturity

_____ 35. Loss of sucking and rooting reflexes

13 Airway Management and Ventilation

Because Chapter 13 is lengthy, it has been divided into parts in this workbook to aid your study. Read the assigned textbook pages, then progress through the objectives and self-evaluation materials as you would with other chapters. When you feel secure in your grasp of the content, proceed to the next section.

Part 1, begins on p. 508

Review of Chapter Objectives

After reading this part of the chapter, you should be able to:

1. Explain the primary objective of airway maintenance. p. 508

The primary objective of airway maintenance is to keep the airway open and clear (patent) so that oxygen can be carried to and carbon dioxide carried away from the alveoli and the capillary beds of the pulmonary tissue.

3. Describe the anatomy and functions of the upper and lower airway structures in detail, including landmarks for direct laryngoscopy. pp. 509–515

The mouth, or oral cavity, is a single cavity that serves as an auxiliary air passage. The posterior upper surface is the soft palate, which moves upward and closes off the passages from the nose to the pharynx during swallowing. The nasal cavity is a hollow two-sided chamber lined with mucous membranes that warms, filters, and humidifies air as it enters the respiratory system. Its anterior openings are the nares, or nostrils. The nasal and oral cavities empty into the pharynx, or throat. The pharynx is a muscular tube that functions as the transitional area for food and air between the nose and mouth and between the esophagus and larynx.

The larynx is the tubular structure that begins the lower airway. It consists of the thyroid and cricoid cartilages, the vocal cords, the arytenoid folds, and the upper portion of the trachea. It is the "Adam's apple" located in the anterior neck. The epiglottis is a flap-like structure covering the opening of the trachea, the glottis. It closes during swallowing to prevent food or fluids from entering the trachea and respiratory system. The vallecula is a fold formed by the epiglottis and base of the tongue. The larynx opens into the trachea, a series of cartilaginous "C" shaped structures that hold the airway open. The trachea divides into two mainstem bronchi at the carina. The bronchi subdivide, finally reaching the respiratory bronchioles, the alveolar ducts, and, finally, the alveoli. The alveoli are the primary exchange structures between the respiratory system and the pulmonary capillaries of the cardiovascular system for oxygen and carbon dioxide.

4. Explain the differences between adult and pediatric airway anatomy. pp. 514–515

The gross anatomy of the infant's airway is very similar to that of the adult but is smaller in size with smaller airway clearances and a greater proportion of soft tissue. The larynx is more superior and anterior than in the adult, and the smallest clearance of the airway is the cricoid cartilage rather than the glottis as it is in the adult. The child's tongue is proportionally larger and more easily obstructs the airway. Because of the smaller lumen size, the soft tissue swelling may obstruct the airway more quickly.

5. Discuss the following functions of the respiratory system:

- **Mechanics of ventilation** pp. 516–517
  Respiration is the exchange of gases between a living organism and its environment. The volume of the thorax expands as the diaphragm contracts and displaces downward. The intercostal muscles contract, pulling the rib cage upward and outward. The muscles of the neck enhance this action as they lift the sternum. The lungs expand with the chest as the pleural seal secures the exterior of the lung to the interior of the thorax. The expansion of the lungs reduces the air pressure within them, and air flows into the alveoli. Gravity and the intrinsic elasticity of the lungs then cause the thorax to settle, the pressure within the lungs to increase, and air to be exhaled.

- **Pulmonary circulation** p. 517
  The right ventricle pumps blood depleted of its oxygen into the pulmonary artery. The blood is directed to the respective lungs through the right and left pulmonary arteries that then divide, ultimately, into the pulmonary capillaries. In the capillaries, the blood releases carbon dioxide and the hemoglobin becomes saturated with oxygen. The blood then returns through the pulmonary veins to the left atrium.

- **Gas exchange in the lungs** pp. 517–520
  The air brought into the lungs contains 21 percent oxygen and very little carbon dioxide. Oxygen diffuses through the alveolar and capillary walls and is bound to the hemoglobin, while carbon dioxide diffuses in the opposite direction. The air exhaled contains about 16 percent oxygen and 5 percent carbon dioxide.

- **Diffusion of the respiratory gases** p. 519
  The oxygen from inspired air diffuses from the alveolar space through the alveolar wall and the pulmonary capillary membrane, where it attaches to the hemoglobin of the blood. Carbon dioxide, mostly transported as bicarbonate, diffuses from the blood plasma across the capillary membrane and through the alveolar wall.

6. Describe oxygen transport in the blood and factors that affect it. pp. 519–520

Oxygen diffuses to the blood and is transported on the hemoglobin molecule. Hemoglobin is a very efficient transporter of oxygen, and each gram holds 1.34 mL of oxygen when fully saturated. As blood passes by well-oxygenated alveoli, between 98 and 100 percent of the hemoglobin is fully saturated and carries 97 percent of the oxygen in the blood. The remaining oxygen is dissolved in the blood plasma. As the oxygenated blood passes through the capillaries and is exposed to the lower oxygen partial pressures found in the tissues, hemoglobin releases oxygen. The oxygen then diffuses through the capillary wall, into the interstitial space, and then through the cell membrane.

The following factors affect oxygen transport.

- **Reduced hemoglobin levels.** Reduced hemoglobin levels caused by anemia or due to hemorrhage reduce the oxygen-carrying capability of the blood and its ability to provide oxygen to the body cells.

- **Inadequate alveolar ventilation.** If the alveolar oxygen level is reduced, it will affect the oxygen saturation. Reduced alveolar oxygen levels may be caused by low environmental oxygen levels, or poor alveolar ventilation may be caused by airway obstruction, respiratory muscle paralysis, chronic obstructive pulmonary disease, asthma, pneumothorax, or hypoventilation due to head injury.

- **Decreased alveolar diffusion.** Pulmonary edema is a condition in which an accumulation of fluid expands the space between the interior of the alveoli and the interior capillary. This increases the distance the oxygen must diffuse and hampers effective exchange.

- **Ventilation/perfusion mismatch.** If some of the alveoli are without air exchange (as in atelectasis), some of the blood will pass alveoli that are not oxygenated and then mix with the oxygenated blood from other areas of the lung. If the circulation to some of the alveoli is obstructed (as in pulmonary embolism), a significant amount of blood is prevented from reaching the alveolar/capillary membrane.

7. Describe carbon dioxide transport in the blood and factors that affect it.   **p. 520**

The blood carries approximately 70 percent of its carbon dioxide as bicarbonate, while 20 percent is transported attached to the hemoglobin and about 7 percent is dissolved in the plasma. Factors affecting carbon dioxide transport include:

- **Hyperventilation.** In hyperventilation, a person exhales carbon dioxide faster than it is produced and transported to the pulmonary system, thereby reducing the blood carbon dioxide levels.
- **Increased CO_2 production.** Carbon dioxide production may increase with fever, extreme muscle use, shivering, and metabolic processes.
- **Decreased CO_2 elimination.** Decreased alveolar ventilation results in increasing alveolar carbon dioxide levels, reduced diffusion, and increases in blood carbon dioxide levels. Such decreases may be caused by drug- or head injury-induced respiratory depression, airway obstruction, asthma, COPD, and impairment of respiratory muscles.

8. Describe the voluntary and involuntary regulation of respiration.   **pp. 521–522**

Respiration is controlled by the autonomic nervous system through the use of stretch receptors in the lung tissue and through chemoreceptors that monitor the oxygen and carbon dioxide levels in the blood and the pH of the cerebrospinal fluid. An increase in carbon dioxide, a decrease in oxygen, or a decrease in pH will increase the stimulus to breathe. Stretching the lung tissue, as with a deep breath, will decrease the stimulus to breathe. The pH level in the cerebrospinal fluid is the primary control over respiration, though blood hypoxia is a strong stimulus to breathe.

Voluntary control of respiration permits speech and somewhat modifies breathing patterns. However, if oxygen levels drop too low, involuntary respiration will occur.

9. List the concentration of gases that comprise atmospheric air.   **pp. 517–518**

Atmospheric air contains approximately 79 percent nitrogen, 21 percent oxygen, and much less than 1 percent carbon dioxide.

10. Define the various measures of respiratory function, and give average normal values for each, including normal respiratory rates for the adult, child, and infant.   **pp. 522–523**

- **Total lung capacity (TLC)** is the volume of air in the lungs after a maximal inspiration, about 6 L in the adult male.
- **Tidal volume (V_T)** is the average volume of air inspired (or expired) with each breath, about 500 mL in the adult male at rest.
- **Dead space volume (V_D)** is the portion of the tidal volume that does not reach the alveoli and is unavailable for gas exchange, about 150 mL.
- **Alveolar volume (VA)** is the amount of air that reaches the alveoli with each breath, about 350 mL.
- **Minute volume (V_{min})** is the amount of air moved in and out of the respiratory system in one minute (minute volume = tidal volume × respiratory rate).
- **Alveolar minute volume (V_{A-min})** is the amount of gas that reaches the alveoli per minute.
- **Inspiratory reserve volume (IRV)** is the amount of air that can be inspired after a normal inspiration.
- **Expiratory reserve volume (ERV)** is the amount of air that can be exhaled after a normal exhalation.
- **Residual volume (RV)** is the amount of air in the lungs after a maximal exhalation.

- **Functional residual capacity (FRC)** is the amount of air remaining in the lungs after a normal expiration.
- **Forced expiratory volume (FV)** is the amount of air a person can exhale after a maximal inhalation, about 4,500 mL in an adult male.

11. Describe assessment of the airway and the respiratory system.   **pp. 525–537**

Assessment of the airway is an integral part of both the initial assessment and the focused examination. During the initial assessment, the evaluation is directed at detecting any potentially life-threatening airway problems. If the patient is not conscious, alert, and demonstrating articulate speech, the airway and respiration are closely evaluated. The rate, depth, and symmetry of respiration are evaluated, as is the presence of any unusual respiratory sounds. During the focused exam, the emphasis is on the finer details of respiratory evaluation including skin color, auscultation of breath sounds, detection of abnormal breathing sounds, palpation of the thorax, and the use of pulse oximetry and/or capnography.

12. Describe the modified forms of respiration and list the factors that affect respiratory rate and depth.   **pp. 528–529**

Forms of respiration

- *Coughing*—the forceful exhalation of a large volume of air to expel material from the airway.
- *Sneezing*—sudden, forceful exhalation through the nose usually caused by nasal irritation.
- *Hiccoughing* (hiccups)—sudden diaphragmatic spasm with spasmodic closure of the glottis that serves no useful purpose.
- *Sighing*—slow, deep involuntary inspiration followed by a prolonged expiration that hyperinflates the lungs and expands collapsed alveoli.
- *Grunting*—forceful expiration against a partially closed epiglottis, usually an indication of respiratory distress.

Factors affecting respiratory rate and depth

- *Kussmaul's respirations*—deep, slow, or rapid gasping respirations commonly associated with diabetic ketoacidosis.
- *Cheyne-Stokes respirations*—progressively deeper, faster breathing alternating gradually with shallow, slower respirations indicating brainstem injury.
- *Biot's respirations*—irregular breathing pattern with sudden episodes of apnea indicating increased intracranial pressure.
- *Central neurogenic hyperventilation*—deep, rapid respirations indicating increased intracranial pressure.
- *Agonal respirations*—shallow, slow, or infrequent respirations indicating severe brain anoxia.

13. Discuss the methods for measuring oxygen and carbon dioxide in the blood and their prehospital use.   **pp. 531–537**

Pulse oximetry is a noninvasive monitoring of the arterial oxygenation of the skin. It accurately reflects the oxygen delivery to the end organs, giving an ongoing evaluation of circulation and respiration. In prehospital care, the oximeter is quick and easy to use and provides an accurate and constant evaluation of the cardiorespiratory system.

Capnography is the noninvasive monitoring of exhaled CO_2 concentrations over time. It can be used to elevate the initial and continuing placement of an endotracheal tube as well as the effectiveness of ventilations and CPR. The device can also monitor the patient's general condition and response to medications. The real-time monitoring of $ETCO_2$ is rapidly becoming the standard of care in emergency medical services.

14. Define and explain the implications of partial airway obstruction with good and poor air exchange and complete airway obstruction.   **p. 523**

Obstruction of the airway by a foreign object or swelling may range from minor to complete. If the airway obstruction permits speech and coughing and you do not notice skin color changes, respiration is probably adequate and intervention may not be needed. However, if the patient has serious dyspnea, cannot speak or cough, is choking or gagging, and you notice skin color changes, intervention is necessary. Continued inadequate respiration will lead to increasing hypoxia. No air movement due to complete obstruction will rapidly lead to serious hypoxia and death.

15. Describe the common causes of upper airway obstruction, including:

- Tongue   pp. 523–524

  The most common cause of airway obstruction is the tongue. In the unconscious person or the supine patient, the lack of muscle tone allows the tongue to rest against the posterior pharynx and thereby obstruct the airway.

- Foreign body aspiration   p. 524

  Large, poorly chewed lumps of food and objects aspirated by children commonly account for airway obstruction. The victim will often grasp his throat, a universal distress signal.

- Laryngeal spasm   p. 524

  The glottis is the smallest part of the airway and may be responsible for obstruction secondary to spasm. Spasm may be caused by stimulation by a foreign object as during endotracheal intubation.

- Laryngeal edema   p. 524

  Because the glottis is the narrowest part of the adult airway, swelling will rapidly reduce the airway lumen size and restrict breathing. Restriction and obstruction may be caused by anaphylaxis, epiglottitis, or the inhalation of toxic substances, superheated steam, or smoke.

- Trauma   p. 524

  Physical injury to the structures of the upper airway may result in loose objects such as the teeth, tissue, or clotted blood obstructing the airway. Further, blunt or penetrating trauma may result in collapse of the airway due to fracture or displacement of the larynx or trachea. Soft-tissue swelling may also restrict the lumen of the airway.

17. Describe causes of respiratory distress, including:

- Upper and lower airway obstruction   pp. 523–525

  Upper and lower airway obstructions range in severity from minor to complete obstructions and may be caused by the tongue, a foreign body, swelling, vomitus, blood, or teeth.

- Inadequate ventilation   p. 525

  Insufficient minute volume compromises respiratory exchange and may be due to bronchospasm, rib fracture, hemothorax or pneumothorax, drug overdose, airway obstruction, renal failure, or central nervous system injury.

- Impairment of respiratory muscles   pp. 516–517

  The respiratory muscles may be impaired by fatigue, central nervous system depression, or spinal injury.

- Impairment of nervous system   pp. 516–517

  Respiratory system control, provided by the central nervous system, may be depressed by drugs or by intracranial or spinal injury

30. Define the following: pp. 511, 512, 514, 520, 521, 528, 529, 596, 600

- Gag reflex

  The gag reflex is a mechanism that stimulates retching to keep foreign material from entering the lower airway.

- Atelectasis

  Atelectasis is the collapse of the alveoli.

- FiO_2

  FiO_2 is the concentration of oxygen in inspired air.

- Hypoxia

  Hypoxia is a generalized oxygen deficiency.

- Hypoxemia

  Hypoxemia is an oxygen deficiency in the blood.

- Pulsus paradoxus

  Pulsus paradoxus is a drop in the blood pressure of greater than 10 mmHg during inspiration.

Case Study Review

Reread the case study on pages 507 and 508 in Paramedic Care: Introduction to Advanced Prehospital Care *and then read the following discussion.*

This study focuses on the variety of techniques that paramedics might be called on to employ to ensure the management of a patient's airway and breathing in an emergency situation.

Crystal and Charlie attend a trauma patient with a mechanism of injury suggesting serious internal injuries. They are immediately obligated to employ spinal precautions, requiring that they position the patient's head and neck in the neutral position and maintain that positioning. As they move to the airway evaluation portion of the initial assessment, Crystal hears gurgling and attempts to clear the airway with positioning (displacing the jaw forward while maintaining the spinal immobilization) and suction. Airway maintenance is more difficult in this trauma patient because of the inability to extend his head and neck due to the potential for spine injury. The landmarks for endotracheal intubation are also more difficult to visualize because the head cannot be brought to the sniffing position and because there is likely to be some blood in the airway. Crystal needs to be very careful to ensure and confirm proper tube placement because unrecognized esophageal placement is deadly.

While the clenched teeth (trismus) prevent insertion of the oral airway, a nasopharyngeal airway could help maintain the airway. However, with the possibility of severe head injury and basilar skull fracture, Crystal must be very careful with its insertion, directing it straight back and along the floor of the nasal cavity.

The Glasgow Coma Score of 5 for this patient mandates field intubation. The rapid sequence procedure is required because of the clenched jaw. Lidocaine is administered to reduce the effects of pharynx, larynx, and upper trachea tissue stimulation during the intubation. This (vagal) stimulation would also cause a possible increase in intracranial pressure, an undesirable circumstance in a patient with possible head injury. Midazolam is a sedative used to lower the patient's level of consciousness before he is paralyzed, reducing his memory of the circumstance (should he be awake) and reducing anxiety. Succinylcholine is a smooth muscle relaxant that relaxes the clenched jaw and permits opening of the mouth for intubation. It also relaxes the muscles of the airway and makes intubation somewhat easier to perform. Succinylcholine may increase intracranial pressure (a possible contraindication for this patient) and may increase the likelihood of vomiting. The greatest benefit to using succinylcholine is its short duration of action. If the rapid sequence intubation fails, it will only be a few minutes until the paralytic effects of the drug wear off. During the time until the jaw relaxes, Crystal ventilates her patient with full breaths at a rate of about 24 times per minute (actually, 24 times per minute might be just slightly too fast for a head injury patient). Any faster would blow off too much carbon dioxide and possibly increase intracranial pressure.

Charles employs Sellick's maneuver, placing posterior pressure on the cartilage ring (cricoid cartilage) at the base of the larynx. This pressure compresses the esophagus between the cricoid cartilage and the vertebral column, holding it closed and thereby preventing any passage of emesis upward and into the pharynx. This procedure will also displace the larynx, somewhat posteriorly, making it easier to visualize during an intubation attempt. Charles must maintain this pressure until the patient is intubated because relaxing it may release emesis into the pharynx.

Once the endotracheal tube is placed, both Charles and Crystal must carefully ensure it is properly located. All signs demonstrate that the ventilations are effective, including bilateral and equal lung sounds with each breath, increasing oxygen saturation, and color change from the $ETCO_2$ detector. Charles and Crystal will carefully secure the tube in place and note the depth of insertion by recording the number on the side of the endotracheal tube. A real danger in prehospital care is the unnoticed dislodging of an endotracheal tube during C-collar placement, immobilization to the long spine board, movement of the patient to the long spine board, or while loading or unloading the patient from the ambulance. Again, the consequence of unrecognized endotracheal tube displacement is patient death. Crystal and Charles will check the breath sounds, oximetry, and the $ETCO_2$ detector after each move and frequently during their care and transport.

Crystal employs a glucose test to rule out hypoglycemia, which could account for the unconsciousness and because hypoglycemia is detrimental in the head injury patient.

Content Self-Evaluation

MULTIPLE CHOICE

_A_ 1. The sinuses help trap bacteria and can become infected.
   A. True   B. False

_B_ 2. The nasal cavity is responsible for all of the functions listed below EXCEPT:
   A. warming the air.   D. cleansing the air.
   B. deoxygenating the air.   E. the sense of smell.
   C. humidifying the air.

_A_ 3. The space located between the base of the tongue and the epiglottis is called the:
   A. vallecula.   D. epiglottic fossa.
   B. cricoid.   E. glottic opening.
   C. arytenoid fold.

_C_ 4. Which of the following is the only bone in the axial skeleton that does not articulate with another bone?
   A. the mandible   D. the thyroid
   B. the maxilla   E. the zygomatic bone
   C. the hyoid bone

_C_ 5. Which of the following correctly lists the order in which air passes through airway structures during inspiration?
   A. trachea, larynx, laryngopharynx, nasopharynx, nares
   B. nares, nasopharynx, trachea, laryngopharynx, larynx
   C. nares, nasopharynx, laryngopharynx, larynx, trachea
   D. laryngopharynx, nares, nasopharynx, larynx, trachea
   E. trachea, nares, laryngopharynx, larynx, nasopharynx

_A_ 6. The narrowest part of the adult airway is the:
   A. cricoid ring.   D. carina.
   B. thyroid ring.   E. tracheal stricture.
   C. glottis.

_E_ 7. Which of the following can be caused by stimulation with a laryngoscope during an intubation attempt?
   A. coughing   D. decreased respiratory rate
   B. bradycardia   E. all of the above
   C. hypotension

_D_ 8. The point at which the trachea divides into the two mainstem bronchi is called the:
   A. hilum.   D. carina.
   B. parenchyma.   E. pleura.
   C. vallecula.

_A_ 9. The mainstem bronchus that leaves the trachea at almost a straight angle is the right mainstem bronchus.
   A. True   B. False

_B_ 10. Beta$_2$ stimulation will cause the bronchioles to:
   A. constrict.   D. stiffen.
   B. dilate.   E. none of the above
   C. shorten.

©2006 Pearson Education, Inc.
Paramedic Care: Principles & Practice, Vol. 1

CHAPTER 13   *Airway Management and Ventilation*   **155**

_____ 11. The tissue covering each lung and the interior of the thorax is the:
   A. hilum.   D. carina.
   B. parenchyma.   E. pleura.
   C. vallecula.

_____ 12. Which of the following is NOT one of the differences in respiration between pediatric patients and adults?
   A. The pediatric airway is smaller in all aspects.
   B. Pediatric ribs are softer and contribute less to respiration than those of adults.
   C. Children rely more on their diaphragms for breathing than adults do.
   D. The glottis is the narrowest point of the pediatric airway, whereas the cricoid cartilage is the narrowest point in adults.
   E. Children's teeth are softer and more prone to damage than those of adults.

_____ 13. Internal respiration occurs in the:
   A. peripheral capillaries.   D. pulmonary capillaries.
   B. airway.   E. both C and D
   C. alveoli.

_____ 14. Which aspect of the respiratory cycle is passive?
   A. inspiration
   B. expiration
   C. neither A nor B
   D. both A and B
   E. both A and B, but only during stress

_____ 15. The oxygenated circulation that provides perfusion for the lung tissue itself flows through the:
   A. pulmonary arteries.   D. bronchial veins.
   B. pulmonary veins.   E. none of the above
   C. bronchial arteries.

_____ 16. The amount of nitrogen in the air is approximately:
   A. 79 percent.   D. 0.04 percent.
   B. 4 percent.   E. 0.10 percent.
   C. 0.4 percent.

_____ 17. The normal oxygen saturation of hemoglobin in blood as it leaves the lungs is about:
   A. 75 percent.   D. 95 percent.
   B. 85 percent.   E. 97 percent.
   C. 90 percent.

_____ 18. The majority of the carbon dioxide carried by the blood is:
   A. carried by the hemoglobin.
   B. dissolved in the plasma.
   C. transported as bicarbonate.
   D. found as free gas in the blood.
   E. carried as free radicals.

_____ 19. Which of the following will reduce the carbon dioxide levels in the blood?
   A. administration of bicarbonate   D. high-flow oxygen
   B. administration of antacids   E. hypoventilation
   C. hyperventilation

_____ 20. Which of the following would NOT increase the production of carbon dioxide?
   A. fever   D. metabolic acids
   B. airway obstruction   E. exercise
   C. shivering

A 21. The primary center controlling respiration is located in the:
A. medulla.   D. cerebrum.
B. pons.   E. cerebellum.
C. spinal cord.

E 22. Which of the following is the secondary or backup stimulus that causes respiration to occur?
A. an increase in pH of the blood
B. a decrease in pH of the blood
C. an increase in pH of the cerebrospinal fluid
D. a decrease in pH of the cerebrospinal fluid
E. reduced oxygen levels in the blood

C 23. The amount of air moved with one normal respiratory cycle is called:
A. minute volume.   D. dead air space.
B. alveolar air.   E. total lung capacity.
C. tidal volume.

C 24. The volume of air contained in a normal inspiration is about:
A. 150 mL.   D. 6,000 mL.
B. 350 mL.   E. none of the above
C. 500 mL.

A 25. Which of the following is the most common cause of upper airway obstruction?
A. the tongue   D. laryngeal swelling
B. foreign bodies   E. aspiration of blood or vomitus
C. trauma

C 26. All of the following conditions may cause reduced inspiratory volumes EXCEPT:
A. pneumothorax.   D. respiratory muscle paralysis.
B. asthma.   E. emphysema.
C. high inspired oxygen concentrations.

B 27. The normal respiratory rate for an adult at rest is:
A. 8 to 12.   D. 24 to 32.
B. 12 to 20.   E. 40 to 60.
C. 18 to 24.

B 28. Which of the following is a breathing pattern associated with flail chest?
A. abdominal breathing   D. intercostal retraction
B. paradoxical breathing   E. both A and C
C. diaphragmatic breathing

A 29. It is unlikely that a patient will have significant hypoxia and not display cyanosis.
A. True   B. False

30. Which modified form of respiration is designed to expand alveoli that may have collapsed during periods of inactivity or rest?
A. coughing   D. grunting
B. sneezing   E. sighing
C. hiccoughing

31. The respiratory pattern that presents with deep and rapid respirations is:
A. apneustic respirations.   D. central neurogenic hyperventilation.
B. Cheyne-Stokes respirations.   E. agonal respirations.
C. Biot's respirations.

32. Stridor is most commonly associated with:
A. laryngeal constriction or edema. D. fluids within the airway.
B. the tongue blocking the airway.   E. foreign bodies in the lower airway.
C. narrowing of the bronchioles.

33. The feeling of flexibility or stiffness associated with the lungs and ventilation is:
A. back pressure.
D. effusion.
B. resiliency.
E. Hering-Breuer reflex.
C. compliance.

34. Pulse oximetry measures the amount of oxygen dissolved in the plasma of the blood.
A. True
B. False

35. The absence of CO_2 in exhaled air, as identified by the end-expiratory CO_2 detector, suggests:
A. ventilation is not deep enough.
B. ventilations are not occurring fast enough.
C. the endotracheal tube may be in the esophagus.
D. the oxygen percentage of inspired air is insufficient.
E. all of the above

36. The normal partial pressure of CO_2 in exhaled air is:
A. 5 mmHg.
D. 45 mmHg.
B. 25 mmHg.
E. 86 mmHg.
C. 38 mmHg.

37. The disposable device that records the level of exhaled CO_2 using pH-sensitive chemically impregnated paper is a:
A. capnometer.
D. colormetric device.
B. capnograph.
E. non-waveform $ETCO_2$ device.
C. capnogram.

38. If the $ETCO_2$ detector becomes contaminated with gastric contents, further readings may be unreliable.
A. True
B. False

39. During CPR, the $ETCO_2$ levels reflect cardiac output and coronary perfusion pressure.
A. True
B. False

40. The value of capnography is that it can assess which of the following:
A. the effectiveness of CPR.
B. proper initial endotracheal tube placement.
C. proper endotracheal tube placement continues.
D. patient responses to medications.
E. all of the above

©2006 Pearson Education, Inc.
Paramedic Care: Principles & Practice, Vol. 1

Label the Diagram

41. Write the names of the components of the upper airway marked A, B, C, D, E, F, G, and H on the diagram below in the spaces provided.

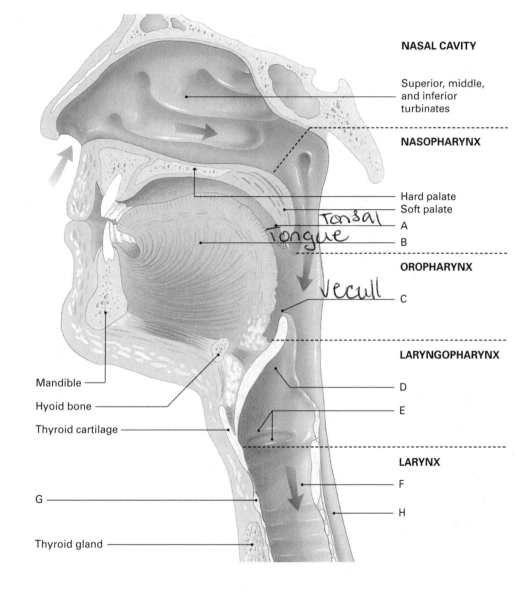

NASAL CAVITY

Superior, middle, and inferior turbinates

NASOPHARYNX

Hard palate
Soft palate
Tonsal — A
Tongue — B

OROPHARYNX

Vecull — C

LARYNGOPHARYNX

D

E

Mandible

Hyoid bone

Thyroid cartilage

LARYNX

F

G

H

Thyroid gland

A. _____

B. _____

C. _____

D. _____

E. _____

F. _____

G. _____

H. _____

Special Project

Airway Obstruction

List the five causes of airway obstruction and identify the mechanism that causes each problem.

1. _____

   _____

2. _____

   _____

3. _____

   _____

4. _____

   _____

5. _____

   _____

Normal Respiratory Values: Identify the normal values for each of the items listed below.

	Inspired Air	Expired Air	
% Oxygen	_____	_____	PaO$_2$ _____
% Carbon dioxide	_____	_____	PaCO$_2$ _____

Normal Respiratory Rates/Volumes:

Infant: _____ to _____

Child: _____ to _____

Adult: _____ to _____

Tidal volume: _____

Alveolar volume: _____

Dead space volume: _____

Minute volume: _____

Part 2, begins on p. 538

Review of Chapter Objectives

After reading this part of the chapter, you should be able to:

2. Identify commonly neglected prehospital skills related to the airway. p. 538

The manual maintenance of the airway, using the head-tilt/chin-lift or jaw thrust maneuver, is one of the most important but often neglected prehospital airway skills. Proper use of these techniques helps ensure an adequate airway early in the care process.

16. Describe complete airway obstruction maneuvers, including:

- **Heimlich maneuver** p. 587
  The Heimlich maneuver involves a forceful upward and backward abdominal thrust using the hands placed halfway between the umbilicus and the xiphoid process. The increased abdominal and thoracic pressures help propel an obstruction up and out of the airway.
- **Removal with Magill forceps** p. 587
  If basic life support measures fail to secure a patent airway, you may introduce a laryngoscope to visualize beyond the oral cavity. If you notice a foreign body obstructing the airway, you may then remove it using the Magill forceps.

18. Explain the risk of infection to EMS providers associated with airway management and ventilation. p. 603

As was mentioned in Chapter 2, "The Well-Being of the Paramedic," there are several diseases that can be transmitted by body fluids and airborne droplet transmission. The pocket mask reduces the contact with the patient and, if equipped with a one-way valve, lessens the exposure to droplet contamination.

19. Describe manual airway maneuvers, including:

- **Head-tilt/chin-lift maneuver** pp. 538–539
  To execute the head-tilt/chin-lift airway maneuver, the rescuer places one hand on the patient's forehead, gently tilting the head back, while the other engages the mandible, displacing it anteriorly.
- **Jaw-thrust maneuver** pp. 539–540
  During the jaw-thrust (or the triple-airway maneuver), the rescuer places his fingers on the patient's lateral mandible, displacing it anteriorly while the thumbs displace it inferiorly. The maneuver may rotate the head and extend the neck. If spinal injury is suspected, the head should not be tilted backward (use the modified jaw-thrust).
- **Modified jaw-thrust maneuver** p. 540
  The modified jaw-thrust (for the trauma patient) requires that the jaw-thrust maneuver be modified by manually securing the head in a neutral position while the mandible is displaced forward.

20. Describe the indications, contraindications, advantages, disadvantages, complications, special considerations, equipment, and techniques of the following:

- **Upper airway and tracheobronchial suctioning** pp. 597–600
  Suctioning is the use of pressures that are less than atmospheric to draw fluids and semi-fluids out of the airway. It should be used any time it can effectively remove material from the airway. Continuous suctioning should be avoided because it draws against the patient's ventilation attempts and generally interrupts artificial ventilation of the apneic patient. Suctioning can be provided by an electric or a mechanical device. Tracheobronchial suctioning passes a lubricated soft suction catheter down the endotracheal tube into the trachea or bronchi to remove secretions. Suction is applied for 10 to 15 seconds while the catheter is slowly turned and withdrawn.

- **Nasogastric and orogastric tube insertion** **p. 600**

Nasogastric tube insertion is recommended for the conscious patient, because it permits him to talk more easily, while the procedure is to be avoided when there is danger of skull fracture and further injury caused by the tube's placement. Both oral and nasal techniques may be used for gastric decompression when patient ventilation is restricted or there is danger of aspiration. The tube is measured for depth of insertion by measuring from the epigastrium to the angle of the jaw and then to the nares. Use a topical anesthetic spray, and then lubricate the distal tip and insert the tube through the nares and along the nasal floor or through the mouth along the midline. Advance the tube, encourage patient swallowing if possible, and then introduce 30 to 50 mL of air while listening over the epigastrium. The absence of gastric sounds and the inability to speak suggests tracheal placement and the need to reattempt insertion.

- **Oropharyngeal and nasopharyngeal airway** **pp. 542–546**

The oropharyngeal airway is designed to maintain an airway by displacing the tongue anteriorly. It should not be used in conscious or semiconscious patients who have an intact gag reflex. Displace the tongue forward with a tongue blade and insert the airway along the base of the tongue. It may also be inserted by placing it, backward, into the oral cavity to the base of the tongue and then rotating it 180° and continuing the insertion. The oral or nasal airway should be used when ventilating the patient using any mechanical device.

The nasopharyngeal airway is inserted into the nasopharynx in the unconscious or semiconscious patient. It is a soft rubber tube that is lubricated and inserted posteriorly in the largest nostril (usually the left). It is indicated in the semiconscious patient or as the oral airway would be used. It should not be used in the patient with possible skull fracture.

- **Ventilating a patient by mouth-to-mouth or mouth-to-nose** **pp. 602–607**

Ventilation by mouth-to-mouth or mouth-to-nose is an easy technique that requires no equipment, though it risks disease transmission. The rescuer seals his mouth over the patient's mouth or nose (or both with the small child or infant), closes the nostrils or mouth with his fingers, takes a deep breath, and inflates the patient's lungs. The procedure induces air with about 15 percent oxygen that will successfully sustain life. When possible, mouth-to-mask or bag-valve mask ventilation is recommended.

Mouth-to-mask

The pocket mask is an adjunct to mouth-to-mouth ventilation that provides some protection against direct contact with the patient and the patient's exhaled air. It is simply sealed to the patient's face with the rescuer's hands and held in place during ventilation. It is recommended for use any time you would otherwise employ direct mouth-to-mouth ventilation. Some masks provide for supplemental oxygen administration that improves the percentage of oxygen provided to the patient.

One/two/three person bag-valve mask

Bag-valve-mask devices are mechanical devices that provide positive pressure ventilation. The mask is sealed to the patient's face with one hand while the other hand squeezes the bag, pushing air into the patient's lungs. The device is best used for the intubated patient because the volume of air and the pressure delivered to the patient is low. If the patient is not intubated, the air exchange achieved by one person may not be enough to sustain life. With two or more persons, one rescuer seals the mask to the face and maintains head positioning while another uses both hands to squeeze the bag. Since the volume of the bag is limited, it is essential to obtain a good seal on the face when using the bag-valve mask. Any time the bag-valve mask is used, it should have the oxygen reservoir attached and oxygen flowing at 12 to 15 lpm.

Flow-restricted, oxygen-powered ventilation device

Flow-restricted, oxygen-powered ventilation devices, sometimes called demand valve resuscitators, ventilate a patient with a flow of oxygen when a button or bar is pushed. They can be used with a face mask, EOA, EGTA, PtL airway, or endotracheal tube. They provide the patient with 100% oxygen. However, the pressures they use may cause gastric insufflation or lung tissue damage. They are not recommended for intubated or pediatric patients.

Automatic transport ventilator

Automatic transport ventilators provide a patient with ventilation with 100% oxygen at a rate and volume determined by the user. Recent advances in technology make automatic ventilators compact and dependable for field use. They are not recommended for children under the age of five years and are dependent upon a good patient airway.

21. Compare the ventilation techniques used for an adult patient to those used for pediatric patients, and describe special considerations in airway management and ventilation for the pediatric patient. pp. 572–576, 605

During bag-valve masking, one rescuer seals the mask to the face and thrusts the jaw anteriorly while the other rescuer compresses the bag. The small (450 mL) bag-valve mask is used for infants, while the standard pediatric bag-valve mask is adequate for children up to eight years old. Ensure the mask seals well and that ventilation achieves good chest rise and breath sounds.

Endotracheal intubation of the pediatric patient is more difficult than for the adult for the following reasons. The airway structures are smaller and more flexible, the tongue is relatively larger, the epiglottis is floppier and rounder, the vocal folds are more difficult to visualize, and the narrowest part of the airway is the cricoid cartilage. A straight laryngoscope blade and uncuffed endotracheal tube are used for patients under eight years of age. The tube is only introduced to 2 to 3 cm beyond the vocal cords (place the black glottic mark at the vocal cords). The procedure is more likely to produce vagal stimulation and may require atropine administration.

22. Identify types of oxygen cylinders and pressure regulators and explain safety considerations of oxygen storage and delivery, including steps for delivering oxygen from a cylinder and regulator. p. 601

Oxygen is commonly available in steel or aluminum cylinders of D (400 L), E (660 L), and M (3,450 L) sizes and is brought to administration pressures by a therapy regulator (50 psi) that allows for the administration of a liter per minute flow rate. Oxygen is a gas that easily supports combustion and should be used with caution near any ignition source or near grease. The pressure in the tank makes rupture an event that may produce serious injury, so tanks must be handled and stored carefully.

23. Describe the indications, contraindications, advantages, disadvantages, complications, liter flow range, and concentration of delivered oxygen for the following supplemental oxygen delivery devices: pp. 601–602

- **Nasal cannula** The nasal cannula is a blind tube with ports to correspond to the patient's nostrils. Oxygen flows into the nares and the patient breathes enriched oxygen when breathing through the nose. The device delivers 24 to 44 percent oxygen with flows of 1 to 6 lpm. The nasal cannula is useful for the patient with anxiety regarding oxygen masks and for prolonged oxygen administration. It is of little benefit if the patient is not breathing through the nose unless the prongs are then placed facing into the mouth.
- **Simple face mask** A simple face mask delivers oxygen into the mask in front of the patient's mouth and nose. The patient inhales 40 to 60 percent oxygen when the device receives an oxygen flow of 8 to 12 lpm. The simple oxygen face mask is useful for the routine administration of oxygen.
- **Partial rebreather mask** The partial rebreather mask is indicated for patients needing moderate concentrations of oxygen. One-way disks limit mixing of oxygen with inspired air and help increase the oxygen concentration. Maximum oxygen flow is about 10 lpm.
- **Nonrebreather mask** The nonrebreather mask consists of oxygen tubing and a face mask with a reservoir. Because of valves in the mask, oxygen flows into the reservoir while the patient exhales and into the patient from the input tubing and reservoir when the patient inhales. If the reservoir does not completely collapse (usually 10 to 15 lpm flow) on inspiration, oxygen delivery is between 80 percent and 95 percent.
- **Venturi mask** The Venturi mask is a high-flow oxygen mask that delivers very precise concentrations of oxygen. The oxygen concentration is generally low, with normal concentrations of 24, 28, 35, and 40 percent. It is often used to treat COPD patients who need supplemental oxygen but who may have respiratory drive problems with high-concentration oxygen.

24. Describe the use, advantages, and disadvantages of an oxygen humidifier.   **p. 602**

Oxygen bubbles through sterile water to obtain humidification. Humidified oxygen administration benefits patients with croup, epiglottitis, or bronchiolitis or patients on long-term oxygen therapy.

25. Describe the indications, contraindications, advantages, disadvantages, complications, equipment, and technique for the following:

- **Endotracheal intubation by direct laryngoscopy**   **pp. 546–563, 572–576**

Endotracheal intubation is the method of choice for the patient who is unable to protect his airway. It may also be considered for the patient who is expected to lose the airway due to swelling, as may occur with inhalation injury or with a trauma patient or with one who is in need of assisted ventilation. The only contraindication to endotracheal intubation is the pediatric patient with possible epiglottitis, unless respirations are worsening. The procedure requires an endotracheal tube, a laryngoscope, and tape to secure the tube once in place. Once the patient is hyperventilated, the laryngoscope is inserted into the right side of the oral cavity, then moved to the left, displacing the tongue. It is negotiated down the airway until it engages the epiglottis (straight blade) or is negotiated into the vallecula. As the tongue and pharynx are lifted to visualize the glottic opening, the endotracheal tube is placed through the opening, then advanced 2 to 3 cm beyond. Placement is checked and then the cuff is inflated to seal the trachea.

- **Digital endotracheal intubation**   **pp. 563–566**

Digital intubation is a blind intubation technique in which the endotracheal tube is guided into the glottis with the fingers of a hand inserted into the oral cavity. One hand is deeply inserted into the oral cavity, and one finger locates the epiglottis while the others direct the tube along its posterior surface and, hopefully, into the trachea. The technique is helpful in the trauma patient whose neck cannot be extended or the patient with a short neck, where visualization of the glottis is very difficult. The fingers of the rescuer must be protected with an oral airway, and great care must be used to ensure the endotracheal tube is correctly placed in the trachea.

- **Dual lumen airway**   **pp. 580–584**

A dual lumen airway, like the Esophageal Tracheal CombiTube, has two lumens, or tubes. The device is inserted blindly through the mouth, and one lumen enters the trachea and the other enters the esophagus. After determining which tube has entered the trachea, the patient is ventilated through that tube. The dual lumen airway is easy to use and does not require special equipment. The device diminishes gastric distention and regurgitation and can be used on trauma patients because the neck can remain in the neutral position during insertion and ventilation. However, maintaining adequate mask seal is difficult, and the device cannot be used with pediatric patients or those with esophageal disease or caustic ingestions, or in conscious patients or those with a gag reflex.

- **Nasotracheal intubation**   **pp. 580–584**

Nasotracheal intubation is a blind intubation technique that is recommended for spinal injury, clenched teeth, oral injuries and swelling, and obesity or arthritis preventing patient positioning in the sniffing position. The patient must be breathing and without nasal or basilar skull fractures. The endotracheal tube is inserted blindly into the largest nares and along the floor of the nasal cavity. Listen to the breath sounds, and once the breath sounds are heard clearly, advance the tube during the next inhalation. Carefully confirm proper tube placement. Once inserted, the tube can be secured more easily and the patient cannot bite or compress the tube.

- **Rapid sequence intubation**   **pp. 576–579**

Rapid sequence intubation is indicated for a patient who has a gag reflex or is likely to fight any intubation attempt but who requires such a procedure. The procedure induces sedation, then muscle paralysis to permit easier intubation. The patient is ventilated while the medications take effect. The procedure requires that care providers continue ventilation during the entire time of paralysis and maintain the airway if endotracheal intubation is unsuccessful. Care must be taken to administer agents that do not cause hypotension and ICP increase in serious trauma patients.

- **Endotracheal intubation using sedation**   **pp. 568–572**

To perform endotracheal intubation using sedation, the caregiver simply medicates the patient without employing a paralytic agent.

©2006 Pearson Education, Inc.
Paramedic Care: Principles & Practice, Vol. 1

- Open cricothyrotomy   pp. 592–596

  Cricothyrotomy is an incision through the cricothyroid membrane to allow the passage of air. It is employed only when complete airway obstruction makes no other means of effectively ventilating the patient possible. The cricoid membrane is located (the first hard ring moving from the mid-trachea upward), then the membrane between it and the thyroid cartilage. The skin above the membrane is incised vertically with a scalpel and then the membrane is opened with a horizontal incision. A 6- or 7-mm endotracheal tube (or tracheostomy tube) is directed down the trachea, and the cuff is inflated. Complications of the open cricothyrotomy include severe hemorrhage, thyroid gland damage, damage to surrounding airway structures, subcutaneous emphysema, and incorrect tube placement.

- Needle cricothyrotomy (translaryngeal catheter ventilation)   pp. 588–592

  Percutaneous transtracheal catheter ventilation (or needle cricothyrotomy) is used only for severe, partial airway obstruction above the vocal cords that is not correctable by other methods. An over-the-needle catheter is inserted through the cricothyroid membrane with a syringe attached. Once the membrane is penetrated, air can be inspired into the syringe to confirm proper placement. The catheter is then directed caudally, the needle is withdrawn, and the catheter is attached to a high-pressure, high-volume oxygen line. High-pressure oxygen (50 psi) is passed through the large (14 gauge or larger) catheter using special equipment and then is allowed to escape. Expiration should take twice as long as inflation. If the chest does not deflate, a second needle or an open cricothyrotomy may be needed.

- Extubation   pp. 579–580

  Extubation is the removal of the endotracheal tube when a patient awakens and is intolerant of the endotracheal tube. Removal calls for the deflation of the cuff and withdrawal of the tube during expiration or a cough. Laryngospasm may occur with the withdrawal of the endotracheal tube.

26. Describe use of cricoid pressure during intubation.   pp. 541–542

Cricoid pressure or Sellick's maneuver places posteriorly directed pressure on the cricoid cartilage, compressing the esophagus and preventing vomit from entering the pharynx. The procedure also may move the structures of the airway so they may be more easily viewed during intubation attempts. Once applied, Sellick's procedure must be maintained until the endotracheal tube is placed, because early release may permit emesis to enter the pharynx. Do not apply excessive pressure, because doing so may obstruct the trachea.

27. Discuss the precautions that should be taken when intubating the trauma patient.   pp. 566–568

The trauma patient may have sustained spinal injury: all airway care must be provided with limited (if any) movement of the head and neck. In addition to the cervical collar, the head should be held in a neutral position manually by an EMT while intubation is attempted. Orotracheal or nasotracheal intubation, lighted stylette intubation, or digital techniques may be attempted.

28. Discuss agents used for sedation and rapid sequence intubation.   pp. 569–571

Midazolam, diazepam, etomidate, ketamine, sodium thiopental, propofol, and fentanyl are used to sedate patients as the first step of rapid sequence intubation. Then paralytics such as succinylcholine, vecuronium, atracurium, and pancuronium are used to relax the skeletal muscles and permit endotracheal intubation. The drugs atropine and lidocaine may also be used as part of the rapid sequence intubation regimen.

29. Discuss methods to confirm correct placement of an endotracheal tube.   pp. 559–563

Verify and document at least three of the following: visualization of the tube passing through the vocal cords, the presence of bilateral breath sounds, absence of breath sounds over the epigastrium, positive $ETCO_2$ change, verification of placement by an esophageal detector device, condensation in the endotracheal tube, absence of vomitus within the endotracheal tube, and the absence of vocal sounds once the tube is in place. It is highly recommended that the patient's chest be auscultated for bilateral breath sounds to ensure the endotracheal tube has not been introduced too far and into the right mainstem bronchus.

30. **Define the following:** pp. 511, 512, 514, 520, 521, 528, 529, 596, 600

- **Gastric distention**
  Gastric distention is an over-expansion of the stomach sometimes caused by air pushed into the stomach by artificial ventilation.
- **Sellick's maneuver**
  Sellick's maneuver is pressure applied posteriorly to the cricoid cartilage to occlude the esophagus and prevent emesis from entering the airway.
- **Laryngectomy**
  A laryngectomy is the surgical removal of the larynx resulting in an opening or stoma where the trachea opens to the outside through the neck.

Content Self-Evaluation

MULTIPLE CHOICE

_____ 1. In the head-tilt/chin-lift maneuver, the fingers under the chin should apply a firm pressure to ensure the jaw remains closed.
A. True
B. False

_____ 2. The intent behind employing Sellick's maneuver is to:
A. displace the diaphragm.
B. increase venous return.
C. prevent regurgitation.
D. clear an airway obstruction.
E. increase blood flow to the brain.

_____ 3. Which of the following is an advantage of the nasopharyngeal airway over the oropharyngeal airway?
A. It has a larger diameter.
B. It is easier to insert.
C. It is blocked less frequently by vomitus.
D. It does not stimulate the gag reflex as strongly.
E. It can be used with a bag-valve mask.

_____ 4. Insertion of the nasopharyngeal airway directs the soft rubber tube:
A. directly up and into the nostril.
B. directly along the floor of the nasal cavity.
C. into the left nostril, most frequently.
D. laterally along the side of the nasal cavity.
E. directly into the vallecula space.

_____ 5. The airway adjunct that acts primarily by displacing the tongue forward is the:
A. oropharyngeal airway.
B. PtL airway.
C. endotracheal tube.
D. nasopharyngeal airway.
E. esophageal gastric tube airway.

_____ 6. The preferred technique of insertion for the oropharyngeal airway in pediatric patients calls for inserting the airway using a tongue blade without rotating the device.
A. True
B. False

_____ 7. The airway technique preferred for use with the patient who is unconscious is:
A. the oropharyngeal airway.
B. the nasopharyngeal airway.
C. endotracheal intubation.
D. nasotracheal intubation.
E. EGTA.

_____ 8. The light of the laryngoscope should be a bright yellow and flicker slightly when pressure is placed on the blade.
A. True
B. False

_____ 9. The tip of the curve of the Macintosh laryngoscope blade is designed to fit into the:
  A. nasopharynx.
  B. glottic opening.
  C. vallecula.
  D. arytenoid fossa.
  E. epiglottis.

_____ 10. The laryngoscope blade considered to be best designed for intubation of the pediatric patient is:
  A. the Macintosh blade.
  B. the curved blade.
  C. the straight blade.
  D. either B or C
  E. none of the above

_____ 11. The pilot balloon of the endotracheal tube should be very firm to ensure there is a good seal between the tube and the interior of the trachea.
  A. True
  B. False

_____ 12. The major purpose for using a malleable stylette during endotracheal intubation is to:
  A. maintain a preset curve in the tube.
  B. keep the tube's lumen open.
  C. stiffen the tube so it can be pushed through the glottis.
  D. prevent foreign matter from entering the tube.
  E. all of the above

_____ 13. Which of the following in NOT an indication for endotracheal intubation?
  A. respiratory arrest
  B. cardiac arrest
  C. inability to protect the airway
  D. obstruction due to foreign object, swelling, or burns
  E. severe epiglottitis

_____ 14. Which of the following is a likely occurrence when using an endotracheal intubation to secure the airway?
  A. Gastric distention is more likely.
  B. Complete airway control is achieved.
  C. The tracheal suctioning becomes more complicated.
  D. Medications can no longer be introduced into the trachea.
  E. It makes obtaining a good mask seal more difficult.

_____ 15. When using the laryngoscope to visualize the glottis, it is best to use the teeth as a fulcrum to increase your ability to lift the tissue.
  A. True
  B. False

_____ 16. To reduce the risk for hypoxia, limit attempts at intubation to no more than:
  A. 15 seconds.
  B. 30 seconds.
  C. 45 seconds.
  D. 60 seconds.
  E. 80 seconds.

_____ 17. Which of the following is NOT an indication for esophageal intubation?
  A. absence of chest rise with ventilation
  B. gurgling sound over the epigastrium
  C. a falling pulse oximetry reading
  D. skin color turning pink
  E. increasing resistance to ventilatory effort

_____ 18. Upon placing the endotracheal tube, you hear very faint breath sounds and some gurgling over the epigastric region. You should next:
  A. advance the tube slightly.
  B. withdraw the tube slightly.
  C. inflate the cuff and auscultate again.
  D. ventilate more forcibly.
  E. remove the tube and re-intubate.

_____ 19. Upon placing the endotracheal tube in a patient, you determine that you can only auscultate breath sounds on the right side. You should next:
   A. withdraw the tube a few centimeters.
   B. withdraw the tube completely.
   C. pass the tube a few centimeters further.
   D. secure the tube and ventilate more aggressively.
   E. check the mask seal.

_____ 20. The purpose of the cuff on the end of the endotracheal tube is to:
   A. help guide the tube to its proper location.
   B. prevent dislodging of the tube after it is correctly placed.
   C. seal the airway.
   D. center the tube in the trachea.
   E. widen the opening of the vocal cords.

_____ 21. What volume of air is used to inflate the cuff of an endotracheal tube?
   A. 2 to 4 mL   D. 10 to 15 mL
   B. 4 to 6 mL   E. 15 to 25 mL
   C. 5 to 10 mL

_____ 22. Confirmation of proper endotracheal tube placement is achieved by:
   A. visualizing the tube passing through the glottis.
   B. hearing clear and bilaterally equal breath sounds.
   C. noting the absence of gastric sounds with ventilation.
   D. observing condensation on the endotracheal tube with exhalation.
   E. any three of the above

_____ 23. Which of the following is NOT a standard procedure when performing endotracheal intubation using the transillumination technique?
   A. cutting the tube to 35 to 37 cm
   B. conforming the stylette and tube to a "hockey-stick" configuration
   C. placing the stylette in the ETT and locking the ETT in place at its proximal end
   D. lifting the patient's tongue and jaw forward with your fingers
   E. advancing the tube/stylette into the mouth and advancing it into the hypopharynx

_____ 24. The pattern of light that indicates that the lighted stylette is in the proper position to advance the endotracheal tube when performing transillumination intubation is:
   A. a very dim and diffuse light.
   B. a circle of light at the Adam's apple.
   C. a light on either side of the Adam's apple.
   D. absent light in the neck.
   E. a bright light above the Adam's apple.

_____ 25. Digital intubation may be indicated in all of the following EXCEPT:
   A. an unconscious trauma patient with suspected C-spine injury.
   B. a patient with facial injuries that distort the anatomy.
   C. an unconscious patient with a gag reflex.
   D. an entrapped patient who cannot be properly positioned.
   E. a patient with copious amounts of blood or other fluids remaining in the airway.

_____ 26. Indications for rapid sequence intubation include which of the following?
   A. impending respiratory failure
   B. acute disorder threatening the airway
   C. altered mental status with risk of aspiration
   D. Glasgow Coma Scale of 8 or less
   E. all of the above

_____ 27. Which of the following is NOT a paralytic agent used for rapid sequence intubation?
   A. succinylcholine
   B. midazolam
   C. vecuronium
   D. atracurium
   E. pancuronium

_____ 28. The duration of action of succinylcholine (Anectine) is approximately:
   A. 1 to 2 minutes.
   B. 2 to 3 minutes.
   C. 3 to 5 minutes.
   D. 4 to 6 minutes.
   E. 10 to 15 minutes.

_____ 29. If you cannot intubate the patient who has been paralyzed, the patient has no definitive airway.
   A. True
   B. False

_____ 30. The reason the succinylcholine is used in prehospital care is that it:
   A. is fast acting and of short duration.
   B. is the easiest to administer.
   C. does not cause muscle fasciculations.
   D. can be used with massive crush injuries.
   E. has a half life of 30 minutes.

_____ 31. It is essential that an adult patient be premedicated with vecuronium before the administration of succinylcholine because fasciculations are otherwise likely to cause musculoskeletal trauma.
   A. True
   B. False

_____ 32. In the intubation of children under eight years old, it is recommended that the paramedic use:
   A. a cuffed endotracheal tube and a straight laryngoscope blade.
   B. an uncuffed endotracheal tube and a straight laryngoscope blade.
   C. a cuffed endotracheal tube and a curved laryngoscope blade.
   D. an uncuffed endotracheal tube and a curved laryngoscope blade.
   E. an uncuffed endotracheal tube and digital technique.

_____ 33. Because of the anterior location of the glottic opening, it is essential to use a stylette with the endotracheal tube during pediatric intubation.
   A. True
   B. False

_____ 34. Which of the following is NOT an advantage of nasotracheal intubation?
   A. It is well tolerated by a semi-conscious patient.
   B. It is easier and quicker to perform than orotracheal intubation.
   C. It can be performed without displacing the patient's head.
   D. The tube cannot be bitten.
   E. The tube can be easily anchored.

_____ 35. Which of the following is NOT required for blind nasotracheal intubation?
   A. a neutral or slightly extended neck
   B. a generally quiet environment
   C. a strong, malleable stylette
   D. a patient who is breathing
   E. a preoxygenated patient

_____ 36. The primary danger associated with extubation is:
   A. laryngospasm.
   B. aspiration.
   C. fasciculations.
   D. tracheal damage.
   E. vomiting.

_____ 37. The major disadvantage to the use of the Esophageal Tracheal CombiTube is that:
  A. the trachea is not isolated.
  B. the tube must be in the trachea.
  C. it is associated with gastric distension and vomiting.
  D. it cannot be used in the trauma patient.
  E. it is somewhat time-consuming to insert.

_____ 38. Which of the following is a feature of the PtL airway?
  A. It can be inserted blindly.
  B. It can seal off the nasal and oral cavities.
  C. The patient can be ventilated regardless of whether the tube is in the trachea or esophagus.
  D. It can be inserted without moving the cervical spine.
  E. All of the above

_____ 39. The only indication for the use of a needle cricothyrotomy is the inability to establish an airway by any other means.
  A. True   B. False

_____ 40. An advantage to the use of a needle cricothyrotomy is that subsequent ventilation of the patient requires no special or additional equipment.
  A. True   B. False

_____ 41. The open cricothyrotomy should not be preformed on the patient under 12 years of age because the cricothyroid membrane is small and underdeveloped.
  A. True   B. False

_____ 42. Which of the following is a part of suctioning the stoma patient?
  A. preoxygenating with 100 percent oxygen
  B. injecting 3 mL of saline
  C. inserting the catheter until resistance is met
  D. withdrawing the catheter while the patient exhales or coughs
  E. all of the above

_____ 43. Which of the following is NOT indicated when suctioning through the endotracheal tube?
  A. Insert the catheter until you meet resistance.
  B. Suction only during insertion.
  C. Preoxygenate the patient.
  D. Rotate the suction catheter while suctioning.
  E. Suction no longer than 10 to 15 seconds.

_____ 44. Nasogastric tube placement is indicated in a patient:
  A. with facial fractures.
  B. with a possible basilar skull fracture.
  C. who is awake.
  D. for whom a relatively large gastric tube is indicated.
  E. all of the above

_____ 45. Which of the devices listed below delivers the highest concentration of oxygen to the patient?
  A. nasal cannula   D. Venturi mask
  B. simple face mask   E. A and D
  C. nonrebreather mask

_____ 46. Which of the devices below delivers the most controlled concentration of oxygen to a patient?
  A. nasal cannula   D. Venturi mask
  B. simple face mask   E. B and C
  C. nonrebreather mask

_____ 47. The bag-valve mask with an oxygen supply attached and oxygen flowing at 15 lpm delivers what percentage of oxygen to the patient?
   A. 21 percent
   B. 40 to 60 percent
   C. 60 to 70 percent
   D. 90 to 95 percent
   E. 99.9 percent

_____ 48. One rescuer bag-valve masking is difficult to perform effectively because:
   A. it is difficult to maintain proper airway positioning.
   B. it is difficult to maintain mask seal.
   C. it is difficult to squeeze the bag.
   D. all of the above
   E. none of the above

_____ 49. Hazards of using the demand valve to ventilate a patient include all of the following EXCEPT:
   A. oxygen toxicity.
   B. gastric distention.
   C. pulmonary barotrauma.
   D. pneumothorax.
   E. subcutaneous emphysema.

_____ 50. Which of the following is NOT an advantage of automatic ventilators?
   A. They free a rescuer when the patient is not breathing.
   B. They are convenient and easy to use.
   C. They are dependable.
   D. They can be used on children younger than age five years.
   E. They are lightweight and tolerant to temperature extremes.

Special Project

Problem Solving: Airway Maintenance

You have been called to a report of a man down and arrive with one EMT and another paramedic. You find bystanders doing CPR on a male in his mid-50s in a parking lot. You take the patient's head and determine the bystanders are doing a fine job of ventilating the patient. You get out your airway bag and prepare to place an endotracheal tube.

1. What equipment would you prepare?

   _____

   _____

   _____

2. How would you check your equipment?

   _____

   _____

   _____

   _____

3. What would you ask the ventilator to do before your attempt?

   _____

   _____

4. Identify the ten steps of the procedure you are about to attempt.

_____

_____

_____

_____

_____

_____

_____

_____

5. You place the endotracheal tube. What actions would you take to ensure it is properly placed?

_____

_____

_____

_____

_____

_____

_____

_____

_____

_____

6. You place the endotracheal tube and notice no chest rise with the first breath. Auscultation reveals diminished breath sounds and gurgling over the epigastric area. What actions would you take?

_____

_____

_____

_____

_____

Drugs Used in the Care of Patients with Airway Problems

Emergency management for patients with airway problems utilizes many of the pharmacological agents that are available to the paramedic. Please review and memorize the various names, indications, therapeutic effects, contraindications, side effects, routes of administration, and recommended dosages for the following medications. You can use the drug cards found at the back of this workbook for review.

Atracurium	Midazolam
Atropine	Oxygen
Diazepam	Pancuronium
Etomidate	Propofol
Fentanyl	Sodium thiopental
Ketamine	Succinylcholine
Lidocaine	Vecuronium

INTRODUCTION TO ADVANCED PREHOSPITAL CARE

Content Review

Content Self-Evaluation

Chapter 1: Introduction to Advanced Prehospital Care

_____ 1. The highest level of prehospital emergency care provider and the leader of the prehospital emergency team is the:
   A. EMT-Intermediate.
   B. paramedic.
   C. EMT-Basic.
   D. medical director.
   E. physician's assistant.

_____ 2. While required to be licensed, registered, or credentialed, paramedics still may only function as approved by and under the direction of the system's medical director.
   A. True
   B. False

_____ 3. The paramedic's traditional role has been that of:
   A. 911 responder.
   B. clinician.
   C. injury and illness prevention advocate.
   D. primary care specialist.
   E. physician's assistant.

_____ 4. The paramedic must ensure that patients receive the best possible care, regardless of ability to pay, as part of his role as:
   A. gatekeeper.
   B. facilitator.
   C. patient advocate.
   D. health resources link.
   E. clinician.

_____ 5. Which of the following is true regarding the 1998 DOT National Standard curriculum?
   A. It increases the educational standards for the EMT-Paramedic.
   B. It increases the understanding of the pathophysiology of various diseases.
   C. It increases the understanding of the pathophysiology of various injuries.
   D. Anatomy and physiology becomes a required prerequisite course.
   E. all of the above

_____ 6. A skill that is infrequently used in your career as a paramedic should be practiced more during ongoing education.
   A. True
   B. False

_____ 7. There are many unanswered questions about paramedic practice, and these can only be answered by sound scientific research.
   A. True
   B. False

8. Ethics can be defined as:
   A. a legal requirement of the profession.
   B. good manners.
   C. right or honorable behavior.
   D. playing the role of a patient advocate.
   E. none of the above

9. Which of the following is NOT an example of an expanded scope of practice for the paramedic?
   A. critical care transport
   B. 911
   C. industrial medicine
   D. sports medicine
   E. primary care

10. Paramedics have played an important role in the industrial setting, providing care on oil rigs, at movie sets, in factories, and in similar settings.
    A. True
    B. False

Chapter 2: The Well-Being of the Paramedic

11. The core elements of physical fitness are:
    A. muscular strength, speed, agility.
    B. muscular strength, good reflexes, speed.
    C. speed, cardiovascular endurance, flexibility.
    D. speed, cardiovascular endurance, agility.
    E. muscular strength, cardiovascular endurance, flexibility.

12. Active exercise performed while moving muscles through their range of motion is called:
    A. isometric.
    B. polymeric.
    C. aerobic.
    D. isotonic.
    E. anaerobic.

13. The target heart rate is:
    A. your ideal resting heart rate.
    B. your objective heart rate five minutes after exercise.
    C. an indicator of good cardiovascular exercise.
    D. a rate to achieve through exercise three times per week.
    E. both C and D

14. Good nutrition is fundamental because food is your fuel.
    A. True
    B. False

15. Which of the following is NOT a major food group?
    A. grains/bread
    B. dairy products
    C. carbohydrates
    D. meat/fish
    E. none of the above

16. The major source of calcium, protein, and vitamins A and D in a healthy diet is:
    A. vegetables.
    B. meat/fish.
    C. fruits.
    D. grains/breads.
    E. dairy products.

17. The old fashioned sit-up, practiced daily and in moderation, is very helpful in reducing the incidence of back injury.
    A. True
    B. False

©2006 Pearson Education, Inc.
Paramedic Care: Principles & Practice, Vol. 1

_____ 18. Which of the following is NOT part of proper lifting?
   A. positioning the load as close to the body as possible
   B. keeping your feet far apart
   C. keeping your back as straight as possible
   D. exhaling during the lift
   E. keeping your palms up

_____ 19. Only those patients with diagnosed HIV/AIDS, hepatitis B, and tuberculosis should be considered infectious and require you to use body substance isolation procedures.
   A. True   B. False

_____ 20. Which of the following items of personal protective equipment would you use with all patients?
   A. gloves   D. both A and B
   B. eyewear and mask   E. both A and C
   C. gowns

_____ 21. Which of the following items of personal protective equipment are recommended when intubating a patient?
   A. gloves   D. both A and B
   B. eyewear and mask   E. A, B, and C
   C. gowns

_____ 22. HEPA and N-95 respirators are to be used when suctioning, intubating, or providing nebulized treatments or just routine care for patients who have or are suspected of having:
   A. HIV/AIDS.   D. tuberculosis.
   B. hepatitis A.   E. bacterial meningitis.
   C. hepatitis B.

_____ 23. Gowns are recommended for which of the following situations?
   A. intubation   D. childbirth
   B. splashing blood   E. B and D
   C. suctioning

_____ 24. Disinfection of EMS equipment is most frequently done using:
   A. bleach.   D. pressurized steam.
   B. radiation.   E. an autoclave.
   C. chemical agents.

_____ 25. Which of the following places the progressive stages of grieving as you would expect to observe them in a patient?
   A. denial, anger, bargaining, depression, acceptance
   B. denial, bargaining, anger, depression, acceptance
   C. anger, denial, bargaining, acceptance, depression
   D. anger, denial, bargaining, depression, acceptance
   E. depression, anger, denial, bargaining, acceptance

_____ 26. A patient experiencing a major loss who puts off dealing with the event is most likely in which stage of loss?
   A. denial   D. bargaining
   B. anger   E. acceptance
   C. depression

_____ 27. Which age-group will most likely to seek out a detailed explanation of death and its difference from just being sick?
   A. newborn to age 3   D. ages 9 to 12
   B. ages 3 to 6   E. ages 12 to 18
   C. ages 6 to 9

_____ 28. When informing the family of the death of a member, use the words "moved on" or "has gone to a better place" rather than being blunt and using the words "dead" or "died."
A. True
B. False

_____ 29. The human response to stress progresses through three stages. They occur in which order?
A. alarm, resistance, exhaustion
B. resistance, alarm, exhaustion
C. alarm, exhaustion, resistance
D. resistance, exhaustion, alarm
E. exhaustion, alarm, resistance

_____ 30. The condition in which coping mechanisms can no longer buffer personal job stressors is called:
A. a critical incident.
B. professional overload.
C. stress.
D. disorientation.
E. burnout.

_____ 31. Which of the following is NOT a healthy behavior to help deal with or reduce stress?
A. controlled breathing
B. taking a few days off
C. reframing
D. having a few drinks to help put it behind you
E. creating a non-EMS circle of friends

_____ 32. An example of an event that is likely to be stressful for an EMS providers is:
A. suicide of an EMS worker.
B. death of a child.
C. bad incident that draws media attention.
D. serious accident with prolonged extrication.
E. all of the above

_____ 33. Recent evidence suggests that critical stress debriefing does not appear to mitigate the effects of traumatic stress.
A. True
B. False

_____ 34. In some societies, lack of eye contact is considered a sign of respect.
A. True
B. False

_____ 35. Death and disability are common results of ambulance crashes when patients are not well secured and care providers do not wear seatbelts.
A. True
B. False

Chapter 3: EMS Systems

_____ 36. In a tiered EMS system, system members have contact with the patient in which order?
A. emergency physician, dispatcher, ALS provider, BLS provider
B. dispatcher, ALS provider, BLS provider, emergency physician
C. dispatcher, BLS provider, ALS provider, emergency physician
D. dispatcher, BLS provider, emergency physician, ALS provider
E. none of the above

_____ 37. The concept of triage had its first use in prehospital medicine during:
A. the Napoleonic Wars.
B. the U.S. Civil War.
C. World War I.
D. World War II.
E. the Vietnam War.

©2006 Pearson Education, Inc.
Paramedic Care: Principles & Practice, Vol. 1

_____ 38. The first federal initiative to begin today's modern EMS system was:
  A. the Emergency Medical Services act.
  B. the Robert Wood Johnson grants.
  C. the National Highway Safety Act.
  D. the Consolidated Omnibus Budget Reconciliation Act.
  E. the Health, Education, and Welfare Act.

_____ 39. Which of the following was NOT a component of the Emergency Medical Services Act of 1973?
  A. communications
  B. standardized record keeping
  C. personnel training
  D. medical direction
  E. system evaluation

_____ 40. The medical director is a physician who has the responsibility to be an advocate for the system to the medical community and an advocate for quality patient care.
  A. True
  B. False

_____ 41. Insufficient research exists to demonstrate a relationship between response times and mortality rates of patients.
  A. True
  B. False

_____ 42. Enhanced 911 provides which of the following?
  A. automatic listing of the caller's location
  B. instant routing to the appropriate agency
  C. instant call-back capability
  D. all of the above
  E. none of the above

_____ 43. Priority dispatching is best described as:
  A. using medically approved protocols to determine response configuration.
  B. giving of prearrival instructions.
  C. ensuring ambulances are staged for response.
  D. both A and B
  E. all of the above

_____ 44. The learning domain associated with facts or knowledge is referred to as:
  A. cognitive.
  B. psychomotor.
  C. affective.
  D. didactic.
  E. dexterity.

_____ 45. The process by which an agency grants recognition to an individual who has met its qualifications is:
  A. licensure.
  B. certification.
  C. registration.
  D. reciprocity.
  E. graduation.

_____ 46. Which of the following is an example of expanded scope of practice for the EMT-Paramedic?
  A. critical care transport
  B. industrial EMS
  C. tactical EMS
  D. primary care
  E. all of the above

_____ 47. Through the National Registry of EMTs, individuals have access to a process tool by which they may receive reciprocity when moving from one state to another.
  A. True
  B. False

_____ 48. The Joint Review Committee on Educational Programs for the EMT-Paramedic does which of the following?
A. provides the principal basis for reciprocity in most states
B. oversees the training of paramedics in several states
C. certifies paramedics
D. establishes standards for didactic and clinical portions of paramedic training
E. serves a national referral agency

_____ 49. The agency responsible for establishing a standard list of ALS supplies and equipment for ambulances is the:
A. American College of Surgeons.
B. American College of Emergency Physicians.
C. Federal General Services Administration.
D. Military Assistance to Traffic and Safety Group.
E. National Department of Transportation.

_____ 50. A hospital designated as a receiving facility for the EMS system should have:
A. an emergency department.
B. 24-hour emergency physician coverage.
C. a documented desire to participate in the system.
D. desire to participate in multiple casualty preparedness plans.
E. all of the above

_____ 51. Which of the following is NOT a part of a well-designed disaster plan?
A. a diverse, noncentralized oversight approach
B. cooperation that supercedes geographical, political, and historical boundaries
C. frequent disaster plan tests and drills
D. integration of all system components
E. all of the above

_____ 52. Which of the following is NOT one of the rules of evidence used to evaluate a proposed change in the EMS system?
A. There must be a theoretical basis for the change.
B. There must be scientific research to support the change.
C. The change must be clinically important.
D. The change must be affordable, practical, and teachable.
E. The change must be approved by a majority of EMS practitioners.

_____ 53. In emergency medical service, customer satisfaction can be created or destroyed with a simple word or deed.
A. True   B. False

_____ 54. In the future, the ability of research to demonstrate the value of prehospital care may be essential to the survival of EMS.
A. True   B. False

_____ 55. The EMS system model that requires a competitive bid and establishes criteria for system performance is the:
A. public utility model.   D. volunteer model.
B. third service model.   E. proprietary model.
C. fire service model.

Chapter 4: Roles and Responsibilities of the Paramedic

_____ 56. As a paramedic, you will often serve people who are unaware of your knowledge and skills.
A. True   B. False

_____ 57. A paramedic unit answering which of the following calls is LEAST likely to require additional assistance?
   A. a motor vehicle collision
   B. reported use of a weapon
   C. a single patient with a medical illness
   D. a hazardous materials spill
   E. rescue situations

_____ 58. Which of the following is NOT a component of the scene size-up?
   A. identifying potential scene hazards
   B. identifying the number of patients
   C. applying a cervical collar
   D. requesting additional services
   E. determining the mechanism of injury

_____ 59. Specialty centers to which you may direct patients include which of the following?
   A. obstetric care centers
   B. trauma care centers
   C. stroke care centers
   D. burn care centers
   E. all of the above

_____ 60. The highest level of trauma center is:
   A. level I.
   B. level II.
   C. level III.
   D. level IV.
   E. none of the above

_____ 61. Which of the following is a statement of opinion that should not be included on a patient care report?
   A. "The patient was intoxicated."
   B. "The patient had the odor of alcohol on his breath."
   C. "The patient's speech was slurred."
   D. "The patient had difficulty walking."
   E. "The patient used inappropriate language when speaking."

_____ 62. As the volume of EMS responses decreases, so should the hours of training.
   A. True
   B. False

_____ 63. The paramedic who wishes to maintain interest in EMS and maintain skills and knowledge might participate in:
   A. in-hospital rotations.
   B. quality improvement activity.
   C. research projects.
   D. professional EMS organizations.
   E. all of the above

_____ 64. In general, a profession has:
   A. established standards.
   B. a specialized body of knowledge.
   C. requirements for ongoing education.
   D. requirements for initial education.
   E. all of the above

_____ 65. The paramedic should always place the needs of the patient above his own needs.
   A. True
   B. False

Chapter 5: Illness and Injury Prevention

_____ 66. Unintentional injury results in about how many deaths per year?
   A. 25,000
   B. 44,000
   C. 70,000
   D. 90,000
   E. 25,000

_____ 67. Injury prevention programs that focus on keeping an injury from ever occurring are examples of:
A. primary prevention.
B. secondary prevention.
C. tertiary prevention.
D. acute prevention.
E. none of the above

_____ 68. Other than the survivors and their families, no one experiences the aftermath of trauma more directly than EMS providers; hence those providers are prime candidates to be advocates of injury prevention.
A. True
B. False

_____ 69. Under the guidelines of the Occupational Safety and Health Administration (OSHA), responsibility for body substance isolation precautions is borne by:
A. the employee.
B. the health department.
C. the state EMS authority.
D. the employer.
E. both the employer and employee.

_____ 70. Which of the following is NOT essential to safe emergency driving?
A. being familiar with and obeying the traffic laws
B. understanding the capabilities and limitations of the vehicle
C. being able to drive at high speed in all conditions
D. using proper sound and visual warning devices
E. all of the above

_____ 71. Which of the following is NOT true of premature and low birth weight infants?
A. There are close to 300,000 of them born each year.
B. They are far more likely to die in the first year of life.
C. More than 4,000 of them die each year.
D. Very few have resulting disabilities.
E. Their conditions often result from inadequate prenatal care.

_____ 72. In children, the percentage of firearm injuries that are unintentional is about:
A. 10 percent.
B. 15 percent.
C. 25 percent.
D. 30 percent.
E. 33 percent.

_____ 73. Alcohol use is a factor in about what percentage of auto collisions?
A. 10 percent
B. 20 percent
C. 25 percent
D. 40 percent
E. 50 percent

_____ 74. The early release of patients from health care facilities to help control heath care costs is NOT likely to cause an increase in the number of EMS responses.
A. True
B. False

_____ 75. An action the EMS responder can take to implement injury prevention strategies might be to:
A. preserve response team safety.
B. recognize scene hazards.
C. engage in on-scene education.
D. know available community resources.
E. all of the above

Chapter 6: Medical/Legal Aspects of Advanced Prehospital Care

_____ 76. Moral responsibilities are best described as:
A. requirements of case law.
B. requirements of statute law.
C. standards of a profession.
D. personal feelings of right and wrong.
E. legal concepts of right and wrong.

©2006 Pearson Education, Inc.
Paramedic Care: Principles & Practice, Vol. 1

_____ 77. The term "judge-made law" is another name for:
   A. constitutional law.
   B. common law.
   C. legislative law.
   D. administrative law.
   E. criminal law.

_____ 78. The regulations that permit a governmental agency to implement statutes are examples of:
   A. constitutional law.
   B. common law.
   C. legislative law.
   D. administrative law.
   E. criminal law.

_____ 79. The type of law that limits the authority of the government is:
   A. constitutional law.
   B. common law.
   C. legislative law.
   D. administrative law.
   E. criminal law.

_____ 80. The division of the legal system that deals with conflicts between two or more parties such as contract disputes and matrimonial issues is:
   A. administrative law.
   B. criminal law.
   C. civil law.
   D. legislative law.
   E. constitutional law.

_____ 81. The individual initiating civil litigation is referred to as the:
   A. victim.
   B. plaintiff.
   C. defendant.
   D. initiator.
   E. damagee.

_____ 82. Which of the following is NOT a component of a paramedic's scope of practice?
   A. protocols
   B. system policies and procedures
   C. certification
   D. training and continuing education
   E. on-line medical direction

_____ 83. The degree of care, skill, and judgment that would be expected under like or similar circumstances by a similarly trained, reasonable paramedic is best defined as:
   A. duty to act.
   B. standard of care.
   C. breach of duty.
   D. proximate cause.
   E. malfeasance.

_____ 84. A paramedic's action or inaction that immediately caused or worsened damages suffered by a patient are referred to as being:
   A. the proximate cause.
   B. _res ipsa loquitur_.
   C. a wrongful tort.
   D. actual damages.
   E. negligible.

_____ 85. If your employer or agency carries insurance coverage, you are not encouraged to purchase your own because your employer's or agency's coverage is most likely adequate.
   A. True
   B. False

_____ 86. Disclosing confidential patient information may expose the paramedic to litigation for:
   A. defamation of character.
   B. breach of confidentiality.
   C. invasion of privacy.
   D. libel or slander.
   E. all of the above

_____ 87. The act of injuring an individual's character, name, or reputation by false spoken statements with malicious intent is called:
   A. slander.
   B. breach of confidentiality.
   C. malfeasance.
   D. misfeasance.
   E. libel.

_____ 88. Before beginning to treat a conscious, alert, and rational patient, you must obtain expressed consent.
A. True   B. False

_____ 89. To give informed consent, the patient must be told and understand:
A. the nature of the illness or injury.
B. the nature of the recommended treatment.
C. the risks of the recommended treatment.
D. the dangers of refusing the treatment.
E. all of the above

_____ 90. A patient who has once given consent may withdraw it at any time.
A. True   B. False

_____ 91. Which of the following would NOT be considered an emancipated minor?
A. a married teenager
B. a pregnant teenager
C. a financially independent teenager living at his parent's home
D. a parent
E. a member of the armed forces

_____ 92. Which of the following patients can refuse care?
A. a severely intoxicated patient
B. a minor
C. a conscious, alert, and rational adult
D. a patient who does not understand the intended treatment
E. a patient who does not understand the risks of treatment

_____ 93. If you leave a patient at the emergency department without ensuring that the staff is able to continue your care, you may be guilty of:
A. negligence.   D. nonfeasance.
B. abandonment.   E. assault.
C. malfeasance.

_____ 94. The unlawful act of placing another person in fear of bodily harm is:
A. assault.   D. slander.
B. abandonment.   E. libel.
C. battery.

_____ 95. If you need to use force to restrain a patient, it is best to achieve it without the assistance of the police, because they are often associated with punishment.
A. True   B. False

_____ 96. For which of the following patients would you attempt resuscitation?
A. one who is obviously dead
B. one with a valid DNR order
C. one with obvious tissue decomposition
D. one who has extreme dependant lividity
E. none of the above

_____ 97. If there is any doubt about the authenticity or applicability of a DNR order, you should initiate resuscitation.
A. True   B. False

_____ 98. At the crime scene, the paramedic's primary responsibility is to protect evidence and then to treat the patient.
A. True   B. False

_____ 99. Which of the following statements regarding a paramedic's responsibility at the crime scene is NOT true?
   A. Contact law enforcement if they are not on the scene.
   B. Do not enter the crime scene unless it is safe.
   C. The paramedic's primary responsibility is patient care.
   D. Take no action to preserve evidence at the crime because patient care is most important.
   E. Document the movement of any scene item.

_____100. Which of the following is NOT required when documenting a patient care response?
   A. Complete documentation promptly.
   B. Ensure it is accurate.
   C. Ensure it is objective.
   D. Maintain patient confidentiality.
   E. Ensure it is concise and brief.

Chapter 7: Ethics in Advanced Prehospital Care

_____101. Which of the following might lead to ethical problems?
   A. patients refusing care   D. confidentiality
   B. advanced directives   E. all of the above
   C. hospital destinations

_____102. Ethics go beyond examining what is right and wrong to consider what is right or good behavior.
   A. True   B. False

_____103. Most codes of ethics for professional groups address broad humanitarian concerns and professional etiquette.
   A. True   B. False

_____104. When faced with an ethical challenge, the best guiding question a paramedic can ask himself is:
   A. "How would I like to be treated?"
   B. "What is in the best interest of the patient?"
   C. "Which actions will account for the greatest good?"
   D. "What would the patient want?"
   E. "What would my supervisor do?"

_____105. The term referring to the paramedic's obligation to treat all patients fairly is:
   A. benevolence.   D. autonomy.
   B. justice.   E. euphylanthropnia.
   C. beneficence.

_____106. The Latin phrase *primum non nocere* is an excellent summation of the concept of:
   A. beneficence.   D. nonmaleficence.
   B. autonomy.   E. none of the above
   C. justice.

_____107. The question that best represents the interpersonal justifiability test for analyzing an ethical situation is:
   A. "Can you justify this action to others?"
   B. "Would you want this procedure if you were in the patient's place?"
   C. "Would you want this procedure performed on you if you were in similar circumstances?"
   D. "Will you likely be questioned about the need for this procedure later?"
   E. none of the above

_____108. When presented with a valid DNR order, the paramedic should:
  A. begin resuscitation immediately.
  B. contact the patient's physician to verify the order's validity.
  C. contact medical direction for advice before beginning resuscitation.
  D. not begin resuscitation.
  E. begin with CPR and delay advanced interventions.

_____109. Appropriate reasons for breaching patient confidentiality include:
  A. particular infectious diseases.
  B. a reporter's request for information.
  C. elderly neglect and abuse.
  D. satisfying a co-worker's curiosity.
  E. A and C

_____110. When presented with orders from a physician that do not comply with your protocols and that you believe are not in the patient's best interest, which of the following should you do?
  A. Follow the physician's order and report your concerns to the medical director.
  B. Ask the physician to repeat or confirm the order.
  C. Ask the physician for an explanation of the order.
  D. Do not follow the physician's order.
  E. all except A

Chapter 8: General Principles of Pathophysiology, Part 1

_____111. The main elements of a typical cell include all of the following EXCEPT the:
  A. cilia.   D. cytoplasm.
  B. cell membrane.   E. all except B and D
  C. organelles.

_____112. Which of the following is NOT an organelle?
  A. Golgi apparatus   D. lysosome
  B. mitochondria   E. cytoplasm
  C. endoplasmic reticulum

_____113. All of the following are common cell functions EXCEPT:
  A. reproduction.   D. conductivity.
  B. secretion.   E. metabolic absorption.
  C. contractility.

_____114. The component of the cell that converts carbohydrates into energy sources is the:
  A. mitochondria.   D. Golgi apparatus.
  B. lysosome.   E. cytoplasm.
  C. nucleus.

_____115. The tissue type that can spontaneously contract is:
  A. epithelial.   D. connective.
  B. cardiac muscle.   E. skeletal muscle.
  C. nerve.

_____116. The tissue type that transmits electrical impulses throughout the body is:
  A. epithelial.   D. connective.
  B. cardiac muscle.   E. skeletal muscle.
  C. nerve.

_____117. The body organ system that plays an important role in regulation of body fluids and electrolytes is the:
  A. muscular.   D. endocrine.
  B. gastrointestinal.   E. lymphatic.
  C. genitourinary.

©2006 Pearson Education, Inc.
Paramedic Care: Principles & Practice, Vol. 1

_____118. The body organ system that releases chemical messengers to affect other organs is the:
   A. muscular.
   B. gastrointestinal.
   C. genitourinary.
   D. endocrine.
   E. lymphatic.

_____119. The term that applies to the building up of biochemical substances to produce energy is:
   A. anatomy.
   B. physiology.
   C. catabolism.
   D. anabolism.
   E. metabolism.

_____120. Ductless or endocrine glands secrete directly onto the surface of the body.
   A. True
   B. False

_____121. The body's major chemoreceptors are located in the:
   A. arch of the aorta.
   B. brain.
   C. lungs.
   D. tongue.
   E. heart.

_____122. Most of the input affecting body organs and homeostasis occurs via the negative feedback loop.
   A. True
   B. False

_____123. The form of cellular adaptation in which cell size decreases due to a decrease in workload is:
   A. atrophy.
   B. hypertrophy.
   C. hyperplasia.
   D. metaplasia.
   E. dysplasia.

_____124. The form of cellular adaptation in which there is an increase in the number of cells due to an increase in workload is:
   A. atrophy.
   B. hypertrophy.
   C. hyperplasia.
   D. metaplasia.
   E. dysplasia.

_____125. The type of cellular injury caused by a hypersensitivity response is:
   A. hypoxic.
   B. chemical.
   C. infectious.
   D. immunological.
   E. hypertonic.

_____126. A pathogen's virulence is related to its ability to:
   A. invade cells.
   B. destroy cells.
   C. produce toxins.
   D. produce hypersensitivity reactions.
   E. all of the above

_____127. The body's natural process for removal of the body's dead and nonfunctioning cells is:
   A. apoptosis.
   B. fatty change.
   C. necrosis.
   D. gangrene.
   E. none of the above

_____128. The form of cell death in which cells take on a cottage cheese–like consistency is:
   A. fatty necrosis.
   B. liquefactive necrosis.
   C. caseous necrosis.
   D. coagulative necrosis.
   E. cellulose necrosis.

_____129. The interstitial compartment contains all the fluids found outside the cellular compartment.
   A. True
   B. False

_____130. The percentage of total body water made up of intravascular fluid is:
   A. 75 percent.
   B. 60 percent.
   C. 25 percent.
   D. 17.5 percent.
   E. 7.5 percent.

_____131. The universal solvent is:
   A. water.
   B. sodium.
   C. plasma.
   D. calcium.
   E. hydrogen.

_____132. Dehydration from plasma loss can result from:
   A. hyperventilation.
   B. poor nutritional states.
   C. pancreatitis.
   D. burns.
   E. all of the above

_____133. A negatively charged ion is called a(n):
   A. anion.
   B. cation.
   C. electrolyte.
   D. dissociated element.
   E. none of the above

_____134. The most frequently occurring anion in the human body is:
   A. magnesium.
   B. chloride.
   C. potassium.
   D. calcium.
   E. sodium.

_____135. Which of the following is NOT an electrolyte?
   A. sodium bicarbonate
   B. calcium chloride
   C. glucose
   D. sodium chloride
   E. none of the above

_____136. A solution that contains a lesser concentration of solute molecules than another is referred to as:
   A. hypertonic.
   B. isotonic.
   C. hypotonic.
   D. osmotic.
   E. hyperbaric.

_____137. When a hypotonic solution is placed in the human bloodstream, water moves in what manner?
   A. into the vascular space
   B. it does not move
   C. out of the vascular space
   D. both into and out of the vascular space
   E. none of the above

_____138. The movement of a solute from an area of higher concentration to an area of lower concentration is:
   A. diffusion.
   B. osmosis.
   C. active transport.
   D. facilitated transport.
   E. oncosis.

_____139. The mechanism by which glucose is transported across a cell membrane using helper proteins is:
   A. diffusion.
   B. osmosis.
   C. active transport.
   D. facilitated transport.
   E. oncosis.

_____140. The pressure pushing water out of plasma and across the capillary wall into the interstitial space is:
   A. osmolarity.
   B. osmotic pressure.
   C. hydrostatic pressure.
   D. oncotic force.
   E. filtration.

_____141. Which of the following is NOT a mechanism that commonly produces edema?
  A. a decrease in plasma osmotic force
  B. an increase in hydrostatic pressure
  C. increased capillary permeability
  D. venous dilation
  E. lymphatic channel obstruction

_____142. The blood component that contains hemoglobin and is responsible for transporting most of the oxygen from the lungs to the body cells is:
  A. plasma.   D. leukocytes.
  B. the platelets.   E. hemoglobin.
  C. erythrocytes.

_____143. The blood component that helps the body fight infection is:
  A. plasma.   D. the leukocytes.
  B. the platelets.   E. hemoglobin.
  C. the erythrocytes.

_____144. The blood component that comprises 99 percent of the formed elements is:
  A. plasma.   D. the leukocytes.
  B. the platelets.   E. hemoglobin.
  C. the erythrocytes.

_____145. Common signs of a transfusion reaction include:
  A. hypotension.   D. vomiting.
  B. tachycardia.   E. all of the above
  C. headache.

_____146. A small volume of colloid solution can be administered to a patient with a greater-than-expected increase in the intravascular volume.
  A. True   B. False

_____147. The solution that will cause a net movement of water out of the erythrocytes is:
  A. a colloid solution.   D. an isotonic solution.
  B. a hypertonic solution.   E. both A and B
  C. a hypotonic solution.

_____148. The solution that will cause a net movement of water into the intravascular space is:
  A. a colloid solution.   D. an isotonic solution.
  B. a hypertonic solution.   E. both A and B
  C. a hypotonic solution.

_____149. An example of a hypotonic solution is:
  A. lactated Ringer's solution. D. D_5W.
  B. normal saline.   E. plasmanate.
  C. dextran.

_____150. The lower the pH value, the lower the concentration of hydrogen ions.
  A. True   B. False

_____151. A pH value that would be considered acidosis in the human is:
  A. 6.9 to 7.35.   D. 7.6 to 7.75.
  B. 7.35 to 7.45.   E. 7.75 and greater.
  C. 7.45 to 7.5.

_____152. An increase in pH of 1 would reflect a concentration of hydrogen ions:
  A. 100 times as great.   D. 1/100th less great.
  B. 10 times as great.   E. a doubling.
  C. 1/10th less great.

_____153. The mechanism that responds most slowly to a change in the pH of the body is:
A. endocrine function.
B. kidney function.
C. the digestive system.
D. the buffer system.
E. none of the above

_____154. The addition of carbon dioxide to the bloodstream will result in an increase in hydrogen ions.
A. True
B. False

_____155. Respiratory acidosis is caused by a retention of carbon dioxide in the lungs.
A. True
B. False

Chapter 8: General Principles of Pathophysiology, Part 2

_____156. Most disease processes are caused by both environmental and genetic factors.
A. True
B. False

_____157. The proportion of the population affected by a disease at a given point in time is that disease's:
A. prevalence.
B. morbidity.
C. mortality.
D. incidence.
E. average.

_____158. Few diseases with a genetic disposition have risk factors that are modifiable.
A. True
B. False

_____159. The percentage of lung cancer in men associated with smoking is:
A. 40 percent.
B. 60 percent.
C. 70 percent.
D. 75 percent.
E. 90 percent.

_____160. Which of the following are associated with ulcer development?
A. stress
B. nonsteroidal antiinflammatory drugs
C. diet
D. alcohol consumption
E. all of the above

_____161. Which of the following may cause hypoperfusion?
A. blood loss
B. spinal injury
C. myocardial infarction
D. severe disease
E. all of the above

_____162. The portion of the cardiovascular system that is known as the capacitance system is the:
A. venous system.
B. heart.
C. arterial system.
D. capillary beds.
E. lymphatic system.

_____163. Cardiac afterload is determined by:
A. peripheral vascular resistance.
B. cardiac output.
C. blood pressure.
D. the Frank-Starling mechanism.
E. all of the above

_____164. When baroreceptors detect a fall in blood pressure, they cause a(n):
A. increase in heart rate.
B. increase in the strength of myocardial contraction.
C. venous constriction.
D. arteriolar constriction.
E. all of the above

_____165. Contraction of the arterial blood vessels will:
   A. increase preload.
   B. decrease arterial pressure.
   C. increase peripheral vascular resistance.
   D. decrease vascular volume.
   E. reduce blood pressure.

_____166. Which of the following is NOT one of the conditions of oxygen movement and utilization that make up the Fick principle?
   A. adequate exhaled carbon dioxide
   B. adequate oxygen diffusion in lungs
   C. proper tissue perfusion
   D. efficient oxygen off-loading
   E. adequate red blood cells

_____167. Hypoperfusion ultimately causes shock at the cellular level.
   A. True   B. False

_____168. Anaerobic metabolism occurs in the absence of:
   A. carbon dioxide.   D. pyruvic acid.
   B. tissue perfusion.   E. nitrogen.
   C. oxygen.

_____169. During hypoperfusion, the catecholamines epinephrine and norepinephrine are responsible for:
   A. increasing heart rate.
   B. increasing cardiac contractile strength.
   C. arteriolar constriction.
   D. increasing blood pressure.
   E. all of the above

_____170. During hypoperfusion, the hormone ADH is responsible for:
   A. increasing red blood cell production.
   B. causing the spleen to release blood.
   C. producing a potent vasoconstrictor.
   D. increasing re-absorption of water by the kidneys.
   E. increasing the heart rate.

_____171. During decompensated shock, which of the following is likely to occur?
   A. myocardial hypoxia and reduced output
   B. a speeding up of sympathetic activity
   C. dilution of the blood
   D. decreased capillary permeability
   E. release of beta$_2$

_____172. The type of shock resulting from severe heart damage from an MI is:
   A. cardiogenic.   D. septic.
   B. hypovolemic.   E. anaphylactic.
   C. neurogenic.

_____173. The type of shock resulting from dehydration from prolonged vomiting is:
   A. cardiogenic.   D. septic.
   B. hypovolemic.   E. anaphylactic.
   C. neurogenic.

_____174. The type of shock resulting from a severe spinal cord injury is:
   A. cardiogenic.   D. septic.
   B. hypovolemic.   E. anaphylactic.
   C. neurogenic.

_____175. Multiple organ dysfunction syndrome is a massive inflammatory response triggered by a severe disease or injury.
A. True
B. False

Chapter 8: General Principles of Pathophysiology, Part 3

_____176. Which of the following are released by bacteria during their destruction?
A. antibiotics
B. gram-negative material
C. exotoxins
D. endotoxins
E. histamines

_____177. The infectious agents that are made almost entirely of protein and do not have protective capsids are:
A. viruses.
B. bacteria.
C. fungi.
D. parasites.
E. prions.

_____178. When the body is infected, the skin provides an:
A. external, specific response to infection.
B. external, nonspecific response to infection.
C. internal, specific response to infection.
D. internal, nonspecific response to infection.
E. both A and B

_____179. The inflammatory response to infection is more rapid than the immune response and is not specific to the invading organism.
A. True
B. False

_____180. The principal agent of the immune response that identifies "non-self" proteins located on the surface of many cells is called a(n):
A. antigen.
B. antibody.
C. B cell.
D. T cell.
E. lymphocyte.

_____181. The type of immunity that is an outcome of an immune response is:
A. primary.
B. acquired.
C. natural.
D. secondary.
E. B and D

_____182. The type of immunity that does not produce antibodies but attacks the invading agent directly is:
A. cell-mediated.
B. humoral.
C. natural.
D. primary.
E. both A and C

_____183. Which of the following is NOT one of the essential characteristics of an immunogen?
A. sufficient foreignness
B. sufficient size
C. sufficient complexity
D. sufficient density
E. sufficient quantity

_____184. The erythrocytes (red blood cells) have HLA antigens on their surface like all other body cells.
A. True
B. False

_____185. Under the ABO classification of blood antigens, the universal blood recipient is blood type:
A. A.
B. B.
C. O.
D. AB.
E. both C and D

_____186. With which of the following blood types would an individual have only the anti-A antibody?
A. A
B. B
C. O
D. AB
E. both B and D

_____187. Infants are given some immunity from antibodies that cross the placental barrier.
A. True
B. False

_____188. Which of the following is NOT a function of the inflammatory response?
A. destroying and removing unwanted substances
B. recognizing "non-self" antigens
C. stimulating the immune response
D. promoting healing
E. walling off the infected and inflamed area

_____189. When cells are injured, the inflammatory response begins within seconds.
A. True
B. False

_____190. The cell that is the chief activator of the inflammatory response is the:
A. mast cell.
B. T cell.
C. B cell.
D. C cell.
E. phagocyte.

_____191. The agent released by mast cells during the inflammatory response that increases blood flow to the injury site is:
A. the chemotaxic factor.
B. IgE.
C. histamine.
D. serotonin.
E. cortisol.

_____192. To help corral an invading organism, the coagulation system produces a protein fiber called:
A. bradykinin.
B. fibrin.
C. fibrous enzyme.
D. fibrinogen.
E. serotonin.

_____193. The collection of white cells along blood vessel walls during the early stages of inflammation is:
A. margination.
B. diapedesis.
C. granulocytosis.
D. active transport.
E. exudation.

_____194. Which of the following cells are involved in the immune response?
A. monocytes
B. neutrophils
C. basophils
D. eosinophils
E. all of the above

_____195. A growth that forms to wall off infection from the rest of the body is:
A. pus.
B. a fibroblast.
C. a granuloma.
D. a granulocyte.
E. a phagocyte.

_____196. Scab generation occurs during which stage of the wound healing process?
A. initial response
B. granulation
C. epithelialization
D. contraction
E. none of the above

_____197. The impaired wound healing experienced by the elderly is most commonly due to the incidence of chronic disease.
A. True
B. False

_____198. The hypersensitivity associated with disturbance in tolerance for one's own "self" antigens is:
   A. allergy.
   B. anaphylaxis.
   C. autoimmunity.
   D. isoimmunity.
   E. monoimmunity.

_____199. Rheumatoid arthritis is a disease involving:
   A. allergy.
   B. anaphylaxis.
   C. autoimmunity.
   D. isoimmunity.
   E. none of the above

_____200. The type of immune deficiencies related to medical treatment is:
   A. nutritional.
   B. iatrogenic.
   C. stress induced.
   D. trauma induced.
   E. all of the above

_____201. The second stage of the general adaptation syndrome in response to stress involves:
   A. exhaustion.
   B. resistance.
   C. adaptation.
   D. alarm.
   E. both B and C

_____202. The category of hormones called catecholamines includes:
   A. epinephrine.
   B. endorphins.
   C. cortisol.
   D. norepinephrine.
   E. both A and D

_____203. Stimulation of the alpha$_2$ receptors will cause:
   A. increased heart rate.
   B. inhibition of norepinephrine release.
   C. vasoconstriction.
   D. bronchodilation.
   E. all of the above

_____204. Stimulation of the beta$_1$ receptors will cause:
   A. increased heart rate.
   B. inhibition of the effects of norepinephrine.
   C. vasoconstriction.
   D. bronchodilation.
   E. lacrimation.

_____205. Cortisol has a harmful immunosuppressive action that may, however, be beneficial in protecting against stress.
   A. True
   B. False

Chapter 9: General Principles of Pharmacology, Part 1

_____206. "Valium" is an example of what type of drug name?
   A. chemical
   B. generic
   C. official
   D. brand
   E. common

_____207. "Diazepam, USP" is an example of what type of drug name?
   A. chemical name
   B. generic name
   C. official name
   D. brand name
   E. common name

_____208. Which of the following is a common source of drugs?
   A. plant
   B. animal
   C. mineral
   D. synthetic
   E. all of the above

_____209. Calcium chloride is an example of a drug from:
- A. plant sources.
- B. animal sources.
- C. mineral sources.
- D. synthetic sources.
- E. all of the above

_____210. A drug that is classified as a Schedule I controlled substance is:
- A. heroin.
- B. morphine.
- C. codeine.
- D. diazepam.
- E. B and C

_____211. The current oversight of narcotics and addictive substances is regulated under the:
- A. Pure Food and Drug Act of 1906.
- B. Harrison Narcotic Act of 1914.
- C. Federal Food and Cosmetic Act of 1938.
- D. Controlled Substances Act of 1970.
- E. Prescription Drug Amendments.

_____212. The bioassay of a drug in a preparation is a test to determine the drug's:
- A. potency.
- B. amount and purity.
- C. effectiveness.
- D. availability in a biological model.
- E. effectiveness compared to other like drugs.

_____213. You should inspect the label of a drug you are about to administer:
- A. when you remove the medication from the drug box.
- B. as you draw up the medication.
- C. immediately before administering to the patient.
- D. both A and C
- E. A, B, and C

_____214. During the last trimester of pregnancy, medication administration does not present as great a risk as earlier in the pregnancy because most drugs will not cross the placenta to the fetus.
- A. True
- B. False

_____215. Drugs confer new properties on cells or tissues through complicated biochemical reactions.
- A. True
- B. False

_____216. Which of the following is NOT one of the processes of pharmacokinetics?
- A. absorption
- B. distribution
- C. biotransformation
- D. antagonism
- E. elimination

_____217. The movement of large molecules through the cell membrane using special carrier proteins is:
- A. diffusion.
- B. active transport.
- C. osmosis.
- D. filtration.
- E. facilitated diffusion.

_____218. The movement of solvent in solution from an area of lower concentration to an area of higher concentration is:
- A. diffusion.
- B. active transport.
- C. osmosis.
- D. filtration.
- E. facilitated transport.

_____219. The breaking down of a drug by the body that facilitates the drug's activity or elimination is its:
A. bioavailability.
B. biotransformation.
C. metabolism.
D. prodrug effect.
E. none of the above

_____220. Which of the following is a medium for elimination of a drug from the body?
A. urine
B. respiratory air
C. feces
D. sweat
E. all of the above

_____221. Which of the following is NOT an enteral route of drug administration?
A. oral
B. intraosseous
C. umbilical
D. sublingual
E. rectal

_____222. The administration route that delivers medication most quickly and specifically to the lungs is:
A. intramuscular.
B. nebulization.
C. topical.
D. intravenous.
E. endotracheal.

_____223. Drugs that are mixed with a wax-like base that dissolves at body temperature are:
A. pills.
B. suppositories.
C. tablets.
D. capsules.
E. suspensions.

_____224. Drugs that are powders or small pills placed in gelatin containers are:
A. pills.
B. suppositories.
C. tablets.
D. capsules.
E. suspensions.

_____225. Preparations of volatile drugs in alcohol are called:
A. solutions.
B. tinctures.
C. suspensions.
D. spirits.
E. elixirs.

_____226. Preparations made using an alcohol extraction process are:
A. solutions.
B. tinctures.
C. suspensions.
D. spirits.
E. elixirs.

_____227. Variables that must be considered when determining the proper method for storing drugs include:
A. temperature.
B. light.
C. moisture and humidity.
D. shelf life.
E. all of the above

_____228. The force of attraction between a drug and its receptor site is referred to as its:
A. affinity.
B. efficacy.
C. agonism.
D. antagonism.
E. none of the above

_____229. A chemical that binds to a receptor site and causes the expected effect is called a(n):
A. partial antagonist.
B. competitive antagonist.
C. agonist.
D. antagonist.
E. noncompetitive antagonist.

©2006 Pearson Education, Inc.
Paramedic Care: Principles & Practice, Vol. 1

_____230. A chemical that binds to a receptor site, causes the expected effect, changes the receptor site, and prevents other drugs from triggering it is called a(n):
A. partial antagonist.
B. competitive antagonist.
C. agonist.
D. antagonist.
E. noncompetitive antagonist.

_____231. Naloxone (Narcan) is a(n):
A. agonist-antagonist.
B. competitive antagonist.
C. agonist.
D. pseudoantagonist.
E. noncompetitive antagonist.

_____232. A rapidly occurring tolerance to a drug is called:
A. idiosyncrasy.
B. tachyphylaxis.
C. antagonism.
D. synergism.
E. potentiation.

_____233. The response in which a drug enhances the actions of another is called:
A. idiosyncrasy.
B. tachyphylaxis.
C. antagonism.
D. synergism.
E. potentiation.

_____234. The time from administration until the drug reaches the minimum effective dose is its:
A. onset of action.
B. duration of action.
C. therapeutic index.
D. biological half-life.
E. termination of action.

_____235. The time it takes to reduce the concentration of a drug in the body by 50 percent is its:
A. onset of action.
B. duration of action.
C. therapeutic index.
D. biological half-life.
E. termination of action.

Chapter 9: General Principles of Pharmacology, Part 2

_____236. Control of the body's automatic functions is provided by the:
A. somatic nervous system.
B. autonomic nervous system.
C. peripheral nervous system.
D. central nervous system.
E. voluntary nervous system.

_____237. Control of the body's voluntary functions is provided by the:
A. somatic nervous system.
B. autonomic nervous system.
C. peripheral nervous system.
D. central nervous system.
E. voluntary nervous system.

_____238. The "fight-or-flight" response is controlled by the:
A. somatic nervous system.
B. autonomic nervous system.
C. sympathetic nervous system.
D. parasympathetic nervous system.
E. voluntary nervous system.

_____239. Anesthetics, as a group, tend to cause:
A. reduced sensation.
B. respiratory stimulation.
C. central nervous system elevation.
D. cardiovascular stimulation.
E. all of the above

_____240. Sedation is a term that describes:
A. decreased anxiety.
B. induction of sleep.
C. reduced sensation.
D. decreased pain sensation.
E. opioid antagonism.

_____241. The class of drugs called amphetamines cause:
  A. the release of norepinephrine.
  B. the release of dopamine.
  C. an increased wakefulness.
  D. decreased appetite.
  E. all of the above

_____242. Extrapyramidal symptoms associated with psychotherapeutic medication administration include:
  A. muscle tremors.
  B. fatigue.
  C. tachycardia.
  D. anxiety.
  E. all of the above

_____243. The side effects of the antipsychotic drugs include:
  A. extrapyramidal symptoms.
  B. orthostatic hypotension.
  C. sedation.
  D. sexual dysfunction.
  E. all of the above

_____244. Which of the following is NOT a sign or symptom of depression?
  A. weight gain
  B. loss of energy
  C. enhanced concentration
  D. suicide attempts
  E. feelings of hopelessness

_____245. Tricyclic antidepressants (TCAs) act by blocking the uptake of serotonin and dopamine, thereby extending their duration of action.
  A. True
  B. False

_____246. When taken in overdose, tricyclic antidepressants can cause:
  A. CNS depression.
  B. respiratory depression.
  C. cardiotoxic effects.
  D. neurotoxic sedation.
  E. none of the above

_____247. Parkinson's disease is an imbalance in the actions of dopamine and acetylcholine.
  A. True
  B. False

_____248. The system that works in opposition to the sympathetic nervous system is the:
  A. somatic nervous system.
  B. autonomic nervous system.
  C. central nervous system.
  D. peripheral nervous system.
  E. none of the above

_____249. The adrenergic neurotransmitter is:
  A. acetylcholine.
  B. epinephrine.
  C. norepinephrine.
  D. muscarinic antagonist.
  E. muscarinic agonist.

_____250. The parasympathetic nervous system originates from which nerve root regions?
  A. cranial and sacral
  B. cranial and lumbar
  C. cranial and thoracic
  D. thoracic and lumbar
  E. thoracic and sacral

_____251. A drug that blocks or inhibits the actions of the parasympathetic nervous system is a:
  A. sympatholytic.
  B. sympathomimetic.
  C. parasympatholytic.
  D. parasympathomimetic.
  E. none of the above

_____252. A drug that stimulates the parasympathetic nervous system is a:
  A. sympatholytic.
  B. sympathomimetic.
  C. parasympatholytic.
  D. parasympathomimetic.
  E. none of the above

_____253. The effects of cholinergic stimulation include all of the following EXCEPT:
  A. salivation.
  B. lacrimation.
  C. defecation.
  D. blurred vision.
  E. emesis.

254. Side effects of atropine include:
  A. blurred vision.
  B. dry mouth.
  C. photophobia.
  D. anhidrosis.
  E. all of the above

255. Epinephrine accounts for what percentage of the neurotransmitters released by the adrenal gland when it is stimulated?
  A. 20 percent
  B. 40 percent
  C. 60 percent
  D. 80 percent
  E. 90 percent

256. Stimulation of which type of receptor causes peripheral vasoconstriction, mild bronchoconstriction, and increased metabolism?
  A. alpha$_1$
  B. alpha$_2$
  C. beta$_1$
  D. beta$_2$
  E. dopaminergic

257. Stimulation of which of the following receptors increases heart rate, cardiac contractile force, cardiac automaticity, and cardiac conduction?
  A. alpha$_1$
  B. alpha$_2$
  C. beta$_1$
  D. beta$_2$
  E. dopaminergic

258. A type of drug that causes peripheral vasoconstriction is a(n):
  A. beta$_2$ agonist.
  B. beta$_1$ antagonist.
  C. beta$_1$ agonist.
  D. alpha$_1$ antagonist.
  E. alpha$_1$ agonist.

259. A type of drug that causes increased heart rate, contractility, and conduction is a(n):
  A. beta$_2$ agonist.
  B. beta$_1$ antagonist.
  C. beta$_1$ agonist.
  D. alpha$_1$ antagonist.
  E. alpha$_1$ agonist.

260. Which of the following is a synthetic catecholamine?
  A. isoproterenol
  B. dopamine
  C. atropine
  D. propranolol
  E. none of the above

261. The order in which an electrical impulse travels through the cardiac conduction system is:
  A. SA node, internodal pathways, AV node, bundle of His, Purkinje fibers.
  B. AV node, internodal pathways, SA node, bundle of His, Purkinje fibers.
  C. internodal pathways, AV node, SA node, Purkinje fibers, bundle of His.
  D. bundle of His, SA node, AV node, Purkinje fibers, internodal pathways.
  E. bundle of His, SA node, internodal pathways, AV node, Purkinje fibers.

262. The unique property of myocardial muscle tissue allowing it to transmit an electrical impulse to adjacent cells is:
  A. inotropy.
  B. automaticity.
  C. contractility.
  D. conductivity.
  E. depolarization.

263. The drug of choice for torsade de pointes is:
  A. atropine.
  B. bretylium.
  C. magnesium.
  D. digoxin.
  E. adenosine.

264. Digoxin has which of the following effects on the heart?
   A. increases the intrinsic firing rate of the SA node
   B. increases conduction through the AV node
   C. decreases the ventricular refractory period
   D. decreases ventricular automaticity
   E. recharges the firing rate of the Purkinje fibers

265. Hypertension is a major contributor to all of the following EXCEPT:
   A. coronary artery disease.   D. blindness.
   B. stroke.   E. all of the above
   C. depression.

266. A diuretic is used to:
   A. reduce circulating blood volume.   D. reduce baroreceptor effectiveness.
   B. dilate the arterial system.   E. increase renal blood flow.
   C. dilate the venous system.

267. Nitroglycerin rapidly loses its potency when exposed to:
   A. humidity.   D. cold.
   B. light.   E. oxygen.
   C. heat.

268. Which of the following statements is true regarding digoxin?
   A. It has a very large therapeutic index.
   B. Individual variability is minor.
   C. Normal use does not cause toxicity in patients.
   D. It may cause the dysrhythmias it is intended to treat.
   E. all of the above

269. The clotting cascade can be interrupted by:
   A. antiplatelets.   D. hemostatic agents.
   B. anticoagulants.   E. antithrombolytics.
   C. fibrinolytics.

270. The major side effect of aspirin when it is used to help prevent the heart attack is:
   A. stroke.   D. tachycardia.
   B. chest pain.   E. metabolic acidosis.
   C. bleeding.

271. Medications that break up blood clots after they have formed are:
   A. antiplatelets.   D. hemostatic agents.
   B. anticoagulants.   E. analgesics.
   C. fibrinolytics.

272. A causative factor for coronary artery disease is:
   A. low-density lipoproteins (LDL).
   B. very low-density lipoproteins (VLDL).
   C. high-density lipoproteins (HDL).
   D. intermediate-density lipoproteins (IDL).
   E. all of the above

273. The pathophysiology of asthma has two basic components, which are:
   A. bronchoconstriction and vasodilation.
   B. vasodilation and inflammation.
   C. sequestration and inflammation.
   D. bronchoconstriction and inflammation.
   E. vasodilation and sequestration.

274. A nonselective sympathomimetic agent used to treat asthma is:
    A. terbutaline.
    B. albuterol.
    C. theophylline.
    D. epinephrine.
    E. ipratropium.

275. Histamine is released during the invasion of an allergen:
    A. when histaminic cells constrict.
    B. as a by-product of antibody-antigen interaction.
    C. when mast cells rupture.
    D. during the histamine cascade.
    E. as a by-product of antigen rupture.

276. Histamine plays a significant role in minor and moderate allergic reactions.
    A. True
    B. False

277. A drug that increases the productivity of a cough is a(n):
    A. expectorant.
    B. mucolytic.
    C. antitussive.
    D. surfactant.
    E. cannabinoid.

278. Antacids are antagonists that block the receptors responsible for the production of gastric acids.
    A. True
    B. False

279. A transmitter associated with the vomiting reflex is:
    A. serotonin.
    B. dopamine.
    C. acetylcholine.
    D. histamine.
    E. all of the above

280. An example of an ophthalmic drug used to treat glaucoma is:
    A. pancreatin.
    B. chloramphenicol.
    C. dronabinol.
    D. timolol.
    E. dopamine.

281. Oxytocin is produced by the:
    A. posterior pituitary gland.
    B. uterus.
    C. adrenal gland.
    D. thyroid gland.
    E. testes.

282. The type of diabetes that typically manifests during adulthood is:
    A. retrograde.
    B. type I.
    C. type II.
    D. insipidus.
    E. one of the above

283. The hormone oxytocin's principal action is to:
    A. relax the uterine muscles.
    B. dilate uterine arterioles.
    C. induce labor.
    D. cause breast enlargement.
    E. none of the above

284. Nonsteroidal antiinflammatory drugs (NSAIDs) are used to treat:
    A. headache.
    B. fever.
    C. arthritis.
    D. orthopedic injuries.
    E. all of the above

285. A solution containing a modified pathogen that stimulates the development of antigens is called a(n):
    A. vaccine.
    B. serum.
    C. immunogen.
    D. rotavirus.
    E. none of the above

_____ 286. The basic processes of pharmacokinetics include all of the following EXCEPT:
  A. absorption.
  B. elimination.
  C. syncretization.
  D. biotransformation.
  E. distribution.

_____ 287. Which of the following is NOT one of the six rights of drug administration?
  A. the right dose
  B. the right person
  C. the right concentration
  D. the right documentation
  E. the right route

_____ 288. Confirmation of a medication order received from medical direction on-line is achieved by:
  A. echoing it.
  B. redundancy.
  C. direct duplication.
  D. indirect duplication.
  E. none of the above

_____ 289. An environment cleaned with material that is toxic to living tissue is:
  A. aseptic.
  B. sterile.
  C. medically clean.
  D. disinfected.
  E. none of the above

_____ 290. A sharps container should be:
  A. puncture resistant.
  B. marked as a biohazard container.
  C. a rigid structure.
  D. capable of holding whole needles and preloaded syringes.
  E. all of the above

_____ 291. One drug commonly administered transdermally is:
  A. sodium bicarbonate.
  B. epinephrine.
  C. nitroglycerin.
  D. aspirin.
  E. magnesium.

_____ 292. The route by which a drug is administered into the ear canal is called:
  A. transdermal.
  B. sublingual.
  C. buccal.
  D. aural.
  E. none of the above

_____ 293. When treating an ear infection with medicated gauze, you should pack the gauze firmly into the ear canal.
  A. True
  B. False

_____ 294. The oxygen flow rate associated with nebulizer use is:
  A. 5 to 8 liters per minute.
  B. 8 to 10 liters per minute.
  C. 10 to 12 liters per minute.
  D. 12 to 15 liters per minute.
  E. none of the above

_____ 295. Nebulizers are preferable to metered dose inhalers for patients with respiratory emergencies.
  A. True
  B. False

_____ 296. Endotracheal administration of medications generally requires increasing the drug dosage by:
  A. 1 to 1 ½ times.
  B. 2 to 2½ times.
  C. 3 times.
  D. 5 times.
  E. none of the above

297. Which of the following drugs is NOT administered via the endotracheal route?
   A. lidocaine
   B. naloxone
   C. atropine
   D. nitroglycerin
   E. epinephrine

298. Which of the following is an advantage of enteral drug administration?
   A. It is convenient.
   B. It is inexpensive.
   C. It requires little equipment.
   D. It requires little training.
   E. all of the above

299. Drugs absorbed by the stomach and small intestine must pass through the portal system and liver.
   A. True
   B. False

300. A drug administered by the oral route should be followed by what volume of water?
   A. 4 to 8 ounces
   B. 8 to 16 ounces
   C. 16 to 32 ounces
   D. 2 cups
   E. no water at all

301. Rectal medications should NOT be administered if you note:
   A. diarrhea.
   B. rectal bleeding.
   C. hemorrhoids.
   D. severe anal irritation.
   E. any of the above

302. A syringe should be chosen for drug administration that is slightly larger than the volume of drug to be administered.
   A. True
   B. False

303. The larger the gauge of a hypodermic needle, the smaller its diameter.
   A. True
   B. False

304. The drug container that must be broken to obtain the drug is the:
   A. vial.
   B. ampule.
   C. Mix-o-Vial.
   D. preloaded syringe.
   E. medicated solution.

305. The total dose of a drug contained in an ampule with 3 mL of a drug in a 0.4 mg/mL concentration is:
   A. 0.3 mg.
   B. 1.2 mg.
   C. 4 mg.
   D. 7 mg.
   E. 12 mg.

306. Which of the following must be screwed together before use?
   A. vial
   B. ampule
   C. Mix-o-Vial
   D. preloaded syringe
   E. both A and C

307. The amount of mixing solution you must remove from a vial for mixing with the powered drug with a nonconstituted drug system is:
   A. 1 mL.
   B. 2 mL.
   C. ½ of the solution.
   D. ¾ of the solution.
   E. all the solution.

308. The administration route in a drug injected just beneath the skin is called:
   A. intradermal.
   B. subcutaneous.
   C. intramuscular.
   D. intraosseous.
   E. none of the above

309. The drug administration route that requires the needle be inserted at 45° is:
   A. intradermal.
   B. subcutaneous.
   C. intramuscular.
   D. intraosseous.
   E. none of the above

A 310. The drug administration route that calls for use of a needle with a lumen gauge of 25 to 27 is:
   A. intradermal.
   B. subcutaneous.
   C. intramuscular.
   D. intraosseous.
   E. none of the above

C 311. All of the following are likely to be acceptable sites for intramuscular injection EXCEPT the:
   A. upper arms.
   B. thighs.
   C. abdomen.
   D. buttocks.
   E. deltoids.

C 312. At which injection site(s) can you administer more than 1 mL of drug?
   A. intradermal
   B. subcutaneous
   C. intramuscular
   D. both B and C
   E. all of the above

D 313. When you pull back on the syringe plunger during subcutaneous or intramuscular injection and blood appears, you should:
   A. inject the drug.
   B. inject the drug followed by a small bubble of air.
   C. insert the needle 1 cm further.
   D. attempt the injection at another site.
   E. ignore it because the appearance of blood has no significance.

E 314. For which intramuscular injection sites can you administer 5 mL or more of the drug?
   A. deltoid
   B. gluteal
   C. vastus lateralis
   D. rectus femoris
   E. all except A

B 315. After injecting heparin intramuscularly, massage the site to enhance systemic absorption.
   A. True
   B. False

Chapter 10: Intravenous Access and Medication Administration, Part 2

B 316. Arterial cannulation presents with fewer hemorrhage control problems but is not used commonly for drug administration because the arteries are difficult to find.
   A. True
   B. False

B 317. Veins of the legs are preferable to those of the arms because they are larger and easier to locate.
   A. True
   B. False

C 318. Which of the following are likely to have fragile veins that are hard to cannulate?
   A. obese patients
   B. pregnant patients
   C. geriatric patients
   D. asthma patients
   E. none of the above

_____ 319. An intravenous fluid that contains electrolytes and water but does not have large proteins is a(n):
   A. colloid.
   B. crystalloid.
   C. isotonic solution.
   D. hypotonic solution.
   E. hypertonic solution.

_____ 320. An intravenous fluid that contains an electrolyte concentration less than that of plasma is a(n):
   A. colloid.
   B. crystalloid.
   C. isotonic solution.
   D. hypotonic solution.
   E. hypertonic solution.

©2006 Pearson Education, Inc.
Paramedic Care: Principles & Practice, Vol. 1

_____321. The most desirable replacement for blood lost during trauma is:
   A. normal saline.   D. 5 percent dextrose in water.
   B. lactated Ringer's solution.   E. normal Ringer's lactate.
   C. blood.

_____322. The most common macrodrip rate equaling 1 mL is:
   A. 10 gtt.   D. 60 gtt.
   B. 25 gtt.   E. none of the above
   C. 45 gtt.

_____323. The administration set that is most appropriate when the overall volume of fluid a
         patient receives must be restricted is a:
   A. macrodrip administration set.
   B. microdrip administration set.
   C. measured volume administration set.
   D. blood tubing set.
   E. none of the above

_____324. The administration set most appropriate to administer intravenous solution to a
         pediatric patient is a:
   A. macrodrip administration set.
   B. microdrip administration set.
   C. measured volume administration set.
   D. blood tubing set.
   E. none of the above

_____325. Blood can be administered with fluids like lactated Ringer's because there is little
         likelihood for coagulation.
   A. True   B. False

_____326. The model of intravenous cannula to use for patients with delicate veins like the small
         child or geriatric patient is:
   A. over-the-needle.   D. angiocatheter.
   B. through-the-needle.   E. both A and D
   C. hollow needle.

_____327. The lumen of an 18-gauge needle is larger than one of a 22-gauge needle.
   A. True   B. False

_____328. When cleansing the site for intravenous cannulation, you should use a povidone-iodine
         or alcohol swab and rub firmly, starting from the center and move outward in
         expanding circles.
   A. True   B. False

_____329. Placing a finger over the exterior skin at the point of the tip of the catheter before
         removing the needle:
   A. stops air from entraining into the vessel.
   B. stops blood from flowing out the catheter hub.
   C. prevents the catheter from coming out with the needle.
   D. prevents the catheter tip from becoming an embolism.
   E. A and B

_____330. The external jugular venous access site is extremely painful for the patient and should be
         used only for patients with a decreased or complete loss of consciousness.
   A. True   B. False

_____331. For the measured volume administration set to work properly, you must fill it with at least:
   A. 10 mL of fluid.   D. 50 mL of fluid.
   B. 20 mL of fluid.   E. 100 mL of fluid.
   C. 30 mL of fluid.

_____332. Which of the following is a factor that may cause problems with the intravenous flow rates?
A. removal of the constricting band
B. IV solution bag placed above the cannulation site
C. the cannula tip up against a vein valve
D. half-full drip chamber
E. all of the above

_____333. Which of the following is a complication of peripheral venous access?
A. thrombus formation
B. thrombophlebitis
C. air embolism
D. necrosis
E. all of the above

_____334. After a bolus of a drug has been administered, you should flush the line with what volume of fluid?
A. 20 mL
B. 30 mL
C. 40 mL
D. 50 mL
E. 100 mL

_____335. An intravenous drug infusion may be administered as either a piggyback or the primary IV line.
A. True
B. False

_____336. If you prepare an intravenous drug infusion, the accompanying label must contain all of the following information EXCEPT:
A. the time and date of mixture.
B. your initials.
C. the total drug weight mixed in the bag.
D. the name of the medical direction physician.
E. the expiration date.

_____337. Which of the following statements is NOT true regarding venous access devices?
A. They permit repeated access to the central circulation.
B. They are of stainless steel or plastic construction with a flexible catheter.
C. They are most often placed in the superior vena cava.
D. They require a standard 1-inch, 23-gauge catheter.
E. They present as a raised circle just beneath the skin.

_____338. Blood analysis can determine the concentrations of:
A. gases.
B. electrolytes.
C. hormones.
D. cardiac enzymes.
E. all of the above

_____339. Drawing blood and injecting it into the blood tubes in the wrong order may:
A. leave the wrong volume of blood in a tube.
B. cross-contaminate the blood with anticoagulants.
C. cause oxidation.
D. cause precipitation.
E. dilute the samples.

_____340. The most ideal veins to use to withdraw blood are those of the back of the hand because their infiltration will least affect future venipuncture sites.
A. True
B. False

_____341. When drawing blood, completely fill the blood tube, because the anticoagulant is measured for that amount of blood.
A. True
B. False

©2006 Pearson Education, Inc.
Paramedic Care: Principles & Practice, Vol. 1

_____342. When drawing blood through a needle that is too small, one possible complication is:
   A. hemoconcentration.   D. hemolysis.
   B. hemoagglutination.   E. hemoconiosis.
   C. hemodilution.

_____343. Any solution that can be administered by intravenous infusion can be administered by intraosseous infusion.
   A. True   B. False

_____344. Proper insertion of the intraosseous needle includes:
   A. introducing it perpendicular to the puncture site.
   B. inserting it with a twisting motion.
   C. inserting it 2 to 4 mm for entry.
   D. feeling for a "pop" or decreased resistance.
   E. all of the above

_____345. It is essential to frequently flush the intraosseous needle to keep it patent.
   A. True   B. False

Chapter 11: Therapeutic Communications

_____346. Which of the following is a reason for failing to communicate?
   A. prejudice   D. internal distractions
   B. lack of privacy   E. all of the above
   C. external distractions

_____347. As a representative of EMS, you are granted a certain amount of the public's trust at each new emergency scene.
   A. True   B. False

_____348. With children, try to use nicknames, because they communicate a more personal and empathetic relationship between caregiver and patient.
   A. True   B. False

_____349. The interpersonal zone that extends 1½ to 4 feet from the patient is:
   A. the intimate zone.   D. public distance.
   B. personal distance.   E. defensive distance.
   C. social distance.

_____350. The paramedic's eye level that indicates a willingness to let the patient have some control is:
   A. higher than the patient's eye level.
   B. lower than the patient's eye level.
   C. equal to the patient's eye level.
   D. both A and B
   E. both B and C

_____351. Eye contact is a powerful means of nonverbal communication.
   A. True   B. False

_____352. It is much better to tell a child that you are "measuring" a blood pressure rather than "taking" a blood pressure.
   A. True   B. False

_____353. Using "why" questions is often important because it causes the patient to focus on the causes of events.
   A. True   B. False

_____354. The stage of childhood development at which a patient uses simple words, short sentences, and concrete explanations is:
- A. infant.
- B. toddler.
- C. preschooler.
- D. school age.
- E. adolescent.

_____355. The forcing of one's own beliefs, values, and patterns of behavior upon people of another culture is:
- A. ethnothictity.
- B. cultural diversity.
- C. ethnocentrism.
- D. cultural imposition.
- E. none of the above

Chapter 12: Life-Span Development

_____356. The preschooler represents a child between the ages of:
- A. birth and 1 year.
- B. 1 and 3 years.
- C. 3 and 5 years.
- D. 6 and 12 years.
- E. 13 and 18 years.

_____357. The infant represents a child between the ages of:
- A. birth and 1 year.
- B. 1 and 3 years.
- C. 3 and 5 years.
- D. 6 and 12 years.
- E. 13 and 18 years.

_____358. The respiratory rate generally falls with age.
- A. True
- B. False

_____359. The pulse rate generally increases with age.
- A. True
- B. False

_____360. During the first 6 months of life, the infant's birth weight is expected to:
- A. increase by 2 kg per week.
- B. decrease by 5 to 10 percent.
- C. double.
- D. triple.
- E. none of the above

_____361. The reflex that causes the infant to turn his head toward a touch to the cheek is the:
- A. Moro reflex.
- B. palmar reflex.
- C. rooting reflex.
- D. sucking reflex.
- E. vagal reflex.

_____362. The formation of a close personal relationship through frequent or constant association is called:
- A. bonding.
- B. secure attachment.
- C. scaffolding.
- D. benchmarking.
- E. modeling.

_____363. By the time an infant becomes a toddler, the respiratory system has matured and is able to maintain an excessive respiratory rate.
- A. True
- B. False

_____364. The age at which children begin to understand the concept of cause and effect is:
- A. 1 to 2 years.
- B. 2 to 3 years.
- C. 3 to 4 years.
- D. 4 to 5 years.
- E. 5 to 6 years.

_____365. The school-age child grows by about what amount per year?
- A. 2 cm
- B. 3 cm
- C. 4 cm
- D. 5 cm
- E. 6 cm

_____366. Male children generally finish growing at the age of:
A. 12.
B. 14.
C. 16.
D. 18.
E. 20.

_____367. The development stage at which smoking and alcohol and illicit drug use is most likely is:
A. preschool.
B. school age.
C. adolescent.
D. early adult.
E. middle-adult.

_____368. The stage of development in which life-long habits and routines are established is:
A. late adult.
B. school age.
C. adolescent.
D. early adult.
E. middle-adult.

_____369. Cardiovascular changes associated with late adulthood include:
A. cardiac valve disease.
B. diminishing of pacemaker cells.
C. decreased tolerance of tachycardia.
D. heart enlargement.
E. all of the above

_____370. In general, the gastrointestinal system shows less age-associated change in function than other body systems.
A. True
B. False

Chapter 13: Airway Management and Ventilation

_____371. By the time air reaches the lower airway, it is at body temperature, humidified, and virtually free of airborne particles.
A. True
B. False

_____372. The order in which air passes through airway structures during inspiration is:
A. trachea, larynx, laryngopharynx, nasopharynx, nares.
B. nares, nasopharynx, trachea, laryngopharynx, larynx.
C. laryngopharynx, nares, nasopharynx, larynx, trachea.
D. nares, nasopharynx, laryngopharynx, larynx, trachea.
E. trachea, nares, laryngopharynx, larynx, nasopharynx.

_____373. The location at which the mainstem bronchi and major blood vessels enter the lung is the:
A. hilum.
B. parenchyma.
C. vallecula.
D. carina.
E. pleura.

_____374. The mainstem bronchus that leaves the trachea at almost a straight angle is the left mainstem bronchus.
A. True
B. False

_____375. Parasympathetic receptors cause the bronchioles to:
A. constrict.
B. dilate.
C. shorten.
D. stiffen.
E. none of the above

_____376. The narrowest part of the pediatric airway is the:
A. cricoid ring.
B. hyroid ring.
C. glottis.
D. carina.
E. tracheal stricture.

_____377. Which of the following is NOT true regarding the adult and pediatric airway and respiration?
A. The pediatric airway is smaller in all aspects than the adult.
B. Pediatric ribs are stronger and contribute more to respiration than ribs in adults.
C. Children rely more on their diaphragms for breathing than adults.
D. The cricoid cartilage is the narrowest point of the pediatric airway but not of the adult airway.
E. Children's teeth are softer and more prone to damage than adults'.

_____378. The active aspect of the respiratory cycle is:
A. inspiration.
B. expiration.
C. neither A or B
D. both A and B
E. resting stage.

_____379. The percentage of carbon dioxide in atmospheric air is approximately:
A. 79 percent.
B. 4 percent.
C. 0.4 percent.
D. 0.04 percent.
E. 0.10 percent.

_____380. The majority of the oxygen carried by the blood is:
A. carried by the hemoglobin.
B. dissolved in the plasma.
C. transported as bicarbonate.
D. found as free gas in the blood.
E. none of the above

_____381. The reflex that responds to the stretching of the lungs by inhibiting respirations is the:
A. apneustic reflex.
B. pneumotaxic reflex.
C. Frank-Starling reflex.
D. Hering-Breuer reflex.
E. baroreceptor response.

_____382. The primary stimulus that causes respiration to occur is a(n):
A. increase in pH of the blood.
B. decrease in pH of the blood.
C. increase in pH of the cerebrospinal fluid.
D. decrease in pH of the cerebrospinal fluid.
E. reduction of oxygen in the blood.

_____383. The amount of air in the lung after a maximal inspiration is called the:
A. minute volume.
B. alveolar air.
C. tidal volume.
D. dead air space.
E. total lung capacity.

_____384. The normal respiratory rate for a child at rest is:
A. 8 to 12 breaths per minute.
B. 12 to 20 breaths per minute.
C. 18 to 24 breaths per minute.
D. 24 to 32 breaths per minute.
E. 40 to 60 breaths per minute.

_____385. The most common prehospital cause of laryngeal spasm is:
A. aspiration of foreign bodies.
B. aspiration of blood or vomitus.
C. overly aggressive intubation.
D. trauma.
E. airway edema.

_____386. The modified form of respiration that is caused by nasal irritation is the:
A. cough.
B. sneeze.
C. hiccup.
D. grunt.
E. sigh.

_____387. The respiratory pattern that displays with an increasing rate and depth of respirations alternating with periods of slow, shallow breathing is:
A. Kussmaul's respirations.
B. Cheyne-Stokes respirations.
C. Biot's respirations.
D. central neurogenic hyperventilation.
E. agonal respirations.

_____388. Snoring is generally related to:
- A. laryngeal constriction or edema.
- B. the tongue blocking the airway.
- C. narrowing of the bronchioles.
- D. fluids within the airway.
- E. foreign bodies in the lower airway.

_____389. When using pulse oximetry to guide care, your objective is to achieve an oxygen saturation level of:
- A. 80 to 85 percent.
- B. 85 to 90 percent.
- C. 90 to 95 percent.
- D. 95 to 99 percent.
- E. no less than 100 percent.

_____390. Capnography is a valuable assessment tool for which of the following?
- A. to ensure proper initial endotracheal tube placement.
- B. to assess the effectiveness of CPR.
- C. to ensure proper endotracheal tube placement continues.
- D. to document patient responses to medications.
- E. all of the above

_____391. When the endotracheal tube is in the esophagus, the esophageal detector device will be difficult to withdraw because the esophagus will seal shut.
- A. True
- B. False

_____392. In the absence of suspected cervical spine injury, the best manual technique for maintaining the airway in the unconscious patient is the head-tilt/chin-lift.
- A. True
- B. False

_____393. Sellick's maneuver is performed by:
- A. displacing the thyroid cartilage upward.
- B. displacing the tongue forward.
- C. depressing the cricoid cartilage posteriorly.
- D. squeezing the trachea between the fingers.
- E. placing pressure on the abdomen to expel air.

_____394. The nasopharyngeal airway should be inserted into the right nostril unless there is resistance to its insertion or the septum is deviated.
- A. True
- B. False

_____395. The preferred technique of insertion for the oropharyngeal airway in pediatric patients calls for partially inserting the airway, rotating the device 180°, then continuing the insertion.
- A. True
- B. False

_____396. Which of the following is NOT true regarding endotracheal intubation?
- A. The laryngoscope is held in the right hand.
- B. The laryngoscope is inserted into the right side of the mouth.
- C. The straight blade lifts the epiglottis.
- D. The curved blade fits into the vallecula.
- E. You should advance the ET tube into the glottis, 2 to 3 cm beyond the tube cuff.

_____397. The tip of the straight laryngoscope blade is designed to:
- A. engage the nasopharynx.
- B. just enter the glottic opening.
- C. fit into the vallecula.
- D. fit into arytenoid fossa.
- E. fit under the epiglottis.

_____398. The pilot balloon of the endotracheal tube should be soft to avoid over-inflating the cuff and damaging the delicate tissue of the trachea.
- A. True
- B. False

_____399. When using the stylette for intubation, the tip of the device:
   A. should extend 3 mm beyond the end of the endotracheal tube.
   B. should be even with the end of the endotracheal tube.
   C. should be recessed at least 2 cm from the tube end.
   D. is moved in or out during the intubation attempt as needed.
   E. none of the above

_____400. Indications for endotracheal intubation include all of the following EXCEPT:
   A. respiratory arrest.
   B. epiglottitis.
   C. inability to protect the airway.
   D. obstruction due to foreign object, swelling, or burns.
   E. pneumothorax with respiratory difficulty.

_____401. Which of the following is NOT an indication of esophageal intubation?
   A. absence of chest rise with ventilation
   B. condensation on the endotracheal tube
   C. a falling pulse oximetry reading
   D. increasing abdominal distention
   E. increasing resistance to ventalitory effort.

_____402. All of the following are dangers to the patient associated with endotracheal intubation EXCEPT:
   A. damage to teeth.
   B. soft-tissue damage to the oropharynx.
   C. patient hypoxia during intubation attempts.
   D. endobronchial intubation.
   E. hyperkalemia.

_____403. Which of the following is NOT used to confirm proper endotracheal tube placement?
   A. visualization of the tube passing through the glottis
   B. the absence of vocal sounds
   C. changing color on a $ETCO_2$ detector
   D. condensation on the endotracheal tube with exhalation
   E. the presence of phonation

_____404. The transillumination technique for intubation works best:
   A. in bright daylight.   D. in a dark room.
   B. on heavy patients.   E. all of the above
   C. with clenched teeth.

_____405. In attempting digital intubation, the fingers of the rescuer must reach to the:
   A. epiglottis.   D. laryngeal opening.
   B. posterior nares.   E. cricoid cartilage.
   C. back of the tongue.

_____406. Rapid sequence intubation is indicated in a patient who has a gag reflex yet who has trouble maintaining his airway or has an inadequate respiratory effort.
   A. True   B. False

_____407. The major difference between succinylcholine and vecuronium as paralytics in prehospital care is that vecuronium:
   A. causes fasciculations.   D. increases intracranial pressure.
   B. has a shorter time to onset. E. all of the above
   C. has a much longer duration.

_____408. The patient receiving rapid sequence intubation is likely to vomit.
    A. True   **B.** False

_____409. It is essential that a pediatric patient be premedicated with vecuronium before the administration of succinylcholine, because fasciculations are otherwise likely to cause musculoskeletal trauma.
    A. True   **B.** False

_____410. The use of a laryngoscope and the passage of an endotracheal tube may cause a child's heart rate to drop dramatically, which may reduce cardiac output and blood pressure.
    A. True   **B.** False

_____411. Which of the following is NOT an advantage associated with nasotracheal intubation?
    A. The head and neck may remain in the neutral position.
    B. The patient cannot bite the endotracheal tube.
    C. The procedure is less time-consuming than orotracheal intubation.
    D. The endotracheal tube can be secured more easily.
    E. The procedure does not stimulate the gag reflex as much as the oral route.

_____412. Nasotracheal intubation is contraindicated for a:
    A. patient with a potential spine injury.
    B. patient not in arrest or deeply comatose.
    C. patient with a fractured jaw.
    D. severely obese patient.
    E. patient with nasal fractures.

_____413. The PtL airway is inserted:
    A. using the nasal route.
    B. using the tongue-jaw-lift maneuver.
    C. with one cuff preinflated.
    D. with the head and neck flexed.
    E. all of the above

_____414. Which of the following is NOT a complication of needle cricothyrotomy?
    A. barotrauma from overinflation
    B. excessive bleeding due to improper catheter placement
    C. hypoventilation from improper equipment
    D. prevention of passage of a subsequent endotracheal tube
    E. tracheal compression from hemorrhage or subcutaneous emphysema

_____415. Needle cricothyrotomy is not indicated if the airway is completely blocked and exhalation through the glottis is not possible.
    A. True   **B.** False

_____416. When performing a surgical or open cricothyrotomy, you first make a small vertical incision through the skin, then a vertical incision through the cricothyroid membrane.
    A. True   **B.** False

_____417. Generally, suctioning attempts should be limited to no longer than:
    A. 10 seconds.   **D.** 60 seconds.
    B. 30 seconds.   **E.** as long as needed to clear the airway.
    C. 45 seconds.

_____418. When no contraindication exists, the nasogastric tube is preferred for gastric decompression.
    A. True   **B.** False

_____419. Adult bag-valve masks do not have pop-off valves because patients with poor lung compliance would likely activate the valves before effective ventilation is achieved.
   A. True   B. False

_____420. The percentage of oxygen delivered to the patient when using the demand valve device is about:
   A. 40 percent.   D. 90 percent.
   B. 50 percent.   E. 100 percent.
   C. 75 percent.

©2006 Pearson Education, Inc.
Paramedic Care: Principles & Practice, Vol. 1

WORKBOOK ANSWER KEY

Note: Throughout Answer Key, textbook page references are shown in italic.

CHAPTER 1: Introduction to Advanced Prehospital Care

CONTENT SELF-EVALUATION

MULTIPLE CHOICE

1. C *p. 5*	6. C *p. 7*	11. C *p. 8*
2. A *p. 6*	7. B *p. 8*	12. E *p. 8*
3. E *p. 6*	8. B *p. 7*	13. E *p. 10*
4. E *p. 6*	9. B *p. 7*	14. A *p. 10*
5. D *p. 6*	10. A *p. 8*	15. E *p. 10*

LISTING

16. Requires an anatomy and physiology course as a prerequisite; requires a more extensive foundation of medical knowledge; provides for improved understanding of the pathophysiology of disease and injury processes
17. A. advanced airway management, ventilator management, fluid and electrolyte therapy, advanced pharmacology, specialized monitoring, operating intraaortic balloon pumps, and various techniques of critical care medicine
    B. industry-specific additional training including knowledge and skills necessary for site safety, performing sick call duty, accident prevention, medical screening, and the administration of vaccinations and immunizations
    C. injury care associated with the sport, injury prevention, pregame preparation, and determinations as to whether the athlete can return to practice or competition

CHAPTER 2: The Well-Being of the Paramedic

CONTENT SELF-EVALUATION

MULTIPLE CHOICE

1. A *p. 16*	15. D *p. 25*	28. D *p. 33*
2. C *p. 17*	16. E *p. 25*	29. D *p. 33*
3. A *p. 17*	17. B *p. 24*	30. B *p. 34*
4. A *p. 17*	18. E *p. 26*	31. D *p. 34*
5. B *p. 18*	19. E *p. 27*	32. B *p. 35*
6. C *p. 18*	20. A *p. 27*	33. A *p. 35*
7. E *p. 19*	21. E *p. 27*	34. A *p. 35*
8. C *p. 19*	22. C *p. 30*	35. E *p. 36*
9. D *p. 20*	23. C *p. 30*	36. B *p. 37*
10. C *p. 20*	24. B *p. 30*	37. E *p. 39*
11. E *p. 21*	25. B *p. 32*	38. B *p. 40*
12. C *p. 23*	26. A *p. 31*	39. D *p. 39*
13. A *p. 23*	27. A *p. 31*	40. B *p. 40*
14. A *p. 24*		

MATCHING

46. A, B *p. 24*	49. A, C *p. 24*
47. A, B, D *p. 24*	50. A, B, D *p. 24*
48. A, B *p. 24*	

SPECIAL PROJECT: PROBLEM SOLVING

1. Immediately clean the affected area, and wash it aggressively at the hospital.
2. Get a medical evaluation (once at the hospital).
3. Make arrangements to take the proper immunization boosters (if yours are not current).
4. Notify your service infection-control liaison or other appropriate person.
5. Document the circumstances of exposure and the steps you took to reduce your chances of acquiring an infectious disease.

CHAPTER 3: EMS Systems

CONTENT SELF-EVALUATION

MULTIPLE CHOICE

1. A *p. 46*	15. B *p. 56*	28. D *p. 64*
2. A *p. 47*	16. A *p. 56*	29. C *p. 64*
3. E *p. 47*	17. C *p. 58*	30. B *p. 65*
4. B *p. 47*	18. A *p. 58*	31. C *p. 66*
5. B *p. 50*	19. D *p. 58*	32. E *p. 66*
6. B *p. 49*	20. B *p. 59*	33. B *p. 67*
7. B *p. 51*	21. A *p. 59*	34. C *p. 68*
8. A *p. 54*	22. D *p. 59*	35. E *p. 68*
9. D *p. 55*	23. D *p. 60*	36. B *p. 69*
10. C *p. 55*	24. E *p. 59*	37. B *p. 69*
11. E *p. 55*	25. C *p. 61*	38. A *p. 69*
12. C *p. 55*	26. B *p. 62*	39. C *p. 71*
13. C *p. 56*	27. A *p. 62*	40. A *p. 72*
14. A *p. 56*		

LISTING

41. U.S. DOT, National Traffic and Highway Safety Administration *p. 59*
42. U.S. General Services Administration *p. 64*
43. American College of Surgeons Committee on Trauma *p. 64*
44. American College of Emergency Physicians *p. 64*
45. Joint Review Committee on Educational Programs for the EMT-Paramedic *p. 62*

SPECIAL PROJECT: The EMS Agenda of the Future

A. The EMS Agenda for the Future was a document pulished in 1996 creating a vision for future EMS in the United States. It identifies 14 EMS attributes and integrates EMS into the health care system.
B. Integration of Health Services   EMS Research
   Legislation and Regulation   System Finance
   Human Resources   Medical Direction
   Education Systems   Public Education
   Prevention   Public Access
   Communication Systems   Clinical Care
   Information Systems   Evaluation

CHAPTER 4: Roles and Responsibilities of the Paramedic

CONTENT SELF-EVALUATION

MULTIPLE CHOICE

1. A	p. 78	10. B	p. 83	18. E	p. 86
2. E	p. 79	11. C	p. 84	19. B	p. 86
3. E	p. 79	12. C	p. 84	20. B	p. 87
4. A	p. 79	13. E	p. 84	21. A	p. 90
5. E	p. 80	14. E	p. 84	22. D	p. 89
6. D	p. 80	15. B	p. 85	23. B	p. 90
7. E	p. 81	16. B	p. 85	24. E	p. 92
8. B	p. 81	17. B	p. 85	25. C	p. 92
9. A	p. 82				

MATCHING

26. J	p. 84	31. A	p. 79	36. G	p. 81
27. F	p. 81	32. D	p. 80	37. A	p. 79
28. G	p. 81	33. E	p. 81	38. J	p. 84
29. C	p. 79	34. H	p. 83	39. C	p. 79
30. I	p. 84	35. B	p. 79	40. E	p. 81

CHAPTER 5: Illness and Injury Prevention

CONTENT SELF-EVALUATION

MULTIPLE CHOICE

1. C	p. 98	8. A	p. 101	15. A	p. 104
2. A	p. 98	9. E	p. 102	16. C	p. 104
3. A	p. 98	10. B	p. 102	17. A	p. 105
4. E	p. 98	11. B	p. 103	18. E	p. 105
5. B	p. 98	12. A	p. 103	19. B	p. 106
6. E	p. 101	13. B	p. 103	20. E	p. 107
7. A	p. 99	14. C	p. 103		

SPECIAL PROJECT: Understanding the Importance of Illness/Injury Prevention Programs

A. Yes, this is a teachable moment for both the families and the community. The tragic loss of children is an event that usually brings forth a concern about child safety and is a good opportunity to promote safe practices and safety education. However, use care not to instill guilt or blame for the incident.

B. $65 - 7 = 58$

C. Possible answers include a water safety course for children, pool fencing and cpr training.

CHAPTER 6: Medical/Legal Aspects of Advanced Prehospital Care

CONTENT SELF-EVALUATION

MULTIPLE CHOICE

1. B	p. 113	8. A	p. 118	15. A	p. 122
2. C	p. 113	9. D	p. 119	16. D	p. 123
3. C	p. 115	10. E	p. 119	17. E	p. 124
4. A	p. 115	11. C	p. 119	18. B	p. 125
5. E	p. 116	12. C	p. 119	19. C	p. 126
6. D	p. 117	13. E	p. 121	20. E	p. 125
7. B	p. 118	14. A	p. 121	21. B	p. 126

22. B	p. 126	27. D	p. 130	32. A	p. 135
23. E	p. 126	28. C	p. 130	33. A	p. 134
24. B	p. 126	29. D	p. 130	34. C	p. 135
25. B	p. 127	30. A	p. 130	35. C	p. 137
26. A	p. 128	31. E	p. 131		

SPECIAL PROJECT: Crossword Puzzle

CHAPTER 7: Ethics in Advanced Prehospital Care

CONTENT SELF-EVALUATION

MULTIPLE CHOICE

1. A	p. 144	5. D	p. 147	8. B	p. 154
2. B	p. 146	6. B	p. 150	9. A	p. 156
3. D	p. 146	7. A	p. 153	10. E	p. 158
4. A	p. 147				

SPECIAL PROJECT: Ethics and the Mass Casualty Incident

A. While the guiding principles of health care involve doing what is in the patient's best interest (beneficence), at the mass-casualty incident the needs of multiple patients often outstrip the care resources available. Decisions must be made to ensure the most patients are benefited (justice). p. 156

B. A patient in cardiac arrest would require at least three care providers (one doing compressions, one ventilating, and one administering drugs and performing other advanced interventions). The result of an attempted resuscitation of an unwitnessed cardiac arrest patient is very likely to be poor, especially when the arrest is due to trauma. In a mass-casualty incident, the three care providers could each attend a patient (or numerous patients) who has serious injuries and increase that patient's chances for survival and reduce the seriousness of any resulting disability.

The triage at a mass-casualty incident presents an ethical dilemma. Prehospital care providers are taught to care for a single patient, doing all they can for him. However, at the mass-

CHAPTER 13: Airway Management and Ventilation

Part 1

CONTENT SELF-EVALUATION

MULTIPLE CHOICE

1. A	*p. 510*	15. C	*p. 517*	29. B	*p. 528*
2. B	*p. 510*	16. A	*p. 518*	30. E	*p. 528*
3. A	*p. 511*	17. E	*p. 519*	31. D	*p. 529*
4. C	*p. 510*	18. C	*p. 520*	32. A	*p. 530*
5. C	*p. 509*	19. C	*p. 520*	33. C	*p. 530*
6. C	*p. 512*	20. B	*p. 520*	34. B	*p. 531*
7. E	*p. 512*	21. A	*p. 521*	35. C	*p. 533*
8. D	*p. 513*	22. E	*p. 521*	36. C	*p. 533*
9. A	*p. 513*	23. C	*p. 522*	37. D	*p. 534*
10. B	*p. 513*	24. C	*p. 522*	38. A	*p. 534*
11. E	*p. 514*	25. A	*p. 523*	39. A	*p. 535*
12. D	*p. 515*	26. C	*p. 525*	40. E	*p. 535*
13. A	*p. 516*	27. B	*p. 525*		
14. B	*p. 517*	28. B	*p. 526*		

LABEL THE DIAGRAM

36. A. Tonsil
    B. Tongue
    C. Vallecula
    D. Epiglottis
    E. Vocal cords
    F. Trachea
    G. Cricoid cartilage
    H. Esophagus

SPECIAL PROJECT: Airway Obstruction

1. **The tongue.** In the absence of muscle tone, the relaxed tongue drops back in the larynx, blocking the airway.
2. **Foreign body.** An object, usually food, becomes lodged in the laryngopharynx and blocks the airway.
3. **Trauma.** Trauma may disrupt the integrity of the airway, thereby allowing it to collapse or physically blocking the airway. Additionally, loose teeth or blood clots may obstruct the airway.
4. **Laryngeal edema or spasm.** Swelling of the laryngeal tissue may occlude the airway, or spasm of the vocal cords may occur secondary to intubation attempts.
5. **Aspiration.** The inhalation of teeth, dentures, blood, food, or vomitus may occlude the airway.

Normal Respiratory Values

% Oxygen: 21% in inspired air; 14% in expired air; PaO_2 is 80 to 100 torr

% CO_2: 0.04% in inspired air; 5% in expired air; $PaCO_2$ is 35 to 45 torr

Normal Respiratory Rates/Volumes

Infant: 40 to 60; Child: 18 to 24; Adult: 12 to 20

Tidal volume: 500 mL

Alveolar volume: 350 mL

Dead space volume: 150 mL

Minute volume: 3000 to 5000 mL

Part 2

CONTENT SELF-EVALUATION

MULTIPLE CHOICE

1. B	*p. 539*	18. E	*p. 555*	35. C	*p. 577*
2. C	*p. 541*	19. A	*p. 556*	36. A	*p. 580*
3. D	*p. 542*	20. C	*p. 559*	37. A	*p. 582*
4. B	*p. 543*	21. C	*p. 559*	38. E	*p. 583*
5. A	*p. 544*	22. E	*p. 560*	39. A	*p. 588*
6. A	*p. 546*	23. A	*p. 561*	40. B	*p. 589*
7. C	*p. 546*	24. B	*p. 561*	41. A	*p. 592*
8. B	*p. 547*	25. C	*p. 563*	42. E	*p. 596*
9. C	*p. 548*	26. E	*p. 568*	43. B	*p. 599*
10. C	*p. 548*	27. B	*p. 569*	44. C	*p. 600*
11. B	*p. 549*	28. C	*p. 569*	45. C	*p. 602*
12. A	*p. 551*	29. A	*p. 570*	46. D	*p. 602*
13. E	*p. 553*	30. A	*p. 570*	47. D	*p. 604*
14. B	*p. 553*	31. B	*p. 570*	48. D	*p. 604*
15. B	*p. 554*	32. B	*p. 572*	49. A	*p. 606*
16. B	*p. 555*	33. B	*p. 573*	50. D	*p. 607*
17. D	*p. 555*	34. B	*p. 577*		

SPECIAL PROJECT: PROBLEM SOLVING: Airway Maintenance

1. suction, laryngoscope, stylette, tape, stethoscope, endotracheal tube, 10-mL syringe, water-soluble gel, Magill forceps, BSI
2. Laryngoscope: Check blade—bright white and nonflickering light. Tube cuff: Inflate with 10 mL of air using syringe. Does cuff hold air? Endotracheal tube: Have one larger and one smaller tube available.
3. Hyperventilate the patient.
4. Fill syringe with 10 to 15 mL of air. Position the patient's head. Grasp the laryngoscope handle in the left hand. Insert blade in the right side of the patient's mouth. Displace tongue to left. Insert blade to the epiglottis. Lift laryngoscope along axis of handle. Visualize the vocal folds and glottis. Grasp tube and pass it between the cords. Inflate the cuff and auscultate.
5. Visualize with the laryngoscope the tube passing through the cords. Check the depth of the tube against the mouth. Auscultate all lung fields for bilaterally equal breath sounds. Auscultate the epigastrium for gurgling sounds. Employ capnography, observe for chest rise.
6. If the tube is placed in the esophagus, leave it in place, hyperventilate the patient, and attempt to place another tube in the trachea. Re-auscultate and assure the new tube is properly placed.

Introduction to Advanced Prehospital Care: Content Review

CONTENT SELF-EVALUATION

CHAPTER 1: INTRODUCTION TO ADVANCED PREHOSPITAL CARE

1. B	*p. 5*	5. E	*p. 8*	9. B	*p. 9*
2. A	*p. 6*	6. A	*p. 7*	10. A	*p. 10*
3. A	*p. 6*	7. A	*p. 8*		
4. C	*p. 8*	8. C	*p. 8*		

CHAPTER 2: THE WELL-BEING OF THE PARAMEDIC

11.	E	*p. 17*	**20.**	A	*p. 24*	**29.**	A	*p. 34*
12.	D	*p. 17*	**21.**	D	*p. 24*	**30.**	E	*p. 35*
13.	E	*p. 17*	**22.**	D	*p. 24*	**31.**	D	*p. 35*
14.	A	*p. 19*	**23.**	E	*p. 24*	**32.**	E	*p. 37*
15.	C	*p. 19*	**24.**	A	*p. 27*	**33.**	A	*p. 38*
16.	E	*p. 19*	**25.**	A	*p. 30*	**34.**	A	*p. 38*
17.	B	*p. 21*	**26.**	A	*p. 30*	**35.**	A	*p. 40*
18.	B	*p. 23*	**27.**	C	*p. 32*			
19.	B	*p. 23*	**28.**	B	*p. 31*			

CHAPTER 3: EMS SYSTEMS

36.	C	*p. 47*	**43.**	D	*p. 58*	**50.**	E	*p. 66*
37.	A	*p. 49*	**44.**	A	*p. 59*	**51.**	A	*p. 67*
38.	C	*p. 49*	**45.**	B	*p. 59*	**52.**	E	*p. 70*
39.	D	*p. 51*	**46.**	E	*p. 61*	**53.**	A	*p. 69*
40.	A	*p. 54*	**47.**	A	*p. 62*	**54.**	A	*p. 70*
41.	B	*p. 56*	**48.**	D	*p. 62*	**55.**	A	*p. 72*
42.	D	*p. 56*	**49.**	B	*p. 64*			

CHAPTER 4: ROLES AND RESPONSIBILITIES OF THE PARAMEDIC

56.	A	*p. 78*	**60.**	A	*p. 83*	**64.**	E	*p. 86*
57.	C	*p. 79*	**61.**	A	*p. 84*	**65.**	B	*p. 92*
58.	C	*p. 80*	**62.**	B	*p. 86*			
59.	E	*p. 83*	**63.**	E	*p. 86*			

CHAPTER 5: ILLNESS AND INJURY PREVENTION

66.	C	*p. 98*	**70.**	C	*p. 102*	**74.**	B	*p. 105*
67.	A	*p. 99*	**71.**	D	*p. 103*	**75.**	E	*p. 105*
68.	A	*p. 99*	**72.**	B	*p. 104*			
69.	E	*p. 101*	**73.**	E	*p. 104*			

CHAPTER 6: MEDICAL/LEGAL ASPECTS OF ADVANCED PREHOSPITAL CARE

76.	D	*p. 114*	**85.**	B	*p. 121*	**94.**	A	*p. 130*
77.	B	*p. 114*	**86.**	E	*p. 123*	**95.**	B	*p. 130*
78.	D	*p. 115*	**87.**	A	*p. 124*	**96.**	E	*p. 131*
79.	A	*p. 115*	**88.**	A	*p. 125*	**97.**	A	*p. 134*
80.	C	*p. 115*	**89.**	E	*p. 125*	**98.**	B	*p. 135*
81.	B	*p. 115*	**90.**	A	*p. 126*	**99.**	D	*p. 136*
82.	E	*p. 115*	**91.**	C	*p. 126*	**100.**	E	*p. 137*
83.	B	*p. 119*	**92.**	C	*p. 127*			
84.	A	*p. 120*	**93.**	B	*p. 130*			

CHAPTER 7: ETHICS IN ADVANCED PREHOSPITAL CARE

101.	E	*p. 144*	**105.**	B	*p. 147*	**109.**	E	*p. 154*
102.	A	*p. 144*	**106.**	D	*p. 147*	**110.**	E	*p. 158*
103.	A	*p. 146*	**107.**	A	*p. 151*			
104.	B	*p. 146*	**108.**	D	*p. 153*			

CHAPTER 8: GENERAL PRINCIPLES OF PATHOPHYSIOLOGY, PART 1

111.	A	*p. 167*	**126.**	E	*p. 177*	**141.**	D	*p. 189*
112.	E	*p. 168*	**127.**	A	*p. 180*	**142.**	C	*p. 191*
113.	C	*p. 169*	**128.**	C	*p. 180*	**143.**	D	*p. 191*
114.	A	*p. 168*	**129.**	B	*p. 181*	**144.**	C	*p. 191*
115.	B	*p. 169*	**130.**	E	*p. 181*	**145.**	E	*p. 192*
116.	C	*p. 169*	**131.**	A	*p. 182*	**146.**	A	*p. 193*
117.	C	*p. 170*	**132.**	D	*p. 183*	**147.**	B	*p. 194*
118.	D	*p. 171*	**133.**	A	*p. 185*	**148.**	E	*p. 194*
119.	D	*p. 171*	**134.**	B	*p. 186*	**149.**	D	*p. 194*
120.	B	*p. 172*	**135.**	C	*p. 188*	**150.**	B	*p. 195*
121.	B	*p. 172*	**136.**	C	*p. 186*	**151.**	A	*p. 195*
122.	A	*p. 173*	**137.**	C	*p. 187*	**152.**	C	*p. 195*
123.	A	*p. 175*	**138.**	A	*p. 187*	**153.**	B	*p. 197*
124.	C	*p. 175*	**139.**	D	*p. 188*	**154.**	A	*p. 198*
125.	D	*p. 178*	**140.**	C	*p. 189*	**155.**	A	*p. 198*

CHAPTER 8: GENERAL PRINCIPLES OF PATHOPHYSIOLOGY, PART 2

156.	A	*p. 200*	**163.**	A	*p. 207*	**170.**	D	*p. 213*
157.	A	*p. 200*	**164.**	E	*p. 208*	**171.**	A	*p. 213*
158.	B	*p. 201*	**165.**	C	*p. 208*	**172.**	A	*p. 214*
159.	E	*p. 203*	**166.**	A	*p. 209*	**173.**	B	*p. 215*
160.	E	*p. 205*	**167.**	A	*p. 210*	**174.**	C	*p. 216*
161.	E	*p. 205*	**168.**	C	*p. 210*	**175.**	A	*p. 219*
162.	A	*p. 207*	**169.**	E	*p. 212*			

CHAPTER 8: GENERAL PRINCIPLES OF PATHOPHYSIOLOGY, PART 3

176.	D	*p. 222*	**186.**	B	*p. 230*	**196.**	A	*p. 251*
177.	E	*p. 222*	**187.**	A	*p. 238*	**197.**	A	*p. 253*
178.	B	*p. 224*	**188.**	B	*p. 241*	**198.**	C	*p. 253*
179.	A	*p. 224*	**189.**	A	*p. 241*	**199.**	C	*p. 257*
180.	B	*p. 225*	**190.**	A	*p. 242*	**200.**	B	*p. 259*
181.	E	*p. 225*	**191.**	C	*p. 243*	**201.**	E	*p. 261*
182.	A	*p. 226*	**192.**	B	*p. 244*	**202.**	E	*p. 263*
183.	D	*p. 227*	**193.**	A	*p. 247*	**203.**	B	*p. 264*
184.	B	*p. 228*	**194.**	E	*p. 248*	**204.**	A	*p. 264*
185.	D	*p. 230*	**195.**	C	*p. 250*	**205.**	A	*p. 265*

CHAPTER 9: GENERAL PRINCIPLES OF PHARMACOLOGY, PART 1

206.	D	*p. 279*	**216.**	D	*p. 289*	**226.**	B	*p. 294*
207.	C	*p. 279*	**217.**	E	*p. 289*	**227.**	E	*p. 295*
208.	E	*p. 279*	**218.**	C	*p. 289*	**228.**	A	*p. 295*
209.	C	*p. 279*	**219.**	B	*p. 292*	**229.**	C	*p. 296*
210.	A	*p. 281*	**220.**	E	*p. 293*	**230.**	E	*p. 296*
211.	D	*p. 281*	**221.**	B	*p. 293*	**231.**	A	*p. 296*
212.	D	*p. 282*	**222.**	B	*p. 294*	**232.**	B	*p. 298*
213.	E	*p. 285*	**223.**	B	*p. 294*	**233.**	E	*p. 298*
214.	B	*p. 287*	**224.**	D	*p. 294*	**234.**	A	*p. 298*
215.	B	*p. 289*	**225.**	D	*p. 294*	**235.**	D	*p. 298*

©2006 Pearson Education, Inc.
Paramedic Care: Principles & Practice, Vol. 1

CHAPTER 9: GENERAL PRINCIPLES OF PHARMACOLOGY, PART 2

236. B	p. 301	253. D	p. 315	270. C	p. 339
237. A	p. 301	254. E	p. 317	271. C	p. 340
238. C	p. 301	255. D	p. 319	272. A	p. 340
239. A	p. 302	256. A	p. 321	273. D	p. 341
240. A	p. 304	257. C	p. 321	274. D	p. 343
241. E	p. 306	258. E	p. 321	275. C	p. 344
242. A	p. 307	259. C	p. 322	276. A	p. 344
243. E	p. 307	260. A	p. 323	277. A	p. 345
244. C	p. 307	261. A	p. 327	278. B	p. 347
245. A	p. 308	262. D	p. 327	279. E	p. 348
246. C	p. 308	263. C	p. 332	280. D	p. 349
247. A	p. 309	264. C	p. 332	281. A	p. 350
248. E	p. 311	265. C	p. 332	282. C	p. 353
249. C	p. 311	266. A	p. 333	283. C	p. 356
250. A	p. 311	267. B	p. 338	284. E	p. 360
251. C	p. 314	268. D	p. 338	285. A	p. 360
252. D	p. 314	269. B	p. 339		

CHAPTER 10: INTRAVENOUS ACCESS AND MEDICATION ADMINISTRATION, PART 1

286. C	p. 289	296. B	p. 384	306. D	p. 397
287. C	p. 372	297. D	p. 384	307. E	p. 395
288. A	p. 373	298. E	p. 384	308. B	p. 399
289. D	p. 374	299. A	p. 384	309. B	p. 399
290. E	p. 375	300. A	p. 386	310. A	p. 399
291. C	p. 376	301. E	p. 390	311. C	p. 403
292. D	p. 379	302. A	p. 391	312. C	p. 403
293. B	p. 380	303. A	p. 391	313. D	p. 405
294. A	p. 381	304. B	p. 392	314. E	p. 405
295. A	p. 383	305. B	p. 392	315. B	p. 405

CHAPTER 10: INTRAVENOUS ACCESS AND MEDICATION ADMINISTRATION, PART 2

316. B	p. 407	326. C	p. 416	336. D	p. 430
317. B	p. 407	327. A	p. 417	337. D	p. 434
318. C	p. 407	328. A	p. 418	338. E	p. 437
319. B	p. 409	329. E	p. 418	339. B	p. 438
320. D	p. 409	330. A	p. 420	340. B	p. 438
321. C	p. 410	331. B	p. 422	341. A	p. 439
322. A	p. 412	332. C	p. 425	342. D	p. 441
323. B	p. 411	333. E	p. 426	343. A	p. 441
324. C	p. 414	334. A	p. 428	344. E	p. 445
325. B	p. 415	335. B	p. 430	345. A	p. 448

CHAPTER 11: THERAPEUTIC COMMUNICATIONS

346. E	p. 467	350. B	p. 469	354. C	p. 475
347. A	p. 467	351. A	p. 471	355. D	p. 478
348. B	p. 468	352. A	p. 472		
349. B	p. 469	353. B	p. 474		

CHAPTER 12: LIFE-SPAN DEVELOPMENT

356. C	p. 484	361. C	p. 487	366. D	p. 494
357. A	p. 484	362. A	p. 488	367. C	p. 495
358. A	p. 485	363. B	p. 490	368. D	p. 495
359. B	p. 485	364. A	p. 491	369. E	p. 497
360. C	p. 485	365. E	p. 493	370. A	p. 498

CHAPTER 13: AIRWAY MANAGEMENT AND VENTILATION

371. A	p. 510	388. B	p. 530	405. A	p. 564
372. D	p. 509	389. D	p. 532	406. A	p. 568
373. A	p. 513	390. E	p. 535	407. C	p. 569
374. B	p. 513	391. A	p. 536	408. A	p. 570
375. A	p. 513	392. A	p. 538	409. B	p. 569
376. A	p. 515	393. C	p. 541	410. A	p. 573
377. B	p. 515	394. A	p. 543	411. C	p. 577
378. A	p. 517	395. B	p. 546	412. E	p. 577
379. D	p. 518	396. A	p. 558	413. B	p. 584
380. A	p. 519	397. E	p. 548	414. D	p. 588
381. D	p. 521	398. A	p. 549	415. A	p. 589
382. D	p. 521	399. C	p. 551	416. B	p. 596
383. E	p. 522	400. B	p. 553	417. A	p. 598
384. C	p. 522	401. B	p. 553	418. A	p. 600
385. C	p. 524	402. E	p. 554	419. A	p. 604
386. B	p. 528	403. E	p. 560	420. E	p. 605
387. B	p. 529	404. D	p. 561		

National Registry of Emergency Medical Technicians

Practical Evaluation Forms

The forms on the next page are provided to help you identify common criteria by which you will be evaluated. It may be valuable to review your practical skills by using these sheets during your class practice sessions and as you review those skills before class, state, and any national testing. Evaluation forms will vary; however, many of the important elements of paramedic practice are common to all forms.

EMT-PARAMEDIC FORMS

The following skill instruments for the EMT-Paramedic level were developed by the National Registry of EMTs and have been approved for use in advanced level National Registry Examinations.

- Bleeding Control/Shock Management
- Dual Lumen Airway Device
- Dynamic Cardiology
- Intravenous Therapy
- Oral Station
- Patient Assessment—Medical
- Patient Assessment—Trauma
- Pediatric Intraosseous Infusion
- Pediatric (less than 2 years) Ventilatory Management
- Spinal Immobilization (Seated Patient)
- Spinal Immobilization (Supine Patient)
- Static Cardiology
- Ventilatory Management—Adult

EMT-Paramedic Form

National Registry of Emergency Medical Technicians
Advanced Level Practical Examination

BLEEDING CONTROL/SHOCK MANAGEMENT

Candidate: _____ Examiner: _____

Date: _____ Signature: _____

Time Start:_____	Possible Points	Points Awarded
Takes or verbalizes body substance isolation precautions	1	
Applies direct pressure to the wound	1	
Elevates the extremity	1	
NOTE: The examiner must now inform the candidate that the wound continues to bleed.		
Applies an additional dressing to the wound	1	
NOTE: The examiner must now inform the candidate that the wound still continues to bleed. The second dressing does not control the bleeding.		
Locates and applies pressure to appropriate arterial pressure point	1	
NOTE: The examiner must now inform the candidate that the bleeding is controlled.		
Bandages the wound	1	
NOTE: The examiner must now inform the candidate that the patient is exhibiting signs and symptoms of hypoperfusion.		
Properly positions the patient	1	
Administers high concentration oxygen	1	
Initiates steps to prevent heat loss from the patient	1	
Indicates the need for immediate transportation	1	

Time End: _____   **TOTAL**   10

CRITICAL CRITERIA

_____ Did not take or verbalize body substance isolation precautions
_____ Did not apply high concentration of oxygen
_____ Applied a tourniquet before attempting other methods of bleeding control
_____ Did not control hemorrhage in a timely manner
_____ Did not indicate the need for immediate transportation

You must factually document your rationale for checking any of the above critical items on the reverse side of this form.

EMT-Paramedic Form

National Registry of Emergency Medical Technicians
Advanced Level Practical Examination

INTRAVENOUS THERAPY

Candidate: _____ Examiner: _____

Date: _____ Signature: _____

Level of Testing: ❑ NREMT-Intermediate/85 ❑ NREMT-Intermediate/99 ❑ NREMT-Paramedic

Time Start: _____

	Possible Points	Points Awarded
Checks selected IV fluid for: -Proper fluid (1 point) -Clarity (1 point)	2	
Selects appropriate catheter	1	
Selects proper administration set	1	
Connects IV tubing to the IV bag	1	
Prepares administration set [fills drip chamber and flushes tubing]	1	
Cuts or tears tape [at any time before venipuncture]	1	
Takes/verbalizes body substance isolation precautions [prior to venipuncture]	1	
Applies tourniquet	1	
Palpates suitable vein	1	
Cleanses site appropriately	1	
Performs venipuncture -Inserts stylette (1 point) -Notes or verbalizes flashback (1 point) -Occludes vein proximal to catheter (1 point) -Removes stylette (1 point) -Connects IV tubing to catheter (1 point)	5	
Disposes/verbalizes disposal of needle in proper container	1	
Releases tourniquet	1	
Runs IV for a brief period to assure patent line	1	
Secures catheter [tapes securely or verbalizes]	1	
Adjusts flow rate as appropriate	1	

Time End: _____   **TOTAL**   21

CRITICAL CRITERIA

____ Failure to establish a patent and properly adjusted IV within 6 minute time limit
____ Failure to take or verbalize body substance isolation precautions prior to performing venipuncture
____ Contaminates equipment or site without appropriately correcting situation
____ Performs any improper technique resulting in the potential for uncontrolled hemorrhage, catheter shear, or air embolism
____ Failure to successfully establish IV within 3 attempts during 6 minute time limit
____ Failure to dispose/verbalize disposal of needle in proper container

NOTE: Check here (_____) if candidate did not establish a patent IV and do not evaluate IV Bolus Medications.

INTRAVENOUS BOLUS MEDICATIONS

Time Start: _____

Asks patient for known allergies	1	
Selects correct medication	1	
Assures correct concentration of drug	1	
Assembles prefilled syringe correctly and dispels air	1	
Continues body substance isolation precautions	1	
Cleanses injection site [Y-port or hub]	1	
Reaffirms medication	1	
Stops IV flow [pinches tubing or shuts off]	1	
Administers correct dose at proper push rate	1	
Disposes/verbalizes proper disposal of syringe and needle in proper container	1	
Flushes tubing [runs wide open for a brief period]	1	
Adjusts drip rate to TKO/KVO	1	
Verbalizes need to observe patient for desired effect/adverse side effects	1	

Time End: _____   **TOTAL**   13

CRITICAL CRITERIA

____ Failure to begin administration of medication within 3 minute time limit
____ Contaminates equipment or site without appropriately correcting situation
____ Failure to adequately dispel air resulting in potential for air embolism
____ Injects improper drug or dosage [wrong drug, incorrect amount, or pushes at inappropriate rate]
____ Failure to flush IV tubing after injecting medication
____ Recaps needle or failure to dispose/verbalize disposal of syringe and needle in proper container

You must factually document your rationale for checking any of the above critical items on the reverse side of this form.

EMT-Paramedic Form

National Registry of Emergency Medical Technicians
Advanced Level Practical Examination
ORAL STATION

Candidate: _____Examiner: _____

Date: _____Signature: _____

Scenario: _____

Time Start: _____

	Possible Points	Points Awarded
Scene Management		
Thoroughly assessed and took deliberate actions to control the scene	3	
Assessed the scene, identified potential hazards, did not put anyone in danger	2	
Incompletely assessed or managed the scene	1	
Did not assess or manage the scene	0	
Patient Assessment		
Completed an organized assessment and integrated findings to expand further assessment	3	
Completed initial, focused, and ongoing assessments	2	
Performed an incomplete or disorganized assessment	1	
Did not complete an initial assessment	0	
Patient Management		
Managed all aspects of the patient's condition and anticipated further needs	3	
Appropriately managed the patient's presenting condition	2	
Performed an incomplete or disorganized management	1	
Did not manage life-threatening conditions	0	
Interpersonal relations		
Established rapport and interacted in an organized, therapeutic manner	3	
Interacted and responded appropriately with patient, crew, and bystanders	2	
Used inappropriate communication techniques	1	
Demonstrated intolerance for patient, bystanders, and crew	0	
Integration (verbal report, field impression, and transport decision)		
Stated correct field impression and pathophysiological basis, provided succinct and accurate verbal report including social/psychological concerns, and considered alternate transport destinations	3	
Stated correct field impression, provided succinct and accurate verbal report, and appropriately stated transport decision	2	
Stated correct field impression, provided inappropriate verbal report or transport decision	1	
Stated incorrect field impression or did not provide verbal report	0	

Time End: _____   **TOTAL**   15

Critical Criteria

_____ Failure to appropriately address any of the scenario's "Mandatory Actions"

_____ Performs or orders any harmful or dangerous action or intervention

You must factually document your rationale for checking any of the above critical items on the reverse side of this form.

EMT-Paramedic Form

National Registry of Emergency Medical Technicians
Advanced Level Practical Examination

PEDIATRIC INTRAOSSEOUS INFUSION

Candidate: _____ Examiner: _____

Date: _____ Signature: _____

Time Start:_____	Possible Points	Points Awarded
Checks selected IV fluid for: -Proper fluid (1 point) -Clarity (1 point)	2	
Selects appropriate equipment to include: -IO needle (1 point) -Syringe (1 point) -Saline (1 point) -Extension set (1 point)	4	
Selects proper administration set	1	
Connects administration set to bag	1	
Prepares administration set [fills drip chamber and flushes tubing]	1	
Prepares syringe and extension tubing	1	
Cuts or tears tape [at any time before IO puncture]	1	
Takes or verbalizes body substance isolation precautions [prior to IO puncture]	1	
Identifies proper anatomical site for IO puncture	1	
Cleanses site appropriately	1	
Performs IO puncture: -Stabilizes tibia (1 point) -Inserts needle at proper angle (1 point) -Advances needle with twisting motion until "pop" is felt (1 point) -Unscrews cap and removes stylette from needle (1 point)	4	
Disposes of needle in proper container	1	
Attaches syringe and extension set to IO needle and aspirates	1	
Slowly injects saline to assure proper placement of needle	1	
Connects administration set and adjusts flow rate as appropriate	1	
Secures needle with tape and supports with bulky dressing	1	

Time End: _____   **TOTAL**   23

CRITICAL CRITERIA

_____ Failure to establish a patent and properly adjusted IO line within the 6 minute time limit
_____ Failure to take or verbalize body substance isolation precautions prior to performing IO puncture
_____ Contaminates equipment or site without appropriately correcting situation
_____ Performs any improper technique resulting in the potential for air embolism
_____ Failure to assure correct needle placement before attaching administration set
_____ Failure to successfully establish IO infusion within 2 attempts during 6 minute time limit
_____ Performing IO puncture in an unacceptable manner [improper site, incorrect needle angle, etc.]
_____ Failure to dispose of needle in proper container
_____ Orders or performs any dangerous or potentially harmful procedure

You must factually document your rationale for checking any of the above critical items on the reverse side of this form.

EMT-Paramedic Form

National Registry of Emergency Medical Technicians
Advanced Level Practical Examination

PEDIATRIC (<2 yrs.) VENTILATORY MANAGEMENT

Candidate: _____ Examiner _____

Date: _____ Signature: _____

NOTE: If candidate elects to ventilate initially with BVM attached to reservoir and oxygen, full credit must be awarded for steps denoted by "**" so long as first ventilation is delivered within 30 seconds.

	Possible Points	Points Awarded
Takes or verbalizes body substance isolation precautions	1	
Opens the airway manually	1	
Elevates tongue, inserts simple adjunct [oropharyngeal or nasopharyngeal airway]	1	
NOTE: Examiner now informs candidate no gag reflex is present and patient accepts adjunct		
**Ventilates patient immediately with bag-valve-mask device unattached to oxygen	1	
**Hyperventilates patient with room air	1	
NOTE: Examiner now informs candidate that ventilation is being performed without difficulty and that pulse oximetry indicates the patient's blood oxygen saturation is 85%		
Attaches oxygen reservoir to bag-valve-mask device and connects to high flow oxygen regulator [12-15 L/minute]	1	
Ventilates patient at a rate of 20-30/minute and assures adequate chest expansion	1	
NOTE: After 30 seconds, examiner auscultates and reports breath sounds are present, equal bilaterally and medical direction has ordered intubation. The examiner must now take over ventilation.		
Directs assistant to pre-oxygenate patient	1	
Identifies/selects proper equipment for intubation	1	
Checks laryngoscope to assure operational with bulb tight	1	
NOTE: Examiner to remove OPA and move out of the way when candidate is prepared to intubate		
Places patient in neutral or sniffing position	1	
Inserts blade while displacing tongue	1	
Elevates mandible with laryngoscope	1	
Introduces ET tube and advances to proper depth	1	
Directs ventilation of patient	1	
Confirms proper placement by auscultation bilaterally over each lung and over epigastrium	1	
NOTE: Examiner to ask, "If you had proper placement, what should you expect to hear?"		
Secures ET tube [may be verbalized]	1	

TOTAL 17

CRITICAL CRITERIA

_____ Failure to initiate ventilations within 30 seconds after applying gloves or interrupts ventilations for greater than 30 seconds at any time
_____ Failure to take or verbalize body substance isolation precautions
_____ Failure to pad under the torso to allow neutral head position or sniffing position
_____ Failure to voice and ultimately provide high oxygen concentrations [at least 85%]
_____ Failure to ventilate patient at a rate of at least 20/minute
_____ Failure to provide adequate volumes per breath [maximum 2 errors/minute permissible]
_____ Failure to pre-oxygenate patient prior to intubation
_____ Failure to successfully intubate within 3 attempts
_____ Uses gums as a fulcrum
_____ Failure to assure proper tube placement by auscultation bilaterally **and** over the epigastrium
_____ Inserts any adjunct in a manner dangerous to the patient
_____ Attempts to use any equipment not appropriate for the pediatric patient

You must factually document your rationale for checking any of the above critical items on the reverse side of this form.

EMT-Paramedic Form

National Registry of Emergency Medical Technicians
Advanced Level Practical Examination

SPINAL IMMOBILIZATION (SEATED PATIENT)

Candidate:_____Examiner:_____

Date: _____Signature:_____

Time Start: _____	Possible Points	Points Awarded
Takes or verbalizes body substance isolation precautions	1	
Directs assistant to place/maintain head in the neutral, in-line position	1	
Directs assistant to maintain manual immobilization of the head	1	
Reassesses motor, sensory, and circulatory function in each extremity	1	
Applies appropriately sized extrication collar	1	
Positions the immobilization device behind the patient	1	
Secures the device to the patient's torso	1	
Evaluates torso fixation and adjusts as necessary	1	
Evaluates and pads behind the patient's head as necessary	1	
Secures the patient's head to the device	1	
Verbalizes moving the patient to a long backboard	1	
Reassesses motor, sensory, and circulatory function in each extremity	1	
Time End: _____ **TOTAL**	12	

CRITICAL CRITERIA

_____ Did not immediately direct or take manual immobilization of the head
_____ Did not properly apply appropriately sized cervical collar before ordering release of manual immobilization
_____ Released or ordered release of manual immobilization before it was maintained mechanically
_____ Manipulated or moved patient excessively causing potential spinal compromise
_____ Head immobilized to the device **before** device sufficiently secured to torso
_____ Device moves excessively up, down, left, or right on the patient's torso
_____ Head immobilization allows for excessive movement
_____ Torso fixation inhibits chest rise, resulting in respiratory compromise
_____ Upon completion of immobilization, head is not in a neutral, in-line position
_____ Did not reassess motor, sensory, and circulatory functions in each extremity after voicing immobilization to the long backboard

You must factually document your rationale for checking any of the above critical items on the reverse side of this form.

EMT-Paramedic Form

National Registry of Emergency Medical Technicians
Advanced Level Practical Examination

SPINAL IMMOBILIZATION (SUPINE PATIENT)

Candidate:_____ Examiner:_____

Date: _____ Signature:_____

Time Start: _____	Possible Points	Points Awarded
Takes or verbalizes body substance isolation precautions	1	
Directs assistant to place/maintain head in the neutral, in-line position	1	
Directs assistant to maintain manual immobilization of the head	1	
Reassesses motor, sensory, and circulatory function in each extremity	1	
Applies appropriately sized extrication collar	1	
Positions the immobilization device appropriately	1	
Directs movement of the patient onto the device without compromising the integrity of the spine	1	
Applies padding to voids between the torso and the device as necessary	1	
Immobilizes the patient's torso to the device	1	
Evaluates and pads behind the patient's head as necessary	1	
Immobilizes the patient's head to the device	1	
Secures the patient's legs to the device	1	
Secures the patient's arms to the device	1	
Reassesses motor, sensory, and circulatory function in each extremity	1	
TOTAL	**14**	

Time End: _____

CRITICAL CRITERIA

_____ Did not immediately direct or take manual immobilization of the head
_____ Did not properly apply appropriately sized cervical collar before ordering release of manual immobilization
_____ Released or ordered release of manual immobilization before it was maintained mechanically
_____ Manipulated or moved patient excessively causing potential spinal compromise
_____ Head immobilized to the device **before** device sufficiently secured to torso
_____ Patient moves excessively up, down, left, or right on the device
_____ Head immobilization allows for excessive movement
_____ Upon completion of immobilization, head is not in a neutral, in-line position
_____ Did not reassess motor, sensory, and circulatory functions in each extremity after voicing immobilization to the device

You must factually document your rationale for checking any of the above critical items on the reverse side of this form.

p312/8-003k

EMT-Paramedic Form

National Registry of Emergency Medical Technicians
Advanced Level Practical Examination

STATIC CARDIOLOGY

Candidate: _____ Examiner: _____

Date: _____ Signature: _____

SET #_____

Level of Testing: □ NREMT-Intermediate/99 □ NREMT-Paramedic

Note: No points for treatment may be awarded if the diagnosis is incorrect.
Only document incorrect responses in spaces provided.

Time Start:_____

	Possible Points	Points Awarded
STRIP #1		
Diagnosis:	1	
Treatment:	2	
STRIP #2		
Diagnosis:	1	
Treatment:	2	
STRIP #3		
Diagnosis:	1	
Treatment:	2	
STRIP #4		
Diagnosis:	1	
Treatment:	2	

Time End: _____   **TOTAL**   12

p307/8-003k

EMT-Paramedic Form

National Registry of Emergency Medical Technicians
Advanced Level Practical Examination

VENTILATORY MANAGEMENT - ADULT

Candidate:_____Examiner:_____

Date: _____Signature: _____

NOTE: If candidate elects to ventilate initially with BVM attached to reservoir and oxygen, full credit must be awarded for
steps denoted by "**" so long as first ventilation is delivered within 30 seconds.

	Possible Points	Points Awarded
Takes or verbalizes body substance isolation precautions	1	
Opens the airway manually	1	
Elevates tongue, inserts simple adjunct [oropharyngeal or nasopharyngeal airway]	1	
NOTE: **Examiner now informs candidate no gag reflex is present and patient accepts adjunct**		
**Ventilates patient immediately with bag-valve-mask device unattached to oxygen	1	
**Hyperventilates patient with room air	1	
NOTE: **Examiner now informs candidate that ventilation is being performed without difficulty and that pulse oximetry indicates the patient's blood oxygen saturation is 85%**		
Attaches oxygen reservoir to bag-valve-mask device and connects to high flow oxygen regulator [12-15 L/minute]	1	
Ventilates patient at a rate of 10-20/minute with appropriate volumes	1	
NOTE: **After 30 seconds, examiner auscultates and reports breath sounds are present, equal bilaterally and medical direction has ordered intubation. The examiner must now take over ventilation.**		
Directs assistant to pre-oxygenate patient	1	
Identifies/selects proper equipment for intubation	1	
Checks equipment for: -Cuff leaks (1 point) -Laryngoscope operational with bulb tight (1 point)	2	
NOTE: **Examiner to remove OPA and move out of the way when candidate is prepared to intubate**		
Positions head properly	1	
Inserts blade while displacing tongue	1	
Elevates mandible with laryngoscope	1	
Introduces ET tube and advances to proper depth	1	
Inflates cuff to proper pressure and disconnects syringe	1	
Directs ventilation of patient	1	
Confirms proper placement by auscultation bilaterally over each lung and over epigastrium	1	
NOTE: **Examiner to ask, "If you had proper placement, what should you expect to hear?"**		
Secures ET tube [may be verbalized]	1	
NOTE: **Examiner now asks candidate, "Please demonstrate one additional method of verifying proper tube placement in this patient."**		
Identifies/selects proper equipment	1	
Verbalizes findings and interpretations [compares indicator color to the colorimetric scale and states reading to examiner]	1	
NOTE: **Examiner now states, "You see secretions in the tube and hear gurgling sounds with the patient's exhalation."**		
Identifies/selects a flexible suction catheter	1	
Pre-oxygenates patient	1	
Marks maximum insertion length with thumb and forefinger	1	
Inserts catheter into the ET tube leaving catheter port open	1	
At proper insertion depth, covers catheter port and applies suction while withdrawing catheter	1	
Ventilates/directs ventilation of patient as catheter is flushed with sterile water	1	
TOTAL	**27**	

CRITICAL CRITERIA

_____ Failure to initiate ventilations within 30 seconds after applying gloves or interrupts ventilations for greater than 30 seconds at any time
_____ Failure to take or verbalize body substance isolation precautions
_____ Failure to voice and ultimately provide high oxygen concentrations [at least 85%]
_____ Failure to ventilate patient at a rate of at least 10/minute
_____ Failure to provide adequate volumes per breath [maximum 2 errors/minute permissible]
_____ Failure to pre-oxygenate patient prior to intubation and suctioning
_____ Failure to successfully intubate within 3 attempts
_____ Failure to disconnect syringe **immediately** after inflating cuff of ET tube
_____ Uses teeth as a fulcrum
_____ Failure to assure proper tube placement by auscultation bilaterally **and** over the epigastrium
_____ If used, stylette extends beyond end of ET tube
_____ Inserts any adjunct in a manner dangerous to the patient
_____ Suctions the patient for more than 15 seconds
_____ Does not suction the patient

You must factually document your rationale for checking any of the above critical items on the reverse side of this form.

p303/8-003k

TERBUTALINE

THIAMINE

VASOPRESSIN

Name/Class: TERBUTALINE (Brethine, Bricanyl)/Sympathetic Agonist

Description: Terbutaline is a synthetic sympathomimetic that causes bronchodilatation with less cardiac effect than epinephrine.

Indications: Bronchial asthma and bronchospasm in COPD.

Contraindications: Hypersensitivity to the drug.

Precautions: The patient may experience palpitations, anxiety, nausea, and/or dizziness. Vital signs and breath sounds must be monitored; use caution with cardiac or hypertensive patients.

Dosage/Route: Two inhalations with a metered dose inhaler, repeated once in 1 min or 0.25 mg SQ repeated in 15 to 30 mins.

Name/Class: THIAMINE/Vitamin

Description: Thiamine is vitamin B_1, which is required to convert glucose into energy. It is not manufactured by the body and must be constantly provided from ingested foods.

Indications: Coma of unknown origin, chronic alcoholism with associated coma, and delirium tremens.

Contraindications: None.

Precautions: Known hypersensitivity to the drug.

Dosage/Route: 50 to 100 mg IV/IM. Ped: 10 to 25 mg IV/IM.

Name/Class: VASOPRESSIN (Pitressin)/Hormone, Vasopressor

Description: Vasopressin is a hormone with strong vasopressive and antidiuretic properties but that may precipitate angina and/or AMI.

Indications: To increase peripheral vascular resistance in arrest (CPR) or to control bleeding from esophageal varices.

Contraindications: Chronic nephritis with nitrogen retention, ischemic heart disease, PVCs, advanced arteriosclerosis, or 1st stage of labor.

Precautions: Epilepsy, migraine, heart failure, angina, vascular disease, hepatic impairment, elderly, and children.

Dosage/Route: *Arrest:* 40 units IV.
Esophageal varices: 0.2 to 0.4 units/min IV drip.

SOTALOL

STREPTOKINASE

SUCCINYLCHOLINE

Name/Class: SOTALOL (Betapace)/Beta Blocker, Antidysrhythmic

Description: Sotalol is a nonselective beta blocker that slows heart rate and decreases AV conduction and irritability.

Indications: Ventricular and supraventricular dysrhythmias.

Contraindications: Hypersensitivity, bronchial asthma, sinus bradycardia, 2nd- and 3rd-degree heart block, long QT syndromes, cardiogenic shock, uncontrolled CHF, or COPD.

Precautions: CHF, electrolyte disturbances, recent MI, diabetes, sick sinus rhythms, or renal impairment.

Dosage/Route: 1 to 1.5 mg/kg IV at 10 mg/min or 80 mg PO bid or 160 mg PO QD.

Name/Class: STREPTOKINASE (Streptase)/Fibrinolytic

Description: Streptokinase is a fibrinolytic that acts by activating the process that converts plasminogen to plasmin and results in the degradation of fibrin and fibrinogen and decreases erythrocyte aggregation.

Indications: AMI, deep vein thrombosis (DVT), or pulmonary embolism.

Contraindications: Active internal bleeding, aortic dissection, traumatic CPR, recent stroke, intracranial or intraspinal surgery or trauma (within 2 months), intracranial tumors, uncontrolled hypertension, pregnancy, hypersensitivity to anistreplase or streptokinase.

Precautions: Recent major surgery (10 days), patients > 75 years, cerebral vascular disease, GI or GU bleeding, recent trauma, hypertension, hemorrhagic conditions, ophthalmic conditions, or oral anticoagulant use.

Dosage/Route: *AMI:* 1.5 million units IV over 1 hour.

DVT and pulmonary emboli: 250,000 units IV over 30 min, then 100,000 units/hr.

Name/Class: SUCCINYLCHOLINE (Anectine)/Depolarizing Neuromuscular Blocker

Description: Succinylcholine is an ultra–short-acting depolarizing neuromuscular blocker.

Indications: Facilitated endotracheal intubation.

Contraindications: Hypersensitivity, family history of malignant hyperthermia, penetrating eye injury, narrow-angle glaucoma.

Precautions: Severe burn or crush injury; electrolyte imbalances; hepatic, renal, cardiac, or pulmonary impairment; fractures; spinal cord injury; dehydration; severe anemia; porphyria.

Dosage/Route: 1 to 1.5 mg/kg IV/IM. Ped: 1 to 2 mg/kg IV/IM.

RACEMIC EPINEPHRINE

SODIUM BICARBONATE

SODIUM NITROPRUSSIDE

Name/Class: RACEMIC EPINEPHRINE (microNefrin, Vaponefrin)/Sympathomimetic Agonist

Description: Racemic epinephrine is a variation of epinephrine used only for inhalation to induce bronchodilation and to reduce laryngeal edema and mucus secretion.

Indications: Croup (laryngotracheobronchitis).

Contraindications: Hypersensitivity, hypertension, or epiglottitis.

Precautions: May result in tachycardia and other dysrhythmias. Patient vital signs and ECG should be monitored.

Dosage/Route: 0.25 to 0.75 mL of a 2.25% solution in 2 mL NS once by nebulizer. Ped: same as adult.

Name/Class: SODIUM BICARBONATE (NaHCO$_3$)/Alkalizing Agent

Description: Sodium bicarbonate provides vascular bicarbonate to assist the buffer system in reducing the effects of metabolic acidosis and in the treatment of some overdoses.

Indications: Tricyclic antidepressant and barbiturate overdose, refractory acidosis, or hyperkalemia.

Contraindications: None when used in severe hypoxia or late cardiac arrest.

Precautions: May cause alkalosis if given in too large a quantity. It may also deactivate vasopressors and may precipitate with calcium chloride.

Dosage/Route: 1 mEq/kg IV, then 0.5 mEq/kg/10 min. Ped: same as adult (may be given IO).

Name/Class: SODIUM NITROPRUSSIDE (Nipride)/Nitrate

Description: Sodium nitroprusside is a rapid-acting hypotensive agent producing peripheral vasodilation and a mild increase in heart rate, a decrease in cardiac output, and a slight decrease in peripheral vascular resistance.

Indications: Hypertensive crisis.

Contraindications: Compensatory hypertension or impaired cerebral circulation (head injury, stroke).

Precautions: Hepatic or renal impairment, hyponatremia, or hypothyroidism.

Dosage/Route: 0.5 to 0.1 mcg/kg/min IV drip. Ped: same as adult.

PROPAFANONE

PROPRANOLO

PROSTAGLANDIN E_1

Name/Class: PROPAFANONE (Rythmol)/Antidysrhythmic

Description: Propafanone is an antidysrhythmic that stabilizes the myocardial membranes, reduces automaticity and the rate of single and multiple PVCs, and suppresses ventricular tachycardia.

Indications: Ventricular and supraventricular dysrhythmias.

Contraindications: Hypersensitivity, uncontrolled CHF, cardiogenic shock, sick sinus syndrome, AV block, bradycardia, hypotension, bronchospastic disorders, electrolyte imbalances, non–life-threatening dysrhythmias, COPD, or nursing mothers.

Precautions: CHF, AV block, hepatic or renal impairment, elderly, or pregnancy.

Dosage/Route: 150 to 300 mg PO/8 hours or 1 to 2 mg/kg IV at 10 mg/min.

Name/Class: PROPRANOLOL (Inderal)/Beta Blocker

Description: Propranolol is a nonselective beta blocker affecting both bronchial and cardiac sites. It reduces heart rate, myocardial irritability, contraction force, cardiac output, and blood pressure.

Indications: Ventricular fibrillation and pulseless ventricular tachycardia refractory to lidocaine and bretylium and selected SVTs.

Contraindications: 2nd- and 3rd-degree heart blocks, CHF, cor pulmonale, sinus bradycardia, cardiac impairment, cardiogenic shock, bronchospasm, or bronchial asthma, COPD, adrenergic-augmenting psychotropic or MAO inhibitors.

Precautions: Peripheral vascular disease, bee sting allergy, mild COPD, renal or hepatic impairment, diabetes, hypoglycemia, myasthenia gravis, WPW syndrome, or major surgery.

Dosage/Route: 1 to 3 mg slow IV (over 2 to 5 min), not to exceed 1 mg/min, may repeat/2 min to 0.1 mg/kg. Ped: 0.01 mg/kg slow IV.

Name/Class: PROSTAGLANDIN E₁ (Prostin VR Pediatric)/Vasodilator

Description: Prostaglandin E_1 is derived from fatty acids and causes vasodilation, inhibits platelet aggregation, and stimulates intestinal and uterine smooth muscles. It also helps maintain ductus arteriosus patency in newborn infants.

Indications: Infant cyanotic heart disease.

Contraindications:

Precautions: Constant respiratory monitoring is required.

Dosage/Route: Infant: 0.05 to 0.1 mcg/kg/min IV/IO.

PROCAINAMIDE

PROCHLORPERAZINE

PROMETHAZINE

Name/Class: PROCAINAMIDE (Pronestyl)/Antiarrhythmic

Description: Procainamide prolongs ventricular repolarization, slows conduction, and decreases myocardial excitability.

Indications: Ventricular fibrillation and pulseless ventricular tachycardia refractory to lidocaine.

Contraindications: Hypersensitivity to procainamide or procaine, myasthenia gravis, and 2nd- or 3rd-degree heart block.

Precautions: Hypotension, cardiac enlargement, CHF, AMI, ventricular dysrhythmias from digitalis, hepatic or renal impairment, electrolyte imbalance, or bronchial asthma.

Dosage/Route: 20 to 30 mg/min IV drip up to 17 mg/kg to effect, then 1 to 4 mg/min. Ped: 15 mg/kg/IV/IO over 30 to 60 min.

Name/Class: PROCHLORPERAZINE (Compazine)/Antiemetic

Description: Prochlorperazine is a phenothiazine derivative similar to chlorpromazine with potent antiemetic properties and fewer sedative, hypotensive, and anticholinergic effects.

Indications: Severe nausea and vomiting or acute psychosis.

Contraindications: Hypersensitivity to phenothiazines coma or depression.

Precautions: Breast cancer, children with acute illness or dehydration.

Dosage/Route: 5 to 10 mg IV/IM. Ped: 0.13 mg/kg IV/IM/PR if > 10 kg or > 2 years.

Name/Class: PROMETHAZINE (Phenergan)/Antiemetic

Description: Promethazine is an anticholinergic agent that enhances the effects of analgesics and is a potent antiemetic.

Indications: Nausea and vomiting, motion sickness, to enhance the effects of analgesics, and to induce sedation.

Contraindications: Hypersensitivity to phenothiazines.

Precautions: Hepatic, respiratory, or cardiac impairment, asthma, hypertension, elderly, or debilitated patients.

Dosage/Route: 12.5 to 25 mg IV/IM/PR. Ped: 0.5 mg/kg IV/IM/PR.

PHENYTOIN

PHYSOSTIGMINE

PRALIDOXIME

Name/Class: PHENYTOIN (Dilantin)/Anticonvulsant

Description: Phenytoin is a derivative related to phenobarbital that reduces the spread of electrical discharges in the motor cortex and inhibits seizures. It also has antidysrhythmic properties that counteract the effects of digitalis.

Indications: Seizures, status epilepticus, or cardiac dysrhythmias secondary to digitalis toxicity.

Contraindications: Hypersensitivity to hydantoin products, seizures due to hypoglycemia, sinus bradycardia, heart block, and Adams-Stokes syndrome.

Precautions: Hepatic or renal impairment, alcoholism, cardiogenic shock, elderly, debilitated patients, diabetes, hyperglycemia, bradycardia, heart block, or respiratory depression.

Dosage/Route: *Seizures, status epilepticus:* 10 to 15 mg/kg slow IV. Ped: 8 to 10 mg/kg slow IV.
Dysrhythmias: 100 mg slow IV (over 5 min) to a maximum 1,000 mg. Ped: 3 to 5 mg/kg slow IV.

Name/Class: PHYSOSTIGMINE (Antilirium)/Parasympathomimetic

Description: Physostigmine inhibits the breakdown of acetylcholine, resulting in prolonged parasympathetic effects. It is sometimes used as an antidote for anticholinergic (e.g., atropine) and tricyclic antidepressant overdoses.

Indications: Tricyclic antidepressant (CNS and cardiac effects) and anticholinergic overdose.

Contraindications: Asthma, diabetes, gangrene, cardiovascular disease, or narrow-angle glaucoma.

Precautions: Reduce dose (or administer atropine) if increased salivation, emesis, or bradycardia develop.

Dosage/Route: 0.5 to 3 mg IV (not faster than 1 mg min), repeat as needed. Ped: 0.01 to 0.03 mg/kg/15 to 20 min to max 2 mg.

Name/Class: PRALIDOXIME (2-PAM)/Cholinesterase Reactivator

Description: Pralidoxime reactivates cholinesterase and reinstitutes the degrading of acetylcholine and restores normal neuromuscular transmission. It is used to reverse severe organophosphate poisoning.

Indications: Organophosphate poisoning.

Contraindications: Carbamate insecticides (Sevin), inorganic phosphates, and organophosphates having no anticholinesterase activity, asthma, peptic ulcer disease, severe cardiac disease, or patients receiving aminophylline, theophylline, morphine, succinylcholine, reserpine, or phenothiazines.

Precautions: Rapid administration may result in tachycardia, laryngospasm, and muscle rigidity. Excited or manic behavior may be noted after regaining consciousness.

Dosage/Route: 1 to 2 g in 250 to 500 mL NS infused over 15 to 30 min; or 1 to 2 g IM/subcutaneous if IV not feasible. Ped: 20 to 40 mg/kg IV/IM subcutaneous.

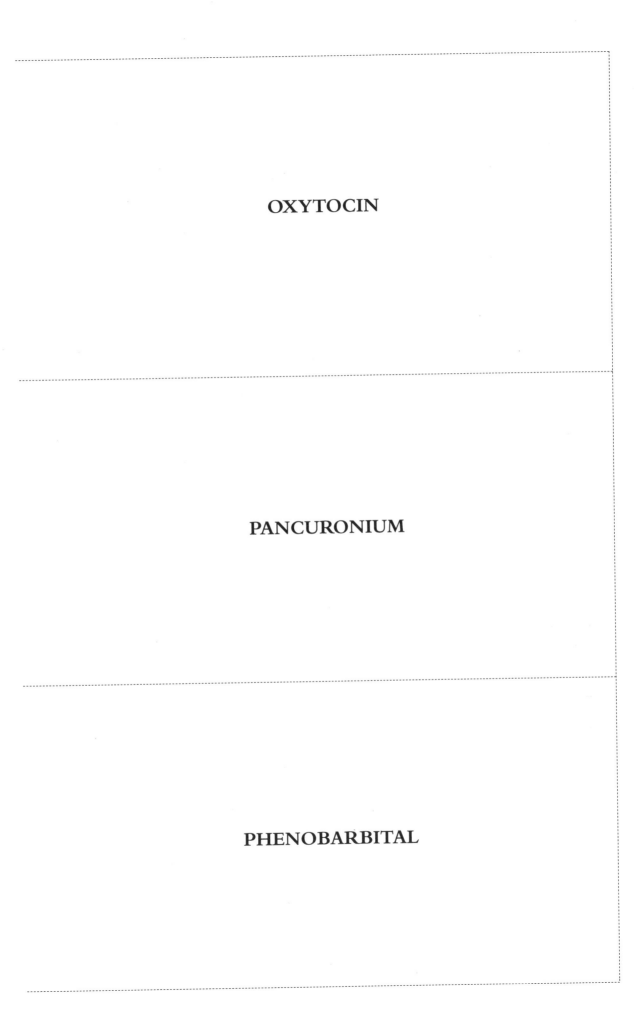

OXYTOCIN

PANCURONIUM

PHENOBARBITAL

Name/Class: OXYTOCIN (Pitocin)/Hormone

Description: Oxytocin is a naturally occurring hormone that causes the uterus to contract, thereby inducing labor, encouraging delivery of the placenta, and controlling postpartum hemorrhage.

Indications: Severe postpartum hemorrhage.

Contraindications: Hypersensitivity, prehospital administration before delivery of the infant or infants.

Precautions: Before delivery may induce uterine rupture and fetal dysrhythmias, hypertension, intracranial bleeding, or asphyxia. Uterine tone, ECG, and vital signs should be monitored during administration.

Dosage/Route: 3 to 10 units IM after delivery of the placenta. 10 to 20 units in 1,000 mL of D_5W or NS IV titrated to effect.

Name/Class: PANCURONIUM (Pavulon)/Nondepolarizing Neuromuscular Blocker

Description: Pancuronium is a nondepolarizing neuromuscular blocker that causes paralysis without bronchospasm or hypotension, it does not cause the fasciculations associated with polarizing agents.

Indications: To facilitate endotracheal intubation.

Contraindications: Hypersensitivity to pancuronium or bromides, or tachycardia.

Precautions: Debilitated patients, myasthenia gravis, pulmonary, hepatic, or renal disease, or fluid or electrolyte imbalance.

Dosage/Route: 0.04 to 0.1 mg/kg IV. Ped: same as adult.

Name/Class: PHENOBARBITAL (Luminal)/Anticonvulsant

Description: Phenobarbital is a long-acting barbiturate anticonvulsant with sedative and hypnotic effects that limits the spread of seizure activity.

Indications: Seizures, status epilepticus, and acute anxiety.

Contraindications: Hypersensitivity to barbiturates.

Precautions: Hepatic, renal, cardiac, or respiratory impairment, allergies, elderly, debilitated patients, fever, hyperthyroidism, diabetes, severe anemia, hypoadrenal function, and during labor, delivery, and lactation.

Dosage/Route: 100 to 300 mg slow IV/IM. Ped: 6 to 10 mg/kg slow IV/IM.

NITROUS OXIDE

NOREPINEPHRINE

OXYGEN

Name/Class: NITROUS OXIDE (Nitronox)/Analgesic (gas)

Description: Nitrous oxide is a self-administered analgesic gas composed of 50% oxygen and 50% nitrous oxide. Its effects last only 2 to 5 minutes after administration ceases.

Indications: Musculoskeletal, burn, and ischemic chest pain and severe anxiety (including hyperventilation).

Contraindications: Possible bowel obstruction, pneumothorax or tension pneumothorax, COPD, head injury, impaired mental status, or drug intoxication.

Precautions: Use in well-ventilated area. It may cause nausea and vomiting.

Dosage/Route: It is self-administered inhalation until the pain is relieved or the patient drops the mask.

Name/Class: NOREPINEPHRINE (Levophed)/Sympathomimetic Agent

Description: Norepinephrine is a naturally occurring catecholamine and causes vasoconstriction, cardiac stimulation, and increased blood pressure, myocardial oxygen demand, and coronary blood flow.

Indications: Refractory hypotension and neurogenic shock.

Contraindications: Hypotension due to hypovolemia.

Precautions: Hypertension, hyperthyroidism, severe heart disease, elderly, MAO inhibitor therapy, patients receiving tricyclic antidepressants. Monitor blood pressure frequently and infuse the drug through the largest vein available as it may cause tissue necrosis.

Dosage/Route: 0.5 to 30 mcg/min IV, titrated to BP. Ped: 0.01 mcg/kg/min (rarely used).

Name/Class: OXYGEN/Oxidizing Agent (Gas)

Description: Oxygen is an odorless, colorless, tasteless gas, essential for life. It is one of the most important emergency drugs.

Indications: Hypoxia or anticipated hypoxia, or in any medical or trauma patient to improve respiratory efficiency.

Contraindications: There are no contraindications to oxygen therapy.

Precautions: Chronic obstructive pulmonary disease and very prolonged administration of high concentrations in the newborn.

Dosage/Route: Hypoxia: 100% by inhalation or IPPV.

NALOXONE

NIFEDIPINE

NITROGLYCERIN

Name/Class: NALOXONE (Narcan)/Narcotic Antagonist

Description: Naloxone is a pure narcotic antagonist that blocks the effects of both natural and synthetic narcotics and may reverse respiratory depression.

Indications: Narcotic and synthetic narcotic overdose, coma of unknown origin.

Contraindications: Hypersensitivity to the drug, non–narcotic-induced respiratory depression.

Precautions: Possible dependency (including newborns). It also has a half-life that is shorter than that of most narcotics; hence the patient may return to the overdose state.

Dosage/Route: 0.4 to 2 mg IV/IM (2 to 2.5 times the dose ET), repeated/2 to 3 min as needed up to 10 mg. Ped: 0.01 mg IV/IM (2 to 2.5 times the dose ET) repeated/2 to 3 min as needed up to 10 mg.

Name/Class: NIFEDIPINE (Procardia, Adalat)/Calcium Channel Blocker

Description: Nifedipine is a calcium channel blocker that reduces coronary artery spasm in angina. It also decreases peripheral vascular resistance, blood pressure, and cardiac workload.

Indications: Severe hypertension and angina.

Contraindications: Hypersensitivity or hypotension.

Precautions: Monitor blood pressure carefully, since it can drop significantly with nifedipine use.

Dosage/Route: One 10 to 20 mg capsule SL/PO.

Name/Class: NITROGLYCERIN (Nitrostat)/Nitrate

Description: Nitroglycerin is a rapid smooth muscle relaxant that reduces peripheral vascular resistance, blood pressure, venous return, and cardiac workload.

Indications: Chest pain associated with angina and acute myocardial infarction, and acute pulmonary edema.

Contraindications: Hypersensitivity, tolerance to nitrates, severe anemia, head trauma, hypotension, increased ICP, patients taking sildenafil, glaucoma, and shock.

Precautions: May induce headache that is sometimes severe. Nitroglycerin is light sensitive and will lose potency when exposed to the air.

Dosage/Route: 1 tablet (0.4 mg) SL. May be repeated/3 to 5 min up to 3 tablets, or ½ inch of topical ointment, or 0.4 mg (one spray)SL up to 3 sprays/25 min.

MILRINONE

MORPHINE SULFATE

NALBUPHINE

Name/Class: MILRINONE (Primacor)/Cardiac Inotrope, Vasodilator

Description: Milrinone is related to amrinone and increases the strength of cardiac contraction without increasing rate, increasing cardiac output without increasing oxygen demand.

Indications: CHF or pediatric septic shock.

Contraindications: Hypersensitivity.

Precautions: Elderly, pregnancy, and nursing mothers.

Dosage/Route: *CHF:* 50 mcg/kg IV over 10 min, then a drip of 0.375 to 0.75 mcg/kg/min IV.
Ped: (septic shock) 50 to 75 mcg/kg IV, then a drip of 0.5 to 0.75 mcg/kg/min.

Name/Class: MORPHINE SULFATE (Morphine)/Narcotic Analgesic

Description: Morphine sulfate is a potent analgesic and sedative that causes some vasodilation, reducing venous return, and reduced myocardial oxygen demand.

Indications: Moderate to severe pain and in MI and to reduce venous return in pulmonary edema.

Contraindications: Hypersensitivity to opiates, undiagnosed head or abdominal injury, hypotension, or volume depletion, acute bronchial asthma, COPD, severe respiratory depression, or pulmonary edema due to chemical inhalation.

Precautions: Elderly, children, or debilitated patients. Naloxone should be readily available to counteract the effects of morphine.

Dosage/Route: *Pain:* 2.5 to 15 mg IV; 5 to 20 mg IM/subcutaneous. Ped: 0.05 to 0.1 mg/kg IV; 0.1 to 0.2 mg/kg IM/subcutaneous.
AMI or PE: 1 to 2 mg/6 to 10 min to response.

Name/Class: NALBUPHINE (Nubain)/Narcotic Analgesic

Description: Nalbuphine is a synthetic narcotic analgesic equivalent to morphine, though its respiratory depression does not increase with higher doses.

Indications: Moderate to severe pain.

Contraindications: Hypersensitivity, undiagnosed head or abdominal injury.

Precautions: Impaired respirations, narcotic dependency.

Dosage/Route: 5 mg IV/IM/subcutaneous, repeat as 2 mg doses as needed up to 20 mg. Ped: 0.1 to 0.15 mg/kg IV/IM/subcutaneous (rarely used).

METOCLOPRAMIDE

METOPROLOL

MIDAZOLAM

Name/Class: METOCLOPRAMIDE (Reglan)/Antiemetic

Description: Metoclopramide is a dopamine antagonist similar to procainamide but with few antidysrhythmic or anesthetic properties. Its antiemetic properties stem from rapid gastric emptying and desensitization of the vomiting reflex.

Indications: Nausea and vomiting.

Contraindications: Hypersensitivity, allergy to sulfite agents, seizure disorders, pheochromocytoma, mechanical GI obstruction or perforation, and breast cancer.

Precautions: CHF, hypokalemia, renal impairment, GI hemorrhage, intermittent porphyria.

Dosage/Route: 10 to 20 mg IM; 10 mg slow IV (over 1 to 2 min). Ped: 1 to 2 mg/kg/dose.

Name/Class: METOPROLOL (Lopressor)/Beta Blocker

Description: Metroprolol is a beta-adrenergic blocking agent that reduces heart rate, cardiac output, and blood pressure.

Indications: AMI.

Contraindications: Cardiogenic shock, sinus bradycardia < 45, 2nd- or 3rd-degree heart block, PR interval > 0.24, cor pulmonale, asthma, or COPD.

Precautions: Hypersensitivity, hepatic or renal impairment, cardiomegaly, CHF controlled by digitalis and diuretics, AV conduction defects, thyrotoxicosis, diabetes, or peripheral vascular disease.

Dosage/Route: 5 mg slow IV/5 min up to 3 times.

Name/Class: MIDAZOLAM (Versed)/Sedative

Description: Midazolam is a short-acting benzodiazepine with CNS depressant, muscle relaxant, anticonvulsant, and anterograde amnestic effects.

Indications: To induce sedation before cardioversion or intubation.

Contraindications: Hypersensitivity to benzodiazepines, narrow-angle glaucoma, shock, coma, or acute alcohol intoxication.

Precautions: COPD, renal impairment, CHF, elderly.

Dosage/Route: 1 to 2.5 mg slow IV; 0.07 to 0.08 mg/kg IM (usually 5 mg). Ped: 0.05 to 0.2 mg/kg IV: 0.1 to 0.15 mg/kg IM; 3 mg intranasal.

METAPROTERENOL

METARAMINOL

METHYLPREDNISOLONE

Name/Class: METAPROTERENOL (Alupent)/Sympathomimetic Bronchodilator

Description: Metaproterenol is a synthetic sympathomimetic amine, similar to isoproterenol that causes smooth muscle relaxation of the bronchial tree, decreasing airway resistance, facilitating mucus drainage, and increasing vital capacity.

Indications: Bronchospasm, as in asthma and COPD.

Contraindications: Hypersensitivity to sympathomimetic agents, tachydysrhythmias, and hyperthyroidism.

Precautions: Elderly, hypertension, coronary artery disease, and diabetes.

Dosage/Route: 0.65 mg via metered dose inhaler (2 sprays); 0.2 to 0.3 mL in 2.5 to 3 mL NS via nebulizer. Ped: 0.1 to 0.2 mL/kg (5% solution) in 2.5 to 3 mL NS via nebulizer.

Name/Class: METARAMINOL (Aramine)/Sympathomimetic

Description: Metaraminol is a sympathomimetic similar to norepinephrine but less potent, with gradual onset and longer duration. It causes systemic vasoconstriction and increased cardiac contraction strength, increasing blood pressure and reducing flow to the kidneys.

Indications: Hypotension in a normovolemic patient.

Contraindications: Hypovolemia; MAO inhibitor therapy; peripheral or mesenteric thrombosis; pulmonary edema; cardiac arrest; untreated hypoxia, hypercapnia, and acidosis.

Precautions: Digitalized patients, hypertension, thyroid disease, diabetes, hepatic impairment, malaria.

Dosage/Route: 100 mg/500 mL D_5W or NS, titrated to blood pressure: 5 to 10 mg IM.

Name/Class: METHYLPREDNISOLONE (Solu-Medrol)/Corticosteroid, Antiinflammatoty

Description: Methylprednisolone is a synthetic adrenal corticosteroid, effective as an antiinflammatory and used in the management of allergic reactions and in some cases of shock. It is sometimes used in the treatment of spinal cord injury.

Indications: Spinal cord injury, asthma, severe anaphylaxis, COPD.

Contraindications: No major contraindications in the emergency setting.

Precautions: Only a single dose should be given in the prehospital setting.

Dosage/Route: *Asthma/COPD/anaphylaxis:* 125 to 250 mg IV/IM. Ped: 1 to 2 mg/kg/dose IV/IM.
Spinal cord injury: 30 mg/kg IV over 15 min, after 45 min an infusion of 5.4 mg/kg/hr.

MAGNESIUM SULFATE

MANNITOL

MEPERIDINE

Name/Class: MAGNESIUM SULFATE (Magnesium)/Electrolyte

Description: Magenesium sulfate is an electrolyte that acts as a calcium channel blocker, acting as a CNS depressant and anticonvulsant. It also depresses the function of smooth, skeletal, and cardiac muscles.

Indications: Refractory ventricular fibrillation and pulseless ventricular tachycardia (especially torsade de pointes), AMI, eclamptic seizures.

Contraindications: Heart block, myocardial damage, shock, persistent hypertension, and hypocalcemia.

Precautions: Renal impairment, digitalized patients, other CNS depressants, or neuromuscular blocking agents.

Dosage/Route: *Ventricular fibrillation or tachycardia:* 1 to 2 g IV over 2 min.
Torsade de pointes: 1 to 2 g IV followed by infusion of 0.5 to 1 g/hr IV.
AMI: 1 to 2 g IV over 5 to 30 min.
Eclampsia: 2 to 4 g IV/IM.

Name/Class: MANNITOL (Osmitrol)/Osmotic Diuretic

Description: Mannitol is an osmotic diuretic that draws water into the intravascular space through its hypertonic effects, then causes diuresis.

Indications: Cerebral edema.

Contraindications: Hypersensitivity, pulmonary edema, CHF, organic CNS disease, intracranial bleeding, shock, or severe dehydration.

Precautions:

Dosage/Route: 1.5 to 2 g/kg slow IV. Ped: 0.25 to 0.5 g/kg over 60 min.

Name/Class: MEPERIDINE (Demerol)/Narcotic Analgesic

Description: Meperidine is a synthetic narcotic with sedative and analgesic properties comparable to morphine but without hemodynamic side effects.

Indications: Moderate to severe pain.

Contraindications: Hypersensitivity, seizure disorders, or acute abdomen prior to diagnosis.

Precautions: Increased intracranial pressure, asthma or other respiratory conditions, supraventricular tachycardias, prostatic hypertrophy, urethral stricture, glaucoma, elderly or debilitated patients, renal or hepatic impairment, hypothyroidism, or Addison's disease.

Dosage/Route: 25 to 50 mg IV, 50 to 100 mg IM. Ped: 1 mg/kg IV/IM.

LABETALOL

LIDOCAINE

LORAZEPAM

Name/Class: LABETALOL (Trandate, Normodyne)/Beta Blocker

Description: Labetalol is a beta blocker with some alpha blocker characteristics. It induces vasodilation, reduces peripheral vascular resistance, and lowers blood pressure.

Indications: Acute hypertensive crisis.

Contraindications: Asthma, CHF, 2nd- and 3rd-degree heart block, severe bradycardia, or cardiogenic shock.

Precautions: COPD, heart failure, hepatic impairment, diabetes, peripheral vascular disease.

Dosage/Route: 20 mg slow IV, then 40 to 80 mg/10 min as needed, up to 300 mg OR a continuous drip 2 mg/min up to 300 mg.

Name/Class: LIDOCAINE (Xylocaine)/Antidysrhythmic

Description: Lidocaine is an antidysrhythmic that suppresses automaticity and raises stimulation threshold of the ventricles. It also causes sedation, anticonvulsant, and analgesic effects.

Indications: Pulseless ventricular tachycardia, ventricular fibrillation, ventricular tachycardia (w/ pulse).

Contraindications: Hypersensitivity to amide-type local anesthetics, supraventricular dysrhythmias, Stokes-Adams syndrome, 2nd- and 3rd-degree heart blocks, and bradycardias.

Precautions: Hepatic or renal impairment, CHF, hypoxia, respiratory depression, hypovolemia, myasthenia gravis, shock, debilitated patients, elderly, family history of malignant hypothermia.

Dosage/Route: *Cardiac arrest:* 1 to 1.5 mg/kg IV repeated every 3 to 5 min up to 3 mg/kg, follow conversion with a drip of 2 to 4 mg/min. Ped: 1 mg/kg IV, repeat/3 to 5 min up to 3 mg/kg, follow conversion with a drip of 20 to 50 mcg/kg/min.

Ventricular tachycardia (w/ pulse): 1 to 1.5 mg/kg slow IV. May repeat at one-half dose every 5 to 10 min until conversion up to 3 mg/kg. Follow conversion with an infusion of 2 to 4 mg/min. Ped: 1 mg/kg, followed by a drip at 20 to 50 mg/kg/min.

Name/Class: LORAZEPAM (Ativan)/Sedative

Description: Lorazepam is the most potent benzodiazepine available. It has strong antianxiety, sedative, hypnotic, and skeletal muscle relaxant properties, and a relatively short half-life.

Indications: Sedation for cardioversion and status epilepticus.

Contraindications: Sensitivity to benzodiazepines.

Precautions: Narrow-angle glaucoma, depression or psychosis, coma, shock, acute alcohol intoxication, renal or hepatic impairment, organic brain syndrome, myasthenia gravis, GI disorders, elderly, debilitated, limited pulmonary reserve.

Dosage/Route: *Sedation:* 2 to 4 mg IM, 0.5 to 2 mg IV. Ped: 0.03 to 0.5 mg/kg IV/IM/PR up to 4 mg.
Status epilepticus: 2 mg slow IV/PR (2 mg/min). Ped: 0.1 mg/kg slow IV/PR (2 to 5 min).

ISOETHARINE

ISOPROTERENOL

KETOROLAC

Name/Class: ISOETHARINE (Bronkosol)/Sympathomimetic Bronchodilator

Description: Isoetharine is a synthetic sympathomimetic with rapid onset and prolonged duration that relaxes the bronchial smooth muscles, decreasing airway resistance and helping clear secretions.

Indications: Bronchospasm in asthma and COPD.

Contraindications: Hypersensitivity to or use of sympathomimetic amines, preexisting tachydysrhythmias, allergy to sodium bisulfite agents.

Precautions: Elderly, hypertension, acute coronary artery disease, CHF, hyperthyroidism, diabetes, tuberculosis, or seizures.

Dosage/Route: 1 or 2 sprays via metered dose inhaler, 0.5 mL in 2 to 3 mL saline via nebulizer. Ped: 0.01 mL/kg of 1% solution (max 0.5 mL) diluted in 2 to 3 mL saline by nebulizer.

Name/Class: ISOPROTERENOL (Isuprel)/Sympathomimetic

Description: Isoproterenol is a synthetic sympathomimetic that results in increased cardiac output by increasing the strength of cardiac contraction and somewhat increasing rate. It also reduces peripheral vascular resistance and venous return.

Indications: Bradycardia refractory to atropine when pacing is not available and for severe status asthmaticus.

Contraindications: Cardiogenic shock.

Precautions: Tachydysrhythmias and those associated with digitalis and acute myocardial infarction.

Dosage/Route: *Bradycardia:* 2 to 10 mcg/min titrated to cardiac rate. Ped: 0.1 mcg/kg/min titrated to cardiac rate.

Status asthmaticus: 1 or 2 sprays, metered dose inhaler. Ped: same as adult.

Name/Class: KETOROLAC (Toradol)/Nonsteroidal Antiinflammatory Drug (NSAID)

Description: Ketorolac is an injectable NSAID that exhibits analgesic, antiinflammatory, and antipyretic properties without sedative effects.

Indications: Mild or moderate pain.

Contraindications: Hypersensitivity to ketorolac, aspirin, or other NSAIDs, and asthma.

Precautions: Peptic ulcers, renal or hepatic impairment, or elderly.

Dosage/Route: 30 mg IV/IM (15 mg > 65 years or weighs < 50 kg)

INSULIN

IPECAC SYRUP

IPRATROPIUM

Name/Class: INSULIN (Regular Insulin, Humulin)/Hormone

Description: Insulin is a naturally occurring protein that promotes the uptake of glucose by the cells.
Indications: Hyperglycemia and diabetic coma.
Contraindications: Hypersensitivity and hypoglycemia.
Precautions:
Dosage/Route: 5 to 10 units IV/IM/SC. Ped: 2 to 4 units IV/IM/SC.

Name/Class: IPECAC SYRUP/Emetic

Description: Ipecac syrup is a gastric irritant and acts on the emetic centers of the medulla to induce vomiting. Emesis usually occurs within 5 to 10 minutes.
Indications: Poisoning and overdose.
Contraindications: Reduced level of consciousness, corrosive ingestion, petroleum distillate ingestion, alkali ingestion, or antiemetic ingestion (especially phenothiazine).
Precautions: Monitor the airway and have suction ready. Administer activated charcoal only after emesis. Caution with heart disease patients.
Dosage/Route: 30 mL PO, followed by 1 to 2 glasses of water, repeat in 20 min as needed.
Ped: 15 mL PO followed by 1 to 2 glasses of water, repeat in 20 min as needed.

Name/Class: IPRATROPIUM (Atrovent)/Anticholinergic

Description: Ipratropium is a bronchodilator used in the treatment of respiratory emergencies that causes bronchial dilation and dries respiratory tract secretions by blocking acetylcholine receptors.
Indications: Bronchospasm associated with asthma, COPD, and inhaled irritants.
Contraindications: Hypersensitivity to atropine or its derivatives, or as a primary treatment for acute bronchospasm.
Precautions: Elderly, cardiovascular disease, or hypertension.
Dosage/Route: 500 mcg in 2.5 to 3 mL NS via nebulizer or 2 sprays from a metered dose inhaler.
Ped: 125 to 250 mcg in 2.5 to 3 mL NS via nebulizer, or 1 or 2 sprays of a metered dose inhaler.

HYDROXYZINE

IBUPROFEN

IBUTILIDE

Name/Class: HYDROXYZINE (Vistaril)/Antihistamine

Description: Hydroxyzine is an antihistamine with depressive, sedative, antiemetic, and bronchodilator properties.

Indications: Acute anxiety, nausea/vomiting.

Contraindications: Hypersensitivity.

Precautions: Elderly.

Dosage/Route: *Anxiety:* 50 to 100 mg deep IM. Ped: 1 mg/kg deep IM.
Nausea/vomiting: 25 to 50 mg deep IM. Ped: 1 mg/kg deep IM.

Name/Class: IBUPROFEN (Advil, Motrin, Nuprin, Excedrin IB)/Nonsteroidal Antiinflammatory Drug (NSAID)

Description: Ibuprofen is the prototype NSAID with significant analgesic and antipyretic properties. It also inhibits platelet aggregation and increases bleeding time.

Indications: Reduce fever and relieve minor to moderate pain.

Contraindications: Sensitivity to aspirin or other NSAIDs, active peptic ulcer, and bleeding abnormalities.

Precautions: Hypertension, GI ulceration, hepatic or renal impairment, cardiac decompensation.

Dosage/Route: 200 to 400 mg PO/4 to 6 hours up to 1,200 mg/day. Ped: 5 to 10 mg/kg PO/4 to 6 hours up to 40 mg/kg/day.

Name/Class: IBUTILIDE (Corvert)/Antidysrhythmic

Description: Ibutilide is a short-acting antidysrhythmic that may convert atrial flutter and fibrillation or may assist with electrical cardioversion.

Indications: Recent onset atrial flutter and fibrillation.

Contraindications: Hypersensitivity, hypokalemia, or hypomagnesemia.

Precautions: CHF, low ejection fraction, recent MI, prolonged QT intervals, hepatic impairment, cardiovascular disorder other than atrial dysrhythmias, or drugs that prolong the QT interval, lactation.

Dosage/Route: 1 mg over 10 min IV. Patients < 60 kg, 0.01 mg/kg IV, may repeat in 10 min as needed.

HEPARIN

HYDRALAZINE

HYDROCORTISONE

Name/Class: HEPARIN (Heparin)/Anticoagulant

Description: Heparin is a rapid-onset anticoagulant, enhancing the effects of antithrombin III and blocking the conversion of prothrombin to thrombin and fibrinogen to fibrin.

Indications: To prevent thrombus formation in acute MI.

Contraindications: Hypersensitivity; active bleeding or bleeding tendencies; recent eye, brain, or spinal surgery; shock.

Precautions: Alcoholism, elderly, allergies, indwelling catheters, elderly, menstruation, pregnancy, or cerebral embolism.

Dosage/Route: 5,000 units IV, then 20,000 to 40,000 units over 24 hours.

Name/Class: HYDRALAZINE (Apresoline)/Antihypertensive

Description: Hydralazine reduces blood pressure by arterial vasodilation, increasing cardiac output and renal and cerebral blood flow.

Indications: Hypertensive crisis and preeclampsia.

Contraindications: Hypersensitivity, coronary artery or mitral valve disease, AMI, tachydysrhythmias.

Precautions: CVA, renal impairment, and MAO inhibitor use.

Dosage/Route: 20 to 40 mg IV/IM repeated in 4 to 6 hours. Ped: 0.1 to 0.5 mg/kg/day IV/IM.

Name/Class: HYDROCORTISONE (Solu-Cortef)/Steroid

Description: Hydrocortisone is a short-acting synthetic steroid that inhibits histamine formation, storage, and release from mast cells, reducing allergic response.

Indications: Inflammation during allergic reactions, severe anaphylaxis, asthma, and COPD.

Contraindications: Hypersensitivity to glucocorticoids.

Precautions: Limited precautions in acute care.

Dosage/Route: 40 to 250 mg IV/IM. Ped: 4 to 8 mg/kg/day IV/IM.

FUROSEMIDE

GLUCAGON

HALOPERIDOL

Name/Class: FUROSEMIDE (Lasix)/Diuretic

Description: Furosemide is a rapid-acting, potent diuretic and antihypertensive that inhibits sodium reabsorption by the kidney. Its vasodilating effects reduce venous return and cardiac workload.

Indications: Congestive heart failure and pulmonary edema.

Contraindications: Hypersensitivity to furosemide or the sulfonamides, fluid and electrolyte depletion states, heptic coma, pregnancy (except in life-threatening circumstances).

Precautions: Infants, elderly, hepatic impairment, nephrotic syndrome, cardiogenic shock associated with acute MI, gout, or patients receiving digitalis or potassium-depleting steroids.

Dosage/Route: 40 to 120 mg slow IV. Ped: 1 mg/kg slow IV.

Name/Class: GLUCAGON (GlucaGen)/Hormone, Antihypoglycemic

Description: Glucagon is a protein secreted by pancreatic cells that causes a breakdown of stored glycogen into glucose and inhibits the synthesis of glycogen from glucose.

Indications: Hypoglycemia without IV access and to reverse beta-blocker overdose.

Contraindications: Hypersensitivity to glucagon or protein compounds.

Precautions: Cardiovascular or renal impairment. Effective only if there are sufficient stores of glycogen in the liver.

Dosage/Route: *Hypoglycemia:* 1 mg IM/SC repeat/5 to 20 min. Ped: 0.1 mg/kg 1 m/SC/IV for child < 10 kg; 1 mg/kg 1 m/SC/IV for child > 10 kg.

Beta-blocker overdose: 50 to 150 mg/kg IV over 1 min. Ped: 50 to 150 mg/kg IV over 1 min.

Name/Class: HALOPERIDOL (Haldol)/Antipsychotic

Description: Haloperidol is believed to block dopamine receptors in the brain associated with mood and behavior, is a potent antiemetic, and impairs temperature regulation.

Indications: Acute psychotic episodes.

Contraindications: Parkinson's disease, seizure disorders, coma, alcohol depression, CNS depression, and thyrotoxicosis, and with other sedatives.

Precautions: Elderly, debilitated patients, urinary retention, glaucoma, severe cardiovascular disease, or anticonvulsant, anticoagulant, or lithium therapy.

Dosage/Route: 2 to 5 mg IM. Ped: Children > 3 years, 0.015 to 0.15 mg/kg/day PO in 2 or 3 divided doses.

FLECAINIDE

FLUMAZENIL

FOSPHENYTOIN

Name/Class: FLECAINIDE (Tambocor)/Antidysrhythmic

Description: Flecainide is a local anesthetic and antidysrhythmic that slows myocardial conduction and effectively suppresses PVCs and a variety of atrial and ventricular dysrhythmias.

Indications: Atrial flutter, atrial fibrillation, AV reentrant tachycardia, or SVT associated with WPW syndrome.

Contraindications: Hypersensitivity, 2nd- or 3rd-degree heart block, right bundle branch block with left hemiblock, cardiogenic shock, or significant hepatic impairment.

Precautions: CHF, sick sinus syndrome, or renal impairment.

Dosage/Route: 100 mg PO/12 hour or 2 mg/kg IV at 10 mg/min. Ped: 1 to 3 mg/kg/day PO in three equal doses (max 8 mg/kg/day).

Name/Class: FLUMAZENIL (Romazicon)/Benzodiazepine Antagonist

Description: Flumazenil is a benzodiazepine antagonist used to reverse the sedative, recall, and psychomotor effects of diazepam, midazolam, and the other benzodiazepines.

Indications: Respiratory depression secondary to the benzodiazepines.

Contraindications: Hypersensitivity to flumazenil or benzodiazepines; those patients who take flumazenil for status epilepticus or seizures; seizure-prone patients during labor and delivery; tricyclic antidepressant overdose.

Precautions: Hepatic impairment, elderly, pregnancy, nursing mothers, head injury, alcohol and drug dependency and physical dependence on benzodiazepines.

Dosage/Route: 0.2 mg IV over 30 sec/min, up to 1 mg.

Name/Class: FOSPHENYTOIN (Cerebyx)/Anticonvulsant

Description: Fosphenytoin is a drug that, once administered, is converted to phenytoin and causes the anticonvulsant properties associated with that drug.

Indications: Seizure control and status epilepticus.

Contraindications: Hypersensitivity, seizures due to hypoglycemia, sinus bradycardia, heart block, Stokes-Adams syndrome, late pregnancy, and lactating mothers.

Precautions: Hepatic or renal impairment, alcoholism, hypotension, bradycardia, heart block, severe CAD, diabetes, hyperglycemia, or respiratory depression.

Dosage/Route: 15 to 20 mg PE/kg IV given at 100 to 150 mg PE/min (PE = phenytoin equivalent).

ESMOLOL

ETOMIDATE

FENTANYL

Name/Class: ESMOLOL (Brevibloc)/Beta Blocker

Description: Esmolol is an ultra–short-acting cardioselective beta blocker that inhibits the actions of the catecholamines.

Indications: Supraventricular tachycardias with rapid ventricular responses.

Contraindications: Cardiac failure, 2nd- and 3rd-degree block, sinus bradycardia, and cardiogenic shock.

Precautions: Allergies or bronchial asthma, emphysema, CHF, diabetes, and renal impairment.

Dosage/Route: 500 mcg/kg/min IV for 1 min, loading dose, then 50 mcg/kg/min for 4 min. If unsuccessful, repeat loading dose every 4 min and increase maintenance dose by 50 mcg/kg to 200 mcg/kg/min.

Name/Class: ETOMIDATE (Amidate)/Hypnotic

Description: Etomidate is an ultra–short-acting nonbarbiturate hypnotic with no analgesic effects and limited cardiovascular and respiratory effects.

Indications: Induce sedation for rapid sequence intubation.

Contraindications: Hypersensitivity.

Precautions: Marked hypotension, severe asthma, or severe cardiovascular disease.

Dosage/Route: 0.1 to 0.3 mg/kg IV over 15 to 30 sec. Ped: children > 10 years, same as for adults.

Name/Class: FENTANYL (Sublimaze)/Narcotic Analgesic

Description: Fentanyl is a potent synthetic narcotic analgesic similar to morphine and meperidine but with a more rapid and less-prolonged action.

Indications: Induce sedation for endotracheal intubation.

Contraindications: MAO inhibitors within 14 days, myasthenia gravis.

Precautions: Increased intracranial pressure, elderly, debilitated, COPD, respiratory problems, hepatic and renal insufficiency.

Dosage/Route: 25 to 100 mcg slowly IV (2 to 3 min). Ped: 2 mcg/kg slow IV/IM.

DROPERIDOL

ENOXAPARIN

EPINEPHRINE

Name/Class: DROPERIDOL (Inapsine)/Antiemetic

Description: Droperidol is related to haloperidol and antagonizes the emetic properties of morphine-like analgesics. It may also produce hypotension and mild sedation.

Indications: Nausea and vomiting (second line), to produce a tranquilizing effect, and in some cases as an antipsychotic.

Contraindications: Intolerance.

Precautions: Elderly, debilitated, hypotension, and hepatic, renal, or cardiac impairment and Parkinson's disease.

Dosage/Route: 2.5 to 10 mg IV. Ped: 0.088 to 0.165 mg/kg IV.

Name/Class: ENOXAPARIN (Lovenox)/Anticoagulant

Description: Enoxaparin is a heparin derivative that prevents the conversion of fibrinogen to fibrin.

Indications: To inhibit clot formation in unstable angina and non–Q-wave myocardial infarction.

Contraindications: Hypersensitivity to the drug, pork products or heparin, major active bleeding, or thrombocytopenia.

Precautions:

Dosage/Route: *Unstable angina and non–Q wave MI:* 1 mg/kg subcutaneously.
Pulmonary embolism: 0.5 mg/kg IV.

Name/Class: EPINEPHRINE (Adrenalin)/Sympathomimetic

Description: Epinephrine is a naturally occurring catecholamine that increases heart rate, cardiac contractile force myocardial electrical activity, systemic vascular resistance, and systolic blood pressure and decreases overall airway resistance and automaticity. It also, through bronchial artery constriction, may reduce pulmonary congestion and increase tidal volume and vital capacity.

Indications: To restore rhythm in cardiac arrest and severe allergic reactions.

Contraindications: Hypersensitivity to sympathomimetic amines, narrow angle glaucoma; hemorrhagic, traumatic, or cardiac shock; coronary insufficiency; dysrhythmias; organic brain or heart disease; or during labor.

Precautions: Elderly, debilitated patients, hypertension, diabetes, hyperthyroidism, Parkinson's disease, tuberculosis, asthma, emphysema, and in children < 6 years.

Dosage/Route: *Arrest:* 1 mg of 1:10,000 IV/3 to 5 min (ET: 2 to 2.5 mg 1:1,000).
Ped: 0.01 mg/kg 1:10,000 IV/IO (ET: 0.1 mg/kg 1:1,000). All subsequent doses 0.1 mg/kg IV/IO.
Allergic reactions: 0.3 to 0.5 mg of 1:1,000 subcutaneously/5 to 15 min as needed or 0.5 to 1 mg of 1:10,000 IV if subcutaneous dose ineffective or severe reaction. Ped: 0.01 mg/kg of 1:1,000 subcutaneously/10 to 15 min or 0.01 mg/kg of 1:10,000 IV if subcutaneous dose ineffective or severe.

DIPHENHYDRAMINE

DOBUTAMINE

DOPAMINE

Name/Class: DIPHENHYDRAMINE (Benadryl)/Antihistamine

Description: Diphenhydramine blocks histamine release, thereby reducing bronchoconstriction, vasodilation, and edema.

Indications: Anaphylaxis, allergic reactions, and dystonic reactions.

Contraindications: Asthma and other lower respiratory diseases.

Precautions: May induce hypotension, headache, palpitations, tachycardia, sedation, drowsiness, and/or disturbed coordination.

Dosage/Route: 25 to 50 mg IV/IM.

Name/Class: DOBUTAMINE (Dobutrex)/Sympathomimetic

Description: Dobutamine is a synthetic catecholamine and beta agent that increases the strength of cardiac contraction without appreciably increasing rate.

Indications: To increase cardiac output in congestive heart failure/cardiogenic shock.

Contraindications: Hypersensitivity to sympathomimetic amines, ventricular tachycardia, and hypovolemia without fluid resuscitation.

Precautions: Atrial fibrillation or preexisting hypertension.

Dosage/Route: 2 to 20 mcg/kg/min IV. Ped: same as adult.

Name/Class: DOPAMINE (Intropin)/Sympathomimetic

Description: Dopamine is a naturally occurring catecholamine that increases cardiac output without appreciably increasing myocardial oxygen consumption. It maintains renal and mesenteric blood flow while inducing vasoconstriction and increasing systolic blood pressure.

Indications: Nonhypovolemic hypotension (70 to 100 mmHg) and cardiogenic shock.

Contraindications: Hypovolemic hypotension without aggressive fluid resuscitation, tachydysrhythmias, ventricular fibrillation, and pheochromocytoma.

Precautions: Occlusive vascular disease, cold injury, arterial embolism. Ensure adequate fluid resuscitation of the hypovolemic patient.

Dosage/Route: 2 to 5 mcg/kg/min up to 20 mcg/kg/min, titrated to effect. Ped: same as adult.

DILTIAZEM

DIMENHYDRINATE

DIMERCAPROL

Name/Class: DILTIAZEM (Cardizem)/Calcium Channel Blocker

Description: Diltiazem is a slow calcium channel blocker similar to verapamil. It dilates coronary and peripheral arteries and arterioles, thus increasing circulation to the heart and reducing peripheral vascular resistance.

Indications: Supraventricular tachydysrhythmias (atrial fibrillation, atrial flutter, and PSVT refractory to adenosine) and to increase coronary artery perfusion in angina.

Contraindications: Hypersensitivity, sick sinus syndrome, 2nd- or 3rd-degree heart block, systolic BP < 90, diastolic BP < 60, wide-complex tachycardia and WPW.

Precautions: CHF (especially with beta blockers), conduction abnormalities, renal or hepatic impairment, the elderly, and nursing mothers.

Dosage/Route: 0.25 mg/kg IV over 2 min, may repeat as needed with 0.35 mg/kg followed by a drip of 5 to 10 mg/hr not to exceed 15 mg/hr over 24 hours.

Name/Class: DIMENHYDRINATE (Dramamine)/Antihistamine

Description: Dimenhydrinate is related to diphenhydramine though it is most frequently used for the prevention and treatment of motion sickness and vertigo rather than any antihistamine properties.

Indications: To relieve nausea/vomiting associated with motion sickness and narcotic use.

Contraindications: None in the emergency setting.

Precautions: Seizure disorders and asthma.

Dosage/Route: 12.5 to 25 mg IV; 50 mg IM/4 hours as needed. Ped: 1.25 mg/kg/4 hours up to 300 mg/day.

Name/Class: DIMERCAPROL (BAL in Oil)/Antidote

Description: Dimercaprol is a dithiol compound that combines with the ions of various heavy metals to form nontoxic compounds that can be excreted.

Indications: Antidote for acute arsenic, mercury, lead, and gold poisoning.

Contraindications: Hepatic and severe renal impairment and poisonings due to cadmium, iron, selenium, and uranium.

Precautions: Hypertensive patients.

Dosage/Route: *Gold and arsenic:* 2.5 to 3 mg/kg IM. Ped: same as adult.
Mercury: 5 mg/kg IM. Ped: same as adult.
Lead: 4 mg/kg IM. Ped: same as adult.

DIAZOXIDE

DIGOXIN

DIGOXIN IMMUNE FAB

Name/Class: DIAZOXIDE (Hyperstat)/Antihypertensive

Description: Diazoxide is a rapid-acting thiazide nondiuretic hypotensive and hyperglycemia agent that reduces BP and peripheral vascular resistance.

Indications: Rapidly decreases BP in hypertensive crisis

Contraindications: Hypersensitivity to thiazides, cerebral bleeding, eclampsia, significant coronary artery disease.

Precautions: Diabetes, impaired cerebral or cardiac circulation, renal impairment, corticosteroid or progesterone therapy, gout, or uremia.

Dosage/Route: 1 to 3 mg/kg IV up to 150 mg, repeated/5 to 15 min, as needed. Ped: same as adult.

Name/Class: DIGOXIN (Digoxin, Lanoxin)/Cardiac Glycoside

Description: Digoxin is a rapid-acting cardiac glycoside used in the treatment of CHF and rapid atrial dysrhythmias. It increases the force and velocity of myocardial contraction and cardiac output. It also decreases conduction through the AV node, thus decreasing heart rate.

Indications: Increase cardiac output in CHF and to stabilize supraventricular tachydysrhythmias.

Contraindications: Hypersensitivity, ventricular fibrillation, or ventricular tachycardia except due to CHF.

Precautions: Reduce dosage if digitoxin taken within 2 weeks. Toxicity potentiated by an MI and with hypokalemia, hypocalcemia, advanced heart disease, incomplete heart block, corpulmonale, hyperthyroidism, respiratory impairment, children, elderly or debilitated patients, and hypomagnesemia.

Dosage/Route: 0.25 to 0.5 mg slowly IV. Ped: 10 to 50 mcg/kg IV.

Name/Class: DIGOXIN IMMUNE FAB (Digibind)/Antidote

Description: Digoxin immune FAB is comprised of fragments of antibodies specific for digoxin (and effective for digitoxin) and prevents the drug from binding to receptor sites.

Indications: Life-threatening digoxin or digitoxin toxicity.

Contraindications: Hypersensitivity to sheep products and renal or cardiac failure.

Precautions: Patients with prior sheep or bovine antibody fragments, renal impairment, and allergies.

Dosage/Route: Dose dependent upon patient digoxin or digitoxin levels.

DEXAMETHASONE

DEXTROSE 50% IN WATER ($D_{50}W$)

DIAZEPAM

Name/Class: DEXAMETHASONE (Decadron)/Steroid

Description: Dexamethasone is a long-acting synthetic adrenocorticoid with intense antiinflammatory activity. It prevents the accumulation of inflammation generating cells at the sites of infection or injury.

Indications: Anaphylaxis, asthma, COPD, spinal cord edema.

Contraindications: No absolute contraindications in the emergency setting. Relative contraindications: systemic fungal infections, acute infections, tuberculosis, varicella, or vaccinia or live virus vaccinations.

Precautions: Herpes simplex, keratitis, myasthenia gravis, hepatic or renal impairment, diabetes, CHF, seizures, psychic disorders, hypothyroidism, and GI ulceration.

Dosage/Route: 4 to 24 mg IV/IM Ped: 0.5 to 1 mg/kg.

Name/Class: DEXTROSE 50% IN WATER ($D_{50}W$)/Carbohydrate

Description: Dextrose is a simple sugar that the body can rapidly metabolize to create energy.

Indications: Hypoglycemia

Contraindications: None in hypoglycemia.

Precautions: Increased ICP. Determine blood glucose level before administration. Ensure good venous access.

Dosage/Route: 25g $D_{50}W$ (50 mL) IV. Ped: 2 mL/kg of a 25% solution IV.

Name/Class: DIAZEPAM (Valium)/Antianxiety, Hypnotic, Anticonvulsant, Sedative

Description: Diazepam is a benzodiazepine sedative and skeletal muscle relaxant that reduces tremors, induces amnesia, and reduces the incidence and recurrence of seizures. It relaxes muscle spasms in orthopedic injuries and produces amnesia for painful procedures (cardioversion).

Indications: Major motor seizures, status epilepticus, premedication before cardioversion, muscle tremors due to injury, and acute anxiety.

Contraindications: Hypersensitivity to the drug, shock, coma, acute alcoholism, depressed vital signs, obstetric patients, neonates.

Precautions: Psychoses, depression, myasthenia gravis, hepatic or renal impairment, addiction, elderly or very ill patients, or COPD. Due to a short half-life of the drug, seizure activity may recur.

Dosage/Route: *Seizures:* 5 to 10 mg IV/IM. Ped: 0.5 to 2 mg IV/IM.
Acute anxiety: 2 to 5 mg IV/IM. Ped: 0.5 to 2 mg IM.
Premedication: 5 to 15 mg IV. Ped: 0.2 to 0.5 mg/kg IV.

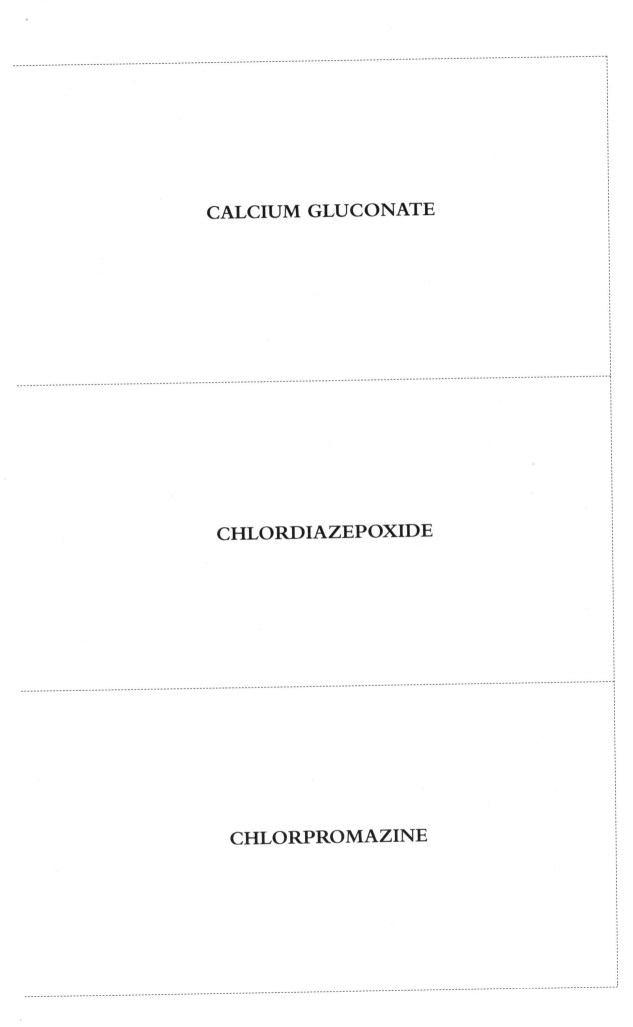

CALCIUM GLUCONATE

CHLORDIAZEPOXIDE

CHLORPROMAZINE

Name/Class: CALCIUM GLUCONATE (Kalcinate)/Electrolyte

Description: Calcium gluconate increases myocardial contractile force and increases ventricular automaticity. It is more potent than calcium chloride.

Indications: Hyperkalemia, hypermagnesemia, and calcium channel blocker toxicity.

Contraindications: Ventricular fibrillation.

Precautions: It may precipitate toxicity in patients taking digitalis, with renal or cardiac insufficiency, and immobilized patients.

Dosage/Route: 5 to 8 mL of 10% solution, repeated as necessary at 10-min intervals.

Name/Class: CHLORDIAZEPOXIDE (Librium)/Sedative, Hypnotic

Description: Chlordiazepoxide is a benzodiazepine derivative that produces mild sedation and anticonvulsant, skeletal muscle relaxant, and prolonged hypnotic effects.

Indications: Severe anxiety and tension, acute alcohol withdrawal symptoms (DTs).

Contraindications: Hypersensitivity to benzodiazepines, pregnant and nursing mothers, children under 6.

Precautions: Primary depressive disorders or psychoses, acute alcohol intoxication.

Dosage/Route: 50 to 100 mg IV/IM.

Name/Class: CHLORPROMAZINE (Thorazine)/Tranquilizer, Antipsychotic

Description: Chlorpromazine is a phenothiazine derivative used to manage psychotic episodes by providing strong sedation and moderate extrapyramidal symptoms. Produces reduced initiative, interest, and affect.

Indications: Acute psychotic episode, intractable hiccups, nausea/vomiting.

Contraindications: Hypersensitivity to phenothiazines, coma, sedative overdose, acute alcohol withdrawal, and children < 6 months.

Precautions: Agitated states with depression, seizure disorders, respiratory infection or COPD, glaucoma, diabetes, hypertension, peptic ulcer, prostatic hypertrophy, breast cancer, thyroid, cardiovascular, and hepatic impairment, and patients exposed to extreme heat or organophosphates.

Dosage/Route: 25 to 50 mg IM. Ped: 0.5 mg/kg IM or 1 mg/kg PR.

BUMETANIDE

BUTORPHANOL

CALCIUM CHLORIDE

Name/Class: BUMETANIDE (Bumex)/Loop Diuretic

Description: Bumetanide is related to furosemide, though it has a faster rate of onset, a greater diuretic potency (40 times), shorter duration, and produces only mild hypotension.

Indications: To promote diuresis in CHF and pulmonary edema.

Contraindications: Hypersensitivity to bumetanide and other sulfonamides.

Precautions: Pregnancy (use only for life-threatening conditions).

Dosage/Route: 0.5 to 1 mg IM/IV over 1 to 2 min, repeat in 2 to 3 hours as needed.

Name/Class: BUTORPHANOL (Stadol)/Synthetic Narcotic Analgesic

Description: Butorphanol is a centrally acting synthetic narcotic analgesic about 5 times more potent than morphine. A schedule IV narcotic.

Indications: Moderate to severe pain.

Contraindications: Hypersensitivity, head injury, or undiagnosed abdominal pain.

Precautions: May cause withdrawal in narcotic-dependent patients

Dosage/Route: 1 mg IV or 3 to 4 mg IM/3 to 4 hours.

Name/Class: CALCIUM CHLORIDE (Calcium Chloride)/Electrolyte

Description: Calcium chloride increases myocardial contractile force and increases ventricular automaticity.

Indications: Hyperkalemia, hypocalcemia, hypermagnesemia, and calcium channel blocker toxicity.

Contraindications: Ventricular fibrillation, hypercalcemia, and possible digitalis toxicity.

Precautions: It may precipitate toxicity in patients taking digoxin. Ensure the IV line is in a large vein and flushed before using and after calcium.

Dosage/Route: 2 to 4 mg/kg IV (10% solution)/10 min, as needed. Ped: 20 mg/kg IV (10% solution) repeat at 10 min, as needed.

ATRACURIUM

ATROPINE

BRETYLIUM

Name/Class: ATRACURIUM (Tracrium)/Nondepolarizing Neuromuscular Blocker

Description: Atracurium is a synthetic skeletal muscle relaxant that produces a short-duration neuromuscular blockade.

Indications: To produce skeletal muscle relaxation to facilitate endotracheal intubation and IPPV.

Contraindications: Myasthenia gravis.

Precautions: Asthma, anaphylaxis, cardiovascular or neuromuscular disease, electrolyte or acid/base imbalance, dehydration, or pulmonary impairment.

Dosage/Route: 0.4 to 0.5 mg/kg IV. Ped: < 2 years 0.3 to 0.4 mg/kg, otherwise same as adult.

Name/Class: ATROPINE/Parasympatholytic

Description: Atropine blocks the parasympathetic nervous system, specifically the vagal effects on heart rate. It does not increase contractility but may increase myocardial oxygen demand. Decreases airway secretions.

Indications: Hemodynamically significant bradycardia, bradyasystolic arrest, and organophosphate poisoning.

Contraindications: None in the emergency setting.

Precautions: AMI, glaucoma.

Dosage/Route: *Symptomatic bradycardia:* 0.5 to 1 mg IV/2 mg ET. Repeat 3 to 5 min to 0.04 mg/kg. Ped: 0.02 mg/kg IV, 0.04 mg/kg ET, may repeat in 5 min up to 1 mg. Asystole: 1 mg IV or 2 mg ET, may repeat 3 to 5 min up to 0.04 mg/kg.

Organophosphate poisoning: 2 to 5 mg IV/IM/IO/10 to 15 min. Ped: 0.05 mg/kg IV/IM/IO/ 10 to 15 min.

Name/Class: BRETYLIUM (Bretylol)/Antidysrhythmic

Description: Bretylium causes a release of norepinephrine, depresses ventricular fibrillation, and reduces ectopy. Bretylium also suppresses ventricular tachydysrhythmias with reentry mechanisms.

Indications: Ventricular fibrillation and ventricular tachycardia refractory to lidocaine.

Contraindications: None in the presence of life-threatening dysrhythmias.

Precautions: Digitalized patients, digitalis-induced dysrhythmias, fixed cardiac output, angina, or renal impairment. May induce postural hypotension.

Dosage/Route: 5 mg/kg IV, then 10 mg/kg/15 to 30 min, to a max 30 mg/kg. Following conversion: 1 to 2 mg/min drip. Ped: 5 mg/kg IV, repeat 10 mg/kg in 15 to 30 min.

ANISTREPLASE (APSAC)

ASPIRIN

ATENOLOL

Name/Class: ANISTREPLASE (APSAC) (Eminase)/Thrombolytic

Description: Anistreplase causes thrombolysis by converting plasminogen into plasmin, which then dissolves the fibrin and fibrinogen of the clot.

Indications: To reduce infarct size in acute MI.

Contraindications: Active internal bleeding, suspected aortic dissection, traumatic CPR, recent hemorrhagic stroke, intracranial or intraspinal surgery or trauma, tumors, pregnancy, hypertension, hypersensitivity to anistreplase or streptokinase.

Precautions: Recent major surgery, cerebral vascular disease, recent GI or GU bleeding, recent trauma, hypertension, patients over 75 years, current oral anticoagulants, or hemorrhagic ophthalmic conditions.

Dosage/Route: 30 units IV over 2 to 5 min.

Name/Class: ASPIRIN (Acetylsalicylic Acid) (Alka-Seltzer, Bayer, Empirin, St. Joseph Children's)/Analgesic, Antipyretic, Platelet Inhibitor, Antiinflammatory

Description: Aspirin inhibits agents that cause the production of inflammation, pain, and fever. It relieves mild to moderate pain by acting on the peripheral nervous system, lowers body temperature in fever, and powerfully inhibits platelet aggregation.

Indications: Chest pain suggestive of an MI.

Contraindications: Hypersensitivity to salicylates, active ulcer disease, asthma.

Precautions: Allergies to other NSAIDs, bleeding disorders, children or teenagers with varicella or influenza-like symptoms.

Dosage/Route: 160 to 325 mg PO (chewable).

Name/Class: ATENOLOL (Tenormin)/Antidysrhythmic, Antihypertensive

Description: Atenolol is a selective beta-blocker that reduces the rate and force of cardiac contraction and lowers cardiac output and blood pressure.

Indications: Non–Q-wave MI and unstable angina.

Contraindications: Sinus bradycardia, 2nd- or 3rd-degree heart block, CHF, cardiogenic failure or shock.

Precautions: Asthma, COPD, or CHF controlled by digitalis and diuretics.

Dosage/Route: 5 mg slow IV (over 5 min), if tolerated, then after 10 min repeat.
Ped: 0.8 to 1.5 mg/kg/day PO (max 2 mg/kg/day).

AMIODARONE

AMRINONE

AMYL NITRITE

Name/Class: AMIODARONE (Cordarone, Pacerone)/Antidysrhythmic

Description: Amiodarone is an antidysrhythmic that prolongs the duration of the action potential and refractory period and relaxes smooth muscles, reducing peripheral vascular resistance and increasing coronary blood flow.

Indications: Life-threatening ventricular and supraventricular dysrythmias, frequently atrial fibrillation.

Contraindications: Hypersensitivity, cardiogenic shock, severe sinus bradycardia, or advanced heart block.

Precautions: Hepatic impairment, pregnancy, nursing mothers, children.

Dosage/Route: 150 to 300 mg IV over 10 min, then 1 mg/min over next 6 hours. Ped: 5 mg/kg IV/IO, then 15 mg/kg/day.

Name/Class: AMRINONE (Inocor)/Cardiac Inotrope

Description: Amrinone enhances myocardial contractility, increasing output, and reduces systemic vascular resistance.

Indications: To increase cardiac output in CHF or children in septic shock or myocardial dysfunction.

Contraindications: Hypersensitivity to amrinone or bisulfites.

Precautions: CHF immediately after MI (may cause ischemia).

Dosage/Route: *CHF:* 0.75 mg/kg IV over 2 to 3 min, then drip at 5 to 15 mcg/kg/min titrated to hemodynamic response (may repeat bolus at 30 min).

Septic shock or myocardial dysfunction in peds: 0.75 to 1 mg/kg IV over 5 min, repeated up to 2 times to 3 mg/kg, then drip of 5 to 10 mcg/min IV.

Name/Class: AMYL NITRITE (Amyl Nitrite)/Vasodilator

Description: Amyl nitrite is a short-acting vasodilator similar to nitroglycerin. Binds with hemoglobin to help biodegrade cyanide.

Indications: Acute cyanide poisoning.

Contraindications: None for acute cyanide poisoning.

Precautions: None.

Dosage/Route: 0.3 mL ampule/min (crushed) until sodium nitrate infusion is ready. Ped: same as adult.

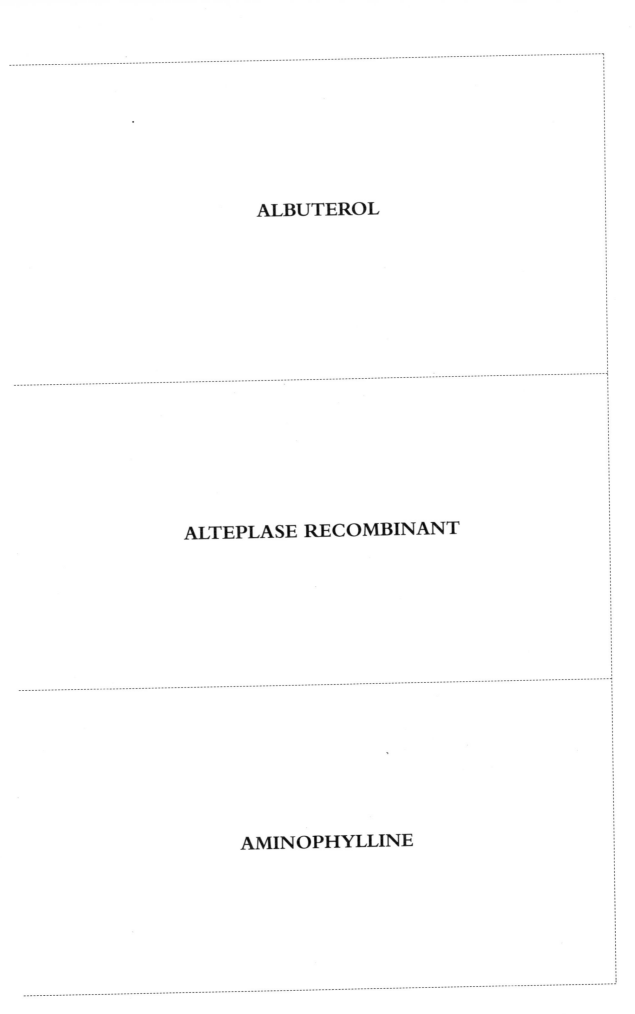

ALBUTEROL

ALTEPLASE RECOMBINANT

AMINOPHYLLINE

Name/Class: ALBUTEROL (Proventil, Ventolin)/Sympathomimetic Bronchodilator

Description: Albuterol is a synthetic sympathomimetic that causes bronchodilatation with less cardiac effect than epinephrine and reduces mucus secretion, pulmonary capillary leaking, and edema in the lungs during allergic reactions.

Indications: Bronchospasm and asthma in COPD.

Contraindications: Hypersensitivity to the drug.

Precautions: The patient may experience tachycardia, anxiety, nausea, cough, wheezing, and/or dizziness. Vital signs and breath sounds must be monitored; use caution with elderly, cardiac, or hypertensive patients.

Dosage/Route: Two inhalations (90 mcg) via metered-dose inhaler (2 sprays) or 2.5 mg in 2.5 to 3 mL NS via nebulizer, repeat as needed. The duration of effect is 3 to 6 hours. Ped: 0.15 mg/kg in 2.5 to 3 mL NS via nebulizer, repeat as needed.

Name/Class: ALTEPLASE RECOMBINANT (tPA) (Activase)/Thrombolytic

Description: Recombinant DNA–derived form of human tPA promotes thrombolysis by forming plasmin. Plasmin, in turn, degrades fibrin and fibrinogen and, ultimately, the clot.

Indications: To thrombolyse in acute myocardial infarction, acute ischemic stroke, and pulmonary embolism.

Contraindications: Active internal bleeding, suspected aortic dissection, traumatic CPR, recent hemmorhagic stroke (6 mo), intracranial or intraspinal surgery or trauma (2 mo), pregnancy, uncontrolled hypertension, or hypersensitivity to thrombolytics.

Precautions: Recent major surgery, cerebral vascular disease, recent GI or GU bleeding, recent trauma, hypertension, patient > 75 years, current oral anticoagulants, or hemorrhagic ophthalmic conditions.

Dosage/Route: *MI and stroke:* 15 mg IV, then 0.75 mg/kg (up to 50 mg) over 30 min, then 0.5 mg/kg (up to 35 mg) over 60 min.
Pulmonary embolism: 100 mg IV infusion over 2 hours.

Name/Class: AMINOPHYLLINE (Aminophylline, Somophyllin)/Methylxanthine Bronchodilator

Description: Aminophylline is a methylxanthine that prolongs bronchodilation and decreased mucus production and has mild cardiac and CNS stimulating effects.

Indications: Bronchospasm in asthma and COPD refractory to sympathomimetics and other bronchodilators and in CHF.

Contraindications: Hypersensitivity to methylxanthines or uncontrolled cardiac dysrhythmias.

Precautions: Cardiovascular disease, hypertension, or taking theophylline, hepatic impairment, diabetes, hyperthyroidism, young children, glaucoma, peptic ulcers, acute influenza or influenza immunization, and the elderly. Watch for PVCs or tachycardia. May cause hypotension.

Dosage/Route: 250 to 500 mg IV over 20 to 30 min. Ped: 6 mg/kg over 20 to 30 min. Max 12 mg/kg/day.

ACETAMINOPHEN

ACTIVATED CHARCOAL

ADENOSINE

Name/Class: ACETAMINOPHEN (Tylenol, Anacin-3)/Analgesic, Antipyretic

Description: Acetaminophen is a clinically proven analgesic/antipyretic with little effect on platelet function.

Indications: For mild to moderate pain and fever when aspirin is otherwise not tolerated.

Contraindications: Hypersensitivity, children under 3 years.

Precautions: Patients with hepatic disease; children under 12 years with arthritic conditions; alcoholism; malnutrition; and thrombocytopenia.

Dosage/Route: 325 to 650 mg. PO/4 to 6 hours. 650 mg PR/4 to 6 hours.

Name/Class: ACTIVATED CHARCOAL (Actidose)/Adsorbent

Description: Activated charcoal is a specially prepared charcoal that will adsorb and bind toxins from the gastrointestinal tract.

Indications: Acute ingested poisoning.

Contraindications: An airway that cannot be controlled; ingestion of cyanide, mineral acids, caustic alkalis, organic solvents, iron, ethanol, methanol.

Precautions: Administer only after emesis or in those cases where emesis is contraindicated.

Dosage/Route: 1 g/kg mixed with at least 6 to 8 oz of water, then PO or via an NG tube.

Name/Class: ADENOSINE (Adenocard)/Antidysrhythmic

Description: Adenosine is a naturally occurring agent that can "chemically cardiovert" PSVT to a normal sinus rhythm. It has a half-life of 10 seconds and does not cause hypotension.

Indications: Narrow, complex paroxysmal supraventricular tachycardia refractory to vagal maneuvers.

Contraindications: Hypersensitivity, 2nd- and 3rd-degree heart block, sinus node disease, or asthma.

Precautions: It may cause transient dysrhythmias. COPD.

Dosage/Route: 6 mg rapidly (over 1 to 2 sec) IV, then flush the line rapidly with saline. If ineffective, 12 mg in 1 to 2 min, may be repeated. Ped: 0.1 mg/kg (over 1 to 2 sec) IV followed by rapid saline flush, then 0.2 mg/kg in 1 to 2 min to max 12 mg.

Emergency Drug Cards

The following pages contain prepared three-by-five-inch index cards. Each card represents one of the drugs commonly used by the paramedic. They identify the name and class of the drug, a brief description, its indications, contraindications, precautions, common dosages, and routes of administration.

Detach and cut out the cards and review each one in detail. Be sure that your instructor identifies which drugs are used in your system and which need to be modified to indicate your system's specific indications, contraindications, precautions, doses, and methods of administration. You may also wish to prepare cards for the drugs used in your system that are not included in this card set.

Once your cards are prepared, begin to familiarize yourself with all of the information contained on the card when presented with the drug name. You will notice that the drug name appears on the back of each card. Working on just a few cards each week and then reviewing them as your course progresses will help you commit to memory the essential information you must know about each drug.